AF324785

TV LOBOTOMY

MICHEL DESMURGET

TV LOBOTOMY

THE SCIENTIFIC TRUTH ABOUT THE EFFECTS OF TELEVISION

Max Milo

Max Milo Editions, Paris, 2023
www.maxmilo.com
ISBN : 978-2-31501-104-9

Warning

The reader will discover, throughout the text, two types of notes. The footnotes, indicated by alphabetical superscripts (example[1]), clarify certain semantic and methodological points that could pose problems for non-specialists. The endnotes, indicated by numerical superscripts (example[1]), present the references of the articles mentioned in support of a given statement. These references are useful on two levels. Firstly, for the author, they constitute a precious safeguard: when each assertion must be supported, it is less easy to say anything and to pass off huckster's junk as proven facts. Secondly, for the reader, they allow to go back to the source of the evidence presented and thus to verify or deepen statements that could be considered suspicious or engaging. These endnotes are in no way necessary for the understanding of the text. They can be totally ignored or consulted on an occasional and parsimonious basis.

INTRODUCTION

"The problem with intellectuals is that they blame television for not being good enough. They are suspected of wanting to put Arte on every channel and impose their cultural preferences on everyone. For my part, I don't believe that there is good or bad television - I prefer that there is no television at all."

(Alexandre Lacroix, philosopher[2])

"Because media influences are subtle, cumulative, and occur over a long period of time, parents, pediatricians, and educators may not be aware of their impact."

(Victor Strasburger, Professor of Pediatrics, School of Medicine, University of New Mexico[3])

I am a researcher. As such, I am listed in the distribution directory of the main scientific journals related to the field of basic and clinical neuroscience[a]. With each new publication, these journals send me their summary, so that I can identify the works that might interest me. For the last 15 years, not a week has gone by without me extracting at least one or two papers relating to the deleterious effects of television on the psychic, cognitive and somatic health of the child. The tendency is so massive that some specialists do not hesitate any more to evoke a true problem of public health[4]. Some voices are even beginning to call for the extension

---

a. The term *neuroscience* refers to all disciplines that study the nervous system (psychology, biology, genetics, physiology, etc.). The journals in question include titles such as *Science, Nature, Lancet, JAMA, BMJ, Pediatrics, Archives of Pediatrics & Adolescent Medicine*, etc.

to the major audiovisual groups of the criminal proceedings originally brought against the tobacco and junk food industries[5]. The analogy is far from incongruous. Indeed, the tobacco industry was condemned in its time for having unduly stimulated the addictive character of products of which it knew the danger[6]. Nowadays, the media-advertising complex spends huge sums of money to identify and manipulate the springs of a cathodic addiction whose existence is becoming more and more difficult to deny[7-12]. Psychology, neuroimaging, ethology, ethnology, sociology, no branch of the human and medical sciences is exempt from contributing to the mercantile cause[13-21]. In recent years, neuromarketing has become the new manipulative grail. Its credo: to go and find the most intimate flaws of our brain to enslave, without our knowledge, our behaviors, our desires, our fears, our impulses, our representations, our decisions. In a recent book, two specialists on the subject summarize the approach as follows: "Aim for the small. Prepare your target. Mark it on the forehead as early as possible. Only the child learns well [...] Cigarette and soft drinks companies know that the earlier the child tastes, the more addicted he will be. Neuroscience has taught companies the ideal ages at which a given learning is most easily achieved."[22] Can we tolerate this kind of abjection? Can we remain impassive when an army of greedy scavengers mobilize all the tools of modern research in order to offer Coca-Cola "available human brain time"[23] ? Can we accept that a "third cathode-ray parent"[24] surreptitiously penetrates the psychic intimacy of our children in order to provoke addictive or purchasing behaviors with devastating health effects? Many people seem to think not, including academics[16,25], journalists[13,17,18,26], specialists in the United Nations Convention on the Rights of the Child[27] and many artists, executives or managers in the audiovisual industry who refuse to hand over their precious offspring to the throes of the "image box"[28-31]. As Liliane Lurçat sums up with her customary talent, "what is the freedom of children, if not to be children, and in the name of what can we allow ourselves to act on them with such power? What is the freedom of adults, if not to be able to understand, and why then target emotion rather than reason?"[25]

Small précis of ordinary nonsense

In theory, the preceding elements should *at least* cause some concern to us parents and spectators. However, in practice, the overwhelming majority of the social body is indifferent to the problem. As disconcerting as it is, this observation is hardly surprising. Indeed, to criticize television is, at the end of the chain, to erode the one who watches it. If you say "TV profoundly affects our relationship to the world", the average consumer will hear "I'm just a dumb, dumb calf". Similarly, if you say "TV is toxic for children", the famous housewife under 50 will translate "I'm a bad mother and I'm not raising my kids well". This kind of idea is all the more difficult to accept when an army of "eminent specialists" is trying to saturate the public space with soothing words and slimy tribunes. Of striking verbiages in tragic logorrheas, our learned diafoirus ardently catechize the praises of cathodic holy Tube. Television helps our children to grow up[32]. It is an extraordinary instrument of democratic culture[33]. The images it produces are beneficial[34]. The deep wisdom of the decision-makers preserves us from the worst[35]. The contemptuous of the small lucarne are demagogues[36], incompetent[37], reactionary[38], hysterical[34], neurotic[39,40], boastful[41], contemptuous[42], jealous[43] and, to say it all, overwhelmed by a "modernity [which] sends us back to the passing of time and to the fear of the unknown"[40]. By denouncing television, the dark preventers of watching in circles "give themselves a good conscience"[36] and try to "remake a virginity on the back of the medias"[34]. The latter are then taken "as scapegoats"[44]. How not to subscribe to these ideas, when one consults the list of the most severe critics of the cathodic thing: Noam Chomsky[45,46], Karl Popper[47], Pierre Bourdieu[48], Liliane Lurçat[25,49-51], Neil Postman[52], Dany-Robert Dufour[24,53], Alain Bentolila[54]. A terrible bunch of illiterate morons (*sic*)! Fortunately, the evangelizers of the audiovisual fact are of a different stature. Take Catherine Muller and François Chemel for example[32]. The first is "a doctor of psychology and psychoanalyst. She intervenes regularly in television and radio programs". The second is "a graduate of Sciences Po, MBA from the CFPJ Paris-Dauphine"[a] and "assistant editor of *Télé 7 Jours*. In television, he participated in the launch of Paris

---

a. If you have no idea what an MBA or CFPJ is, don't panic, these acronyms are not there to be clear, but to sound pompous. There is no point in giving the meaning of these acronyms (MBA: Master of Business Administration - all this is so much more ronflant in English! -CFPJ: Centre de Formation et de Perfectionnement des Journalistes).

Première". With such an enthusiastic pedigree, one could not expect anything less than a documented, objective and loyal statement. A statement whose recent publication offers worried parents the keys to "good use" of the television. In reading the words of Muller and Chemel, we learn, for example, that television is "attentive to the needs of children", that it helps "to raise awareness by showing the world as it is, in its reality, not always easy to accept", that it is "a social lubricant [...] It is a fantastic pedagogical support when it stimulates "our two brains" and allows children to acquire new knowledge more easily by associating it "with happy memories, privileged moments when they felt big and strong. Like when they learned to read effortlessly by watching *Numbers and Letters* with Grandma and Grandpa. Analyzing signs, memorizing them and learning to put them together to make sense: cerebral cortex. Feeling happy to share a good time: deep brain". It does not matter that the well-being of children is of little importance to the commercial interests of advertisers and other shareholders[16,55-60]. It does not matter that TV distorts the reality of the world to the point of creating a world without reality[61]. It doesn't matter that TV is a notable vector of social isolation[12,29,62,63]. It doesn't matter that TV is one of the most bitter enemies of learning the written language[64]. Never mind that the ability to decipher letters says nothing about the ability to read[54,65,66]. Finally, it does not matter how ridiculous this fable of two brains is, no doubt intended to give credibility to a proposition that is too absurd to be presented without a healthy pseudo-scientific patina[a]. No matter! Have confidence, parents, and "don't feel vain guilt if you put your children in front of a DVD and you spare yourself a little calm. TV reflects. It "reflects" like a mirror by sending back to its audience an image of the world and of itself"[32]. Even reality TV hides a noble project! Did you think, like Michel Meyer, that it was a kind of "low-end for invertebrates", a "machine to stultify without precedent"[28] ? Like Alain Bentolila, you considered it to be a "great nauseating fair", a "mediocre mush of banalities and approximations"[54]. You were wrong! Reality TV is basically a "social elevator, [...] [raised] within a society that offers nothing else to give equal opportunities to all its young members". Reality TV is "a lesson in life, a new version of the

---

a. Memory, emotion and cognition solicit, obviously, a large network of interconnected cortical and subcortical structures. The "most recent works on the brain" that our eminent specialists in neurophysiology evoke in support of their theses, surely go back to Descartes, Galen, Hippocrates or Plato! For some less prehistoric research, see for example[67-69].

TV Lobotomie

adage *'love one another'* that Jesus preached on the mountains of Galilee"[32]. Poor us, to murder the test pattern would be like crucifying the Son of Man a second time! Only a deep psychic disorder could justify such madness. It is not Michael Stora, "psychologist, psychoanalyst", founder of the Observatory of digital worlds in human sciences who will contradict me[40]. Our man is "suspicious of speeches that tend to demonize images [...] When parents insist on the "bad" character that they attribute to images, [Stora] always asks himself what is "bad" in them". Thus, for example, this "father of a family wanted to [...] say all the bad things he thought about TV and the danger it represented for the youngest. In the course of the conversation, he ended up explaining that his military career required him to be away from home for several months a year. Some of his children were not well. He didn't see them much, and had to put one of his sons in a boarding school... The bitterness he felt in front of the images, "bad" according to him, was in fact the expression of a personal suffering linked to his long absences. And thus to his absence of "image". Michael Stora advised his interlocutor to "communicate with his children by webcam". It is beautiful as Freud and clear as Goethe. "The spirit finally enlightens me. Inspiration descends on me, and I write comforted"[70]: without television, no salvation for our children! Do not laugh because the hour is serious! Did you know that "there is a link between self-confidence and relation to the images [...] Just as we could, baby, be admired by our mother without that this one confirms, by tender gestures, hugs, kisses, the love which she carried to us, in the same way we can adopt the same attitude of admiration, contemplation, even of fascination, in front of images which, by essence, do not have body, neither arm, nor mouth"[40]. Faced with such evidences (*sic*)[a], one can frankly wonder if the apostles of a severe cathodic restriction measure well the danger that they make run to the humanity. The case of those parents who would like to limit the exposure of their children to violent programs is particularly telling from this point of view. This restrictive approach, Serge Tisseron tells us, "an entire people tried it not so long ago [...] It was the German people between 1918 and 1945 [...]. From the moment when Germany was accused en bloc of having behaved inhumanely and pilloried by all the nations, it became [due to the absence of an

---

a. If you have not understood anything, don't worry, neither have I! Psychoanalytic pompous verbiage is generally not very accessible to the common mind. For a very entertaining demonstration of this point, see [71].

image] impossible for a veteran of the Reich to recognize that he had behaved inhumanly [...] There was therefore only one thing left for former German soldiers of the Great War to do: bury deep within themselves the fascination with evil and the joy of killing [nothing less! They had discovered it"[34]. By wanting to control the content of the programs we give to our children, it is therefore their appetite for violence and barbarism that we could inflame! It is just a pity that scientific work shows a rigorously opposite risk, concerning a desensitization to violence and a criminal facilitation in the presence of unpleasant images[72]. Among the thousands of research studies conducted in this field, none has shown a reduction in violent behavior in the short or long term, after exposure to violent audio-visual content[72]. This conclusion seems to be shared by Michael Stora, who insists, however, on the dark danger of induced addiction. Thus, as our eminent specialist writes docently, "among the patients who come to see me for a problem of addiction to video games, some [a little? a lot? 1, 2, 3, 10, 100?] were not allowed, as children, to watch television and were pushed to read very early. Their parents, who often [1, 10, 50, 80 % of the "some" cases?] exercise so-called "intellectual" professions, hate television. It is in their eyes a stultifying, degrading object"[40]. Intellectual pigs! It is to wonder what waits the services of the DDASS[a] to intervene.

*

* *

There is no one so blind as the one who does not want to see

"Nerd"! It is curiously the first word that came to Sylvain[b] when I spoke to him about this book! His exact phrase was, I think, "your thing is a nerd-bobo catch! Anyway, it's all very complicated and there is no simple answer". A happy observation, which reminds me of a superb text by my friend Zorn. "In my family," says this son of fine lineage, "when it came to taking sides, one of the most fashionable recourses was 'complicated'. Complicated" was the magic word, the key word that allowed to put aside

------

a. Departmental Directorate of Health and Social Affairs.
b. All first names have been changed to preserve the anonymity of the persons mentioned.

all the unresolved problems [...] It was enough to discover that a thing was "complicated" and already it was taboo [...] One said "complicated" to the people who were in charge.One said "complicated" about a thing as if one pronounced on it an incantation, and it disappeared [...] To find everything "complicated", that seemed to be the proof of a superior level [...] This superiority [...] was most convenient [...] : we never had to commit ourselves; it was enough for us to always find everything "complicated."[73] Many specialists of the cathodic thing seem to have been raised in Zorn country! If we believe our powerful theorists, everything is in fact so complicated that the very question of the influence of the media ends up becoming "not very relevant", except of course for the sketchy minds of a few "*physicists* or biologists that their reputation often leads them to develop points of view that they think are authorized"[37]. I am one of them, I confess... and from the depths of my inscience, I even dare to persist. I persist not out of rigorist stubbornness but out of simple submission to the obvious! Whoever is a little bit attentive to the daily events cannot, indeed, I believe, ignore the deep impact of the audiovisual media on our behaviors. I remember, for example, a captivating morning trip to the breakfast section of a large supermarket. While everything was relatively quiet, my 3-year-old niece suddenly started rolling around on the floor to get the purchase of the cereal labeled "Seen on TV". Only this (prodigiously expensive) brand found favor in her eyes. The presence on the box of a little TV hero, familiar to children, had obviously produced the desired effect! It didn't take long for my own daughter, Valentine, to express the same impression. When she was only 30 months old, she suddenly started frantically singing "maaf maaf" when she saw the logo of the famous insurance company on the windshield of a car. I suppose she must have seen (and seen again) this gem of an advertisement at her nanny's house[74]. Only a few days after the episode, it was her sister Charlotte's turn (7 years old, 1.26 meters, 19 kilos) to show the first symptoms of intense formatting. While watching a "youth" program[75], the little girl suddenly said to her mother, without looking away from the screen: "Say Mommy, am I fat?" At the next meal, she began her first low-calorie diet and refused to eat a single crumb of bread! There was also this psychology student who declared at the end of a course on the acquired and the innate that homosexuality was "in an established way" a genetic trait. Our proud descendant of the Enlightenment was sure of his sources. Television had said so. "Frankly, you should have watched it mister, it was super documented!" Two other zealous telephonists confirmed the facts to me, without unfortunately being able to recall the exact references of the program. A third explained to me that anyway it was "the same for pedophilia", he had heard it on the 20 hours news[a]! Stupendous abolition of understanding[77], especially from students in the humanities whose critical spirit should be the cardinal attribute! As Jean-Paul Brighelli says with talent, these kids "with still soft skulls" only seem to analyze the world with "a lot of television programs, rumors and hearsay. A soft opinion, a loukoum thought. To think, to weigh, to debate, that supposes work, knowledge, will. All these values are beaten down by the ready-to-think that today takes the place of culture"[78]. 78 Even journalists are not immune to the disaster, as the Greek correspondent for the newspaper *Metro* wrote about a series of particularly violent urban riots: "Everyone is sitting in front of their television sets trying to understand what is going on."[79] This is a remarkable investigative strategy, reminiscent of the heyday of the wars in Kosovo, Afghanistan and Iraq.[80] With such examples, it is difficult to be surprised when two 15-17 year old girls involuntarily testify to the distressing restriction of their cultural field to the audiovisual space alone. I was sitting in a streetcar when the conversation started. Excerpts. The (fake) blonde, Dior cap, Diesel pants, Vuitton clutch: "I have to do the presentation on *Germinal*, the mine thing." The (real) brunette, Adidas tracksuit, Quicksilver tee-shirt, fluorescent Nike shoes : "Great, I saw him on TV, with the singer, but I don't know what his name is." The blonde (depressed): "Yeah, I didn't even know they had made a book about it." The brunette (didactic): "Well, when it works, they do everything, it's business, like *Star'Ac.*" Beyond its entertaining aspect, the exposure of this incredible inculture has, I find, something a little desperate. A despair that reminds me of a magnificent quote from Natacha Polony writing in her superb essay, *Nos enfants gâchés*: "And *Star Academy* becomes the horizon of the children of the bourgeoisie, as much as of the children of the people. Ministers' daughters are paraded as models. The social divide is resolved in the common dream of a whole society to dance on a television set. Tonight, there is a ball on the deck of the Titanic."[81]

On the bottom, this allusion to the famous liner seems to me all the more appropriate as television does not limit its disastrous influences to a few frivolous anecdotes. It manages, with a disturbing constancy, to

a. I suppose that our young man had taken as "information" the evocation of the appalling remarks of Nicolas Sarkozy on the genetic bases of suicide and pedophilia[76].

TV Lobotomie

erode our very humanity. I remember, for example, this 3 year old kid, just operated of a cerebral tumor and crying sadly in front of an empty screen because his mother had left him alone to go see elsewhere *Plus belle la vie*[a]. "You understand, the stepmother explained to me on his return, here it's impossible to watch, he won't stop moaning." Poor kid forced to cry alone in the middle of overflowing white coats because his mother had not had her cathode ray. There was also this game, obviously fake, but which the participants believed to be real and which revealed that out of 10 candidates, 8 consented, when a TV hostess ordered it, to torture a person in an electric chair[82] . Without worrying about the victim's tears and cries, our budding Mengeles proved capable of inflicting potentially lethal currents of 460 volts on an unknown man. These "Mr. and Mrs. Everyman" went through with the "experiment". They obeyed without fail to the injunctions of the priestess animator. One player commented: "I was told to do it like this. Well, the guys who told me that, they know what they are doing! I do. I knew it would burn out in there. But that's not my problem."[83] This appalling barbarity is to some extent reminiscent of the brutal rape of a 10-year-old child by two apparently harmless preadolescents. Our young torturers (one of whom was the victim's brother) had just watched a pornographic movie and apparently couldn't resist the pleasure of a little private best-of. In order not to frustrate anyone, they decided to broadcast the scene in their school, *via* a mobile phone[84]. Some will say (in defiance of the most elementary scientific evidence[85]) that television has nothing to do with this kind of brutality because "behind these dramas, we *always* discover family dramas"[34] and "in our relationship to images, *everything is a* matter of links, whether familial or convivial"[40] (my emphasis). However, the same authors also explain that "adolescents are looking for models to approach the other sex [and that] these images offer them some"[34]. If the contradiction tickles your brain, don't get formal. The "specialist" likes to sing the palinody! For those who might doubt this, let me give you just one more (small) example, just for fun. Faced with a substantial body of alarming data, the American Association of Pediatrics firmly recommended to parents, as early as 1999, that children aged 2 and under be withdrawn from all television exposure[86,87]. In 2002, Serge Tisseron, in a chapter entitled *Du bébé gribouilleur au bébé zappeur (From the scribbling baby to the zapping baby)*, spoke out strongly against this

---

a. A sitcom broadcast on France 3 around 20:15.

recommendation and against those "parents [who] want to prevent their child from exercising his or her talents as a baby zapper. What a mistake! However, it was enough for the scientific community to be moved by the creation of two television channels aimed at the youngest children, for our doctor Proteus to quickly turn around and co-sign a vengeful article explaining how "it is urgent to mobilize for the creation of a moratorium that forbids such channels to exist, before we know a little more about the relationship between young children and screens"[88]. As Edgar Faure, former president of the National Assembly, academician, minister and senator, liked to point out, "it is not the weathervane that turns, it is the wind". That being the case, there is nothing like a gaudy flow of verbiage to avoid this wind. To peremptory and hazardous assertions, the "specialist" of the small TV channel will thus often prefer a subtle tongue in cheek. He will not say brutally: "Television seriously harms the mental and somatic health of the young child". He will declare modestly: "Television is not *a priori* the best ally in this phase of development."[32] In the same way, the skilful semanticist will never claim directly that "TF1 is a mephitic channel". He will just concede cautiously that "TF1 is globally a difficult channel to watch"[90]. In his mouth, the most sordid and vulgar reality show will become a simple "slightly transgressive entertainment"[91]. How elegantly these things are said!

*
* *

The hidden face of the iceberg

Some unhappy people may think that the previous illustrations are too vaporous to be convincing. Let them reassure themselves. It is the case with television as with icebergs: the emerged fragment is rarely the most fatal and the most decisive. In this field also, "the essential is invisible for the eyes"[a]. The problem, unfortunately, is that this invisible is in fact very difficult to explore, and this because of a double limitation. First, almost everyone watches television. The estimated impact of a risk factor tends to be mechanically underestimated when this factor is uniformly distributed

---

a. To quote the famous sentence of the fox to the Little Prince[92].

in the reference population, i.e., when all subjects are affected and only variations in the level of exposure (high *versus* low)[93,94] can be compared. Second, a causal mechanism cannot be identified directly, by simple phenomenological observation, when it acts on an asynchronous basis. A brief example should convince us of this. Let us imagine that your horn sounds instantaneously each time you insert a key into the lock of your car. It will not take you long to associate these two events[95]. Now let us imagine that a transmission bias introduces a latency that can range from a handful of milliseconds to a few hours or even several years, between the sounding of the horn and the unlocking of the door. It will then become very difficult to identify the source of the problem (if the horn is sounding when you have been driving for more than two hours, the lock will not spontaneously appear as a plausible hypothesis). Only a "hard" experimental approach will eventually unravel the ball of wax. This is exactly what happens with television. Indeed, in this case, the lack of temporal coincidence between exposure and behavior tends to hide the causal chain that leads from the media to the symptoms. My friend Sophie's denials illustrate this point, I think, beautifully. When I tried to explain to this bubbly thirty-something the reasons for my anti-cathodic hobby, I only received a laconic echo: "You're completely paranoid, my poor fellow. Frankly, I've been watching TV since I was a fat kid, and it hasn't made me stupid." Apart from this wonderful slip of the tongue, which I will come back to, the assertion is not false. Sophie is a nurse's aide in a hospital department. Her human qualities and her professionalism are unanimously recognized. However, she would have liked to be a nurse. Unfortunately, the written tests for access to the profession rejected this project three times. One wonders if Sophie's early cathodic diet did not cost her that little extra soul that sometimes makes the difference between failure and academic success. In line with this idea, a number of studies have denounced the negative impact of television on attention, learning skills and long-term academic success[64]. Regarding the latter, it has been shown, for example, that "the average time spent watching television during childhood and adolescence was significantly associated with leaving school without qualifications and negatively associated with attaining a university degree. The risk factors for each hour of television watched per weekday evening, adjusted for IQ and gender, were 1.43 and 0.75, respectively. The results were similar for males and females and persisted after further adjustment for socioeconomic status and behavioral problems in early childhood."[96a] 43% more chance of leaving school without a degree and 25% more chance of never sitting in college for every hour of television watched daily during the elementary school years, let's face it, these numbers are pretty good! But back to Sophie. In another area, she also complains loudly about her small size (1.68 meters!) and her overweight (54 kilos!). She finds herself "terribly fat", which leads her to pile up the most disastrous diets. An impressive amount of research suggests that a slight audiovisual withdrawal would have allowed her not only to have a less biased image of her body stature[3,97-105] but also, potentially, to gain a few centimetres (television acts negatively on sleep, which itself acts positively on growth[106]). By a sad coincidence, it turns out that Sophie's father recently developed Alzheimer's disease. The man was also a heavy consumer of audiovisual media. We can think that this concomitance is not totally fortuitous. In fact, recent studies have established that the use of cathode ray tubes accelerates the cognitive decline of senior citizens[107]. It has also been shown, after taking into account a large list of potential covariates, that the probability of contracting Alzheimer's disease increases by a solid 30% for each hour of television consumed between the ages of 40 and 60[108]. To understand this last result, it should be noted that Alzheimer's disease is less likely to occur the more our cognitive functions are actively solicited[109]. This solicitation is challenged by cathode ray exposure. The

---

a. The notion of adjustment (which we will also refer to as "accounting for potential covariates") refers to complex statistical procedures that allow the contribution of television to be isolated precisely. Take school performance, for example. Academic performance can be affected by a number of factors, including gender, intelligence quotient (IQ), socio-economic characteristics of the household, or the existence of behavioral problems (such as hyperactivity). Clearly, not all of these factors are independent of each other. For example, children from more socially advantaged homes also tend to watch less television and have higher IQ test scores. Therefore, if we simply observe that an increase in audiovisual exposure time leads to a decrease in school results, we cannot exclude the possibility that this relationship is only due to the effects of the socio-economic status of the household. Indeed, when the socio-economic status of the household increases, school performance increases and audiovisual exposure time decreases. To overcome this, researchers have at their disposal statistical methods that allow them, if I may say so, to render to Caesar what belongs to Caesar, that is, to identify the specific role of a factor (such as audiovisual exposure time) on the variable studied (such as school performance), independently of the influence of all the other factors that may act on this variable (such as IQ, socio-economic category, etc.). Thanks to these procedures, we obtain, in the end, for the example that concerns us here, a reliable and precise measure of the effect of audiovisual exposure on school results, all other things being equal. In concrete terms, we can imagine this measure as the difference in school results between two children with no behavioural problems, from the same background, of the same sex, with the same IQ, living in similar neighbourhoods, etc., one of whom spends one hour more per day watching TV than the other.

message is therefore quite simple: if you want to preserve your old age, avoid slouching in front of the television like amorphous cattle[110,111].

What is true for old age is also true for childhood. Consider my friend Gilles by way of illustration. Like Sophie, this divorced father thinks I am a dangerous maniac. His favorite argument: "My son has been watching television since he was very young and he's not crazy about it, quite the contrary. However, you don't have to push Gilles very far to learn that his genius teenager has major school discipline problems, poorly contained aggressiveness, a chronic inability to concentrate for more than a few minutes on a given subject, an alarming addiction to brands, a tendency to obesity and a disturbing attraction to alcoholic products. He even, in the words of his father, "started smoking joints this jerk". Far from any moral judgment[a] , we can think that the audiovisual diet of the young man is not totally unrelated to these manifestations. Indeed, the most recent scientific research has largely confirmed the repercussions of television consumption on obesity[106] , the development of attentional disorders[64], the emergence of aggressive behaviors[72] , the emergence of consumerist social values[16,55,112-114] and the appearance of risky health behaviors (tobacco, alcohol, unprotected sexuality, drugs, etc.)[106]. As Andreas Kappos summarizes after a broad review of the literature: "There is no doubt that television and other electronic media negatively influence the mental and physical well-being of children". Television may be one of the triggers for this condition in susceptible children.[116]

*
* *

Not seen, not taken

The data are therefore apparently solid. However, everything is done to discredit their scope. The slightest negative sentence on the audiovisual fact provokes an avalanche of infamous epithets: prohibition, demonization, fundamentalism, moralism, self-righteousness, dishonesty, archaism, etc.

---

a. It may or may not be legitimate for a teenager to gorge himself on sweets, to refuse to wear anything other than jeans and branded shoes, to smoke firecrackers all the time, to drink alcohol in profusion or to immerse himself without health precautions in the pleasures of the flesh. My purpose here is not to pass judgment on this point. Each person must decide for himself or herself. My purpose is simply to underline the link between these behaviors and television exposure.

The Kriegel report on violence on television is sadly symptomatic of this propensity[117]. This firmly documented and rather temperate work called for "no prohibition". It just called for "an expanded program to keep violent entertainment out of the hands of children" and for more precise signage "close to the European average". Intolerable for the thurifers of the cathode god. Blandine Kriegel was dragged to the Place de Grève and stoned without weakness for the price of her infamous book. It was accused of wanting to "worry to control"[38]. He was accused of insidiously leading to censorship[118] and to the reinforcement of the power of the State[38]. It was attempted to divert the debate by pointing out the potential responsibility of advertisers[119]. It was argued that the arguments put forward were insufficient and simplistic, because Blandine Kriegel had mentioned the role of television without mentioning the possible influence of social factors such as precariousness or poverty[38]. It does not matter that most of the scientific studies cited in the report have integrated these factors into their statistical framework by showing that the substantial impact of violent images existed independently of intelligence, sex, socio-professional category, parents' level of education, etc.[72a]. When television is in danger, one must know how to work a little on the truth and subvert the aridity of the facts... and if that is not enough, one can always discredit at a low cost by stigmatizing here an innocent lack of agreement[38] and there an obvious lack of empathy: let's see Blandine, why so much hatred, "we are all responsible adults, we also have children"[118]. If all this proves insufficient, we can ultimately plead technical nullity, on the grounds that the works cited come mainly from America, a barbaric country where "there is [...] much less distance than elsewhere between the desire to kill and the act of killing"[38]. Here again, it does not matter what the facts are. It does not matter that similar studies have been carried out in Eastern, Western, Central, Northern and Southern Europe, Japan, Israel, Australia, Argentina, New Zealand, etc.[120-122]. It does not matter that these studies have shown, according to the conclusions of a report presented by Jo Groebel to the Director General of Unesco, that beyond local cultural variations, "the overall pattern of the implications of media violence is similar throughout the world"[123]. Who has the time anyway to go and check the source of the peremptory assertions of our great specialists? Not seen, not taken! However, this phenomenon of denial is not specific to France. It strikes all the world's

a. See note p. 24.

media places. Thus, as Victor Strasburger, researcher and professor of pediatrics at the University of Medicine in New Mexico, writes at the end of a well-documented review: "In 1954, Senator Estes Kefauver, chairman of the Senate Subcommittee on Juvenile Delinquency, was the first official to openly question the need for violence in television programs. The industry responded that there may be some risk, but that more research was needed. Today, after hundreds of studies, the industry denies that media violence has any effect on children and adolescents. Yet no other area of media has been so thoroughly studied with such compelling results. The relationship between media violence and real-life violence is in fact about as strong as the relationship between smoking and lung cancer."[3] It is difficult to be clearer without openly talking about "misinformation", which is what Brad Bushman and Craig Anderson recently did after analyzing, in detail, the gap between the available scientific knowledge on the one hand, and the soothing claims propagated by the media and their army of devoted pipe-heads on the other.[124]

Let us remain one moment more on the subject of the violence, since this one seems to concentrate an important part of the debates on the television. To change, however, let us evacuate the question of images and contents, to invest the ontogenetic space. As Marie Winn points out, "when television first appeared, parents were quick to recognize the incredible opportunity it offered: a flick of the switch could change their child, albeit temporarily, from an energetic, noisy, intrusive creature eager for activity and experience and demanding constant supervision and attention, into a docile, silent, undemanding presence." Yet, Marie Winn continues, what we fail to consider when we flip that switch is that "those very things that children do that cause so much difficulty for parents, those explorations, manipulations, and incessant experiments with cause and effect, are beneficial and even necessary for children. It might give parents pause to consider that dealing with their children's difficult behaviors by eliminating them completely *via* television is not entirely different from suppressing a child's natural behavior by threatening physical retalia-tion. It is strikingly similar to what happens when a child is drugged into inactivity with laudanum or gin. This developmental violence, strangely enough, is not mentioned (or almost not mentioned[25]). While everyone seems to be concerned about the content, no one seems to be concerned about the nature of the medium. Yet, by keeping our children in front of the television, we not only expose them to more or less adapted programs, but we also deprive them of a large number of cardinal experiences. From then on, a fear could refer, not to what TV induces, but to what it hinders and prohibits by the simple fact of its presence. Let us consider, as an illustration, the process of language acquisition. Here is a domain that suits, we are told, perfectly to the television. The loud didactic claims of the publishers and broadcasters of audiovisual contents for the little ones are edifying in this respect. At Brainy Baby, for example, they claim that a video for 6-36 months teaches children "language and logic".[125] At Baby Einstein, they explain that this DVD for ages 1 and up "enriches the child's vocabulary through the beauty of poetry, music and nature".[125] At BabyTV, a channel for the youngest children, they announce that "stories and rhymes help children learn language".[126] To give substance to this claim, a video for the second year of the series *"Leni" is shown on the television.* 126 To give substance to this statement, a wide range of enthusiastic testimonies is presented. For example, according to Christine, "my daughter is six months old and since she was born she has been watching BabyTV. And since recently she has her favorite cartoons and in the evening she loves the magic lantern. It's a channel that should have been created earlier"[a]. "Of course, Laura adds, like many parents, I'm not really in favor of children staying too long in front of the TV, but this is an educational channel, so there's no need to worry, as long as you stay for a long time."[b] An idea that is generally in line with the statements of my friend Veronique stating that she is "still not going to kick Paul [her 2-year-old son] out of the living room when she watches cooking shows, games or series. I don't see what the problem is if he's there, whether he's watching or not. Often he comes up with phrases he's heard on TV. It just blows me away every time. Frankly, I don't see how it can be bad, he learns a lot of stuff. A lot of stuff, indeed, if we fail to consider the evidence of the most recent research showing a strong positive association between the onset of language disorders in children and early exposure to "educational" DVDs/videos, entertainment cartoons, "all-audience" programs, or simple background screens.[64] For example, every hour of daily content that children watch on television is a significant factor in their development. For example, every hour per day of "educational" content between 8 and 16 months of age results in a 10% lexicon depletion[128]. For example, every hour of "educational" content per day between 8 and 16 months of age results in a 10% decrease in lexical

---

a. Uncorrected text as presented on the BabyTV[127] website.
b. *Ibid.*

proficiency.[128] Similarly, 2 hours of exposure to "all-ages" programming per day between 15 and 48 months of age results in a 3-fold increase in the risk of language development delays.[129] The factor is as high as 6 when the child is in the first year of life. The factor even reaches 6 when the initiation to the position takes place before 1 year. As I will show in detail later, these initial deficits are likely to persist over time and to have a long-term negative impact on the academic and social integration of children[64]. This is indeed a reason to be enthusiastic and to proclaim with Serge Tisseron, "*Long live the zapper babies*! In fact, the concept of the "self-zapping baby" would be more appropriate if we consider that one of the primary effects of television is to drastically reduce the volume and quality of parent-child interactions[130-134]. These interactions are essential for language development[135-143]. "But at least it trains the ear," Isabelle said to me in a spirit of hope. Since giving birth, this single mother with a degree in international business has given her 10-month-old son English-language videos. "It's important, she says to anyone who will listen. Look at your example, after eight years in the U.S., you still have a potato accent and can't tell the difference between *beach* and *bitch*." This is true! Yet no amount of early audiovisual exposure could have saved me. As one ingenious study showed, when 9-month-olds were exposed to native Mandarin, they retained a broad ability to distinguish the sounds of that language. When these children are placed in front of a video of this same Mandarin, they preserve nothing at all.[144] All that Isabelle's son has gained from his mother's almost obsessive concern is the usurpation of precious time by an activity that is, at best, devoid of interest and, at worst, frankly deleterious. This is all the more damaging because young children easily sleep 16 hours a day[145], which, when physiological time is subtracted (meals, baths, diaper changes), leaves little time to wire the brain by acting on the real[a]! Taxing this time, even to the extent of one or two "small" hours per day, is to do a great deal of harm to the child. The tragedy, once again (it cannot be repeated enough!), lies in the obscure nature of the causal chains involved. Television exposure does not make children visibly stupid or retarded. It does not overtly dumb them down. It just narrows the field of their experiences and, *de facto,* the universe of their possibilities.

---

a. This does not mean, of course, that nothing happens during these physiological times, particularly in terms of parent-child interactions. It does mean, however, that the child carries out specific activities outside of physiological time that are fundamental to his or her development.

Had they had 150 IQ[a], they might have had to settle for 110. Had they had the literary audacity of a Thomas Mann, they might have been satisfied with a barely honest pen. If they had the vista of a Federer, they would be satisfied with playing only second-rate satellite tournaments. How do we know, afterwards, how high the mountain would have risen if it had been protected from the cathodic wind? The vox populi will obviously deny the existence of any detriment: look, they will tell us, they watched TV and they did not do badly, they are not stupid. But no one will ask: What did that screen they watched so much steal from them? Obviously, the relevance of such a question is not limited to the case of toddlers. It is also of interest to school-age children and adolescents. It is then the spaces of creativity, of onirism, of sociability, of schooling, of reading, of culture and of motricity that it is appropriate to question. We will have the opportunity to come back in detail on these points throughout this book.

*
* *

Living without TV

In light of the above, my wife Caroline and I decided almost two years ago to drastically restrict our television consumption and to control our children's audiovisual exposure. We thought we could, without too much effort, prune the content and dominate the time. Like so many others before us[29], we quickly became disillusioned. The switch was too tempting, too common, too convenient to allow a painless weaning. All rationalizations were good to turn off the children by taping them in front of the television. All excuses were welcome to question the most elementary rules of use that we had given ourselves (no TV during the meal; no turning on blindly, etc.). A long day at work, a disagreement, an argument, a temporary asthenia and the screen came to life to extract us from the world. Often in the evening, I would slump into the couch like an apathetic dung beetle, cursing the frenzy of an existence that left me "no time to do anything"! Obviously, I had not fully understood the meaning of the sentence: "A 'typical' viewer over 15 years of age spends 3 hours and 40 minutes a day in front of the tele-

----

a. Intelligence quotient.

vision."[146] Just think about it: 3 hours and 40 minutes a day is roughly 20 to 25% of our waking time[147] and 75% of our free time[148]! That's also 1,338 hours per year, or 56 days (almost 2 months!). If you live to be 81 years old, as you are statistically entitled to expect[149], you will have given up 11 years of your life to television (excluding videos and other DVDs)[a]. 11 complete years, that is to say more than 4,000 days and as many nights spent scrutinizing the viewfinder like a flaccid slug. Not even a pee break in the middle of the event. Of course, we can also consider that sleep is essential and propose to count the use of the cathode-ray in "waking time", that is to say on the basis of 16 hours 30 minutes per day[147]. We then arrive at just 16 years. 16 years of a precious existence abandoned to TF1 and company! If we reason on the scale of the French population, we obtain the pharaonic figure of 77 billion hours squandered each year in front of the television set[b], that is to say, almost all the hours lived in one year by 9 million individuals! Unfortunately, our children are not left out: a primary school child spends, every year, more time in front of the cathode ray tube than in front of his teacher (956 hours against 864)[c]! But, obviously, as Luc Ferry wrote one day when he was Minister of Youth, National Education and Research, to agitate these "frightening statistics" is to make of television "an easy scapegoat"[33]. Could we not consider instead that not stirring up these appalling statistics is to offer television a guilty indulgence?

After many difficulties, my wife and I finally succeeded in reducing our family's television consumption. Unexpectedly, the lack of images did not create any crisis. On the contrary, the more intense the withdrawal became, the less painful it became. When Valentine took advantage of a moment of inattention to try out his new indelible markers on the

---

a. This figure does not take into account consumption before the age of 4 (Médiamétrie gives no figures for this age group). It reflects the cumulative total over 77 years (81 - 4) of the average usage published by Médiamétrie for those aged 4 and over, i.e. 3.25 hours per day[146].

b. This figure only takes into account the 61.5 million individuals aged 4 and over[150] who, on average, watch television for 3 hours and 25 minutes a day.[146]

c. School time: 864 hours per year[151]; television time: 797 hours (2 hours 11 minutes per day between 4 and 14 years old[146]); DVD/video time: no reliable data seems to be available in France in the public domain. However, studies conducted in the United States estimate that the consumption of videos increases the time spent watching television by one fifth for 8-10 year olds[152]; in France, this amounts to a little over 26 minutes per day, or 159 hours per year. This gives a total of 956 hours of "TV + videos". This figure is lower than the one proposed by Mr. Meyer (1,400 hours). However, this author does not cite the sources of his estimate[28]. The European Eco-Conseil institute reports a figure of 1,200 hours, but again without an identifiable source[153].

flat screen, the idea of buying a television didn't even cross our minds. Bye-bye *Punchy*. No more *Secret Story*. No more *CSI*. Ciao *Josephine. So long* Champions League. As I took the set down to the basement, I remembered the famous sentence of the *Punchy Guignols*: "You can now turn off the television and resume normal activity!" That's an understatement! 12 months of abstinence have really transfigured our lives. Conflicts about using the remote control have disappeared. Within the family circle, words are exchanged more easily, especially at meal times. The girls seem calmer, more attentive to their environment. They do not seem to miss television. In any case, they do not ask for it. The eldest daughter has stopped (for the most part) harassing us with consumerist demands and her school results have improved substantially. There is no indication that she is "out of step" with her peers. On the contrary, her social life has grown in proportion to her distance from the television. In the evenings, instead of slouching in front of the screen, she reads, paints, draws, heckles, does her homework, brings her plastic figurines to life, plays with her dolls, builds all sorts of haphazard constructions, or more simply, takes the time to do nothing. This "free" time has allowed her to access a strange experience that television had previously deprived her of: boredom. This experience is not insignificant in the sense that it is the basis for desire, creativity and forward thinking.[29,154-156] According to a recent study, when the mind wanders and wanders, there is a strong activation of brain areas involved in projective reasoning and problem solving processes[157]. The effect is even more pronounced when subjects are unaware of their mental wanderings. In other words, while we are bored, our brain is working without our knowledge. The "lost" time is therefore not empty. It is deeply creative. As Miguel de Unamuno wrote in his magnificent *Fog*, "Boredom is the foundation of life; it is boredom that has invented all games and distractions, novels and love."[158] Even Cioran seemed to believe it when he attested from the depths of his irrevocable nihilism that "boredom works wonders: it converts emptiness into substance, it is itself a nourishing void.

Even if she doesn't say it yet, Valentine also seems to be "bored" at times. She sits on the couch and strokes her face with her comforter's ear. A few months ago, these moments were simply unattainable, filled as they were with a constant stream of images and noise. Since the departure of the television, the little one seems less agitated, she accepts bedtime more easily. When she is not "bored" she acts, moves, talks, questions, tests, experiments; in short, she builds herself by experiencing her universe. It happens of course that this forced dynamism makes us regret our audiovisual laudanum. However, nothing could incite us to turn back. As Alexandre Lacroix, philosopher and fervent apologist of the No TV, writes: "To decide to live without TV, I had a serious reason. But this reason is personal and existential. It is a matter of feeling. According to me, things can be summarized as follows: life seems to me more beautiful without TV."[160]

Am I, as I often hear, excessive, paranoid, hysterical and reactionary? Perhaps. However, before concluding in the affirmative and sweeping away the present work as one would dismiss an evil dipteran, I would like the reader to ask himself three small questions: does television really deserve that we abandon 16 years of our waking life to it? Do our children have no other vocation than to offer Coca-Cola "available brain time"? Isn't the scientific evidence against us sufficiently worrying in terms of language, school success, social integration, culture, health, well-being or aggressiveness, to justify the application of a strict precautionary principle? It is up to each person to decide for themselves and their children. As far as I am concerned, the die is cast!

CHAPTER I

TV EVERYWHERE AND AT ANY TIME

"Television requires only one act of courage from the viewer - but it is a superhuman one - and that is to turn it off."

(Pascal Bruckner, philosopher[161])

"The important decision is whether to have a television or not, whether to expose children to almost everything that television offers, or nothing at all."

(Joshua Meyrowitz, Professor of Communication,
University of New Hampshire[162])

"Whereas until now, television chained its viewer [...], tomorrow it will accompany him wherever he goes."

(François Jost, media specialist,
professor at the University of Paris 3-Sorbonne[60])

Where, when, how, why, how and how often do we organize our audiovisual consumption and that of our children? The big media, advertising and industrial groups have long been addressing these questions. Unfortunately, our friends are not very generous when it comes to sharing the fruit of the data they have collected. In the overwhelming majority of cases, their research remains "proprietary," that is, inaccessible to the general public.[57,163] When I asked an acquaintance working for TF1 if she could get me information on children's audiovisual behavior, the lady kindly replied that this information was available, but confidential, reserved for the top hierarchy, and in any case "insortable" on pain of being "kicked out. Following this refusal, I contacted Médiamétrie, Ifop, TNS-Sofres, the CSA institute and the Junior City group (which produces a "playground observatory"), hoping to obtain some data. Success, to say the least, was not forthcoming! However, it is difficult to blame these private companies who owe their clients reserve, confidentiality and loyalty. I also asked several journalists and essayists to find out the source of several figures published in the press, on the Net or in various books. The answers were strangely rare and unsatisfactory, which raises some questions about the deontology and intellectual rigor of a certain number of "professionals"[a]. This left academic research[b]. In many countries, including Germany, Holland and the United States, this is remarkably active. Unfortunately, this is not the case in France, where the effort made is more reminiscent of the Gobi desert than the lush Amazon. Such a shortage is obviously very regrettable. However, it is in no way dramatic if one accepts to consider that there is a very strong general coherence in the audiovisual behavior of young Westerners. Thus, when we compare the data obtained in different countries, either directly (cross-national studies) or incidentally (independent national studies), it turns out that the framework of use set by parents and the details of consumption by children are largely comparable[115,165-170]. As George Comstock and Erica Scharrer have pointed out in a well-documented and widely cited synthesis of the scientific literature: "Precise comparisons [...] are not possible because of methodological variations, and even when the method is the same, uncertainties about the comparability and representativeness of the samples. Yet, large patterns are easily discernible. The most indelible impression refers to the degree to which children's television use is largely the same in all countries."[169] I emphasize this point so strongly primarily to clarify the use of a wide range of academic data from different countries in this chapter. It is also to dispel the myth of a strict cultural relativism that television advocates are so fond of evoking when it comes to evading unwelcome data.[38] Now that all this has been made clear, it is important that we take into account the fact that television is a very popular medium. Now that all this has been clarified, we can calmly attack the heart of the matter.

*

* *

---

a. There are however notable exceptions. The press service of *Télérama* sent me a very complete file through Carole Favier. Sylvain Michelet also replied to me in detail following an excellent paper published in *Psychologies magazine*[164].
b. All the researchers and academics I have contacted to ask for details of their work or copies of their publications have responded, without exception. Many journalists and other essayists would benefit, I believe, from being inspired by this ethic. It would, I am sure, reduce the volume of empty and fanciful assertions.

The TV, master of time and space

In the history of humanity, no consumer good has colonized human life as quickly as television. In the United States, just after the Second World War, it took only seven short years for the rate of household equipment to rise from 1 to 75 percent.[12,171] To reach the same level of coverage, the radio took 14 years, the refrigerator 23, and the television was the first to be installed. It took radio 14 years, the refrigerator 23, the vacuum cleaner 48, the automobile 52, the telephone 67[12] and the book several centuries[62] to reach the same level of coverage. Today, more than 99% of American households are equipped with at least one television. A similar figure applies to France[172,173] and all developed countries[165,166]. Even Africa, an economically disadvantaged continent, has an average penetration rate close to 85%, according to a transnational Unesco study.[165] As Jo Groebel, author of this study, points out: "The screen has become a universal medium throughout the world. Whether in the favelas, an island in the South Pacific, or a skyscraper in Asia, television is ubiquitous."[121] It has become "a major factor in socialization and dominates the lives of children in urban and rural electrified areas around the world."[123] It is hard to argue with this statement when nearly 90% of the world's children recognize Terminator and Rambo[121]. A percentage that takes on its full meaning when one measures, for example, that a quarter of American teenagers do not even know who Hitler is[174]. This is about as many as the number of young Englishmen who make Winston Churchill into a fictional character who never existed[175]. We obviously don't learn that much from television.

Basically, to say that the small screen is everywhere is insufficient. If we wanted to be precise, we should rather say that the small screen is everywhere *in a central position.* Thus, in the overwhelming majority of homes, the living room is designed, not to stimulate interpersonal exchanges, but to facilitate access to the television set[101,176]. In the same way, family planning (meals, bedtime, homework time, etc.) is mainly punctuated, not by physiological rhythms, but by television time[101,177,178]. For example, in France, according to Crédoc, the television news serves as a real "temporal reference"[179]. According to the latest estimates of this organization, "2 out of 3 households dine in front of [the television], and 43% even use it at lunchtime [...] On weekdays, people dine in 35 minutes (33 minutes in 1995), which is the same amount of time as the television news"[180]. Liliane Lurçat was probably not wrong when she wrote a few years ago: "Television in the home, or domestic television, tends to become the mistress of the house around which daily life is organized and deployed."[5]

It must be said that our dear mistress spares no effort to be seductive and penetrate ever further the intimacy of our homes. At the forefront of the strategies implemented by the beautiful one to win our favors, is a large effort of programmatic diversification. When the Rolling Stones were born in 1962, the French audiovisual offer was still limited to a single channel broadcasting, at best, from noon to midnight. Not very stimulating! The landscape began to change slowly in 1963, with the arrival of "2". In 1972, "3" made its appearance. Canal + arrived 12 years later, just before "5" and "6" emerged. Satellite, cable and DTT emerged in the next two decades. Today, a package like Canalsat boasts nearly 300 channels.[182] Information, cinema, sports, music, history, travel, horseback riding, hunting, fishing, shopping, cooking, manga, adults, teens, children, newborns, there is something for everyone. But it's hard to avoid conflicts when Dad wants to watch Eurosport, Mom wants to watch Planet, the kid wants to watch Teletoon and the teen wants to watch MTV. Monique Dagnaud, director of research at the CNRS and former member of the Conseil supérieur de l'audiovisuel (CSA), observes that "television has become one of the greatest sources of tension in families"[183,184]. To avoid the problem, the most direct solution is obviously to multiply the number of receivers. In the United States, for which we have the most accurate public figures, 79% of households have at least three sets and more than 70% of children aged 8 and over have a television in their bedroom[152]. The figure is 43% for 4-6 year olds, 29% for 2-3 year olds and 19% for 0-1 year olds[185]! As a recent Inserm report[a] points out, France has not yet reached these heights, but it is getting closer[186]. Thus, 57% of adults have a television in their bedroom[187], compared to 41% of 13-14 year olds and 25% of 6-8 year olds[188]; proportions comparable to those of Germany [115] and Belgium[189]. A study conducted in 2008 among French pupils aged 6 to 13 with learning difficulties established a higher penetration rate, quite close to that of adults (53%).[190] If we accept that these pupils are also the least socially privileged, this figure overlaps with other data showing that a child is significantly more likely to have a television in his or her room if he or she comes from a modest and/or poorly educated background.[191-193] This relationship explains, in part, the higher penetration rate of children with

------

a. National Institute of Health and Medical Research.

learning difficulties. This relationship explains, in part, the tendency of disadvantaged children to consume more television than their affluent counterparts[167,169,194-198]. Indeed, a "discretionary" TV translates into a frighteningly increased exposure time. Depending on age, the increase can be as high as 60-75%[192]. A teenager who used to watch TV for two hours a day will find himself, for example, at 3.30 a.m. as soon as a receiver is placed in his room[192]. Such amplification is not harmless. It leads to decreased physical activity, poorer eating habits, less time spent reading, impaired sleep, poorer school performance, and a drying up of intra-family interactions.[192,199-201] Although each of these points is discussed in detail in the following sections, they are not necessarily the same. Although each of these points will be discussed in detail in later chapters, it seems appropriate to point out now that the finding of impoverished intra-family exchanges is basically quite trivial. Indeed, when parents choose to place a television in a child's room, it is most often, according to them, to get rid of a cumbersome and painful presence[185,202]. As Nathalie admitted to me with a deep dose of discouragement: "I'm tired, I can't do it anymore between the twins [3 years old], work, the house, my divorce. At least now they stay in their room, I don't see them, I'm a bit quiet." This admission is in line with several quantitative studies showing that the more depressed a mother is, the more her children are exposed to high volumes of television, especially before the age of 3-4 years[203,204]. Alone in front of the television set, the children watch what they want, without supervision, at times that suit them. It is also striking to note that children who have a television available to them are also the ones who have the fewest rules imposed on them by their parents.[192] As Jean-Pierre confirmed to me, the children who have a television are the ones who have the fewest rules. As Jean-Pierre confirmed to me about his teenage daughter, "she has her TV, she doesn't bother me anymore with her stupid series" (*sic*). A bit crude in form, but clear in content.

In apparent contrast to the elements that have just been mentioned, I frequently hear that the audience for the small screen is waning among adolescents and other young adults. They would have "deserted their TV for the Net"[205,206]. Television would have become "an old man's medium", holding "the role of a wallpaper hanging on the wall"[207]. It is necessary to face the evidence, we are told everywhere, young people "almost do not watch television anymore when they are less than 15 years old, and this worries the telecrats very seriously"[208]. In fact, "today, the French are turning away from television and books, and devoting themselves more to this new medium [the Internet]. In agreement with these theses, Médiamétrie data show that the viewing time of 15-24 year-olds has dropped by 22% in 10 years on terrestrial channels[205]. Figures from a private lobby dedicated to the development of Internet advertising confirm this trend, indicating that young Europeans (aged 16-24) now spend more time on the Web than watching television.[205] Continuous observation of the behavior of five families [what a sample!] for a week would also corroborate this pattern. According to the director of the marketing agency that carried out this "study": "The children have not put down their school bags and are now jumping on the Internet. Often, when the television is on, it is behind their back. They watch it with their ears. It's just part of the décor. The conversations they have on MSN [an instant messaging system] seem more entertaining than any soap opera. There's no doubt about it: this is a generation lost to Daddy's television." [210] No doubt? That sounds optimistic! Indeed, according to the most recent estimates, we have never spent so much time in front of our TV. In 2009, worldwide consumption reached an all-time high of 3 hours 12 minutes per day per person[211]. According to the World Health Organization (WHO), nearly 60% of French adolescents aged 15 watch more than two hours of television a day on weekdays[167]. Comparable proportions are observed in countries with high digital penetration such as the United States, Sweden and England. Germany is close to 70%. The Netherlands is over 75%. This picture doesn't change much when you consider a wider demographic range, like Médiamétrie. According to this audience measurement institute, the audiovisual consumption of 15-24 year olds is well over two hours a day in Germany, England, Spain, Italy, the United States and France[212]. For Médiamétrie, "a focus on these young adults reveals that despite the demands they are subjected to, Internet, digital entertainment and especially games, they are far from abandoning their television viewing habits. It is not because they have an Internet screen that they are less of a television fan. *In the end, there is no real competition between the screens.*"[173] The audience share lost by the major terrestrial channels would, in this context, be largely captured by thematic channels on satellite, cable or DTT[212-215]. Several academic studies confirm these conclusions for the United States. No more than in France, there is "support for the speculation that newer media, such as computers, the Internet and video games, are supplanting older media such as television. Not only does television consume almost three times the time of the next closest medium, but the next closest category consists of videos and movies - arguably just another form of television. In other words, exposure to a TV screen, in one form or another, accounts for more than half of young people's exposure to electronic media.[216] This is fully confirmed by a recent report from the highly regarded Nielsen firm[217]. The original purpose of the report was, in the words of the investigators themselves, to "shatter the myths and give [the reader] *hard facts*. In the executive summary, the following conclusions were made: "Teens are NOT abandoning TV for new media: in fact, they are watching more TV than ever, an increase of 6% over the past 5 years in the U.S. Teens love the Internet... but spend far less time browsing than adults: teens spend 11 hours and 32 minutes per month online - well below the average of 29 hours and 15 minutes."

We are thus far from the announced cataclysm. You really have to be desperately blind, candid and ignorant to claim that young people have deserted television. It remains at the heart of their lives and the least we can say is that the trend does not show any inflection. Indeed, the previous data do not take into account the new modes of audiovisual consumption. With the constant diversification of access portals, the programmatic offer will become more and more universal, not to say invasive. In this respect, a significant part of our usage already involves the Web, in parti-cular through so-called *catch-up TV* services[152,218-224] (which, incidentally, renders the often evoked opposition between computer and television largely obsolete). The latest tidal wave to date is *Secret Story*, whose videos totaled 28 million accesses in July 2009 alone.[220] Another example is Dailymotion, where 8 out of 10 of its users consult television programs.[219] Recently, channels have even begun to develop programs specifically for the Net[225]. To this, we must also add the cell phone. This now allows live access to several dozen channels. In 2008, an operator marketed the first cellular device capable of receiving free DTT programs.[226] The 16 channels of personal mobile television will also be available (normally) soon[227,228]. Our audiovisual leash is getting longer and longer to follow us everywhere: in the toilet, on the bus, in the train, in the restaurant, in the stadium, at work, in church, at school or college: "Everywhere at all times, on all screens![218] the National Union of Television Advertising (SNTA) enthuses in a text with an evocative headline: "Television as the first screen of the French: some people would like to make you doubt. In short, TV in all places and at any time; the perfect ubiquity, the absolute nightmare. As

Dimitri Christakis and Frederick Zimmerman, specialists in the subject at the University of Washington, say, "It was already alarming (to some) that two-thirds of teenagers have televisions in their bedrooms. Soon they will have them in their pockets.[4] I can confirm this because I recently saw a student in a neurophysiology lecture watching a soccer game on his laptop. This must be what we call bringing new technologies to the university. It is worth noting that according to a recent study by the Kaiser Foundation, audiovisual consumption linked to new media is already approaching one hour per day in the United States among 8-18 year olds, including 24 minutes for the Internet, 15 minutes for cell phones and 15 minutes for iPod/MP3[152] type systems.

So, contrary to a widely spread discourse, teenagers and other young adults are far from deserting the small screen for video games, instant messaging, forums or blogs. Television remains, by far, the favorite leisure activity of the new generations. And don't think that they watch their programs with a distracted eye. 70% to 80% of the time spent in front of the screen is exclusive of any other activity, except for snacking (15% of the time spent watching TV is also spent eating, I'll come back to that). When television agrees to share itself, it mainly invites to its table household chores (4%), music (4%), the computer (4%), the telephone (4%) and schoolwork (7%).[229] Sometimes, all this beautiful world mixes together in a joyful chaos. For example, this 17-year-old said, "When I'm online, I'm constantly multitasking. At this very moment, I'm watching TV, checking my email every two minutes, checking a news forum about who killed JFK [John Fitzgerald Kennedy], burning music to a CD, and writing these words."[230] Progressive do-gooders, of course, do not miss an opportunity to acclaim this remarkable talent,[231] while at the same time crying harum-scarum at those adults who shy away from the virtual thing because they are "a tad jealous of the ease with which their children handle computer tools."[40] Unfortunately, as we will see in the next chapter, these positions are completely unfounded. The computer expertise of teenagers is a myth. Their ability to do several things at once is a sad chimera. To be convinced of this, it is enough to listen to my 13-year-old niece's good-natured lament that she doesn't understand anything about a German assignment, which she is facing at the same time as TF1's *Gossip Girl*, cell phone SMS and MSN instant messages. But as her mother (an excellent German speaker) says: "What can you do, young people are like that nowadays, they all do the same, you have to live with the times." The ugly reactionary that I am tends to think that it should still be possible to require a teenager or kid to turn off the TV, cell phone and computer for a few minutes. But, apparently I'm wrong. The "experts" are clear: we must not force our youngest children to do anything. Take this mother for example. After having asked her 6 year old son three times to turn off the television, she finally disconnects the power herself. A terrible blindness that led to a terrible caprice, nicely named "crying fit" by the hilarious Catherine Muller and François Chemel. According to these two authors, "if you turn off the television set with authority and walk away, [the child] will be in such a state of frustration and anger that he or she will then be suspicious of all other attempts you might make.[32] A prospect, let's face it, that is hard to sustain! But don't worry, there is a way out. To get out of it, you have to be cunning. Like the fox in the fable, you have to lure the child into another activity.[32] To tame the kid's ardor, take him to the park, offer him a construction game, take him out for a snack. If you're lucky, he'll agree for a few minutes, without a "crying fit", to take off his post. Let's face it, though, it might be hard to lure our young phone-goer back to his multiplication tables or history lesson with this kind of cheese.

*
**

From children's programs to general audience programs

Fortunately, there is still a practical approach that is much safer than trickery to avoid the whims of our children when the set goes out. The only way to get away with it is to curb the early addiction. A recent study has shown that adverse reactions do occur around the age of 6 in response to intransigent disconnections. However, these reactions are very hete-rogeneous. The more children have been exposed to a heavy audiovisual regime before the age of 4, the more likely they are to vehemently oppose the abrogation of the cathode ray when they enter the first grade[232]. In itself, this result is hardly surprising, given the abundance of data showing that television use is acquired by impregnation during the initial stages of life[12,29,169,185,194,233]. It has been shown, in particular, that the volume of television absorbed during early childhood generally predicts adolescent consumption, which in turn predicts adult exposure[196,234-236]. However, it is striking to note that the use of the small screen is not originally the result of a spontaneous demand by the child, but rather of heavy parental pressure. In other words, it is not the children who naturally go to the television. It is the adults who insist and do everything possible to make the meeting happen. A Sofres survey underlines that only 15% of very young children (1-4 years) regularly ask for television. 61% never ask for it! The remaining 25% are divided into rare (10%) or occasional (15%) requesters.[198] Individual or group qualitative interviews largely confirm these data by underlining the natural disinterest of children in television and by stigmatizing the incentive function of parents. For many parents, TV is certainly a way to obtain free time to satisfy various hobbies or household chores: "When he's watching TV," says, for example, this mother of a 1-3 year old[a], "I can do other things.[185] The same is true of this Colorado woman: "They get up and watch TV while I shower and get dressed.[185] Other parents are quick to acknowledge a more general goal of turning their restless brats into lovable, apathetic cattle. For example, this Ohio mother said of her 4-6 year old son, "He's a good little boy. He doesn't bother anyone. He doesn't do anything stupid. He's glued to the TV."[185] Similarly, for this California resident, also the mother of a 4-6 year old: "The media makes my life easier. We are all happier. He doesn't throw tantrums. I can get some work done."[185] And what about this lovely matron, recounting the long road of crosses she had to endure to finally turn her 2-year-old into a zealous telephobe. "When he was 18 months old] I started by trying *Sesame Street*[b]. I would make an effort to get him interested in the program. I would turn on the set and say, "Look! There's a car," or whatever [...] Then I bought a book on *Sesame Street* and we would watch it together. I think that helped get him interested. It took from October to Christmas. Finally "it took". It was very gradual. But now he watches every day, always with a bottle, in the morning and in the afternoon [...] I know that television is not really good for children, but a few hours a day really can't be that bad. I guess if I didn't have a TV, I would have tried to establish a quiet time routine in his room, something like a nap-game. But that would have been difficult."[29]

I confess to remain speechless, not to say featherless, by visualizing this poor amorphous kid, slumped in front of the TV set, "a few hours a

---

a. The study from which this quote is taken[185] does not specify the exact age of the children, just a range: 1-3 or 4-6 years.
b. *1 Sesame Street.*

day", a bottle in his hand. Welcome, dear friends, to the wonderful world of TeleValium: guaranteed tranquility, flawless stultification. If the symptoms persist, consult the program and increase the dose.

The extent of the incentive strategies exerted on children, to lead them to the television set, proves to be all the more difficult to understand as the vast majority of adults seem to be fully aware of the potentially harmful character of television. Thus, between 85 and 90% of parents of children aged 2 to 17 admit to being worried about the cathode ray tube[191] and more generally about electronic media[237,238]. In the apprehension contest, television is far ahead of all its other competitors, including the Internet and video games[191,237,238]. More than the amount of time spent in front of the screen, it is the nature of the programs watched that mainly alarms parents[191]. 75 to 80% of them say they are concerned about their offspring being overexposed to inappropriate sexual, violent and semantic content. More than 80% believe that this content substantially influences children's behaviour. 77% consider that advertising influences the food choices of young people. 66% admit that they are regularly asked to buy products "seen on TV"[237,238]. A set of fears summarized with great lucidity by this mother who stated bluntly: "[Television] makes my life easier, but in the long run, when [the children] are older and start encountering all these problems, I think I wish I hadn't let them do it when they were five."[185] Helen's testimony, as collected by Marie Winn, sadly validates this omen, while showing that it becomes terribly difficult to stop the spiral once it has begun. At the beginning of her story, this *musician* tells us that she deliberately placed her two children in front of the television set when they were very small.[29] Initially, she tells us, their children were not allowed to see the television. Initially, she tells us, their consumption consisted of *Mister Rogers' Neighborhood*, an "educational" series lasting about thirty minutes. Then, after a few months, *Sesame Street* was added. When the children were 4 years old, *Mister Rogers' was* considered too bland and was rejected in favor of *Batman*. Then came two more cartoons, *Underdog* and *The Flintstones*. It was then," says Helen, "that I started to feel a little uncomfortable about television... You see, I was in complete control at first. Then slowly these other programs crept in and the kids seemed to want to watch so much! [...] What began to bother me was that John often refused to go out and ride his bike in the afternoon, because he preferred to watch TV. [...] I talked to the school psychologist about the TV problem and she told me not to worry about it, that if John wanted to watch two or three hours of TV that was probably the best thing for him. It went against all my instincts, but it was the easiest thing to do, just let him watch." Later, John and his sister discovered Saturday morning cartoons. "It was great for us," Helen confesses, "because it kept us in bed nice and long while they watched TV." During the week, new programs were gradually added. Getting the kids to leave the TV and come to dinner became more and more difficult. After several requests," says Helen, "I would always have to come in and turn it off, and they would get very angry about it. They would say 'I hate you' and come to dinner pushing and hitting each other, angry and sulky, very, very angry. As a result, dinner was very unpleasant for all of us. They stayed grumpy throughout the meal. It was the worst part of the day, really! [...] It's a terrible saga, right?" Terrible, I don't know, but ordinary, no doubt. Like many parents, Helen will probably end up letting her children eat quietly in front of the television. Obesity will set in and the tantrums will fade away.[239-242]

Like Helen, most families begin their television history with good intentions. As long as the offspring is not yet 5 or 6 years old, it is subject to relatively close surveillance and its audiovisual consumption is constrained both in terms of programming space and time. However, the latter is substantially less regulated (56% *versus* 81% of households)[185a], which is hardly surprising given that parents are much more sensitive to the problem of content than to the question of duration (see *above*). This being said, it should be kept in mind that the rules of use applied to content do not necessarily imply a strict exclusion of "all audiences" programs from the cathodic diet of very young children. In fact, before the age of 5-6 years, they consume a large number of programs that are not specifically intended for them, but which seem acceptable to adults in terms of language, violence or sexuality[115,185,193,197,198,244]. When children enter the first grade, this eclecticism becomes more widespread until the main barriers to parental supervision are broken down[192,193]. We can identify two major reasons for this regrettable collapse. Firstly, the resistance of our young telephonists to exogenous constraints is becoming more and more acute, and parents do not necessarily want to go systematically to conflict (Helen's story bears witness to this). Second, adults generally see age as reducing the risk of ontogenetic damage. On average, more than half of the homes with minors aged 8 to 18 provide them with completely free televi-

---

a. See also for a comparable trend (69% versus 90%), RIDEOUT V.J. and VANDEWATER E.A., Zero to Six: Electronic Media in the Lives of Infants, Toddlers and Preschoolers.[243]

sion use[192,193]. In the remaining homes, there are rules, but they are mostly virtual and applied at the whim of the children. The proportion of families that actually impose restrictions on the use of television on their school-age children is less than 20 percent. This percentage varies, of course, with the age of the protagonists. The 8-10 year olds are the most controlled (26%), followed by the 11-14 year olds (22%) and the 15-18 year olds (13%)[192]. If you put it differently, these figures indicate that 3/4 of 8-year-olds and 8/10 of 11-year-olds are not restricted in their use of the station! Everything is allowed with no time limit. From series to movies, games and reality TV, nothing is banned. This astonishing permissiveness no doubt explains why children's television consumption resembles that of adults at a very early age.[171,173,197,244-246] "Contrary to what is commonly believed, children are not allowed to watch television. Contrary to what one might think," explains Monique Dagnaud, "children watch very few programs intended for young people, such as cartoons. It is estimated that 80% of the time spent in front of the television by children aged 4 to 10 is spent in front of "all audiences" programs. 25 to 30% of 8-12 year olds are still watching TV at 8:30 pm. They therefore see series, films or the news at a very young age, which are all forays into the adult world."[183] In line with this statement, data published by Médiamétrie show that nearly 1.5 million children aged 4 to 10 are in front of the TV at 8 pm. At 10 p.m., the figure is still 800,000 individuals! This value is identical to the one observed in the morning at around 8[247]. It is therefore hardly surprising that children's favorite programs include a number of "all-audience" series such as *Grey's Anatomy*, *Desperate Housewives*, *Prison Break* or *CSI*[238]. According to Catherine Muller and François Chemel, citing Médiamétrie, it has even been established that certain first half of the evening shows, such as Joséphine[32], manage to attract more than 50% of the 4-14 year olds, which guarantees *roughly* (if the figure is valid) 4 million zombies for the next morning's teachers[150]! In the same age group, the daily show of *Secret Story* would have an audience share of 50% at 6pm, between exposed breasts, watery frolics, striptease, banana tasting with suggestive sauce, insults, low blows and high-flying tirades such as "they treated us because FX almost went into an elitist coma", "I'm unable to go to confession", "I don't give a fuck even if I don't have any balls", "he forgot that he has scabs on his ass", "you're a son of a bitch", or "the ugly one, the big disgusting cow who gets naked in the shower with her boobs rubbing her toes"[248-251]. These words and contents are obviously remarkably suitable for kindergarteners!

Having said that, I recognize that it is possible to find much worse in the land of parental irresponsibility, including, for example, this mother who is as proud as she is enthusiastic: "*The Punisher*[a], my son [4 years old!] loves this film."[185] There are also all those adults who are largely unaware of what their children are watching, like this woman who declared in dismay: "I recently paid attention to what [my son (4-6 years old)] was watching and I saw. I said, "What the hell is this?" I couldn't believe it."[185] In keeping with this salutary amazement, a recent academic study found that adults knew less than half of the programs commonly viewed by their children[253]. Further work has established that parental ignorance was not homogeneous, but modulated in inverse proportion to educational level. In other words, the more educated parents are, the better they know what their children watch[192]. It is probably no coincidence that the level of education also modulates the probability that a child has a personal television in his or her bedroom (see *above*). Basically, this lack of knowledge on the part of adults about their children's television viewing habits is largely due to the fact that the latter are very often left to their own devices[12,171,192,198,254]. One large study estimated the proportion of co-viewing in the presence of a parent to be 19% for 2-7 year olds, 6% for 8-13 year olds and 2% for 14-18 year olds[193]. During "parent-free time," zapping becomes the rule for selecting programs, without supervision or concern for appropriateness.[255] Everything is good, even (and especially) when it is not. Everything is good, even (and especially) the worst. Dominique Poussier, head of youth programs at TF1, confirms these data in a captivating testimony recently given to journalist Jean-Philippe Desbordes[44]: "We must," says this woman of influence, "reach children aged 4 to 10. Advertisers think that children are prescribers from the age of 4, and that they are interested in things that are for older children. It's like the phenomenon of little girls wearing thongs at 12... I think we have a big responsibility in several ways: they are still small and very malleable, mothers don't care what they watch, they are future citizens and we can send them messages through the programs[b] [...] Basically, I think that the criticisms that we are receiving are perhaps indicative of the resignation of parents who seem to have given up saying no, they prefer that there is no advertising so they don't have to say no. I think the channel is taking responsibility. It would be good for parents to take theirs [...] We have regular studies by the playground observatory: we

---

a. A particularly violent film that is forbidden to children under 16 in France[252].
b. Like putting on thongs at age 12?

realize that mothers don't know what their children are watching. For children's programs, because they are reassured that there is no danger, they do not know what they are watching. Parents do not watch cartoons[a], or watch them only for a short time. Mothers know what their children are watching when they share while watching Star Academy. The last study we have is for children ages 4 to 14. They watch *Desperate Housewives, Star Ac', CSI* and *FBI: Missing Persons*. For these series, it's joint viewing with mothers or both parents, and it's much more worrisome than watching cartoons... The attacks [suffered by TV stations] are commensurate with the resignation of parents." Simply put, commercial television is there to sell advertisers "human brain time"[b]. If parents have given up, if they let their children watch anything, it is neither the problem nor the responsibility of the channels. They do their job and they do it, as it should be, as well as possible. The argument is as implacable as it is irrefutable. Indeed, one cannot reproach a company for being efficient, sustainable and profitable! By attracting each day in its nets a large mass of immature neurons, TF1 only answers its mercantile vocation. If an educational program of high lineage captivates the customer, then so much the better, it will see the air. If it doesn't and the audience explodes in response to the most distressing contents, then too bad, they will take the focus. It is important not to be misled here: the viewer is not the customer, he is literally a commodity that the channels sell to advertisers. Beyond the façade speeches, all this beautiful world does not care about children. They are only a target, a market, a source of profit. A recent episode in our parliamentary life illustrates, I believe, perfectly this truism[256,257]. On the night of March 9-10, 2009, while a bill was being debated to combat alcoholism, smoking and obesity among young people, the deputies had to vote on an amendment aimed at prohibiting, before and after youth programs, all advertising for fatty and sugary snack products. This is an obvious measure when we know the massive deleterious impact of advertising on children's eating habits[106]. This measure has been called for by the French National Institute for Medical Research (Inserm) and the French Agency for Food Safety (Afssa), and is supported by a number of learned societies and associations, including, for example, the French Pediatric Society (SFP), the French Society of Nutrition (SFN), the French Federation of Cardiology (SFC), the Federation of Parents of Public Schoolchildren (PEEP), the Federation of

---

a. Nor, in fact, the floods of advertising that accompany them.
b. In the words of Patrick Le Lay, who was once the boss of Ms. Poussier [23].

Parents of Schoolchildren (FCPE), and the French Association of Diabetics (AFD).[258] Our deputies rejected the text without any qualms, under the combined pressure of the audiovisual, advertising and agri-food industry lobbies. However common it may be, this appalling and stupid political cowardice will never cease to amaze me. Preserving the profits of a few food groups undoubtedly justifies the aggravation of the obesity epidemic that is currently hitting all developed nations and costing our health systems billions of euros every year[106].

*
**

Rewriting reality

Are we, as parents, as cowardly as our dear deputies? Are we really "resigning" as Dominique Poussier suggests? The idea might be plausible if human behavior always had an informed and rational basis. This is clearly not the case. First, as I have had occasion to point out at length in the introduction, parents find their legitimate fears diluted in a steady stream of servile and sycophantic talk. Second, our most random actions are not, in the overwhelming majority of cases, the result of Cartesian impulses. They are the fruit of psychic arbitrations inaccessible to the Ego. Obviously, the emotional conflict felt by the parents with regard to the use of the post is effectively dissolved in the subterranean action of defensive mechanisms dear to Freudian metapsychology.[259,260] In the rationalization department[a], for example, how can we not think again of the example seen above of this mother explaining that her 4-year-old son is very mature for his age and that he can therefore, without any problem, watch films as frighteningly violent as *The Punisher*. How can we not also think of all those adults whose children are crazy about documentary channels such as Planète, Voyages or Animaux. These "educational" channels are so popular that their audience is, at best, three or four tenths of a percent[262]. Let us repeat once again: from the age of 4-5, children spend most of their time watching

------

a. Rationalization is defined as a "process by which the subject seeks to give a logically coherent, or morally acceptable, explanation for an attitude, action, idea, feeling, etc., whose true motives are not perceived".[261]

"all-audience" programs (see *above*), and the few children's programs they do watch consist mainly of recreational series and cartoons.

According to a report by the Collectif interassociatif enfance et média (CIEM) for the Ministry of Health, "more than 90 percent of the programming for children on all terrestrial channels is fictional"[59]. To evoke the didactic power of television to justify the cathodic use of our kids seems therefore a little extravagant. All the more extravagant as the pedagogical potential of these postulated "educational" channels remains to be established, to say the least.

We will have the opportunity to reconsider this point in detail in the next chapter. Before we get there, however, let's look back for a moment at our "rationalization" strategies and consider the case of those unfortunate adults "obliged" to give in to audiovisual demands so as not to turn their unfortunate offspring into real social pariahs. A necessity perfectly summarized by *Parents* magazine on its website[263]: "One can be anti-TV, but one must know that it remains a factor of socialization. At school, what do the children talk about? Franklin, Dora, Bob the Builder, the Winx, etc. And anyone who doesn't know these heroes, which children need to identify with, risks feeling excluded from their peer group." May I be forgiven for my outburst but frankly, what a load of crap! Not only is there no data to support this kind of nicely peremptory assertion, but all the available evidence clearly tends to invalidate the relevance of the statement. First of all, as we shall see in detail in Chapter III, children identify much more easily with an "imaginary" character from the words of a book or a story than with an embodied subject whose features are irremediably defined. Then, all the kids know Dora and her kind. Those who don't have TV have frequently seen a DVD somewhere (and as the episodes all look the same...)[a], they have often been in contact with a derivative product of some kind (a book in particular) and/or they have generally talked about the program with their friends in the school yard. Valentine has, moreover, on this subject, like all the kids who do not have TV, a remarkable secret weapon that could be summarized as follows: "What is Dora?" His girlfriends are happy to explain it to him and I do not have the impression that the exchanges that I can then observe are poorer than those that two girls who would regularly see this program on TV. On the contrary! In this respect, many case studies emphasize the excellent social integration of

---

a. Valentine saw Franklin in the podiatrist's waiting room. She met Dora at her cousin Eva's house.

children raised away from television[16,29,183,264]. According to several studies, these children are more satisfied with their lives and happier than their counterparts who watch television[55,152,192,193,265]. This is not really surprising, because by avoiding television, these kids also avoid, to a large extent, this "youth culture" that is so alienating because of its dress diktats, its morphological injunctions, its consumerist imperatives and its sad sabir. As Hannah Arendt wrote in a famous essay dedicated to *The Crisis of Education*, "freed from the authority of adults, the child has thus not been liberated but subjected to a much more frightening and truly tyrannical authority: the tyranny of the majority. We shall return to this later. For the moment, let us remain for a moment faithful to the defense mechanisms of the Ego and let us be interested, after Lady Rationalization, in Sir Denial[a]. The latter is widely used by parents to refute the extent of their children's cathode consumption. How many times have I heard mothers explain in a huff that their children "hardly" watch television. Take Astrid, for example, whose 5-year-old daughter only wants to wear pink and glitter. Yes," says this mother in an amused tone, "I made a slut. I don't know where it comes from. The TV? She hardly watches it."[267] There is also Amaury, a charming little 5-year-old boy, whose mother recently explained to me that he had very little audiovisual consumption, limited to "a few cartoons in the morning before going to school and a DVD in the evening while preparing dinner." I didn't dare to point out to the lady that this represented about 2 hours, 2.5 hours per day! I courteously acquiesced to the speech that was proposed to me, while thinking about this study carried out on children from 10 to 13 years old and showing that 81% of the mothers and 87% of the fathers minimize the duration of their offspring's listening. On average, the latter exceeded parental ratings by 56%.[253] A comparable value (63%) was reported in another study for children aged 6 to 13 years. This means that each hour of television postulated corresponds roughly to 1 h 35 of television consumed. This underestimation is all the more critical because it is coupled with an overestimation of the duration of exposure of third-party children [69]. Parents tend to think that "their children watch less than the average time; the estimated average viewing time for other children is 73% higher than the actual average time. The more their own children watch, the more parents think the average viewing time for other children

---

a. Denial is defined as "a defense mode consisting of a refusal by the subject to recognize the reality of a traumatic perception"[261].

is high. In other words, adults believe that their kids watch TV, but not as much and in any case less than other kids.

In fact, the idea that "others" are collectively permeable to the influence of television that leaves us personally unscathed is hardly new. Nor is it specific to the parental institution. By vanity, naivety or blindness, we like to exclude ourselves from the telephonic herd. This psycho-defensive safeguard is functionally necessary to us. Without it, how could we let our children watch the television so assiduously? How could we, ourselves, give up so much screen time? By recognizing that television models not only the behavior of our fellow human beings, but also our own behavior, we would put ourselves in a position to reject either the addictive pleasure of our audiovisual consumption, or the inalienable requirement of our freedom. Cruel dilemma that it is better to deconstruct than to face. "I am different from the others" is the saving credo of the cathodic bovine. For example, 78% of teenagers say that their sexual behaviour is not influenced by television. Seventy-two percent consider that the same is not true for their peers[273]. Similarly, only 10% of users say they are addicted to television. The question of whether the others are addicted to television receives 70% approval.[288] On another level, an overwhelming majority of French people say they prefer documentary and cultural programs to reality shows.[289,274,275] This trend is so massive that it is not surprising that the majority of French people prefer to watch television. This trend is so massive that French television viewers regularly place Arte far ahead of TF1 in the satisfaction ratings[276-278]. However, in terms of audience share, the mephitic first channel systematically pulverizes its elitist little sister, without the slightest ambiguity (26.1% *versus* 1.7% in 2009)[146]. Of the 50 best ratings in 2009, all produced by TF1, there were no documentaries to accompany American series (38), soccer matches (4), mainstream films (3), entertainment programs (3), a news program and an intervention by the Prime Minister.[279] This is not for lack of trying, however, to find a way to make the channel's ratings more attractive. However, it is not for lack of having had a few potentially eligible educational programs, including, for example, a trilogy on the Second World War (*Apocalypse*[a]) and an ecological "event" film broadcast simultaneously in 130 countries (*Home*[b]). In addition, in 2007, TF1 had the 100 highest ratings of all channels combined[281] . In 2008[282] and 2009[283], our glutton had to be content with a

---

a. Broadcast on September 8, 15 and 22, 2009 on France 2.
b. Broadcast on June 5, 2009 on France 2[280].

modest 96 out of 100. In 2006 we were at 98[284]. In fact, the French so vomit the first channel and the values it embodies that they recently watched 7.6 million interviews with the head of state on the latter. At the same time, the beloved public service channel achieved a score almost half that (4.1 million)[285] with exactly the same program. The figures sometimes speak for themselves, especially when they have the bad habit of repeating themselves.[286]

*
**

The unattainable myth of "quality"

To sum up, while the average viewer is resolutely eager for knowledge and culture, he concentrates his audiovisual time on the most inferior channels. Day after day, these channels offer him a wide mix of stupid series, rudimentary information, indigent debates and promotional TV shows. Perfectly primary programs, made of sticky emotions, nauseating voyeurism, pitiful stereotypes, distressing approximations and consumerist injunctions[16,28,287]. I often hear it said that the channels are in no way responsible for this state of affairs, that they are not competent to shape the taste of viewers, and that they merely follow the demand of a public which, according to Patrick Eveno, "ultimately determines the nature of the media, their content, their ways of saying and doing. The argument is convenient. It is nonetheless largely fallacious. Indeed, the content that inhabits our airwaves depends less, for the most part, on the expectations of a hypothetically prescribing population, than on the intrinsic characteristics of the small screen. All the contents are not soluble in the television. Frustrated emotions, Manichean worlds and concrete spaces are much better suited to television than complex fields, subtle analyses and abstract universes.[289,290] This is an assertion that it is probably not useless to support briefly, by questioning some of the structural constraints that enslave audiovisual production.

The first of these constraints is the incredible density of the broadcasting network. Already in 1953, a Unesco report pointed out that it was "difficult, if not impossible, to produce every day of the week good drama series, good entertainment, good educational programs, and good children's programs. The result of long hours of broadcasting is guaranteed to make quality the exception".[290] Today, Europe alone is said to have nearly 600 TV channels,[291] half of which are available on a bouquet such as Canalsat.[182] Even assuming that these channels are broadcasting on a single channel, the number of TV channels in Europe is still very small. Even if we assume that these channels broadcast part-time over a limited period of 18 hours a day, this represents nearly 4 million hours of programming to be provided annually. This is a staggering figure, which can be measured by considering, for example, *L'Odyssée de l'espèce*, the solid 90-minute documentary initially broadcast on France 3[292]. Two years of hard work were necessary to finalize the project. France Télévisions piloted the adventure "alongside Canada, Germany, Belgium, Spain, but also Americans, Swiss, Chinese, Australians, New Zealanders, British, Russians and Slovaks. [...] The film [required] 100,000 km of location scouting around the world, and [mobilized] 150 actors, as well as 200 extras in Europe, North America and South Africa"[293]. These orders of magnitude are comparable to those of another educational program: *Home*. This one-and-a-half-hour film, broadcast for the first time in June 2009, required a budget of 12 million euros, 120 filming locations in 54 countries, 500 hours of recordings on 733 cassettes, and 217 days of filming in 18 months.[280] The quality of the film is difficult to imagine! The quality is heavy to conceive! Filling 4 million hours with well-crafted programs therefore seems like an impossible challenge. Fortunately, mediocrity does not have this time-consuming side. It allows the channels to fill the airwaves with agrarian programs, made up of reality shows, variety shows, games, soap operas, soccer matches or coffee shop debates. To this catalog are added of course the series, films and other cartoons eternally rebroadcast on all the waves of the universe. Last night at the hotel, while zapping a bit, before and after a visit to the local pizza shop, I was entitled to *Rick Hunter, Little House on the Prairie, Mission Impossible, Friends, Camera Café, Rambo III, Stargate SG-1* and the inevitable *DragonBall Z*[a]. Not exactly newcomers to the year. In fact, as Bill McKibben humorously and skilfully sums up, "There's no doubt about it - there's good stuff on TV. But even there, there's a trick. Even great

---

a. June 9, 2009, *Rick Hunter*, RTL9, 7:15 p.m.; *La Petite Maison dans la prairie*, Téva, 7:40 p.m.; *Mission impossible* (the series), Direct 8, 7:50 p.m.; *Friends*, RTL9, 8 p.m.; *Caméra café*, Paris Première, 8:20 p.m.; Rambo III, 13ᵉ Rue, 8:45 p.m.; *Stargate SG-1* (the series), Serieclub, 11:30 p.m.; *DragonBall Z*, AB1, 11:40 p.m.

programs, or the good little things that happen every day, are doomed, I think, to make no difference. [...] If something exceptional happens it makes almost no difference - it is quickly forgotten, leveled, eroded by the endless flow. [...] Hoping that an exceptional program will make a difference is like hoping that you can eat French fries and gravy all week and then lower your cholesterol with a simple broccoli flower on Sunday night. [...] If God decided to deliver the Ten Commandments on the *Today Show*, it's true that he would have a huge audience. But the minute he was done, or maybe after he'd gone through six or seven, it would be time for a commercial and then a discussion with a pet psychiatrist about how to introduce your dog to your new baby.[290] In short, there are undoubtedly a few gems of exceptional quality on the small screen, but these can only be missed, drowned as they are in an inescapable ocean of inanity.

A second major structural constraint imposed on television lies in the plural nature of its audience. This *de facto* confronts channels with a painful choice: either to privilege "divisive" content and limit the audience potential to a small sub-population, or to opt for highly inclusive programs and offer themselves a large recruitment capacity. In the first case, quality programs will inevitably be difficult to produce or purchase because of limited financial resources. The latter will not be a problem. However, the latter will impose the almost exclusive selection of "soft" programs, which are both consensual and easily accessible.[60,287,288,290] A sort of lowest common denominator of individual intelligences which led, for example, France 3 to reject a subject on euthanasia in the first half of the evening, because, in the words of one of the company's journalists, "to devote an entire program to such a weighty question, in prime time, when children and grandmothers must be attracted... we did not feel it. In the same vein, while the debate on violence in the suburbs was raging, the channel consi-dered dedicating a program to the problem. The idea was rejected: "Too focused on young people! A few months later it was the turn of a subject on pensions to be scrapped.[287] This phobia of "segmenting programs," as Hélène Risser calls them in her remarkable book *L'Audimat à mort*, obviously does not only concern the thematic field. It also affects the cognitive space. It is important not to overload the brains of our brave viewers, otherwise we will trigger a frenzied zapping attack[52]. From the lowest common denominator, we then move quickly to the lowest common brain, also called the primacy of the darkest moron. This evolution was theorized by Luc Ferry, Minister of Education, who tactfully declared: "We must understand that [television] must remain essentially an entertainment and a show. It cannot replace a course at the Sorbonne without running the risk of zapping on other channels.[33] This judicious observation is obviously strongly expressed in the field of language. It would indeed be disastrous for the ratings to lead our valiant telephonists astray in the meanders of semantic space. To avoid the pitfall, there is only one rule: to produce speeches of modest syntax and poor lexicon[65,81]. On the big channels, the linguistic nothingness reigns in master, the confusing constructions are forever proscribed and "the long presentations which make the viewer flee have no place"[288]. This reality finds its clearest expression in the political arena. In the space of a few decades, the small screen has taken us from the Gaullian poise - "and you, my dear old country, here we are again, both of us, facing a great test" - to the attractive Raffarinade - "the road is straight but the slope is steep".[81] In fact, when we analyze the political situation, we can see that it is not the case that the government is the only one that has a role to play. In fact, when we analyze the discursive habits of the presidents of the Fifth Republic quantitatively, it appears that the length of sentences and the lexical amplitude have progressively decreased since de Gaulle. Of all the presidents of the Fifth Republic, the last one - Nicolas Sarkozy - is the one who has the shortest sentences, the least varied vocabulary,[294] and undoubtedly the most pronounced propensity to speak like "the man in the street", happily abusing the language.[295] Of course, the latter is sometimes the case. Of course, it happens that the latter rebels and presents itself, like the village of Asterix, in an irreducible form. It is then summarily evacuated. For example, when a journalist suggested to Patrick Poivre d'Arvor that the TF1 8 p.m. newscast should mention the epidemic of resignations from Rachida Dati's ministerial cabinet, the response was not long in coming: "Viewers don't know what a cabinet is; it's very technical, we don't have any pictures."[296] Apparently, we are still quite a bunch of nuts! Fortunately, PPDA and his ilk take care to avoid any neuronal overload by protecting us from overly complex content. As far as complexity is concerned, let's also point out the need to keep everyone in their roles. According to a scriptwriter quoted by Hélène Risser, "we must [for television] create normative characters, banish everything that is complex"[287]. The story of Eric Kristy provides us with a good example. Our man is at the origin of a "demanding" film telling the story of a left-wing teacher who discovers that his son is active in a neo-Nazi group made up of good-natured academics led by a revisionist history professor. Eight years after its production, TF1 had still not broadcast the film. According to Éric Kristy, the "choice of presenting clean-cut 'bad guys' was probably too complex, not Manichean enough for TF1, which aims to attract 10 million people. 287 In essence, the idea fits quite well with the words of Claude de Givray, who spent 12 years at the head of the channel's dramas: "You can't attract nine million people with immoral characters. In short, the networks need a dichotomous world of black and white, a world without gray or complexity, a world in which the good guys are totally good and the bad guys unanimously evil. In this world, "all the details of the films are calibrated to the millimeter in order to cater to the needs of the old farmer from Correze to the young mother from Paris. Surprise, the unexpected, the startling, are formally banished. These features could, by their audacity, strip away the audimat. Predictability is more serene. It reassures by giving to those who watch television, "our children and ourselves, this guarantee - how precious! that we will never run the risk of not understanding"[54]. An experiment conducted by Alain Bentolila and his team confirms this point to the point of caricature, by demonstrating the frightening predictability of audiovisual fictions[54]. A class of fourth graders was presented with the first part of a TV series spread over eight episodes. When the students were asked to imagine the entire plot based on this first episode alone, 80% of them predicted more than 70% of the events that would occur! Once this data was collected, the children were allowed to watch episode 4, and 90% of them were able to reconstruct at least 80% of the events in episodes 2 and 3. Bentolila and his collaborators repeated the experiment four more times, always with the same result. Differences arose, however, when a similar investigation was conducted using eight sections of a children's book. The average prediction from reading the first section was found to be less than 30% for 85% of the students. After reading the fourth passage, only 50% of the students were able to find more than 50% of the events developed in sections 2 and 3. This says a lot about the nature of audiovisual fiction, which is formatted to be understood even before it is seen. A sort of zero degree of intelligibility that of course also concerns Hollywood blockbusters, reality TV, entertainment shows, games and soccer or tennis matches[a]. Let us repeat: without poverty of language, without narrative conformism, without stereotyped characters, it would

---

a. Of course, in this case, we don't know who will win, but we know everything about the plot, the place, the rules, the scene. In the heart of the sports world, the risk of not understanding the script is almost zero. The only unpredictability is the name of the winner.

be totally impossible to aggregate each evening several million profoundly dissimilar people in front of a single program. People are not shown what they want to see, but simply what they can share, a sort of lowest common denominator of singular aspirations and intelligences. That's not much when you think about it. By focusing on our similarities alone, the small screen irreparably drains away most of our identity. As Bill McKibben beautifully explains, "Television tells us that we have everything in common. But we don't. As we lose our particularity, we lose prodigious amounts of information. [...] We can only find subjects of interest to everyone by amputating content, by dismembering information - things that interest me may not interest you, or even be understandable to you. [The only solution is to simplify."[290] From this process of simplification a uniform world is mechanically born, spewing out absolute platitude and profound mediocrity.

A third structural constraint imposed to television resides in the necessarily dynamic nature of the image. On the small screen, slowness is prohibited, there is no room for inaction. Those who have tried to watch *Sleep* or *Empire* by Andy Warhol know this better than anyone. In these two (very) long films, the filmmaker films, in a fixed shot, a drowsy man and the exterior façade of the Empire State Building. Scenes of such boredom that one has to do violence to keep from falling asleep. Scenes that testify to the disgust of the dullness of ordinary daily life. As Benjamin Castaldi, a (apparently) well-known television presenter, recently pointed out, reality TV programs would obviously be "very boring" if they were presented as they are, without timely editing[297]. From *Secret Story*[297], to *Pékin Express*[298,299], or the opening ceremony of the 2008 Olympic Games[300,301] , via animal reports[290], the validity of the statement seems almost unanimous, even if some people would prefer more ambitious terms such as *"macking"*, *"rigging"*, *"fiddling"* or *"faking"* to *"editing"*. The latest contentious case to date is *Le Grand Frère*, a reality show in which a special educator helps young people who have broken with their family environment. Two days before the filming of an episode, the discovery of a script that was precise to say the least, caused a stir in the media circles.[302,303] Here are some excerpts (remember that the program is supposed to capture the reality of a family environment): October 29, "*12:30 p.m.*: Lunch [...] It's still not good enough for Dylan today". "*3 p.m.*: Dylan needs money and Marianne refuses. [...] Marianne and her son clash." "*6:30 p.m.*: Marianne tells her son that if it doesn't work out with Pascal, she will place him in a home." "*7:30 p.m.*: Marianne tries to watch a TV program, but she can't count on Dylan's despotic character, who shamelessly zaps." November 7, "*1 p.m.* [...] All the family is gathered, Dylan apologizes to his mother and his father-in-law. Michel takes the opportunity to ask for Marianne's hand again!!! Happy ending!"[304]. Inevitable scripting according to a producer "familiar with this type of program", interviewed by *Le Parisien*: "We don't have the means to shoot reality. It costs too much. With the budgets allocated, we can't wait a month to have the right scenes. As a result, we regularly ask the witnesses to replay or show us how their daily lives are going. We film life in accelerated form, so to speak.[302] Naturalist documentaries, so prized by the cohorts of cathodic self-righteousness, testify to the generality of the subject. Examples. You want to show off some black-footed ferrets (an infinitely rare lineage on the verge of extinction)? Buy a few common ferrets at the local pet store and comb their feet. Want to show what a voracious critter the piranha is? Identify a few representatives of the species, starve them for a while and throw them (finally) some food. Same thing for tarantulas. Throw a few small (not too fast) birds at them and if you are lucky, they will be promptly swallowed. You want to film a wild jaguar? Go to the nearest zoo, commandeer a tame specimen (preferably declawed) and put it in a tree. A few tricks, among others, that Wolfang Bayer, a fertile professional, acclaimed by his peers, easily justifies: "If we showed viewers the natural, unaltered films, wildlife filmmakers would be out of work in a year, it would be so boring."[290] An idea widely echoed by Bill McKibben, to a blunt conclusion: "Naturalistic documentaries are as absurdly action-packed as soap operas, in which entire lifetimes of divorce, adultery, and sudden death are packed into a week's viewing - trying to understand 'nature' by watching Wild Kingdom [*La Vie Sauvage*] is as difficult as trying to unders-tand 'life' by watching *Dynasty*."[290] One might indeed think that "real" nature must appear terribly boring to the audience of Planet, Journey, or Animals, so much so that it moves in the midst of a frenzied kinetic rush. That being said, without speed of scrolling, without pictorial hysteria, without precipitation of images, shots, and scenes, it is probable that the attention would erode very quickly. Watching a tiger sleeping, a lion yawning or a crocodile lanternizing is not very exciting. Movement awakens interest as surely as rain invigorates a snail. In line with this idea, it is now widely accepted that the rapid changes in our audiovisual universe literally contribute to glueing the brain to the screen, *via* a persistent solicitation of the physiological reflex of orientation (a kind of "change reflex" sometimes called "what's that" reflex)[9,19,305-307]. Confronted with the incessant flow of emergences, attention is monopolized. It then becomes a real invisible leash, by which the station keeps us under its control, far from zapping, from "real" life and from Morpheus' arms. A "cult" series such as *DragonBall Z* is remarkably successful from this point of view[264]. As Bermejo Berros explains in an exhaustive and thorough study, this series "provokes in the spectator long periods of concentration, of absence of movement, of verbal and sound comments. This long period of concentration weakens at certain moments. The children relax not so much because the narrative plot diminishes but because the concentration they are subjected to is prolonged. These brief moments of relaxation end with the appearance on the screen of a visual or sound[a] *clincher,* which has the effect of recovering the child's attention. On the other hand, the dialogues also tend to decrease the attentional intensity of the child viewer. It is as if *DragonBall Z* was designed to deal with this eventuality, since at the end of the dialogues there is usually a clincher that has the immediate effect of increasing the child's attentional level. Over time, it becomes more and more difficult to escape this formal control by virtue of a widely demonstrated principle of inertia[308,309] according to which "the more people watch television, the greater the likelihood that they will continue to do so".[310] In fact, this kinetic martingale was discovered some forty years ago during research aimed at optimizing children's attention to "educational" programs.[29,311] The basic hypothesis was that the more people watch television, the greater the likelihood that they will continue to do so. The basic hypothesis was that increasing the attentional acuity of young viewers could improve learning. The results were consistent with the prediction, but only for simple, low-cognitive-load content.[312,313] As soon as the message became a little more complex, the children's attention span was increased. As soon as the message became somewhat complex or rich, the artificial increase in attentional level caused an impairment of comprehension and memory functions. To put it simply, we could say that the brain no longer had enough resources to process everything. It was therefore content, as its functional architecture dictates, to pay attention to the incessant changes in the audiovisual scene, without being able to really decode and store the content observed. In the long run, this inability to

---

a. This anglicism defines a particularly salient perceptual element (visual or sound).

follow the flow of events resulted in a heavy attentional dropout. It appears that exogenous factors are not the only ones to determine the level of attention of the subjects. The degree of understanding of the message also plays an important role[311,314,315]. Homo Cathodicus flees from what he cannot understand! Consequently, simple contents, delivered on the basis of rapid audiovisual changes, must be privileged in order to catch the viewer's attention and to prevent any audience effusion. As Neil Postman had already underlined with a lot of force, more than 25 years ago, in his remarkable book *Entertaining to Death*, everything that is slow and complicated has no place on the small screen[52]. But let's not fool ourselves. The need for understanding can sometimes be exercised in a very local and partial way. For example, a 6- or 7-year-old watching *DragonBall Z will* usually not understand the overall plot at all. Yet he or she may understand what is going on within each sequence and remain glued to the screen like a mussel to its rock.[264]

The possibility of gluing the child to the set, based on formal subliminal manipulations, did not come without its problems. The BBC, for example, initially refused to broadcast *Sesame Street on the* grounds that it knowingly manipulated children's attention.[29,305] In the words of one BBC executive at the time, "the programme is a very good example of the kind of manipulation that can be done. In the words of a BBC official at the time: "We don't try to tie children to the television screen. If they go away and enjoy themselves during half of our programs, that's fine."[29] Unfortunately, such scruples were not long in dying out. If an executive dared to advocate such a policy today, he or she would be promptly and unceremoniously sent back to the "mentally ill seeking employment" box! The *blitz* would be all the more swift since the principle of frenzy has been expanding ever since the original *Sesame Street* stammering. This principle, which allows channels to sell their advertisers a large panel of available, captive and meditative brains, now affects almost the entire television universe. Thus, for example, in debate programs, instead of inviting two or three people to speak on the substance, they prefer to solicit 10 or 12 to whom they give just enough time for a futile discussion, because "as soon as we stay more than 15 minutes on the same guest, [the audience] gives up. One is obliged to accelerate the rhythm, to shorten the interviews"[316]. 316 The same is true for television news. As Sébastien Bohler, a subtle and informed observer of the media universe, explains: "Take the case of any individual placed in front of his television set during the 8 o'clock news. Successively, he or she will learn of the death of a child in a house fire in the Doubs region, the explosion of a bomb in Bali, the opening of a psychiatric clinic for dogs in a Florida hospital, the failure of Israeli-Palestinian negotiations, the result of a match between an Italian and a French soccer club, the new record made by a fashionable actress, and the progress of medicine in the treatment of a hereditary disease. It is a mess in which it is difficult to get to the bottom of. A study carried out in America is quite revealing from this point of view. In this country, in 1968, the broadcasting time of the speeches presented by the different candidates to the presidential election amounted on average, on the main evening newspapers, to 42.3 seconds. By 1988, this had dropped to 9.8 seconds[317,318]! Gone are the days of long explanations, sometimes tedious, but always very useful. Here comes the era of tumultuous brevity. Yet, as Félicité de La Mennais wrote almost two centuries ago, "the mind is called upon from too many sides at once; it must be spoken to quickly or it will pass. But there are things that cannot be said or understood so quickly, and these are the most important for man. This acceleration of movement, which allows nothing to be chained, nothing to be meditated upon, would alone be enough to weaken and in the long run completely destroy human reason"[319]. Perhaps we are now not very far from this breaking point.

*
**

To conclude

Thus, in half a century, television has imposed itself in almost all our homes. It has colonized our domestic space and taken possession of our schedules. Schoolchildren spend more time in front of the screen than with any adult, including the teacher. Surprisingly, it is not the children who originally demanded the television. It is the parents who prescribe its use and anchor the habit. It must be said that TV has an amazing magic: it is able to offer us, in profusion, a perfect and idyllic tranquility. A simple press of the switch and our most excited kids are transformed into pleasantly apathetic cakes. We can note on this subject, in opposition to a very widespread fable, that Lady Television is far from having been supplanted by Internet or video games. The small screen remains *the* dominant leisure activity whatever the age group. Even teenagers spend more time looking at the screen than surfing the Web or playing with the PlayStation. And clearly, the trend shows no signs of abating. Indeed, channels are now able to follow us everywhere thanks to laptops, cell phones and other small dedicated terminals. TV without constraints of time or place, here is a perspective that should intoxicate our brain sellers. They will soon be able to contemplate their victory with satisfaction. An army of coprophagous spirits, stupefied by stale programs and decaying shows. An ecumenical droppings which, contrary to what we would like to believe, does not result from a deliberate editorial choice, but from the intimate structure of the television medium. It is the case of the television like the scorpion of the fable, it manufactures mediocrity because "it is its nature". The drama without doubt, it is that it goes of this mediocrity as of the hardest drugs: more we undergo precociously the assault of its flavors, more we accustom our life to its anesthetizing presence and more it becomes difficult for us to withdraw our spirit to the weight of its hold.

CHAPTER II
TV STIFLES INTELLIGENCE

"To listen to TF1 you don't need a brain, a digestive tube is enough."
(Didier Daeninckx, writer [320])

"The large number of children who are poor readers rightly worries teachers and parents. But curiously, the school is blamed solely for this state of affairs. To avoid blaming television, the failure has paradoxically been attributed to traditional methods of teaching reading."

(Liliane Lurçat, doctor in psychology,
honorary director of research at the CNRS[25])

"We give them what they want" they say in chorus. Translate: "It's not our fault they're so dumb.""

(Alain Bentolila, linguist, university professor[54])

In the etymological sense, many of our children have become barbarians[a] . They no longer speak the language of the City and no longer share the culture of their Fathers. They do not know how to think anymore. They read with difficulty, write laboriously and count with great difficulty. This observation is not new. Teachers, parents and journalists have been making this observation for nearly 15 years, pointing out the dysfunction of a school system that is riddled with pedagogical[54,65,78,81,322-326] and political[327,328] excesses. Such a stigmatization of the school seems to me to be totally justified. Nevertheless, it also seems to me to be largely fragmentary, in the sense that it eludes the potential involvement of a second agent of influence: television. A number of experimental data show that television plays a critical role in the difficulties experienced by many children and adolescents with regard to school, language and thought. To put it in

---

a. Let us recall that in its etymological sense this term refers to "the name given by the Greeks and Romans to all peoples who did not speak their language"[321].

prosaic terms, recent research establishes television as a gigantic machine for dumbing down, an incredible organ of decerebration of which our kids are the first victims. Of course, this statement may shock us, as it is in direct contradiction with the zeitgeist and the slimy dogma of political correctness. The self-righteous tartufes, the grandiloquent culturalists, the psycho-pipalists of all kinds and other saltimbanques of the cathodic thing will say it outrageous. With a backhand they will evacuate it as one removes a slag. They will mock the form to avoid the substance. However, the substance is there, persistent, persuasive and implacable! However, those who refuse to believe it can rest assured that I am not claiming any positive presumption. I do not hope to be taken at my word. I simply hope that everyone can take hold of the available scientific evidence, in order to take a position, not on backyard judgments, but on objective facts. For the sake of clarity, these will be presented in three main parts in this chapter. The first will look at the alarming academic skills of our children and adolescents, especially in language. The second will show that television has a strong negative, causal effect on these academic skills. The third will establish the functional substratum of this action by exposing the deleterious effect of the small screen on attention, conceptual thinking, language and higher cognitive functions (those which distinguish us from our friends the chimpanzees!).

*
**

This time it is sure, the level drops

Vanessa is a third year psychology student. A short while ago, she left a note in my mailbox: "Sir, would you please send me the article you talked about". Sonia works in STAPS[a]. She could not come to the appointment she had requested "because my mother is sick". Farida and Jean are aiming for a master's degree in biology. The first one prides herself on never having read a book ("it's too boring") and thinks that the expression "Cartesian geometry" has its origin in the sweet city of Carthage. The second is capable of making 11 gross errors in 4 handwritten lines and 31 words (a solid 35%

---

a. STAPS: Sciences and Techniques of Physical and Sports Activities.

error rate)[a]. Julien Courbet is a well-known TV host who has an obvious love for Naples. "Naples, ah Spain," he enthused recently on a major national radio station. Michele attends a renowned business school. She "finds it good that the President of the Republic has dissolved the Church of Scientology"[b]. X has a bachelor's degree. When asked about ecology during the oral exam for the nursing school entrance exam, she said she was very interested in the subject because "it is important to think about how schools work. Jean would like to get an MBA. He is on the waiting list for a prestigious institution and feels "the feet of Damocles over his head." In a recent e-mail, the boy was angry about the "lack of pride of a socialist party that is incapable of resonating. Ms. Anonymous is a French teacher. At the beginning of 2005, she was asked to give a course in conjugation to students preparing for the CAPES[c] of letters [324]. Gilbert is a doctor. His last two secretaries, recruited on completion of the BTS, proved incapable of archiving patient files. They had not mastered alphabetical order.[81] Justin Bieber, 16 years old, is a successful singer for prepubescent girls[332]. In an interview in New Zealand, the teenager was asked a very difficult question: "Justin, does *Bieber mean* 'basketball' in German? Obviously, the young man did not know the latter term, which the somewhat embarrassed presenter struggled to repeat in every possible way. In desperation, Bieber was finally presented with the card with the question on it to read. Perhaps the trouble was, after all, just a faulty accent on the part of the master of ceremonies. Unfortunately, his hopes were dashed. At the end of his reading, our budding star offered a blunt answer: "I don't know what that means. We don't say that in America. Desperate, but not exceptional, as demonstrated by the performance of three pretty young girls crossed one morning in the Lyon-Paris TGV, as they were on their way, if I understood correctly, to a casting. Let's name our girls Fanni, Irène and Laure. The first one had not yet filled in her questionnaire. Here are some selected pieces. Fanni (hesitant): "I followed, it's "-it" isn't it? Irene (affirmative): "Well no,

---

a. This is the first paragraph of the young man's final exam paper. The mistakes are underlined in italics. *"From the time of* the *Greeks* the notion of attention has been the subject *of much reflection*. It is *considered* by *some* as the *return of* consciousness. *Others consider* it as a supramodal function.

b. These remarks were made when the public prosecutor had just demanded the dissolution of the Church of Scientology during a trial [330]. In addition to her grammatical wanderings, our student has some lexical weaknesses since she seems to confuse president/prosecutor and requisition/conviction!

c. CAPES: Certificat d'Aptitude au Professorat de l'Enseignement du Second degré (i.e., the national competitive examination used to recruit teachers).

it's "-e", because it's "I" who followed [...]" Fanni (a few miles later): "What's my favorite director, I don't know." Irene (after some thought): " Well, you just have to say Molière, it's classic [...] " Fanni (suddenly very annoyed): " What is the range of my voice? " Irene (who apparently has already filled out the questionnaire at home): "It's how you sing." Fanni (surprised): "Well, I sing well." Laure (suddenly waking up): "I think it's the number of bytes [*sic*] you can do with your voice, whether it's serious or not." Fanni (worried): "Why do you say that my voice is deep, I assure you I sing well", etc. It is rare, I admit it, that two hours of TGV fly away so quickly. I almost envy Michel Mathieu-Colas, a university professor, for whom it is obviously TGV every day! This trained linguist has made a habit of evaluating the lexical competence of his literature students. Among the most entertaining answers given by the latter were: *hexagon*, "triangle with many sides"; *polygamous*, "which combines several games"; *hemicycle*, bicycle with one wheel; *autochthonous*, "which likes to live at night"; *omnipotent*, "which has all its members"; *sporadic*, "sports junkie"; *gerontology*, "science of fossils"; *xenophobic*, "which is afraid when it is locked up "[333,334]. For this last word, 25% of the respondents failed miserably. Michel Mathieu-Colas concluded that "a whole generation is having difficulty with the French language. Conjugation, syntax and morphology were not immune to the disaster. The "il fesait", "j'envoyerai", "je découvrerai", "j'aura", "je venis", "ils tenèrent", "vous disez" and other "je mourrirai" populate the copies with an edifying constancy[335,336]. Birds "supposedly healthy" can easily become, according to the individual options, "without its mancins", "without loving breast" or "without cerning saints"[337]. Formulas as happy as "give me your drawing, I have to veil it" are cheerfully popularized by inventive teachers.[322] In this enchanted world of the beautiful, theatrical, theatrical, theatrical, theatrical, theatrical, theatrical, theatrical, theatrical, theatrical, theatrical, theatrical, theatrical, theatrical, theatrical. In this enchanted world of the beautiful language, "the Nazi heap" advantageously replaces euthanasia, Martinique is populated with happy "Martinikés" and Schubert offers us a very astonishing symphony "inHeV"[338].

Of course, it is tempting to dismiss the above examples on the grounds that they have no proven generality. In support of this argument, one might point out that the only quantitative study that allows us to evaluate, on a broad basis, the ability of our students to produce written work is the bac. And this one offers results that are more than flattering. Today, nearly 65% of a given age group and 86% of applicants pass[339]. However, many observers refuse to give these figures the slightest significance. The level of requirement of the exam has become too low to be meaningful[78,326,327,340,341]. It must be noted that there is no lack of evidence to support the idea. Thus, for example, what can we say about this student who got a solid 11/20 in French, after having smeared his copy with more than 200 mistakes[322]? Similarly, what about the 180 new baccalaureate holders who were subjected to a simple dictation of about twenty lines at the beginning of their university studies and who managed to produce an average of 10 to 15 gross errors[335]? Comparable figures were reported by Jean-Marie Réveillon, following a detailed quantitative analysis of all the "invention stories" contained in a pile of copies of the general bac[a]. This analysis identified an average of 17 errors per test, for texts of about 40 lines. The author concludes: "The predominance of grammatical errors over usage errors is obvious. It is to be found in all the packets of papers, and immediately cancels out all the soothing considerations about the secondary character of mastery of spelling: what is in question here is a very deficient handling of the language.[336] An observation shared by Patrick Porcheron, vice-president of the prestigious Pierre et Marie Curie University[343]. For this biologist, "for the last 15 years, it has been a real drift. If only it were a spelling problem! But it goes far beyond that: words are used in the wrong way and sentences are constructed without any head or tail. It's a permanent blooper. The disaster is such that our man has recently supported, as is now done in about twenty other French universities, the setting up of language courses intended to teach students the rudiments of French[344]. The teaching of fifth grade on the benches of the Sorbonne is not without a certain cachet. This is undoubtedly what is called structuring excellence, to use a fashionable expression in high ministerial circles. That being said, the problem is obviously identifiable well before access to the university world, as indicated by a recent study of tenth-grade students conducted by the collective Save the Letters. In this study, 1,348 students took the French test for the 1976 brevet des collèges (a dictation of a dozen lines, of average difficulty, followed by vocabulary and grammar questions).[345] Eighty-six percent of the candidates did not obtain an average score on the dictation. Nearly 60% simply got a zero. For

---

a. The S (Scientific) and ES (Economic and Social) streams were concerned. The French test offers a choice of three subjects: commentary, essay and "invention" subject. The latter involves writing a text within a certain number of constraints (for example, for the papers discussed here: "Loti went to Stamboul in search of Aziyadé, without any result. You will write the excerpt from the travel journal that he was able to write on the boat on the way back, confronting his dreams with reality.")[342].

each usage error, four grammar errors were listed. In the sentence: "The machines, the hammers, the tools, the chain motors, the saws mixed their infernal noises and this unbearable din [...] seemed inhuman to me", 60% of the students proved to be ignorant of the word *chain*, 41% could not define the adjective *infernal*, 33% failed on the word *din*. The authors of the study concluded: "The result is catastrophic [...] All these students, who neither know nor respect the rules of agreement and conjugation, show themselves incapable of agreeing what precedes with what follows, thus testifying to a real logical infirmity: what apprehension, what understanding of the world can a being have who isolates each perception, without putting it in relation, in a consecutive process, with what precedes and what follows? A point widely discussed since the 18th century by the Abbé Étienne de Condillac, writing forcefully in his famous *Cours d'étude pour l'instruction du Prince de Parme*: "I regard grammar as the first part of the art of thinking."[346]

All the above observations are unfortunately not isolated. They have been largely confirmed by several international studies of reading comprehension disorders. The first of these studies was carried out between 1994 and 1998, under the aegis of the OECD[347]. It focused on the 16-65 age group. To simplify the analysis of the data, five ability ranks were defined. The first denoted "very low skill level. The second denoted "reading only simple, explicit text for low complexity tasks". The third was "considered to be a suitable minimum for coping with the demands of daily life and work in a complex and advanced society". The fourth and fifth showed "mastery of higher information processing skills". The primary data proved to be absolutely catastrophic. 62% of our youth (16-26 years) were associated with levels 1 and 2[348]. The French government, which had participated in the implementation of this work, suddenly argued that the methodology was flawed. It withdrew from the project and prevented the publication of the data.[347] Insee and a number of other *ad hoc* organizations were quickly commissioned to carry out a counter-assessment. The result: "only" 20 percent of young adults in levels 1 and 2[348]. The honour was safe! Unfortunately, the lull was short-lived. The OECD quickly went back to the drawing board with a new study aimed at "determining the extent to which young adults aged 15 are prepared to meet the challenges of the knowledge society as they approach the end of their compulsory schooling, if not at the end of it"[349]. The results for France were again alarming: 53% of our young people were positioned in the middle of levels 1 and 2. Only 9% of students were deemed worthy of levels 4 and 5[349]! These figures are entirely consistent with those recently presented for elementary school by the High Council for Education. The report sent by this advisory body to the Minister of Education underlines that "4 out of 10 pupils, i.e. about 300,000 pupils, leave CM2 each year with serious shortcomings: nearly 200,000 of them have fragile and insufficient knowledge of reading, writing and arithmetic; more than 100,000 have not mastered the basic skills in these areas. Since the end of CM2 is no longer the end of compulsory schooling, their deficiencies will prevent these students from continuing their education normally in middle school.

When one moves from a static picture to a longitudinal viewpoint, it becomes clear that the previous deficits have become more pronounced in recent years. As Emmanuel Davidenkoff, a recognized specialist in the field of education, points out: "This time, it is clear that the level is falling, and at all levels. Thus, for example, for Sophie Lefèvre, a literature teacher: "Among the large number of students from privileged, even very well-to-do backgrounds, most of whom are surrounded by attentive and cultured parents, one out of 69 wrote in French. And none of these teenagers speaks French like their parents, or has the culture that their parents had at their age [...] I have the impression that we are dealing with intelligences locked in an inability to express themselves."[324] This feeling is widely echoed quantitatively in several statistical studies of governmental[352,353], academic[354], institutional[355-357] and associative[358] origin. Consider, for example, the recent work of the Direction de l'évaluation de la prospective et de la performance (DEPP). In order to estimate the evolution of calculation, reading and spelling skills of CM2 pupils, this official body repeated, in 2007, a survey initially conducted in 1987. The results showed "over 20 years, a significant decline in student performance in all three skills. For reading, "twice as many students (21%) were at the same proficiency level as the lowest 10% of students in 1987. [...] The average decline is observed regardless of the type of skills involved (immediate comprehension, construction of information and meaning, etc.). [...] For questions requiring the writing of a constructed response, the non-response rate increased steadily from 1987 to 2007. This phenomenon has already been highlighted, in particular by the recent PISA and PIRLS international assessments[a]. It refers to the fact

a. PISA: Program for International Student Assessment - international assessments of 15-year-olds.
PIRLS: Progress in International Reading Literacy Study - international assessments of 10-year-olds.

that French students tend to refrain from answering questions requiring a writing effort. For spelling, "the same dictation was given to students in 1987 and 2007, using a text of about ten lines (85 words and punctuation marks[a]). The number of errors (number of misspelled words or incorrect punctuation) increased on average: from 10.7 in 1987 to 14.7 in 2007. The percentage of students who made more than 15 errors was 26% in 1987; it is now 46%. Grammatical errors have increased from an average of 7 in 1987 to 11 in 2007. For example, 87% of the students conjugated the verb "tombait" correctly in the sentence "le soir tombait"; today, only 63% of the students do so. In the field of mathematics, "a significant decline in calculation scores was observed between 1987 and 1999. This decline affects all skill levels. From 1999 to 2007, there was a "settling down" of results: the average score fell slightly, but not significantly"[b]. Taken as a whole, these changes are, without a doubt, far-reaching. The deficits they induce can be measured in whole years. On the question of spelling, for example, Danièle Manesse and Danièle Cogis have obtained results that are quite similar to those of the DEPP[354]. After quantification, the authors show that this represents two levels, all round! Thus, in 2005, the results of 5th grade middle school students were similar to those presented by 5th grade students in 1987. In the same way, the performance of 3rd graders reached that of 5th graders 20 years earlier. It can be noted here that the downward trend in the language and mathematical skills of the younger generations is not specific to France. It also affects other countries with school systems that are very different from ours. The United States is the best documented example[29,361,362].

Of course, all these data do not prevent our pipefitters from being serene. Thus, for example, the hilarious Michael Stora "does not share the

---

a. The dictation was: "It was getting dark. Mom and Dad were worried and wondered why their four boys hadn't come home. - The kids must have gotten lost," said Mom. If they haven't found their way home by now, we'll see them arrive home very tired. - Why don't you call Martine? She might have seen them! No sooner said than done! At that moment, the dog started barking."

b. The joint impairment of arithmetic and language skills is consistent with PISA data showing that adolescents' reading performance is correlated with their science and mathematics scores.[349] Although many parameters can explain this correlation, it has been proposed that the syntactic system may, through its formal organization, represent a kind of precursor to mathematical reasoning. Although many parameters may explain this correlation, it has been proposed that the syntactic system may, through its formal organization, represent a kind of precursor to mathematical reasoning. However, recent studies have failed to validate this hypothesis by showing the existence of a divergent brain substrate for computational and grammatical processes[359,360].

generalized pessimism about the future of writing and reading. We have never written as much as we do now, by SMS, in chat rooms, on blogs [...] Moreover, we are witnessing a real staging of the written word, with the possibility of choosing different fonts, of intervening on the shape of letters, on their colors...".[40]. What wonderful progress! Long live the new technologies! Our kids will now be able to display their cyber-sabir in 3-D and in polychromy! By the way, for those who don't know, this cyber-sabir has a name. It is, says the sociologist Nathalie Brion, "what we call the world novlanguage. [This language is the language of the Internet, the language of SMS, a language that completely defies spelling rules, a language of dialogue for exchange, whatever the language. And in the end it serves everyone and it serves the kids because it teaches them to speak English that is not perfect but is understandable, French that is full of mistakes but is understandable, and to exchange with each other, and in the end it is also important. The analysis is roughly in line with that of Clara Dupont-Monod. Frankly, says this journalist, "is it because we are not good at spelling that we are not equipped for life? I don't think so [...] It's a bit absurd to go crying over the form, when in fact it seems to me that the substance is the same"[364]. 364 Obviously, this kind of pacifying and merciful discourse is very popular in the muffled world of the bobos-humanists[365]. Nowadays, the "Young" is untouchable, certified prodigious by his condition alone. He is a veritable sacred cow, a paragon of creativity, a phoenix of nonconformism.[81] As Pascal Bruckner points out, the "young" is a "new" person, a "new" person, a "new" person. As Pascal Bruckner points out, no one dares to say any more "of our little savages that they are ill-formed. Their slightest nonsense is venerated as a treasure of depth, an abyss of spontaneous poetry, their scribblings are the object of a cult reserved for masterpieces. (And one knows these thousand pedagogical reforms intended, not to educate the child, oh sacrilege, and even less to guide him but to promote his free expression, his "genius")"[161]. Should we congratulate ourselves on this incredible leniency? I really don't think so. Basically, if our "formidable youth" were to evoke any feeling in me, it would be more concern than admiration. Indeed, to mystically celebrate the child in order to spare him the pain of having to build himself, we do him a great disservice. Language, for example, is extraordinarily difficult to master in its most intimate subtleties. Yet, it is the ultimate rampart of our intelligence. It is also the first factor of our social insertion and consequently the first avenue of our potential exclusion. When a child loses the use of words, all the fields of his professional, communicative and cognitive life are threatened.

The professional world, for example, shows no mercy for the spelling impaired. Mistakes are paid for in cash, even (and especially) when they are harmless. So, when I receive a cover letter full of mistakes, I throw it away without any qualms. The "Dear Sir, I am sending you my CV" or "I am writing to you again to ask you to accept me as an intern" inspire me with limited confidence. Several press articles have recently shown that I am not alone in this case. Companies, too, are quite allergic to dysorthographics in their staff[366-373]. This is not surprising when one considers that an employee's lack of mastery of the written code seriously undermines not only his or her career plan, but also the credibility of the company. When the educational director of a private distance learning institution sends me a letter of a few lines to tell me about "these lessons that we know require a certain amount of effort", I must admit that it does not look good. More generally, when an executive sends his clients e-mails, notes or projects full of mistakes, it looks bad and can cause the loss of a contract, a tender or a business deal. Similarly, when a communications agency has to scrap 450,000 copies of an advertising brochure because of the spelling incompetence of certain employees, it is a bit embarrassing, not to mention costly. More prosaically, when a salesman fresh out of private school goes from the verbal directive "if they take more than 300, you give them 5%" to the written proposal "under 300 units, 5% discount", it is not without consequences and we should not be surprised to see the Pôle emploi enriching its herd with an additional young unemployed person. That said, it is fortunate that the threat does not affect our ministers, otherwise Luc Chatel, newly appointed to the Ministry of Education, would have had some worries. At the start of the 2009 school year, our man sent the media a press kit riddled with "dozens of spelling mistakes".[374] "Forgotten accents, trampled conjugation, syntax errors", nothing was spared to the reader, according to the very words of a major national weekly.[375] A wandering that, let's face it, is a bit of a surprise. A wandering which, let us admit it, does not reassure us much about the competence and seriousness of our educational elites.

At the communicational level, we should perhaps not forget that spelling serves precisely to ensure the legibility of the messages sent by the speaker. If everyone starts, tomorrow, to write as he or she likes, our whole capacity to exchange meaning will be dismembered. Just a small example for my friends who are thurifers of the spelling card[365]: "Pouxremwa ç a demi. The mayor hates Dinieu. The mayor hates Dinieu. She addor the tails of village praicekotant that the breast of france. Some assholes talk to her, wing raipon that she m the fat and enjoys on maurain. She likes to swallow herself and to climb on your that breve en oscène. Enough to occupy a few exegete monks for an hour or two (for the "translation"[a]). Having said that, I agree that spelling is not everything. To exchange, one must first have words and syntax. However, the "world novlanguage" so dear to Nathalie Brion is totally foreign to these attributes (cf. *above*). What can one exchange with such a sabir? A few banalities, no doubt, such as "hello", "bye-bye", "I'm fine", "I'm laughing out loud", "cool", "very expensive", or "I'm from the nine cube" (understand Seine-Saint-Denis [93]). But what about, beyond this semantic nothingness? Communication is like my old legos: the fewer the pieces, the more rudimentary the construction. As we have just seen, the grammatical and lexical skills of our children have dramatically decreased over the last two decades, reaching an alarming level today. It should be remembered that nearly 40% of CM2 pupils do not know how to conjugate the verb of the first group *tomber* in the sentence "le soir tombait"[352], that 45% of pupils in seconde are unable to express in the third person plural verbs initially conjugated in the simple past tense in the third person singular (he opened => they opened; he left => they left)[345], that 85% of these same students are unable to find the subject of the verb to *work* in the sentence "in front of the rows of machines where a large number of men were working"[345], that 60% of these students (still them) do not know how to define an assembly "line"[345], that 25% of the students in literature (!) have not mastered the term *xenophobia*[333,334], that 97% of the pupils in a third grade class in Evry do not know the word louche[376], that 98% of a group of 50 students from very privileged backgrounds and aiming for business or engineering degrees are totally unaware of the meaning of the expression "the religions of the Book"[81], that 19 out of 26 aspiring psycho-logists do not know what a "manant" is,[377] and that my 18-year-old bacca-laureate babysitter is unable to solve middle school arithmetic problems because she does not know what "an equally distributed debt" is and

---

a. "For me, it is admitted. The mother is dignified. She looks like the bonace [term for a perfectly calm sea] in the harbor. She adores the queux [cooks] of her village almost as much as the saints of France. When spoken to, she answers that she loves Greece and Jouy-sur-Morin [a commune in Seine-et-Marne]. She loves her valley and climbing the valleys that give her healthy water."

---

cannot determine whether or not the price of an order takes into account a discount in the phrase "the bill is only €321 because the bookstore has given a €43 discount[a]. At this stage of linguistic decay, it is no longer lexical weakness that we should speak of, but almost communicative asthenia. When language is so deeply affected, it inevitably loses its power of transfer and becomes a mere recording chamber for common experiences[54,379-381]. As Alain Bentolila points out with his usual clairvoyance, "the more we know someone, the more we have in common with him and the less we will need words to communicate together. [...] When you have to address people you don't know, when these people don't know in advance what you're going to say to them, it becomes a completely different challenge. Unable to find his words and understand the lofty verbiage of the prosecutor, our defendant ends up jumping on the prosecutor to express with his fists what he could not say with words. Everyone who has lived abroad has, I think, at one time or another, felt this inner violence, this frustration of not being able to express one's thoughts. With my "basic" English, I can allow myself "basic" communication. Nothing more. As soon as I have to debate, argue, support, go beyond the obvious to discuss abstract things and obscure emotions, I suffer martyrdom. Without words to say it, there is nothing to communicate, nothing to share.

That being said, my main problem with English is not really communicative. It is cognitive! Because upstream of their translational power, words have an obvious generative function. They serve to think[65,382,383]! Therefore, before singing the praises of the "new world novlanguage", perhaps we should reread *1984* and go back to the sources of the concept[384]. In the words of its founder, George Orwell, "apart from the desire to eliminate words whose meaning was unorthodox, the impoverishment of the vocabulary was considered an end in itself and no word was left to be dispensed with. Novlanguage was intended not to expand but to diminish the realm of thought, and the reduction of word choice to a minimum indirectly helped to achieve this goal. When this process of lexical impoverishment was completed, all that was to remain was a people of enslaved

---

a. The problems were [378]: (i) "Mr. Genay is saddled with debts; he owes a total of 298 i of which: 121 i to the butcher, 54 € to the pork butcher and 23 € to the dry cleaner, the rest of his debt being equally divided between the garage owner and the grocer. How much does he owe to each of these last two shopkeepers?"
"A teacher bought 28 reading books. The bill only amounts to 321 € because the bookstore gave a 43 € discount. How much were all the books worth? What is the marked price of a book?"

calves, a herd of amorphous morons, permeable to all manipulations and incapable of the slightest critical thought! Seventy years ago, Victor Klemperer was able to observe the relevance of this approach by analyzing precisely the process of appropriation of the German language by the propagandists of the Third Reich[385]. According to the conclusions of this Jewish professor at the University of Dresden: "Nazism insinuated itself into the flesh and blood of the many through isolated expressions, turns of phrase, and syntactic forms that were imposed on millions of people and adopted mechanically and unconsciously [...] [The Third Reich had] subjected language to its terrible system, gained with language its most powerful, most public, and most secret means of propagation." We find the same idea in Umberto Eco, a fine connoisseur of Mussolinian totalitarianism: "All Nazi or Fascist school texts were based on a poor lexicon and elementary syntax, in order to limit the instruments of complex and critical reasoning."[386] Huxley, too, had told us: "To learn freedom (and the love and intelligence that are both its conditions and results) is, among other things, to learn to use language."[387] When words are emptied of their substance, "most men and women will come to love their servitude without ever thinking of revolution."[387] In this sense, preserving the richness of language is to defend our humanity and our ability to reflect the world around us. I know that it is customary to praise the mad semantic creativity of the younger generation. Imagine: "wack" for "crazy," "slack" for "heavy," "hard" for "hard," "bad-tripper" for "worry," and "serious" for just about every possible emotion or judgment. "It's too creepy," a potential 17-year-old babysitter told me not long ago after learning that there was no television in my house. Why "creepy"? "Well, because it's creepy, you know, it's bad, not cool. Not cool? "Are you looking for me? Am I speaking French or what?[a] Apparently, when linguistic inventiveness reaches such heights, it understands itself and loses even the need to see itself defined! Perhaps, however, we should compare the talents: "surgical strike" for "bombing"; "collateral damage" for "blunders", "civilian casualties", "innocent deaths"; "homeless" for "excluded", "vagrant", "beggar", "tramp"; "emerging" for "underdeveloped", "miserable"; "flexicurity" for "evolution", "precariousness", "unemployment"; "flexibility" for "fluidity", "redeployment", "restructuring", "adjustment", "dismissal"; "decision-maker" for "employer", "head of a company", "boss", etc. By its capacity to shape

a. "Pas glop" takes up, I suppose, the binary vocabulary "glop-glop" = good, "pas glop" = not good, of my friend Pifou, hero of the comic strip of my childhood *Pif et Hercule*.

our vision of the world in depth,[80,388,389] this novlanguage is far more effective than its "youthful" counterpart. Who can believe, among other examples, that expressions like "surgical strikes" or "collateral damage" do not profoundly soften our perception of the effects of war? The more our children's lexical competence erodes, the more difficult it will be for them to decipher this type of manipulation, which the advertising and political worlds are extraordinarily fond of. As Christian Delporte recently wrote in the heart of a remarkable book dedicated to the language of wood, "words have a capital function: their acceptance is the key that opens all the locks of thought. One begins by spreading them, one trivializes their use; soon the consciences conquered, they will command all reason"[389].

In light of the elements that have just been mentioned, one might reasonably have thought that everyone would agree on the need to rethink our young people's relationship to knowledge and language. In other words, one would have thought that the social body would quickly go beyond the question of diagnosis to finally address the subject of curative options. This is a foolish hope, as the clan of pipe-ologists seems to be clinging to its flourishing business of "good words". In fact, for our friends, the level is going down... but up. The concept may seem complicated at first, but the recent explanations of Clara Dupont-Monod should allow us to understand it without too many problems. According to this journalist, focusing on a few spelling mistakes "means not seeing what the teenagers have gained, without a doubt. [At this point, if we really have to make a comparison with the past, they are much more resourceful, especially with the new technologies, they are much more curious thanks to the Internet, there is a kind of agility, there is a liveliness"[364]. 364 In line with this kind of hypothesis, many observers have recently claimed that the brains of the new generations have changed[390], that they are now better adapted to *multitasking* and more capable of selecting, analyzing, sorting and synthesizing large flows of information[231]. The fable is very kind. Unfortunately, it is also terribly misleading. For example, when it comes to the handling of computer tools, the technological superiority of the "Google Generation" is relative, to say the least. According to the conclusions of a solid study recently commissioned by the British Library, the "old-timers" have largely caught up with their cyber-lag. This has not been difficult, since "the majority of young people tend to use much simpler applications with far fewer features than most of us think. 391 In fact, the Internet diet of our teens is not fundamentally different from that of their elders[217] and consists mainly of e-mailing, playing online games, chatting *via* instant messaging, downloading and listening to music or videos, and visiting shopping, sports or entertainment sites.[222,392,393] This is not much of a stretch. Not much to write home about. In fact, as Jean-Michel Fourgous explains in a recent parliamentary report, "studies show that [young people] have only a superficial mastery of these [digital] tools.[394] If this observation only concerned the "technical" domain, it would be a lesser evil. Unfortunately, this is not the case. It also affects the cognitive field. Thus, for many (real) specialists, the ability of the new generation to find information on the Web is quite limited[395]. According to the British Library study, it is a "dangerous myth" to believe that young people are experts in this field.[391] Net-boomers have difficulty formulating their requests, sorting the results obtained and prioritizing sources. It makes little difference whether the information comes from a major scientific journal such as *Science*, a recognized daily such as the *New York Times*, a weekly magazine with generally rigorous references such as *Télérama*, a community encyclopedia open to the four winds such as Wikipedia, an uncertain blog, or a totally nebulous site. To be adopted, an "information" must simply be accessible, i.e. appear among the first three or four links returned by the search engine (usually Google or Yahoo). Subsequent answers are simply ignored, which effectively facilitates the synthesis work. The most distressing thing is that this kind of aberration is starting to invade our most reputable media. This morning, for example, I came across an article in *Le Figaro* by Delphine Minoui. This undoubtedly talented young woman was writing about the "mysterious" assassination of an Iranian academic and explained that one plausible lead referred to the victim's recent anti-government remarks. In support of this thesis, the journalist wrote, "an Iranian man introducing himself as one of his students also confirms on his personal blog (ehsan63.blogs-pot.com) the affinities that his professor had with the Iranian protest. He recounts the memory of the large gathering on June 15, when, despite calls from opposition leaders not to take to the streets, Massoud Ali Mahammadi [the victim] had incited his students to demonstrate [...]"[396]. If this kind of rumor, written by an unidentified and unidentifiable stranger on an untraceable blog, is newsworthy in a major national newspaper, then I'll have to give my concierge the Pulitzer Prize for her coverage of the Iraq war. Mind you, our political friends are not to be outdone, as evidenced by a superb flight of lyricism from Ségolène Royal citing as an example, on her Facebook page, a historical figure, a courageous opponent of slave capitalism. The only problem is that this hero has never existed except in the uncertain mind of a contributor to the (self-proclaimed) free encyclopedia Wikipedia[397].

That being said, the difficulties of net-boomers do not stop, unfortunately, as I have already mentioned, with a concern for prioritizing information flows. They also concern other important elements of documentary research, such as the selection of relevant keywords and the use of adapted Boolean operators (AND, OR, ()). Take Noël, for example, a thesis student who is a "new technology" enthusiast, permanently connected to the Internet *via* his iPod and all the wi-fi's in the world. To search a medical database[398] for articles published by Angela Sirigu between 2004 and 2005, the young man tried four times without ever succeeding in obtaining anything other than a polite embarrassment from the search engine[a]. The most annoying thing about this case is that Noël is not unique among the (*a priori* most educated) offspring of the "Google Generation". A recent study conducted on young people entering higher education in Belgium has delivered some quite frightening results regarding the ability of students in the Flat Country to extract information from the Net. For example, only a quarter of the respondents were able to correctly answer the question: "To find a large number of documents on my subject, I can include synonyms (words that have the same meaning) in my search. To bring these synonyms together I use (only one possible answer): 'and', 'except', 'or', '+', 'don't know', 'other (please specify)'." In the words of the study's rapporteurs, "it is disturbing to realize that this notion [Boolean operators], which is basic for documentary research, is so poorly understood [...] The use of the Internet does not seem to promote students' informational skills."[399] The same observation can be found in a text by the collective Save the Letters. According to the authors, "in the first year of secondary school, a large number of students do not know the difference between 'or' and 'therefore'"[345]. Under these conditions, it is not easy to structure a line of reasoning or research.

The alleged capacity of young adults to acquire and synthesize, thanks to the Net, large flows of information is thus a very sad mirage. This conclusion

---

a. The correct formulation was: Sirigu A [author] AND (2004 [date of publication] OR 2005 [date of publication]). 11 results were then obtained. Our friend Noël tried in turn: Sirigu A 2004 2005, for 4 results; Sirigu A [author] AND 2004 [publication date] AND 2005 [publication date], for 1 result; Sirigu A [author] AND 2004 [publication date] OR 2005 [publication date], for 692 570 results; Sirigu A [author] AND 2004 [publication date] OR Sirigu A [author] AND 2005 [publication date] for 4 results.

seems all the more inescapable that the myth of the *"geek"*[a] is largely based on the folklore, already mentioned, of *"multitasking"*. New technologies have, we are told, taught their followers the art of doing more than one thing at a time. In 10 years, our young people would have become true experts in parallel processing. This is a nice story, but unfortunately it does not hold water, as several press articles have recently admitted.[400-405] Watching television while doing algebra homework and keeping three MSN chat windows open is not something any human can do[406-408]. All the brain knows how to do in these situations is to switch from one activity to another, sequentially. However, each transition costs errors and time[409-414]. Moreover, a good part of the brain's resources is taken up, not by carrying out the task, but by managing the multitasking process.[415,416] A neuroimaging study has even shown that learning and memory mechanisms are altered, at the most basic neuronal level, when a subject has to juggle two simple tasks[417]. At the behavioral level, *"multitaskers"* develop, in the long term, serious attentional problems, a high degree of distractibility and, quite unexpectedly, a reduced ability to juggle several cognitive tasks[418]. Specific research has shown that the completion of schoolwork was significantly impaired, both in terms of time spent and degree of accuracy, in 14-year-old students when they worked with a television on in the background.[419-422]

Thus, the proportion of children, teenagers and young adults who have difficulty with academic knowledge (spelling, reading, arithmetic) has grown steadily over the past 20 years. This evolution has not been compensated, as the fable would have it, by an expert mastery of digital tools or the advent of a multitasking mind filled with non-standard calculation and information skills. Faced with this general observation, many specialists have denounced the shortcomings of a school system that has been subjected for two (or even three) decades to improbable pedagogical experiments [54,65,78,81,322-326] and political experiments [327,328]. Without calling this hypothesis into question, several voices have recently been raised to suggest the possible involvement of another potential factor: television [25,29,54,65,81]. It seems high time to explore the merits of this proposal in detail.

*
**

---

a. Anglicism designating a kind of genius of the Internet and new technologies.

A major barrier to academic success

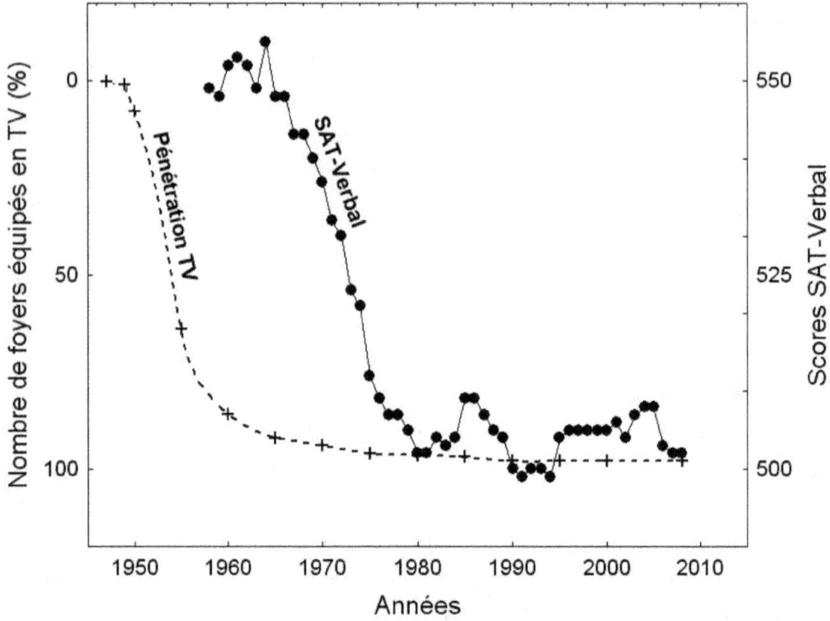

Figure 1: *Comparative evolution of the level of audiovisual penetration (left vertical scale inverted - i.e. increasing downwards -, dotted curve) and of the SAT-Verbal score (right vertical scale, continuous curve) as a function of time (horizontal axis). Note that the two curves move in parallel with a time lag of about 17-18 years, which corresponds to the time it takes for children who have grown up with television to take the SAT exam[a].*

The SAT-Verbal[b] is a standardized test of language proficiency that most American students take before entering college. Between 1965 and 1980, scores on this test plummeted. Various hypotheses were put forward to explain this strange phenomenon: less funding for the school system, increasing incompetence of teachers, the arrival of large numbers of black and Hispanic minority students, the increasing complexity of the test, and so on. None of these proposals proved satisfactory.[362] In fact, it was not until Marie Winn and the recent republication of her book *The Plug-in*

---

a. Penetration Data: Effect of Televised Violence on Aggression[423]; SAT Data: Digest of Education Statistics 2008[424].
b. SAT: Scholastic Aptitude Test, which recently became the SAT Reasoning Test.

Drug that a possible solution to the problem emerged.[29] Winn observed that the collapse of the U.S. economy was a major factor in the decline of the U.S. economy. This author observed that the collapse of the SAT-Verbal reproduced, with a necessary incubation period, the curve of television penetration on the American territory. This concomitance is easily visible on the figure opposite (Figure 1). As one can see on this last one, the language drop began 17-18 years after the beginning of the process of universalization of the post. This latency represents precisely the time required for children born with television to arrive at the SAT.

Of course, isochronism is not the same as proof, and to accuse the small window on the sole basis of the preceding elements would be a bit cavalier. Let us therefore say, in order not to upset anyone, that these elements are only a graphic appetizer. The bulk of the evidence is to be found elsewhere, in the field of experimental sciences. A first illustration of this assertion can be found in an enormous work whose roots go back to the year 1973.[425] At that date, there was a Canadian city of medium importance, named NoTel. This town, located at the bottom of a valley, could not receive television. A group of 13 researchers incidentally learned that the installation of a relay antenna was envisaged to put an end to this incongruity within 12 months. A large study was then implemented to measure the influence of television on fields as diverse as learning to read, aggressiveness, creativity, leisure, etc. Adults and children were tested just before (Pre-TV) and two years after (Post-TV) the arrival of the set. The tests were both longitudinal (the same subjects were assessed before and after TV) and instantaneous (different but comparable subjects, e.g., second graders, were tested before and after TV). To ensure optimal coverage of the data collected, the work was extended to two "control" cities with the same sociological and demographic characteristics as NoTel. One of these cities, UniTel, received a single channel (Canadian Broadcasting Corporation - CBC). The other, MultiTel, received four (CBC plus three major American commercial channels - ABC, CBS, NBC). Academic competence was assessed in its simplest written form, using a symbolic decoding task[426]. Subjects were asked to read words (such as *red*), phrases (such as *the car is red*) and non-words (such as *sked*) presented for a variable duration, ranging from 10 to 2000 milliseconds. Initial results (Pre-TV) showed that after one year of learning to read, NoTel children significantly outperformed their MultiTel and UniTel peers when they entered second grade.

This difference was still present two years later (after TV), when they entered fourth grade. The MultiTel and UniTel children had slightly lower average performance than the NoTel children in second grade! This observation corroborates other data showing that early deficits in learning the written code are very difficult to erase [350,427,428]. It also shows that the late introduction of television does not degrade the acquired ability to decode language signs. Interestingly, when a new cohort of second graders was tested in the After-TV phase, the three cities showed perfectly equivalent results. It only took two years for NoTel to lose its original advantage. It is difficult to deny the causal role of television in these data.

As the NoTel campaign came to an end, five major epidemiological studies were conducted in the United States. Hundreds of thousands of children were tested, from the fourth grade to the master's degree. The conclusion of all these studies was clear: "The amount of time American children and adolescents spend watching television is negatively associated with their academic performance... The quality of the measurements, the size and completeness of the samples, and the consistency of the results make this conclusion irrefutable.[429] Consider, for example, to illustrate this claim, the data on written expression[a] . The data showed that, for children in the sixth grade (age 12), the success rate on a standardized test dropped by nearly 8 percent when daily television viewing increased from one hour or less to four hours or more. For high school seniors (18 years old), on the same basis of exposure, we obtained a significantly higher dropout rate of about 13%. The assessments conducted in mathematics and reading revealed similar trends. However, this general picture proved to be very sensitive to socio-economic influences. Indeed, it was shown that the deleterious effect of the small screen increased with social affluence and parental education. In other words, the more the child came from a privileged (or educated) environment, the more the negative correlation between television and school performance intensified. Slightly positive trends were even observed, in some cases, for the most modest households, below 4 hours of daily use. The TV/performance curve then appeared as a very flattened inverted U. The results obtained by 12-year-olds on a standard reading test illustrate these statements[b]. Among the offspring

---

a. California Assessment Program, 1980, 282,000 12-year-olds; 227,000 18-year-olds[429].
b. *Ibid.*

TV Lobotomie

of the most affluent backgrounds, it was shown that the success rate fell monotonically with the degree of exposure, reaching a maximum of 8% when small (< 1 h/day) and large (= 4 h/day) users were compared. Conversely, in the most disadvantaged subjects, it was found that achievement levels remained stable as long as daily exposure did not reach 4 hours. Beyond this threshold, the curve began to fall to a ceiling deficit of 2% (< 1 h/day *versus* = 4 h/day). To explain these data, it can be suggested that television alters children's cognitive development by substituting functionally poor practices for intellectually formative experiences. To the extent that the latter are more accessible to socially advantaged subjects, it seems normal that they are the most affected. In other words, "the role of television depends on what is displaced. When it brings to the child's experience stimuli and information that are educationally equivalent or superior to those in the environment, its effect is positive or nil. When it fails to match the environment its effect is negative."[429]

Since their collection nearly 30 years ago, the previous data have been largely confirmed[430-434]. This remarkable stability could have provided the basis for a solid consensus. This was not the case, on the contrary. The profusion of evidence was matched by a profusion of polemics. Three points were particularly debated: (1) the observed effects concern only recreational programs, not the so-called educational programs; (2) the link between television and school performance is not causal, it simply reflects the fact that children who fail at school are more likely to watch television than others; (3) the observed effects are so weak that they can safely be neglected. Distractive claims that are not difficult to refute.

Let's start with the content objection. This objection fails on two levels. First, children spend the overwhelming majority of their audiovisual time on recreational programs.[435] They are only marginally exposed to so-called educational programs. It is difficult to imagine that these programs can have a significant influence on intellectual development. Secondly, even if one accepts axiomatically that certain productions have a formative potential, one may wonder about the capacity of these productions to reach a large public. It is already difficult for a primary school teacher to fruitfully nourish the intelligence of 25 six-year-olds from roughly homogeneous backgrounds, so imagine how impossible it can be for a single program to significantly fertilize the brains of several million kids of varying ages and disparate social origins. The "bottom-up" formatting of content is the only acceptable compromise under the sacrosanct principle of the lowest common intelligence.[435] In line with this assertion, it is widely accepted that the positive effect of so-called "educational" programmes is concentrated (when it is pointed) on the least socially advantaged children[433,436]. Middle- and upper-class offspring gain nothing from the game, except probably an intense waste of time, intelligence and money. As Manon, 6 years old, a fan of Dora and a big consumer of derivative products (including shoes, pencil case, T-shirt, dress, barrettes, schoolbag, scooter, doll, DVD, water bottle, cap, yoghurts… and others no doubt) says: "Mom, I answered everything well to Dora."

Beyond the problem of contents, the hard test of causality arises. This one proposes a factorial reversal. It would not be television that would lower school performance, but rather the existence of school difficulties that would push the child towards television. This argument is invalid for at least four reasons. Firstly, the NoTel study and the SAT data clearly show that the TV/achievement association moves, at least partially, from television to the school field (see *above*). Secondly, when the time of audiovisual exposure is reduced, the academic and cognitive performance of pupils improves rapidly, both for children in preparatory classes[437] and for adolescents in secondary schools[438]. Third, there are clear behavioral[439] and biological explanations that causally link the use of the set to impaired academic performance. Biologically, for example, it appears that television negatively affects sleep time and quality[440-443], which has the effect of disrupting cognitive functioning [444] and thus ulti- mately academic output[445]. When audiovisual exposure is experimen- tally reduced, sleep becomes regularized,[440,446] inducing normalization of cognitive functioning[444] and ultimately optimization of academic perfor- mance.[445] Fourthly, longitudinal research has established the existence of remote effects that are not compatible with the reverse causality thesis. For the avoidance of doubt, this research is based on relatively complex statistical procedures that allow the influence of the audiovisual factor to be identified, independently of the contribution of other potentially influential covariates (age, gender, socio-economic status, IQ, number of siblings, parents' education level, school level at the start of the study, etc.)[a]. In other words, thanks to adapted numerical treatments, the role of the audiovisual factor can be isolated and, in a way, extracted from the

---

a. See note p. 24.

influence of the other causal factors. This type of approach has recently made it possible to show that high audiovisual consumption at the end of kindergarten predicted reading difficulties at the start of fourth grade[447]. This finding is consistent with the results of another study that found a significant relationship between the number of hours spent in front of the television before age 3 and success on standardized reading and memory tests at age 6-7.[233] The same negative relationship was identified in a study of children who had been exposed to television for at least three years. The same negative relationship was identified between the level of television exposure recorded at 29 months and demonstrated mathematical ability at 10 years[448]. In another particularly impressive study, nearly 1,000 individuals were followed for 21 years 96 and it was shown that the magnitude of childhood television consumption (5-11 years) was significantly associated with the probability of obtaining a university degree in adulthood. A comparable study of nearly 700 families showed a similar relationship between adolescent television consumption (age 14) and the probability of having a post-baccalaureate diploma at age 33.[438] Again, biological substrates are important in deter-mining the probability of obtaining a university degree. Again, there is no lack of plausible biological substrates to explain these phenomena. For example, it has been established that the use of television heavily alters the deployment of language,[128,129,131,133] the development of formal intelligence,[406,449] and the time devoted to school work.[192,199,438,450] A set of handicaps which results *de facto in* limiting the academic horizon. We shall return to these points in detail later.

After the questions of content and causality, we come to the subject of magnitudes. The hypothesis defended is quite simple: there is indeed a significant causal link between audiovisual consumption and school performance, but it is so weak that it borders on the ridiculous[430,434,451]. However frequent it may be, this statement is nonetheless seriously misleading. Its main shortcoming relates to the very notion of "weakness". Indeed, can we say that an influence is weak when 8-year-olds without a television in their room show, compared to their peers equipped with one, after taking into account a large number of potential covariates (parents' level of education, language spoken at home, sex, age of the child, etc.), performances that are 21% higher in reading, 26% higher in verbal competence and 34% higher in mathematics[200]? This last figure means, to be concrete, that the averages out of 20 of 2 identical children in all points will be established at 9 and 12 according to whether or not a television is present in their room. This effect is in line with the conclusions of a recent study which showed, after taking into account a wide range of potential covariates, that each additional hour of television consumed at the age of 2.5 years resulted in a 6% drop in the child's mathematical skills at the age of 10 years[448]. Still on the same topic, can it be argued that an effect is marginal when the daily addition or subtraction of one hour of television can, after controlling for a large matrix of sociodemographic, psychological, and personal covariates, multiply or divide the risk of school failure by 2? To demonstrate this point, a study recently analyzed the academic performance of 16-year-old middle school students.[438] The study found that, among the participants who had a high school diploma at age 14, there was a significant increase in the risk of academic failure. Among the participants who had a reasonable level of use at the age of 14 (< 2 h/ day), those who had reduced their time of use by 1 hour in 2 years also reduced their chances of failing in school by 50% (repeating a year, grades in the E-F range, leaving the academic system). Unsurprisingly, subjects who increased their time of use by one hour recorded a doubling of the risk factor. In a similar vein, can we say that only psychopaths in need of media recognition are concerned about the audiovisual issue, when it has been shown, after adjustment for IQ and sex, that each hour of television consumed daily, during the week, when the child is in elementary school, increases by 43% the probability of seeing the child leave the school system one day without the slightest qualification[96]? When, in addition to gender and IQ, the socio-economic status of the family and the potential existence of early behavioural problems in the child are taken into account, this probability value decreases slightly, while remaining staggering (34%). Basically, if all these values are so impressive (and infinitely more important than those obtained in the large epidemiological studies described at the beginning of this section), it is because the longitudinal approach that generated them allows, by stubbornly following the same group of individuals over a long period of time, to accumulate the deleterious effects of the position. By definition, this cumulative attribute escapes the traditional studies, whose approach consists essentially in measuring the link between audiovisual exposure and school performance at a given moment (for example at age 15). By considering only a small part of the equation, these studies, which are widely cited in support of the harmlessness of television, dangerously minimize the deleterious effects of television[a]. Longitudinal estimates are infinitely more reliable. Unfortunately, they remain rare. It is indeed expensive and complicated to follow, without losing them, several hundred individuals for almost a quarter of a century!

Thus, there is undoubtedly a strong causal link between television exposure and academic performance. In fact, this is hardly surprising since it seems to be established that television profoundly alters several pillars of academic success. Diligence, intelligence, reading, language, attention and imagination do not emerge unscathed from the cathodic current. This one proves all the more vigorous that it proceeds, as we will see, according to multiple and additive ways. The post is a thief of time. It is also a cause of social isolation, a source of intellectual laziness, an agent of cognitive sterility and a vector of psychic destructuring. At a time when parents are spending huge sums of money on tutoring to ensure the academic success of their children,[452-456] one can be surprised at the impunity granted to Lady Television. It is a strange schizophrenia that demands an education of excellence and delivers our children to the most debilitating media content.

*
**

____

a. In order for the influence of early use (5-10 years old) to have a perfect impact on the school performance of children aged 12, 15 or 18, it would be necessary for early audio-visual consumption to completely condition later use. However, this is not the case. The link between initial and late exposure is significant (cf. chapter II), but not complete. Its strength remains, in part, subject to the vagaries of life. For example, it seems likely that the audiovisual consumption of an adolescent will increase if he suddenly sees the old family television in his room. In the same way, it is likely that some children who are exposed to a lot of television at a very early age will see their use reduced later on if a passion for tennis, soccer or theater comes to light in their lives. This means that a fraction of the early heavy consumers may turn into average consumers at age 15 and that, conversely, a fraction of the early average consumers may turn into heavy or small consumers at age 15. This partial mixing will lead to the loss, over time, of some of the influence of initial audiovisual exposure. This will mechanically result, for one-off studies carried out at 12, 15 or 18 years of age, in a significant under-evaluation of the effects of television on school results.

Effort, intelligence, reading, language, attention, imagination. All of them are hit

Self-discipline, conceived as the ability to put the necessary before the pleasurable, is a central factor in academic success.[457] This reality, which is certainly trivial, is found in particular in the field of homework.458-460 In this area, however, television tends to seriously corrode our children's enthusiasm. This reality, which is certainly trivial, is found in particular in the field of homework.[458-460] In this area, however, television tends to seriously corrode our children's ardour. The first studies were conducted in the 1950s. At that time, the small screen was only beginning its colonizing work and researchers could still construct experimental groups that were identical in terms of their socio-demographic characteristics, but different in terms of their audiovisual equipment. This approach made it possible to measure the impact of television "all things being maintained equal"[a] and thus to pronounce unambiguously on the orientation of the causal chains. The data showed that the small screen diverted a substantial part of the time normally devoted to homework[461,462] to itself. A Boston study of 4-17 year olds found, for example, that 54% of schoolchildren living in an equipped home did not do any work the day before they encountered the experimenter. The percentage was only 43% for students living in families without a station. On weekdays, the average time spent on homework dropped by 20% when television was available (41 minutes *versus* 51 minutes). On weekends, the average time spent on homework dropped by 80% (7 minutes *versus* 34 minutes).[463] These values are exorbitant, especially if we consider that the audiovisual offer was limited to two generalist channels at the time of the study. These are values that the multiplication of offers and channels has not helped to erode. On the contrary. Today, after half a century of research, there is no longer any doubt about the deleterious effect of television on homework[132,192,199,245,438,450,464]. The most recent study found that each hour of weekday television viewing reduces homework time by 14% (4-6 year olds) to 18% (9-12 year olds)[132]. If we consider that the average daily exposure to television is just over 2 hours for 4-14 year olds,[146] this implies a net cut of 28% to 36%. With this in mind, Christine has scaled back her "old school" claims. Our teacher now separates compulsory homework (no more than 8-10 minutes per day) from

---

a. According to the formula canonically used by statisticians.

TV Lobotomie

optional exercises (15-20 minutes). Before," she likes to explain, "I never made a distinction, I gave the homework and that was it, but now the parents are complaining more and more aggressively. They tell me that it's too much, that the children don't have time to do their homework, that the workload is too heavy and that the official texts forbid homework anyway - that's their big thing, the official texts. So for the last 3 years, I've been giving a little bit of homework and the rest is marked "optional". Only 4 or 5 students do everything regularly. The others "didn't have time", which doesn't prevent them from spending recess talking about all the stupid shows they watched on TV the day before. It's really a disaster. Last year, a colleague tried to replace some of the homework with ten minutes of reading. Two nights a week, she gave the children a short playful text. When they returned to class, they had obviously not read it. They were, however, well-versed in the latest *Secret Story* and the latest episode of *CSI*.

This last observation is unfortunately hardly surprising. It simply reflects the gradual displacement of books by mail over the past 40 years. According to the terms of an analysis published in 2007 by the very official Department of Studies, Forecasting and Statistics (DEPS), "the retrospective analysis [...] carried out on a dozen cultural and media practices confirms the generational nature of most of the changes observed since the early 1970s : Whether it is the progression of screen culture, the generalization of listening to recorded music, or the decline in reading daily newspapers or books, each time the changes were initiated by a new generation, before being continued and amplified by the following ones."[465] The figures show, for example, that the proportion of 15 to 24 year olds who regularly read newspapers or consume 20 books a year has fallen by almost 50 percent in a quarter of a century (books: 33 percent to 17 percent; newspapers: 30 percent to 18 percent). Over the same period, the number of viewers who spend at least 3 hours a day watching TV has risen by more than a third (24% to 32%). These transformations have affected all social groups, but with a predilection for the more privileged, who are slowly seeing their historical appetite for the written word eroded. Similar results have been obtained in the United States.

Beyond these statistical facts, the deleterious effect of television on reading has been widely validated by academic research. The latter has shown that if a city is connected to a television set, the entire population sees its reading time drop considerably, often approaching 50%.[462,463,466] This trend even affects the operation of libraries, which are affected by the arrival of the small television set. This trend affects even the functioning of libraries, which, following the arrival of the small screen, are experiencing a drastic reduction in use, with a consequent drop of more than 20% in the number of books borrowed per year and per inhabitant.[467] This reduction applies in proportions that are not always easy to measure. This reduction applies in similar proportions to general and children's books. However, if coercive measures are taken to limit children's audio-visual consumption, the time spent reading rebounds quickly.[29,437,468] This result is fully reflected in several studies of the literature. This finding is fully supported by several recent studies showing that the more television a child watches, the less reading he or she does[185,199,243,245,246,447,450,464,469]. A study carried out by Elizabeth Vandewater's team illustrates this point nicely on the basis of a rather clever experimental protocol[470]. The authors were interested not in individual exposure times, but in households in which the TV is almost always on, regardless of whether anyone is watching it or not. According to the adults, the TV set represents a "company", a "presence", as if silence were a source of intolerable anxiety. For example, this mother of a child under 3 years old confided to us: "I leave it on all the time."[185] For another woman, also the mother of a preschooler, "[the television] is on all the time, mainly because my husband likes to turn it on and go. It's just on. It's background noise. In other words, in 4 out of 10 households, the television is almost always on, even if only in the background, which is hardly surprising when we know, for example, that 44% of French people over 15 years of age say that they turn on the TV immediately when they get home.[471] Children are then subjected to a bombardment of noise and noise. Children are then subjected to a constant bombardment of sounds and images. This is not without consequences for reading. In fact, after taking into account a large number of socio-demographic, psychological and personal covariates (parental education, income, family structure, ethnicity, etc.), it appears that children who are subjected to the omnipresence of audiovisuals are three times more likely not to be able to read at the end of the first year of primary school[470]! This deficit is easily understood if one considers that a permanent cathodic flux multiplies almost by 2 the daily audiovisual consumption of 5-6 year olds (52 minutes *versus* 94 minutes), while decreasing their reading time by almost 30% (49 minutes *versus* 35 minutes). Quite a handicap at the age when one is learning to read! A handicap that is all the more important because it is preceded by a serious familiarization deficit. In fact, when the post saturates the family space with its presence, 3-4 year olds spend substantially less time each day with books (43 minutes *versus* 34 minutes), not only by themselves but also in the company of their parents.[470,472] This early relationship with the written word is a major handicap for children. Yet this early relationship with the written word plays a key role in learning to read.[473]

That being said, let's face it, it would take a pretty messed up brain for our kids to prefer books to television, at least in the early formative years. Indeed, reading requires a much more intense intellectual effort than television. Several studies have shown that the written word imposes a greater tax on brain resources than television[474-476], with the result that the feeling of drudgery is exacerbated[29,169,477]. A survey carried out in the United States among 500 primary school pupils revealed that they all preferred television to reading, whatever the nature of the programmes offered[29]. This plebiscite, which is truly Stalinist, shows how boring and unpleasant reading can seem to our children. It must be said, and all the specialists agree, that the path that leads to a book is no easy matter[29,54,65,81,324]. Charlotte, who is nine years old, can attest to this. She is a very good student and, in the most mechanistic sense of the word, an excellent reader. No sign escapes her sagacity. However, even the simplest books of the famous Pink Library remain, for her young mind, a formidable challenge. *Fantômette contre le géant* is a good example of this.[478] This text, theoretically intended for 8-9 year olds, often refers Charlotte to the dictionary. When the definition provided by the latter proves to be comprehensible, all is well. If it is not, it is necessary to go back to the words and/or to ask for parental guidance. At the end of the day, it can take 20 to 30 minutes of hard work to understand even the smallest paragraph. There is nothing scandalous about this, if one admits that writing is a specific space whose syntax and lexicon must be tamed. Even a modest *Fantômette is* full of puzzling expressions that are unfamiliar to the oral world: "missal lover", "quintessence of their subtle effluvia", "neophyte hunters", "cynocephalus with a prognathic face", "pebbles that dot the outskirts of the ruins", "bewildering articles", "fills a timbale", "rather soporific grammar course", "leveling the median", "aerial bugs, whose name only an entomologist could have told", "countryman between two ages", "lecture on how to handle the hoe", "hobbled players", "Gargantua, who fought against Picrochole", etc.[478]. Examples which show, I believe, that if one needs a lot of words to read[479], one also needs to read a lot to acquire more than the terms of everyday life[65]. This being said, it should probably be made clear here that not all reading is equal from a strict educational point of view. I find the argument that it is okay for kids to read fewer books than they used to because they are making up for it in comics, celebrity magazines, blogs, and manga incredibly misleading. One wonders if the proponents of this incredible compensatory theory have ever read *Voici*, *Closer*, my niece's blog, *DragonBall* or *Naruto*. Take *Voici*, for example. For the purposes of this book, I decided to buy the week's copy[481]. I wasn't expecting great literature, but I didn't think I would have to face such a grammatical Waterloo either! In fact I only got through a single page[481]. That proved to be more than enough for my edification. I started with the small insert on the right. A man named Jonathan philosophically explained that "getting married only means living under the same you [goodbye my t]." "At worst," the young man added, "I'd go back [s included] to a food job." In the adjacent article, his colleague Emily claimed to have "the same [singular is so much more reasonable] delusions" as her boyfriend Leo. Not much compared to Romain, Cindy and Angie who "had a lot of good [plural is so much better] time" in the bathroom. In any case, Émilie knew that her ex was now with Vanessa. "I was laughing my ass off when I saw the pictures of the two of them in the middle of the dead leaves." With this kind of story, this syntactic rigor and this ultimate spelling, our teenagers are undoubtedly in good hands. A way out on the manga side? To find out, I went to Decitre in Lyon. The judgment of a saleswoman, as charming as enthusiastic, was without appeal: "*Naruto*! It's the bible, you'll enjoy it." As a treat, I mostly encountered the pangs of an ineffable boredom. Fortunately, Charlotte was much more enthusiastic. She swallowed the story voraciously. It must be said that her trip to Naruto's country was done without any dictionary or external help. A feat that can easily be explained with the help of a small passage selected at the goodwill of Mr. Random[a]: "Fwam. Shuuuf. Tchak. Slash. Svaf. Hung. Shrap. It is only an illusion! I can overcome the pain!...! Slap. Slap. Slap. Zrax. Zrax. Zrax. Gwaaaah!!! Hung!!! Stak. Last time I couldn't finish you off... Gatch. Wooo! Stack. I trusted you... Why didn't you stop Sasuke? Zouip. Wooop!!! Wooo. I was counting on you... I'm so disappointed in you... You couldn't even protect your friend... You're always the one who gets to be happy... Kshik. You are always the one who takes advantage of everything... Hh... Hh... Hh... Hh... Hng... Hh... Hh... Hh...!... I... Are you okay Naruto? It's not

____

a. Entire text between pages 119 and 125 [482].

limited to Dojutsu... You suffered a Genjutsu attack[a]... But it's over... Well, let's get down to business! Get ready Naruto !"[482] It is difficult to pretend that this kind of text can feed the language and replace the prognathic cynocephalus or other missal fans of this brave Fantômette! Reading *Naruto* is undoubtedly worthy, commendable and respectable. It is possible that this type of work feeds the imagination and the onirism of the customer. The fact remains that *Naruto* and his followers will never make a child a seasoned reader.

Moreover, at this point, it might be a good idea to say a word about the vigorous post-Sixties' elan according to which our unfortunate young heads should not be rushed in order to avoid irreversible traumas. For example, "Don't force them to read" implored a recent issue of the monthly *Psychologies magazine*.[480] In the words of this issue, "Françoise Dolto was the first to believe that it was not essential to read before adulthood." Moreover, "some children hate reading because they have painful memories of learning to read". It is true, I admit, that without learning, the memory is not likely to be very painful. That said, hoping that a child will swallow the briny potion that makes a reader out of a codebreaker seems slightly optimistic, especially if the television is blaring in the house. Obviously, it is much more engaging, at the ages when one is learning to read, to slump in front of *Secret Story* than to sweat over *Fantômette*. Without early learning, there is no possible future in the written world. In contradiction with the assertions attributed to Mme Dolto, a recent report by INSEE has shown that "the practice of reading in adulthood has its roots in childhood. The fact of having read even occasionally during childhood strongly increases the probability of reading as an adult. Moreover, the more regular the reading, the more likely it is to have been retained. When parents also discussed their reading with the child, the child is almost certain to become an adult reader."[483] We force children to eat properly, to take showers regularly, to follow certain rules of behaviour in public, to get up in the morning to go to school, to play sports on Wednesdays, not to cross at red lights, but we could not force them to read a little? Why on earth would it be scandalous to steal even 30 minutes a day from TV to give it to books? 30 minutes is not even a quarter of the brain time our children give to TF1, M6, France 2 and their affiliates every day. However, the idea has difficulty in passing. "You're seriously fascist," Annie told me,

---

a. Charlotte didn't seem to be fazed by these words (Dojutsu, Genjutsu). It's like taekwondo, she said.

for example, just before her 17-year-old daughter assailed me with an irrevocable: "Fuck, you're seriously prehistoric. An affirmation quite close to Serge Tisseron's positions, welcoming "the abandonment of coercive methods" and lyrically declaring that "those who do not have a privileged relationship with the verbal and the acoustic no longer find themselves obliged, as in the past, to learn by force through fear and tears [*sic*]. They turn away from those forms of learning that have never suited them, and to which they have previously complied only for fear of punishment. This is why those who dream of reinstating more restrictive methods of teaching children to read and write would do well to think twice. Times have changed! Children who have a privileged relationship with images are no longer ready today to renounce them as easily as in the past, insofar as the audiovisual environment confirms them every day"[34]. Poor mistreated youth, living in fear and tears, whimpering in their notebooks, stunned by superhuman labor. One wonders how I was able for so long to escape the torments of shame, how I was able without flinching to bear the infamous image of this poor Charlotte chained to her books, like the convict to his galley. Unfortunate child, delivered thus to the barbaric yoke of immoral Thénardier of the reading. Her life would be so much happier and more fulfilled with TF1 in intravenous mode!

Perhaps we should consider paying the young lady in hard cash to give some humanity to her terrible ordeal. After all, isn't it fashionable to pay students to go to school[a]? Despairing as it may seem, when you think about it, this proposal is in perfect harmony with the disastrous effects of the cathodic feeding that we subject our children to every day. Indeed, television literally conditions them to immediacy. It only takes a few moments for the most pathetic moron to become a "star" and to occupy the front page of celebrity magazines. An IQ of a badger is enough to understand, without effort or delay, 99.9% of the programs of the PAF[b]. A deluge of advertising injunctions, largely subliminal, irrevocably impregnates our "available brains" with a model of non-deferred happiness, based on instant access to the most diverse goods. The terms of a report written for the Ministry of Health by the Collectif interassociatif enfance

---

a. In France, you can win trips, driving hours or tickets to see a soccer game. In the United States, it's more direct. In some colleges, an accommodating teenager can expect to earn $50 a week. In elementary school, a clean dictation can be worth up to $25. In England, it's up to £30 per week of attendance[484-487].
b. French Audiovisual Landscape.

et média (CIEM) are edifying in this respect. After having stigmatized the incapacity of the social body to take "the measure of the role of the media in the development of young people and the construction of their identity", the authors conclude without hesitation that television "functions on values that are often opposed to those of the school: promotion of spectacular success without effort, promotion of the exposure of intimacy, functioning in the instantaneous and the immediate satisfaction"[59]. Many teachers openly denounce these evils through the firm stigmatization of a generation that has lost the taste for and the power to learn. Young people, Natacha Polony tells us, "are not ready [...] to accept with humility the time necessary for learning, a time that is generally not that of enjoyment and fulfillment. What makes television the public (or private) enemy number 1 of education," Alain Bentolila continues, "is that it manages to dissuade children and their parents from any desire for curiosity and conquest by making what is not already seen and known unworthy of their intellectual ambition."[54] "The habit of 'flipping' on the remote control," adds Véronique Bouzou, "of passively watching programs that do not require any intellectual quality, has been to the detriment of lessons to be learned or homework to be done. More and more teenagers are unable to concentrate for more than a few minutes on a written text or on any kind of reasoning"[41] "We are trained to want everything, immediately and without effort," says Sébastien Clerc. This is what we can call the zapping syndrome, because television is (along with the game console and the Internet) the basic propaganda organ for this frenzy [...] We stick to immediate enjoyment, and delayed pleasure is no longer of interest. Thus accustomed to not wasting any more time with information that is not striking or very exciting, a part of our youth makes itself less and less available for the slow and progressive acquisition of abstract knowledge [...] Only education can make us understand that a certain amount of displeasure can lead to a greater pleasure than those immediately accessible. To put it simply," summarizes Jean-Philippe Testefort, "what these difficulties show, and what is at stake here, is the students' poor taste for knowledge.[491] Interestingly, these assertions overlap with the results of a recent study which established, after taking into account a wide range of socio-demographic, psychological and personal covariates, that the more a child watched television before the age of 3, the less involved he or she was in school work at the age of 10, in terms of participation, effort or curiosity.[448] This conclusion is compatible with a solid body of research on the subject. This finding is consistent with a strong body of experimental evidence showing that the small screen increases children's behavioral and cognitive impulsivity, while decreasing their propensity for perseverance, their appetite for intellectually demanding tasks, and their ability to concentrate.[29,58,65,437,450,492-494] This last point has been particularly well studied. This last point has been particularly well studied. It has been shown, for example, that the most telephobic students were consistently identified as the most impulsive and inattentive by teachers.[495,496] Similarly, it has been shown that the most telephobic students were the most impulsive and inattentive by teachers. Similarly, it was established that early television consumption profoundly altered the development of attentional functions[497,498]. Longitudinal research published in the Journal of the American Association of Pediatrics is particularly interesting in this respect.[499] Rather than looking at audiovisual consumption, it is important to consider the impact of television on the development of attention. Rather than looking at children's audiovisual consumption syncretically, the authors distinguished between recreational programs with low (e.g., *Babe, The Razmoket, The Flintstones*) *versus* high (e.g., *The Lion King, Video Gag,* or *Scooby-Doo*) violent content. The results showed that each hour of non-violent programming swallowed daily before 3 years of age increased the probability of occurrence of attentional problems at 8 years of age by almost 75%, after taking into account a wide range of socio-demographic, psychological and personal covariates (age, gender, place in the sibling group, place of residence, parents' education, early cognitive stimulation, etc.) When the child was confronted with violent content, the risk level was multiplied by 2.2! Other studies confirmed and extended these results to older subjects, without distinguishing, however, in this case, between different types of content. For example, one study revealed that each hour spent in front of the television between the ages of 5 and 11 increased the probability of developing attentional problems by almost 50% at the age of 13, after taking into account a large number of potential covariates, including the existence of any initial attentional deficits[234]. This last point is extremely important. It ensures that the reported impact is independent of prior influences. In other words, the impairment observed at age 13 does not take into account disorders inherited from early childhood. To put it simply, one could say that early (< 3 years) and late (5-11 years) impacts do not overlap, but are cumulative. This additive principle unfortunately also applies to adolescent influences. According to a recent study, each hour spent in front of the television at 14 years of age increases the probability of developing attentional problems at 16 years of age by 44%, after taking into account, among a wide range of covariates, possible initial attentional deficits.[438] For those who would tend to judge this to be a mistake, it is important to note that the probability of developing attentional problems is higher than the probability of developing them. For those who would tend to consider these effects to be trivial, it is perhaps worth remembering that learning and memory functions depend directly on attention[500-503]. When attention is impaired, all cognitive functioning is compromised. It has been established, to take just one example, that the existence of attentional problems at the age of 16 increases the risk of academic failure by a factor of almost 4, after taking into account a large number of potential covariates (age, sex, socio-economic status, audiovisual consumption, etc.)[438]. A figure that is, let us agree, relatively far removed from the homeopathic field!

For more than 40 years, many authors have emphasized the central role of fast-paced audiovisual formats in the emergence of attentional disorders in children and adolescents[65,305,504,505]. From a theoretical point of view, this idea is based on a large body of experimental evidence showing that there are two distinct attentional systems, carried by different neural circuits and solicited either automatically-exogenously or voluntarily-endogenously[503,506-508]. Audiovisual exposure would lead to a hypertrophy of the first of these systems, to the detriment of the second. Two complementary processes would then be brought into play. Firstly, by being subjected to a frenetic succession of lapidary sequences, the developing brain would become accustomed to continually modifying its cognitive focus and intellectual commitment. Second, by being confronted with an uninterrupted cascade of racy stimuli, the developing mind would learn to rely on external perceptual stimuli to boost its alertness and maintain its interest. The validity of these hypotheses was recently confirmed by Bermejo Berros, in a remarkable experimental work carried out with children aged 6 to 10 years, with reference to the *DragonBall* Z[264] series. This series was selected, not for its fictional interest, but for its capacity to concentrate (if I may say so) all the captative tricks of the trade: sound variations, visual flashes, changes of shots, multiplication of the angles of view, high-pitched sounds, rapid entanglement of the narrative sequences, etc. After having analyzed in detail the level of attention and comprehension of the children to several episodes of the series, Bermejo Berros clearly shows the incredible power of flabbergasting of the latter and he concludes to the devastating role of this kind of programs on the organization of the thought. In the words of this researcher, "since [the child] has not understood the internal relationships between the plot elements of the story he has seen on television, nor does he know how to situate in time and space the events that occur, nor their causes, he gets used to 'thinking horizontally'. This means that he limits himself to reasoning by contiguity and analogy, and when children do not understand the vertical structure of the story, they end up giving greater importance, not to the facts that structure the plot, but to the formal features that have perceptual salience, even if they are not important for that plot [...] Their thinking, with such an influence, ends up being fed only by what is immediate, rapid. [...] In this way, they construct a world of thought of immediacy, dependent on pure perception and emotion, which will serve them little, for example, in many academic tasks that require precisely to overcome perception and to use vertical thinking. In short, series [such as *DragonBall Z*], which are increasingly present in current television, lead to the dislocation of the child's thinking insofar as they do not contribute to the adequate construction of his or her knowledge structures and narrative thinking. They do it in a fragmented and disarticulated way"[264]. To make matters worse, it is to be feared that this process of dislocation does not act in a unidirectional way. Indeed, it is likely that the influence of television resonates with the aforementioned abandonment of certain intellectually structuring practices, such as reading, playing or doing homework.[29,132,461,463,509] The more thought is dislocated under the influence of television, the more it is likely to be disrupted. The more thought is disrupted by the small screen, the poorer these activities become. At the same time, however, the more these activities become impoverished, the more the structuring of thought is called into question[65,406,510-513]. A terrible vicious circle from which it seems very difficult to escape.

For a long time, the deleterious impact of television on attention could not be explained beyond the above. This etiological bottleneck was finally overcome in the early 2000s, when a group of researchers undertook to study the influence of television on the spontaneous activities of young children[130,514]. A fairly simple experimental design was then employed. Subjects aged 1 to 3 years were placed in a room with toys and a television. The television could either be turned off or on. In the latter case, a general public entertainment program was presented (*Jeopardy*). The results showed that the television seriously disturbed the children's spontaneous activity. The children looked at the screen very little (less than 5% of the time), but each glance resulted in an abandonment of the current behaviour. In the end, children with background audiovisual presence changed toys more frequently, showed less rich play patterns, had shorter play periods, and were less focused during these periods. Interestingly, a number of studies have shown that these types of alterations predict poor long-term IQ outcomes[515,516] and are commonly found in children with cognitive delays[500,517-519]. It is therefore not entirely incongruous to suggest that the frequent presence of background television[a] may disrupt intellectual development by distorting some of the activities that constitute that development. To ensure a good understanding of this point, it is undoubtedly not useless to say a few words on the nature of the spontaneous behaviors of the young child[519-521].

Before 12 months, babies are usually content to physically explore objects. They touch them, look at them, and manipulate them. During this first year, attention becomes progressively more sustained and the interaction phases become more complex. Several objects can then be used together and stacked or lined up. Between 12 and 24 months, the initial manipulations give rise to functional activities of use. The child then plays with the doll's hair, puts it to bed or gives it a bottle. With time, these scenarios coordinate with each other to give rise to clearly anticipatory behaviors. For example, the child pretends to take out a pan, fill it with milk, heat it up, pour the result into a bottle and give it to Miss Barbie. In the final stage, symbolic representations arise. The child becomes a cat or an airplane while the matchbox becomes an iron or a race car. Of course, it frequently happens that the adults intervene to enrich these conducts. For example, Dad may ask who is driving the car, prompting his offspring to place an eraser on the matchbox to represent an indispensable driver.

Clearly, many parents do not appreciate the extent to which the skills developed through these early activities are essential to the development of "higher" cognitive functions.[511,513,521-523] It is now known, for example, that there is a strong relationship between the degree of spontaneous play and certain aspects of language development.[510,519,524] It is now known, for example, that there is a strong relationship, first, between the degree of evolution of spontaneous play activities and certain aspects of language

---

a. Remember, as discussed above, that in 40% of homes, the set is constantly on.

development[510,519,524-528] and, second, between intelligence as assessed by IQ tests and language ability[529]. Thus, disrupting a young child's play can ultimately only penalize intelligence. As a concrete illustration, let us imagine a baby in the middle of his playpen. At 8 months old, taken by an irrepressible impulse, our little guy suddenly attacks the cube that was lying next to him. He manipulates it for a few seconds, then he hears a loud belch and turns his head towards the TV. The cube is then "forgotten". When the child returns to the game, he grabs a giraffe, then pauses again in response to a flash of light. The giraffe is lost, too. Eventually, these constant interruptions prevent the development of sustained, endogenous attentional focus. This initial deficit, of course, affects later stages of development. Thus, when children cannot sustain their attention, they inevitably have difficulty coordinating several tasks within complex scenarios. Their games then lose their richness and diversity. This alteration is all the more marked as the deleterious influence of television spreads well beyond the first ages. Let's imagine, to convince us, that Paul decides to feed his Barbie. The young man will grab a pan, put it on the stove, take out the milk... and will stop to locate the origin of the exclamation produced by the set. This interruption will signal the end of the previous operations. When Paul returns to his sheep, he will start a new sequence, which will not fail, in turn, to be quickly suspended. It is then the working memory, conceived as the capacity to select, conserve and process several pieces of information necessary to carry out a complex task, which will be affected. This memory is involved in a number of mental processes including language, reading, calculation and reasoning.[530,531] As if all this were not enough, it turns out that television also affects parents' attention to their children. When the television is on, adults are less likely to interact with their offspring and thus enrich their children's play and language patterns[133,134,532]. In addition, several studies have shown in animals[533] and humans[534,535] that arrhythmic ambient noise can seriously disrupt brain development.

In recent years, the multiplication of programs aimed at young children has seriously exacerbated the fears mentioned above. Indeed, these programs strongly amplify, thanks to their formidable capturing potential, the deleterious power of television. When Baby watches programs that are directly aimed at him, he does not just briefly glance at them. He clings to the image in a sustained manner. Several studies have shown that subjects aged 2 years and under can spend more than 70% of their time staring at the screen in the presence of *ad hoc* content.[130] This figure, which is close to the values observed in adults,[536] greatly exceeds what the scientific community considered plausible only a few years ago.[130,314,537,538] This is another "infant skill" that can be applied to children. This is another "child skill" that the tribe of brain sellers has been able to identify and exploit shamelessly. By shrewdly formatting its contents, the television of the newborns succeeded, in the first sense of the term, in enslaving the child on the basis of a true attentional rapture. Glued to the set, our young telephonist suspends, well in spite of him, the course of his development to the benefit of an infamous and corrosive cathodic mush. And obviously, this mush is not in the process of dissipation. Since the nineties, the proportion of children under 1 year old exposed daily to television has almost quadrupled to reach today the 60%[185,194]. 40% of the newborns of 3 months watch TV! The daily viewing time is around 1 hour, including 30 minutes of educational programs, 10 minutes of baby videos, 10 minutes of recreational youth programs, and 10 minutes of adult content.[269] At 24 months of age, the proportion of television viewers who watch television is almost twice as high as the proportion of children who do not. At 24 months, the proportion of viewers rises to 90% and the daily viewing time rises to 1 hour and 40 minutes, including 55 minutes of educational programs, 30 minutes of recreational children's programs, 5 short minutes of videos for babies and 10 minutes of adult content. After 24 months, the percentage of consumers stabilizes while the exposure time continues to increase slowly to finally reach a little more than 2 hours at age 3[185a]. For the sake of completeness, it should be noted that these values are likely to be underestimated for at least two reasons: firstly, because of a chronic minimisation of the exposure time of children looked after by a childminder[540] and secondly, because background consumption is not taken into account. Of course, times of 1 to 2 hours may seem reasonable at first glance. However, in reality, these values are astronomical. Indeed, the exposure amplitudes should not be related to the total daily time, but to the useful time, i.e., the time effectively allocated to ontogeny, after subtracting physiological activities (diapers, meals, baths, sleep - a child of 6 months-1 year sleeps easily 16 hours per day[145])[b]. A recent study addressed this issue in detail[132]. The authors measured the influence of television on various activities identified as important for the development of language, intelligence or

---

a. For similar consumption estimates between 0 and 35 months, see also: [539].
b. See note a p. 30.

motor skills. The results were impressive, to say the least. Between the ages of 0 and 2 years, each hour spent watching television each day reduces the duration of parent-child interactions by 16%, the duration of exchanges between siblings by 31% and the time spent on creative games (drawing, coloring, dolls, small cars, using toys, etc.) by 10%.

Obviously, the above elements do not please the brain sellers. To avoid any threat to their lucrative business, they have therefore developed a remarkable psychogenetic mythology whose message can be summed up in a few simple words: television is neither good nor bad, its influence depends on the content; when the content is adapted, it effectively supports the intellectual development of the child[a]. Consider, for example, BabyFirst. This channel, which, in the words of its creators, "watches over your baby's development", explains through its website that "from the very first hours of its life, a young child already possesses several billion neurons. Only, these are, at the beginning, of little use to him since most of them are not connected. In reality, to perfect these connections, the brain of the little man must be stimulated. Stimulated by sounds, by colors. Because his daily environment is not always rich enough to awaken him and to participate naturally in his development, the television can represent for him a formidable source of positive action"[b]. If one wants to put aside the (very entertaining) theory of the unconnected neuron, this paragraph is rather clever. In fact, it creates a clever confusion by mixing, under the generic term of *stimulation*, two very disparate realities. *To stimulate* can mean "to subject to an excitation, to the action of a stimulus"[542]. However, it can also mean "to put someone or something in the right conditions to make it act or react; to arouse or reinforce a movement"[542]. Ontogeny specifically implies this second meaning. Television offers only the first, and even then, in a very partial way. This is an unfortunate limitation that our friends at BabyFirst skilfully circumvent by making certain specific stimuli (sounds, colors) the essential elements of infantile development. With this premise in mind, it becomes quite simple to explain that children are not always optimally stimulated by their environment and that television is an effective tool for enriching the environment. Of course, there is no logical connection between these propositions. The television set cannot be elevated to the status of a competent tutor just because some children do not have an optimal developmental environment. Yet the artificers

a. For a detailed analysis of this kind of discourse, see [125].
b. Original text, uncorrected [541].

at BabyFirst are quick to link the two ideas by cleverly using the causal conjunctive phrase *because*. The purpose of this fallacy is obvious: to lend credibility to a fallacious thesis by associating it with an indisputable statement. It is not a thin line, but it is enough to fool many parents unfamiliar with the intricacies of ontogeny. The following elements should solve part of the problem by showing that television represents an outrageously debilitating developmental space for toddlers, regardless of the nature of the content considered.

In order to establish the inevitable educational vacuity of television, it is absolutely necessary to make a small detour by the cerebral physiology. However, the walk should not be too painful, so much this field of study is rich of formidable data. Ontogeny is a wonder that has never ceased to amaze specialists for 100 years. As everyone knows, it all starts when Mr Spermatozoon meets Miss Ovum. After a little DNA mixing, the baby is given a genetic capital, that is to say, in the final analysis, a potential space for development. For a long time, the expression of this potential was associated with essentially endogenous factors. The idea was that intelligence was an inheritable, genetically determined trait. At the heart of this vision was an English psychologist named Cyril Burt. During his career, this university professor studied several dozen pairs of identical (homozygous) twins, separated at birth and raised in profoundly different environments. He showed that the IQ of these twins was very strongly correlated, independently of their developmental conditions. In other words, geniuses and morons always went in pairs, education did not change anything. This pleased the Queen of England, who ennobled Burt, and the liberal politicians, who jumped at the chance to "reform" the educational system so that too much money would not be wasted on educating an army of genetically stupid poor people.[543] Unfortunately, Burt was only a boy. Unfortunately, Burt was a vile fraud. He had made it all up. Twins, collaborators, trips, statistics, none of it was true.[544-548] This fraud was recognized all the more so because of the fact that Burt was not the only one to have made it up. This fraud was recognized all the more easily because animal neurophysiology had already begun, for some years, to shake up the fabrications of our IQ sourpuss. The first blow was struck by Donald Hebb at the end of the 1940s[549]. This eminent researcher had brought home some baby rats. When they became adults, they proved to be infinitely more agile and clever than their laboratory counterparts. This informal observation was followed by dozens of rigorously controlled studies in rodents, cats and primates. The animals were then raised under different environmental conditions: (1) Deficient - some sensory or social elements were absent or presented in limited amounts (e.g., animals were raised in the dark for varying lengths of time at different stages of their lives); (2) Standard - each cage housed a single subject and a few unchanging objects (such as a wheel for rodents); (3) Enriched - each cage housed several subjects and a large number of regularly changed attractive objects (such as balls, colored objects, ladders for rodents). The deficient condition earned David Hubel and Torsten Wiesel a Nobel Prize. They demonstrated that the brain does not develop normally when the animal does not receive the necessary sensory stimulation at certain critical periods of its development. The deficits that occurred were largely irreversible[550,551]. The enriched situation showed an opposite pattern[552-556]. Subjects raised in stimulating conditions with many people proved to be more intelligent, more skilful, more sociable and less sensitive to stress in adulthood than their counterparts in standard environments. A direct correlate of this superiority was observed at the most intimate neurophysiological level. The animals in the enriched condition showed, at autopsy, a heavier and larger brain, a thicker cortex, a greater number of neurons, a greater number of connections per neuron (synapses) and a larger intracerebral vascularization. The magnitude of the differences was sometimes staggering. For example, in the number of synapses per neuron, increases of 20-25% were commonly reported[557,558]. On a human scale, this represents several trillion additional intercellular connections[552].

It would of course be ethically unacceptable to extend to man the experimental manipulations just described in animals. This being said, it is not unusual for the vagaries of life to prove infinitely more harsh than the researcher's hand. When this happens, it appears that man is indeed, in physiological terms, a mammal like any other. Adoption studies are revealing in this respect[554,559]. They are based on a fairly simple protocol: to examine the emotional and cognitive development of adopted children at different ages and to compare the performance of these children with the achievements of other subjects who have not found an adoptive family (non-adopted children) or who have always lived with their parents (control children). The implicit assumption, which has been widely tested experimentally,[559] is that adoption moves children from an unstimulating institutional or family environment to an enriched environment with ample opportunities to play, explore the world, and interact with adults.

All studies conducted in this context have reached similar conclusions: non-adopted individuals, even if they have not suffered any health or nutritional damage, show severely disturbed emotional development and a much lower IQ than control children or adopted subjects. For the latter, the extent of long-term sequelae is proportional to the level of deficiency in the original environment ("feral children"[560] or those deprived of access to language[561] being extreme cases), to the socio-economic characteristics of the foster family[562] and to the age of adoption. Regarding this third point, recent research has shown that individuals adopted before the age of 1 year retained few (if any) identifiable long-term deficits compared to a control population, based on nearly 18,000 subjects examined in 62 studies. Conversely, adoptions completed in the second year or beyond were predictive of persistent impairments in academic achievement, learning function, and language.[559] These data are consistent with the superb findings of a few longitudinal studies showing that the quality of the early school environment profoundly transforms individual outcomes.[563-565] In one of these studies, the quality of the early school environment was found to be significantly different from that of the later school years. In one of these studies, 123 three-year-olds from very disadvantaged backgrounds were randomly divided into two equal experimental groups[566]. About sixty of the lucky ones were then enrolled for two years in a kindergarten of very high standing. The others remained in the indigent school in their neighbourhood. At the end of the study, all the children were returned to their original environment and evaluated at regular intervals. The results showed that the experimental group outperformed their control counterparts in cognitive, affective, occupational and social domains. These differences were still evident 40 years after the program ended. At that time, children who had received 2 years (!), had higher academic achievement (65% with a bachelor's degree vs. 45%), lower unemployment (24% vs. 38%), lower median monthly earnings ($1,856 vs. $1,308), lower levels of jail time (28% vs. 52%), and less use of family mediation (13% vs. 24%), psychotropic drugs (17% vs. 43%), or other drugs (marijuana/hashish 48% vs. 71% ; heroin 0% versus 9%).

In view of these data, it is not easy to deny the founding role played by the early environment in the construction of an individual's affective, social and cognitive skills. Contrary to what the fable of merit, so dear to our "elites"[543], work is not everything. A child who grows up in a sub-optimal environment will never be able to express his full potential. In the primary sense, he or she will become an underdeveloped adult, like Hubel and Wiesel's deficient kittens, Hebb's "standard" rats and the poor children of our urban ghettos. This is of course a non-exhaustive list, to which it is time to add, I believe, all the budding zappers. Indeed, television constitutes from the ontogenetic point of view a sterile time, perfectly useless. It teaches nothing, cables nothing and, in the last analysis, does not solicit any of the fundamental competences that the brain in formation must build. This assertion undeniably refers to an obvious fact that all developmental specialists agree on: the brain does not organize itself by observing reality, but by acting on it[65,528,567-569]. In his superb work entitled *De l'acte à la pensée (From Act to Thought)*, Henry Wallon shows clearly, for example, that "intelligence, an instrument of knowledge, comes out of action and returns to it"[523]. This idea is also found at the heart of the work of Jean Piaget. As Jean-Marie Dolle, a great specialist in the subject, summarizes, "Piaget bases psychology on the adaptation of man to the environment and thus creates the epistemology of the interaction between subject and environment. This means that, all knowledge being the product of interactions between a subject and his environment, knowledge comes from the activity of the subject and, particularly, from his capacity to extract from the element of the environment or object its properties. But to know in this sense comprises, on the one hand, what is drawn from the object itself, its own qualities graspable by perceptive activity, and, on the other hand, what the subject introduces into it by transforming it"[570]. From then on, a simple observation of reality cannot be a factor of development. For example, contemplating *Gribouille*[a] for hours on end will not make Valentine (3 years old) a skilled draftsman. Only assiduous graphic exploration will allow her to acquire a sure hand. Similarly, watching the specialized programs that flourish on BabyFirst, BabyTV or various *ad hoc* videos will never teach James (16 months) the art of language. Only effective communication with a third party will enable him to acquire the rules of syntax[571,572], to discriminate the sounds of his language[144,573,574] and to organize his phonatory apparatus[573,574]. For adults who doubt this, we can suggest that they start learning German, cycling, skiing or tennis, *via* television, by watching Angela Merkel give a speech in front of the Bundestag, Eddy Merckx escape on the slopes of the Ventoux, Patrick Ortlieb descend the face of Bellevarde or Rafael

a. A program from the former *L'Île aux enfants* where we saw a little man drawing various characters or objects.

Nadal slap a solid forehand. Our aspiring experts will then quickly realize that their approach is futile for the simple reason that they do not possess any of the cognitive, sensory and motor structures necessary to achieve the targeted skills[a]. Take Nadal, for example. To reproduce (even from a distance) his forehand, you will need an exceptional physical strength (to make the ball move forward by giving it such a power of rotation requires a titanic force), a surgically precise representation of the organization of your body in space (where is my hand that I do not see in relation to the ball, how is my screen oriented), an exceptional segmental dissociation (when I open my arm I must not rotate the whole body), an extremely early reading of the ball trajectory (where and how it will bounce, in which zone the impact will take place), a perfect ball-racket coordination (when do I have to start the striking movement to arrive in the impact zone with a temporal precision of less than a few tens of milliseconds), a rigorously exact predictive model of the body dynamics (according to its speed and its trajectory, the racket modifies the movement of the arm and the body balance; if I don't anticipate these effects, my shot is likely to land in the stands). None of these skills can be learned by observation.[567] This does not, of course, prevent the brain dealers from explaining to us that the screen represents a fantastic opportunity for sensory-motor and linguistic development because man is, from his earliest childhood, a virtuoso of imitation. We learn, for example, from the BabyFirst website, that "the young child learns mainly by miming. Mom smiles at him and he suddenly tries to reproduce that slight pucker of the lips... by grimacing. Also, the small screen, which broadcasts images, represents for him a permanent source of learning in the broadest sense of the term. All that is good to imitate, it imitates it! Once again, the channel mocks us by playing a clever semantic amalgam. The fact that a young child is able to copy a behavior that he has already mastered (such as sticking out his tongue), does not mean that he will be able to reproduce a new behavior. Similarly, the fact that it can artificially repeat an isolated sound/word does not mean that it is learning to speak (or my parrot is more human than I thought).

At the experimental level, several works in animal psychology have established the validity of the preceding considerations by showing that a naïve subject could not benefit from an enriched environment, in an indirect way, by observing the activity of his fellow creatures "as if

____

a. This does not prevent many tennis or ski teachers from continuing to show up to hope to teach. (See for a discussion[567].)

on TV"[575,576]. Typically, two conditions were considered. The first used a small, transparent individual box, placed in a large "enriched" cage housing several animals and a large number of shimmering objects. The second used standard cages housing a single animal and a few poor, unchanging objects. The "lodge" condition invariably produced pallid rats with atrophied brains and behavior compared to the enriched and, to a lesser extent, standard animals. This observation was beautifully generalized by Held and Hein from a sensory restriction protocol[577]. Kittens were reared in the dark for the first four weeks of life. From then on, they were placed, in pairs, for 3 hours a day in a circular carousel. One of the animals ("Leader") moved around the carousel, driving a small basket in which was installed his companion ("Spectator"). At the end of the experiment, the "Leader" behaved almost normally, unlike the "Spectator". The latter literally behaved like a blind cat. It ran into obstacles, could not place its paws correctly when placed on the corner of a table, had no pupillary blink reflex when a finger was brought close to its eye, and was unable to locate objects in its environment. This last deficit led the poor animal, when placed in height, to jump into the void without taking into account the depth of the ground. Goethe was therefore right: "in the beginning was action"[70] !

In humans, the preceding data have been largely validated through the demonstration of what researchers call a "video deficit"[130]. Behind this learned expression lies a rather simple idea: if you put the child in front of a TV, he will sometimes learn something, but this something will always be notably inferior to what he would have learned from an effective interaction with his environment. For example, take a doll with a glove attached to its hand *via* a piece of Velcro and hide a bell inside the glove. Stand in front of a 12 or 15 month old child, detach the glove, shake it to tint the bell, put it back in place and put the doll on the floor. The child will usually grab the doll and try to remove the glove and dye the bell. Surprisingly, if you perform the same demonstration through a television, Baby watches but then does nothing. When the experimenter places the doll on the floor right after the video, the child does not try to remove the glove or tint the bell. He behaves like a totally naive subject who has never seen the doll[578]. This video deficit remains largely present in children aged 18, 24 or even 30 months[578,579]. It is also found in other types of cognitive tasks involving, for example, finding an object that the experimenter has just hidden. If the child can see the action taking place directly in front of him or her, or in a nearby room *through* a window, everything is fine. On the other hand, if the observation takes place indirectly *via* a television, things get seriously complicated and our budding Sherlock Holmes derives almost no benefit from the information he is given[580-582]. Interestingly, these shortcomings do not diminish in the presence of verbal instruction. This was recently demonstrated in a rather clever protocol involving 2-year-old subjects[582]. At the beginning of the study, the experimenter is in the room where a target object is to be hidden. The child is then presented with a Snoopy doll and four potential hiding places. These are named. Snoopy is then hidden in front of the child and easily found by the latter. Then, the experimenter checks that the child correctly identifies the different hiding places by asking him to hide Snoopy in such and such a place. When this is done, everyone moves to a nearby room. The experimenter then tells the child, "I'm going to go hide Snoopy in his room and then I'll come back and tell you where to find him. Then you can go find Snoopy. I'll be right back. While the experimenter hides Snoopy, an assistant reinforces the instruction: "Now [first name] hides Snoopy. I wonder where he's hiding him." After a few moments, the experimenter can either return or go and stand in front of a video camera connected to a screen positioned in front of the child. The same words are then spoken to the child: "I put Snoopy in [location]. Snoopy is hiding in [location]. Can you find him? Remember he is [location]. In the direct condition, the child finds the coveted object more than 3 times out of 5. In the screen condition, although our young viewer looks at the image and listens to the soundtrack, this proportion drops to 1 in 5, which brings us roughly to the threshold of chance (i.e., the performance of a child who would search for the object completely at random).

Interestingly, the existence of a video deficit is not limited to the manipulation and research activities just mentioned. This phenomenon also affects the core business of specialized channels and other organizations producing dedicated videos: language. However, in this field, the brain sellers are not short of laudatory speeches.[125] "Age-appropriate educational television programs have been associated with significant improvements in a young child's spoken vocabulary," explains BabyFirst,[583] for example, in line with the claims of the BabyTV channel, whose programs "created with the help of child specialists [...] are concerned with associating a visually presented object with its spoken name - a ball appears on the screen, and the narrator says 'ball. This is the first stage in the development of the toddler's vocabulary"[584]. The same is true of Brainy Baby, whose *Left Brain* DVD "teaches your child [as young as 6 months] language and logic skills. Baby Einstein is not to be outdone. The product *Baby Shakespeare,* recommended from the age of 1, modestly proposes to "enrich the child's vocabulary through the beauty of poetry, music and nature"[125]. A whole program, which it is undoubtedly not easy to resist when one is a parent. I was able to see this recently, during the Christmas holidays, in a large shopping center in the Lyon area. A woman was holding a DVD from the Baby Einstein collection. It's good for learning," insisted the woman in order to win the approval of a tall dubious man, visibly chilled by the price of the product. A lively discussion followed, which ended with a definitive "you really don't give a damn about your daughter, you, apart from your soccer and your PlayStation, have no interest in her". Visibly touched, the man lowered his head, grunted for form and took the DVD. It's a sad outcome when we know that all the recent academic studies have underlined the uselessness, at best, and at worst, the deleterious character of this kind of programs. For example, it has been shown that young children do not manage, even at the most basic level of phonics, to take advantage of cathode-ray speech. The basis for this result is the observation that human beings lose their ability to discriminate sounds that do not belong to the repertoire of their language at an early age. For a Japanese adult, audibly differentiating *mali* from *mari* is almost impossible. For Robert, my American friend, a *street* and a *wheel* sound the same. For me, the English words *bitch* and *beach* refer to one and the same reality. Faced with these shortcomings, Patricia Kuhl and her colleagues thought that television might be useful. To test the hypothesis, these researchers from the University of Washington exposed 9-month-old American children to Mandarin language in 12 25-minute sessions spread over 4 weeks[144]. In one experimental condition, a native speaker physically appeared before the children. In the other, this same speaker appeared on a video. It does not take a rocket scientist to guess that this second situation had, contrary to the first, no protective effect. While the subjects in the "real" group had, at the end of the experiment, retained an excellent discriminatory capacity, those in the video group had not benefited from their exposure. They were, after 12 sessions, as deaf to Mandarin as totally naïve children. Other studies have generalized this pedagogical infirmity to the lexical domain, showing that videos for young children are, in practice, totally useless[586,587]. A recent study by Judy Deloache's team seems, in this respect, particularly interesting[588]. 72 children aged 12 to 18 months were divided into 4 groups of 18 units. (1) "Video": the children were placed in front of a widely circulated commercial "educational" video that was supposed to develop language. This 39-minute video showed a house and its garden through different scenes. 25 objects were clearly named as they appeared (tree, table, chair, etc.). To facilitate lexical encoding, each object was presented and named 3 times during the projection. (2) "Video-Parents": the children saw the above video with their parents. The parents were invited to intervene during the projection to stimulate the child's attention by pointing to the objects and repeating their names. (3) "Real": the parents were given a list of the 25 words treated in the video with the objective of teaching these words to their children during their daily interactions. (4) "Control": the children lived normally and were simply evaluated at the end of the experiment Both video groups were subjected to a regimen of at least 5 screenings per week for 4 weeks. At the end of this impregnation, the children's knowledge of the target words was tested. The results showed that the subjects in the Real group had learned significantly more words (53%) than those in the other three groups, all of whom had statistically similar levels of performance (32%). Thus, in the words of the study authors, "children who were extensively exposed to a popular children's video for an entire month, either alone or with their parents, did not learn a single new word more than children who were not exposed to any video. This conclusion seriously relativizes the observations of an earlier, frequently cited work, which had shown, in the very short term, a positive effect of certain audiovisual content on lexical learning[589]. In this work, involving subjects aged 15 to 24 months, the authors compared the acquisition of a target word under several experimental conditions, three of which are of particular interest to us here. (1) "Real": the child was challenged by the experimenter in the mode "look, I have toys". These were then taken out of a drawer and placed on the table. Then, when the child looked at the target object, the latter was lifted and named. This visuo-verbal concomitance, frequently observed during early natural interactions between mother and child, is supposed to promote lexical learning.[136,585] (2) "Video experiment": a video screen was placed in front of the child. A short film was shown. The experimenter was seen calling out to the child, saying "look, I have toys". Then, on 5 occasions, the target object was lifted and named, exactly as in the previous condition (except that, in this case, there was obviously no consideration of the child's attentional focus). (3) "Video-

Educational": the child saw an episode of *Teletubbies* in which an object emerged from the ground 5 times and was then named by a soundtrack embedded in the video. 30 seconds after the end of each condition, learning of the target word (unique) was tested. For the youngest children (15-21 months), 52% of the sample learned the target word in the Real condition versus 40% in the Video-Experimental condition and 23% in the Video-Educational condition. The older children (22-24 months) did slightly better, but still had a large video deficit with learning levels of 93%, 55% and 62% in the Real, Video-Experimenter and Video-Educator conditions respectively. This didactic weakness of the audiovisual conditions was all the more striking as everything had been set up, by the authors of the study, to maximize the probability of restitution of the target word. Of course, faced with such a result, it is possible to emphasize only the "positive" side of things, by arguing the existence of significant lexical learning *via* television. It is easy to imagine how useful this kind of claim can be in convincing parents and in driving business. After all, why should we bother pointing out that language acquisition does not persist over the long term and is infinitely faster and more populous when children are kept away from the set and put in a position to interact directly with their surroundings? For those who still doubt this last statement, the recent work of Frederick Zimmerman's team should prove edifying[128]. These authors used a large experimental sample (n > 1000) to investigate the existence of a statistical link between lexical development and the consumption of specialized educational videos. After controlling for a large number of sociodemographic, psychological and personal covariates (age, family income, parents' education, siblings, ethnicity, etc.), this link was found to be effective and significantly negative. One hour of "educational" screen time consumed daily between 8 and 16 months of age cost children almost 10% of their lexicon! One hour is, let us remember, the average daily exposure of subjects of this age having access to a television[269]. For individuals aged 2 to 4 years, the dose is at least doubled[185]. Not surprisingly, a recent study conducted on this age group (15-48 months) showed, again after taking into account a large number of potential covariates, that 2 hours of daily television resulted in a 3-fold increase in the probability of language development delays. In subjects who started watching television before 1 year of age, the risk increased by 6129 times. When the children were left alone in front of the sight, it was beyond 8 that the cursor should be placed. It should be noted, however, that the content concerned came from "all-audience" programs and not from programs specifically labelled "youth" or "educational". It should also be pointed out that other data from Mayeux and Naigles made it possible to extend these observations to the grammatical field, by showing, in children aged 3-4, the existence of a negative correlation between the degree of success in certain tests of syntactic aptitude and the extent of audiovisual consumption.[572] Overall, all these results are compatible with the conclusions of an earlier work, carried out on the basis of the exceptional case of two brothers, aged 2 and 4, who were followed for 6 years and whose parents were deaf.[571] The mother, who was responsible for almost all of the children's education, was the only one who was able to read and write. The mother, who was almost exclusively responsible for the educational process, did not speak and only *exceptionally* used sign language with her children. When the authors of the study asked her why she did not use sign language more, at least with her older son, she seemed surprised and replied "he can hear". By the time they were examined by specialists, both children had had access to language only through television and, for the older child, some interaction with other children in his building during outdoor play. Assessments showed that the younger child did not speak at all. The older child had significant articulation problems. He had some words, but far fewer than his peers. He did not speak spontaneously and rarely made statements of more than one or two words when questioned. He also showed a complete lack of syntactic and, more generally, grammatical competence. This kind of weakness also characterizes, it may be interesting to underline, the learning of foreign languages by older subjects, with the help of subtitles. In this field, studies have shown that spectators managed to learn a few words[590], but failed miserably to acquire any syntactic competence[591].

In summary, the preceding elements clearly show that television is a very inefficient teacher of language. Its didactic aptitude excludes completely the phonological and syntactic spaces. It is limited, at best, to the lexical field and to the teaching of a few scattered words that the child could have learned infinitely more quickly and in much greater numbers through real interpersonal exchanges[65,572]. In practice, the more a young human wastes his time watching television, the more he expresses important delays in linguistic development and the poorer his lexicon turns out to be. This is all the more alarming because early language damage is both detrimental to the future of children[592,593] and extremely difficult to remedy. This last point was recently emphasized again in a remarkable synthesis by Ghislaine Dehaene-Lambertz and two of her colleagues. According to the conclusions of these internationally recognized specialists in language development, "the level of mastery of a language depends crucially on its age of acquisition and contrary to the assertions of older studies, the decline in learning ability is observed very early, from the first years of life"[594]. As if this were not enough, there is also reason to fear that early language deficits may mechanically deepen in the long term, through the emergence of difficulties in accessing the written world. Indeed, the written world seems to be necessary for intimate learning of the language, beyond the most utilitarian daily uses[65].

Television is thus heavily detrimental to linguistic development. Without wishing to be a killjoy, it should be pointed out that this conclusion is more of a predictable truism than a stunning surprise. Indeed, the station lacks, and will always lack, a founding faculty attribute: interactivity. Not the one that bleeds the decerebrate cohorts of *Star Ac'* nights with overtaxed phone calls, but the one that pushes reality to change the course of its operations when the child acts. Let's try for a moment, to understand the problem, to put ourselves in the place of a young spectator. When he calls, *Fred and Fiona*[a] do not answer. When he smiles, *Bloop and Loop*[b] are unmoved. When he calls out to the *Wordies*[c], they don't lift an eyelid. When he babbles, the other babies (in the TV)[d] do not flinch. When he tries to reproduce a sound or an action, *L'Ami Jacques*[e] never stops to listen, to take back, to help, to support or to encourage. Frankly, it can't be very easy to learn to communicate under these conditions, suffering the cold indifference of a speaker who is both deaf and blind. Obviously, with Mom, things are fundamentally different. As soon as the child acts, she reacts. For example, when Baby makes sounds, Mom imitates them (during the first postnatal year, over 90% of verbal imitations are initiated

---

a. A series that "conveys the concept that everything around us has its own place" (BabyFirst[595]).
b. A series through which "young viewers learn to use their imagination and at the same time enter new worlds" (BabyFirst[596]).
c. "A simple series that develops toddlers' vocabulary in imaginative and creative ways" (BabyFirst[597]).
d. *The Babies,* a program that shows Baby other babies and "promotes socialization. Toddlers play with other children [*sic!*], learn about small animals, and cuddle with mom and dad" (BabyFirst[598]).
e. *L'Ami Jacques* "is a very active mime [who] [...] shows young viewers everything you can say without ever making a sound" (BabyFirst[599]).

by Mom!)[136]. When he looks at or points to objects, Mom names them and hands them to him[136,585]. When he shows improvement in his comprehension skills, Mom adjusts the pace and complexity of the utterances made[136,585]. When he turns his mouth away to indicate that he is no longer hungry, makes a face to signify how vile his broccoli purée is, clutches his stuffed animal to attest that he is not willing to let go, or claps his hands because he has seen the cat go by on the balcony, Mama adapts and responds with words and movements.[136,140,141,585,600] Later, beyond 18-24 months, when the little man begins to speak, Mama encourages him, solicits him and frequently takes up his statements to reformulate them, even correct them[136,601]. All these conducts are absolutely essential to full linguistic development[135-141,143,571,600]. However, once again, their expression is impossible within the audiovisual universe. The television does not nod to accompany positively an action of the child. It does not adapt its words to the expressions of incomprehension that the latter can produce. It does not name the objects he is looking at. She does not imitate the words he articulates. She does not correct the statements he makes. She does not respond to the vocalizations he develops. In the end, all these shortcomings contribute to making the post not only a pathetic pedagogical blunderbuss, but also, more broadly, a powerful linguistic destroyer. Concerning this point, it appears in particular that television is not satisfied to act, by default, by pouring its vile incompetence on our children. It also operates in a more profound way by mutilating the intrafamiliar sociability. When the set is on, whether in the foreground or background, the child hears fewer words, expresses himself more sparingly and briefly, and engages in fewer two-way exchanges.[131-133,142,602] The number of words heard by the child is not the same as the number of words heard by the parent. The number of words heard and spoken before age 3 is a major predictor of future language and cognitive performance[142,143,603]. In other words, fewer words in the early stages of development ultimately mean less language and less intelligence for the child. Of course, we can reassure ourselves by saying, like my friend Marie, that a few more or fewer words cannot be that bad. This is not false. However, we are not talking here about "a few words", but about a real attack of aphasia. Far from being benign, the television effect is absolutely colossal. For example, a child under the age of 4 hears an average of 13,500 words every day. If the television is left on for four hours in the home, this figure falls to around 10,000 words, i.e. a drop of 25%, quantitatively equivalent to the total number of words spoken daily by the father in the presence of his child[133]. In other words, 4 hours of television is equivalent to wiping out the equivalent of the father's linguistic contribution! At age 3, this amputation will represent a cumulative net deficit of nearly 4 million words. And really, 4 hours is not an abracadabratic amount of exposure when you add to the first-order consultations the background workings[a]. In the "first-order" condition, it is simple to imagine an operating mechanism based on a difficulty in sustaining a dialogue in the presence of a film, series or entertainment. In the "background" condition, it is equally easy to assume the existence of an indirect process acting according to rules similar to those already mentioned about the game. With each sound or visual peak, attention is drawn away and the flow of interpersonal exchanges is interrupted.

One could think, in view of the preceding elements, that the debate is now settled: television is a real developmental plague from which it is wise to protect our children. Attention, intelligence, language, reading, taste for effort, sensory-motor skills, none of this resists the cathodic current. However, many pseudo-specialists continue to assert with obstinacy that we should not turn our children away from the screen because images represent a central element of human cognitive activity. They are said to be "the natural support of our imagination, our dreams, our memories, our fantasies".[40] They are said to be "beneficial".[34] They are said to be "the equivalent for our mind of food for our body". Ultimately, they would constitute "a means of knowledge and the whole of the medical imagery shows the importance taken in our society by the image as a means of knowing and understanding"[34]. I must say that I particularly like this last quotation from Serge Tisseron, as it is so representative of the dubious amalgams that the coterie of media thurifers feeds us. Frankly, in all objectivity, what relationship can there be between an anatomical MRI and television? It is not because the former is useful for therapeutic diagnosis that the latter is beneficial to intellectual development! This kind of confusion, skilfully maintained, is a real logical swindle. Obviously, talking about images is meaningless if we do not specify which image we are talking about. In particular, it is unthinkable not to distinguish between endogenous images created by the cognitive, dreamlike or phantasmatic activity of the subject, and exogenous images imposed by

---

a. Let's remember once again that in almost 40% of the households, the television is on all the time and that the average daily consumption per household amounts to almost 5 hours and 40 minutes.

TV Lobotomie

the external world[25,29,65,289]. This conceptual segregation has been establi-shed by the experimental sciences for decades. It is found, for example, at the heart of the definition of the concept of imagination, as proposed in 1951 by Henri Piéron in his indispensable *Vocabulary of Psychology*: "Imagination: a thought process consisting of an evocation of mnemonic images (reproductive imagination) or a construction of images (creative imagination)"[604]. Reading and medical imagery (to take our superb previous example) belong to this second creative category, whereas the small screen belongs mainly to the first reproductive group. In this sense, it is tempting to plagiarize somewhat a splendid quotation of Alain Bentolila to affirm that if "we inhabit a book; the television, it, inhabits us"[a]. Let's take just one example. *Harry Potter* is a superb text. By reading it, each kid creates his own images of Harry, Hermione or Hagrid. There are then as many different representations as there are actual readers and instances of evocation. This is clearly not the case with the film version. In the film version, Harry, Hermione, Hagrid and the others have a literal "human face". They are unambiguously embodied in the features of particular actors, with specific morphological characteristics. Once you have seen the film, Harry ceases forever to be an undefined possibility. He becomes a personified reality. He has a physiognomy, a stature, a vocal intonation and small round glasses. All this imposes itself on the spec-tator and deeply constrains the imaginary field. As Jerry Mander, who as an advertising executive spent more than 15 years of his professional life trying to embed images in our children's brains, says: "[If you read the book], Marjorie Morningstar was an image in your mind before you saw the movie. Then you saw the movie with Natalie Wood playing Marjorie. After seeing Natalie Wood in the role, were you able to recapture the image you had constructed? Marjorie became Natalie Wood at that point [...] [Similarly], Moses is Charlton Heston. Buffalo Bill is Paul Newman. McMurphy is Jack Nicholson [...] Let me ask you the question in reverse. If you saw the movie *Gone with the Wind*, before reading the book, did you manage to develop your own image of Rhett Butler? Or did he remain Clark Gable? Did you see Natalie Wood before reading Marjorie Morningstar? If so, did you manage to erase Natalie to build your own Marjorie? I doubt it very much." [289] I confess that I do too, especially when I think back to my daughter Valentine's last school party. A seven- or eight-year-old had won

---

a. Original quote: "We inhabit a book; the virtual inhabits us."[54]

some sort of magic wand in a duck-fishing competition. Our young man was thrilled and immediately said to one of his classmates, "Come on, I'm doing Harry Potter. The answer came in the second: "Yeah yeah, great, just take my glasses, they are round"; as if the film version had magnified this formal attribute, secondary all in all, to the point of making it indispensable. The rest took place on the squares of a hopscotch. "Harry" had placed several of his comrades on different available cells to reproduce the chess game with living pieces from the first filmed episode of the series[a]. There was no creativity here, just a banal process of reproduction. According to Jane Healy, who worked extensively on the subject in the late 1980s, this phenomenon seems neither new nor isolated. In fact, according to this author, "one of the most disturbing statements to come out of interviews with kindergarten teachers is that children today no longer construct their own 'scripts' for play. Instead of spontaneously creating open-ended frames and actions ("you're a dad and I'm a mom"; "you're a bad guy, I'm a good guy"), they replay the ones they've already seen, even repeating the dialogue ("you're Bill Cosby in the one where...", "we're the Mario brothers when they're chasing the...")"[65].

Unfortunately, the thesis of a castrating action of the television on the child's imagination finds a wide echo in the scientific literature. The most direct evidence was provided by a Canadian study whose protocol, described above, involved three sociologically similar cities, but different in terms of their audiovisual access. NoTel received no channels, OneTel received one and MultiTel received four. The domain of creativity was addressed in 9- and 12-year-old subjects, using a standard "alternative uses" protocol.[605] The task was to imagine, without the need for a computer, a new channel. The task was to imagine, without time limit, the different possible uses of five objects (a magazine, a knife, a shoe, a button or a key). The results showed that the children in NoTel far outperformed those in the other two cities. On average, the absence of television resulted in a 40% increase in the number of possible uses mentioned. When the experiment was repeated, with subjects of similar age, 2 years after the arrival of the small window in NoTel homes, no more differences were observed between the different cities. It didn't take long for the station to dry up the imagination and creativity of NoTel children. From a functional point of view, two complementary mechanisms can

---

a. *Harry Potter and the Philosopher's Stone.*

be considered to explain this disaster. First, television drastically reduces the amount of time children spend on play activities that can stimulate creativity and imagination[29,132,461,463,509]. Second, the audiovisual medium only weakly solicits imaginary and creative spaces. This second point was highlighted using a fairly simple protocol, consisting of presenting the same story to primary school children in different formats: (i) film (or cartoon) (ii) told verbally and/or (iii) told in writing[509]. Following the presentation, the subjects were asked either to reconstruct the story or to invent an ending for it. It then appears, in the words of Caroline Meline, who conducted a seminal study on the subject, that "children's creative thinking is more stimulated or less inhibited by audio and written media than by audiovisual media"[606]. 606 The case of incomplete stories underlines this particularly well by showing that the endings invented by children are less varied, less unexpected and less lexically rich for the film condition than for the situations told[607-609]. Bettelheim was right: "Television captures the imagination but does not set it free. A good book immediately stimulates and frees the mind."[610]

Recently, a study conducted by two German physicians generalized the previous data from the imaginary field to the more general space of symbolic representations[449]. In this study, nearly 2,000 5-6 year old students were given a redesigned version of the famous[611] man test. This version simply required participants to draw a man. The result was then rated out of 13, based on objectively quantifiable physical elements (presence of hair, 1 point; ears expressed as dots, semi-circles or circles, 1 point; legs represented by an outline rather than a line, 1 point; etc.). Analyses showed that the richness of the drawing dropped progressively as a function of audio-visual exposure. Small users (30 minutes or less) peaked at 10 points, while large users (3 hours or more) peaked at 6. Average telephoners (2 hours) were around 8.5. The qualitative meaning of these numerical variations can be easily understood from the following drawings, presented as typical by the authors of the study (Figure 2)[a]. Looking at the figure, I tend to think of all those kids confidently abandoned to the care of TéléNourrice. The laudatory speeches of the psycho-pipeaulogues of the image suddenly seem infinitely less funny.

---

a. This figure is taken from Figure 1 of the original work by Winterstein and Jungwirth[449]. Figure reproduced with permission of the publisher.

Figure 2

*
**

To conclude

Thus, this charming little window, which seems so harmless to parents, is a real ontogenetic disaster for young children. If you want your offspring to fully express their developmental potential, don't let them grow up next to a TV, whether it's actively watched or just turned on in the background. Again, the TV doesn't make kids look stupid or visibly dumb, but it certainly hinders optimal brain function. All fields are affected, from intelligence to imagination, language, reading, attention and motor skills. At the end of the day, the child's entire intellectual, cultural, academic and professional future is irrevocably compromised. For those who may have forgotten, let us just remember, by way of conclusion, that each hour of television consumed during the week while the child is in elementary school increases by more than a third the probability that the child will leave the school system without any diploma[96]. In applied terms, this means that if we take measures today, collectively, to divide by two the audiovisual consumption of primary school children (slightly more than 2 hours per day[146]), not 65 (the current level[339]) but 74% of an age group will obtain the baccalaureate in 10 years. A miraculous increase that will occur "naturally", without the need to fiddle with the tests, bribe the admission juries, recruit thousands of teachers or spend pharaonic sums at Acadomia!

Chapter III
TV threatens health

"Watching TV...kills!"

(Danièle Ohayon, journalist[612])

"The media must be recognized as a major public health issue."
(Christakis & Zimmerman, Center for Child Health,
Behavior and Development, University of Washington[4])

"Reducing time spent watching television should be a health priority for the population."
(Hancox *et al.*, Dunedin Medical School, New Zealand[196])

Imagine a recreational substance whose ingestion would significantly increase the prevalence of obesity, smoking, alcoholism, sleep disorders, suicidal acts, risky sexual behavior, and eating disorders (anorexia/bulimia). Would you consider opening your home to this substance? Would you allow your children to be subjected to its influence? I doubt it very much. If I'm right about this, then it becomes clear that the overwhelming majority of avid viewers and devoted parents do not fully appreciate the toxicity of the small screen. Indeed, dozens of studies show with terrifying regularity that there is no difference between the latter and the recreational substance mentioned above. Television is not a harmless leisure activity. It constitutes a major health problem[4]. Of course, the pipe-heads of all obediences will say that the statement is very exaggerated and that television has never killed anybody. They will claim docently that "if we reason in terms of "dangers", alcohol and tobacco are far more worrying than images because of the number of deaths and invalids that can be attributed to them"[34]. This is a remarkable lobbying effort that just forgets to mention that these dear "images" represent one of the favorite recruiting sergeants of obese, alcoholic and nicotined armies. Let's try a little math to illustrate this point. In the United States, smoking causes an estimated 435,000 deaths per year[613]. A longitudinal study, discussed below, showed that 17% of adult smokers had succumbed to the siren song of smoking because they had watched more than 2 hours of television per day between the ages of 5 and 15.[196] The results of this study are not surprising. Coupling our two measures, then, suggests that television kills nearly 75,000 Americans each year, just by its ability to make a child a smoker. Add to this the post-adolescent influences and deaths due to obesity, alcohol, drugs or risky sexual behavior and it will undoubtedly appear that reasoning in terms of "dangers" is not so stupid after all when we talk about "images". An Australian study, published in one of the most highly regarded international medical journals, has recently confirmed this by including sedentary behaviour in the spectrum of lethal influences of television. A large sample of nearly 9,000 adults aged 25 years and over was studied[614]. After taking into account a wide range of social and individual factors (age, sex, education, waist size, diet, smoking status, alcohol consumption, hypertension, physical exercise, etc.), it appeared that the risk of death increased by nearly 10% for each hour of television consumed daily. The chances (if I may say so) of dying from cardiovascular disease rose by almost 15%! Based on these data, the authors of the study carried out new analyses in order to define, compared to a "moderate" audiovisual consumption (less than 2 hours per day), the increase in the risk of death associated with average consumption (between 2 and 4 hours) and strong consumption (more than 4 hours). Overall result: 13% additional risk of death for moderate use and 46% for heavy exposure. Result for cardiovascular damage alone: 19% and 80%. In other words, an individual who watches television 4 hours a day multiplies by almost 2 his chances of dying from a cardiovascular disease, compared to a fellow human being whose exposure remains lower than 2 hours a day! This heavily negative influence of television on cardiac pathologies has recently been confirmed by three other large epidemiological studies[615-617]. Perhaps we should finally plagiarize the anti-smoking health strategies for TV and write on the bottom of the screens: "Watching TV kills" or "Sitting in front of the TV seriously harms your health".

In short, television is far from being a harmless leisure activity, in health terms. The morbid potential of this evil machine is considerable. In order to facilitate the optimal apprehension of this point, the present chapter is divided into five main parts dealing successively with obesity, smoking, alcoholism, sexuality and sleep. This list is obviously not exhaustive. It does, however, reflect the main areas of concern to the scientific community.

*
**

Eat more, move less

Adrien is 8 years old. He is very overweight. His mother, Jacqueline, refused to admit the problem for a long time. When she finally agreed to open her eyes, under pressure from the family doctor, it was to mention genetic factors. Look at his father," she said, "Adrien will always be well and if he is happy like that, why should I bother him? It is true that the young man seems fulfilled, if not talkative. Television represents, without possible discussion, his favorite leisure. He has a home cinema in his room and a collection of films that would make any local media library green with envy. His latest acquisition is *The Lord of the Rings*[a]. In his own words, Adrien "loves it. It's better than even *Spider-Man.*

In relation to the issues at hand, this example is significant for at least two reasons. First, it confirms the difficulty a majority of parents have in admitting their children's obesity[618-620] and in recognizing that excess weight is often related more to lifestyle options than to innate factors. Second, it outlines a possible relationship between childhood audiovisual practices and the overweight epidemic that has plagued our Western societies in recent years. Nearly 1.7 billion humans are now overweight[622]. In the United States, 68% of adults (> 20 years)[623] and 32% of children (2-19 years)[624] are affected. In France, these proportions are still "only" 49% (adults 18-74 years) and 18% (children 3-17 years)[625]. Several epidemiological studies have shown that excess weight represents a major health hazard (diabetes, stroke, coronary heart disease, cancer, joint damage,

---

a. When I asked Adrien's mother if this film [that I went to see in the cinema] was not a little "violent" and "complicated" for an 8 year old, she answered that no, that this film was for all audiences, and that in any case Adrien was very advanced for his age. As I found it hard to believe that such an epic could be allowed to the youngest children, I went to the Fnac. Adrien's mother was right. On each of the three discs of the collector's box set, there was a green sticker stating "all audiences". Am I the only one who is concerned by this?

---

etc.)[163,626-628]. Overweight is estimated to be responsible for 300,000 annual deaths in the United States[629] or in the late Europe of 15[a]. In France, it is estimated to be the cause of nearly 6% of all deaths,[630] or about 30,000 deaths per year.[631] In terms of costs to the community, overweight now tends to exceed tobacco and alcoholism[632]. In the United States, health care expenditures attributable to obesity were $117 billion in 2000[633] and $147 billion in 2010 when inflation is taken into account.[634] This represents a budget of approximately $500 per year per capita (400 euros)[b].

Over the past 25 years, an impressive body of work has examined the effects of television viewing on obesity[3,637-642]. The overwhelming majority of these studies have shown, after taking into account a large number of sociodemographic, psychological and personal covariates, that the more an individual watched the small screen, the more likely he or she was to be obese[94,643-654]. Thus, for example, an initial study published in 1985 on adolescents aged 12 to 17 years established that each daily hour of television resulted in a 2% increase in the number of obese individuals[655]. A decade later, another study confirmed this point, in subjects aged 10 to 15 years, showing that heavy television consumers (>5 h/day) were 5 times more likely to be overweight than reasonable users (<2 h/day)[656]. 656 Consistent data were recently reported in research involving 15- to 18-year-old high school students showing that simply spending more than 2 hours per day in front of the television increased the risk of being overweight by 55%.[657] Interestingly, a substantial increase in the latter percentage was observed in preschoolers, consistent with the idea that the younger the viewer, the greater the deleterious effect of television. At 36 months of age, the risk of being overweight increased by a factor of 2.6 when daily audiovisual exposure exceeded 2 hours[658].

Clearly, the above evidence poses a problem of causal ordering. Indeed, it is quite possible to argue that television exposure is not a cause, but a consequence of obesity. In this case, the child would not be fat because he watches TV, but he would watch TV because he is fat. Two lines of evidence refute this hypothesis. First, when experimental measures are taken to decrease children's TV viewing, the level of overweight rapidly decreases[645,659-661]. Secondly, when a subject has been abandoned as a child

---

a. Austria, Belgium, Denmark, Finland, France, Germany, Greece, Holland, Ireland, Italy, Luxembourg, Portugal, Spain, Sweden[630].
b. As of today (September 3, 2010), the United States has a population of 310 million[635] and the exchange rate is $1.28 to 1€[636].

to the torments of television, he or she remains more exposed to weight risk once he or she has become an adult, regardless of the evolution of his or her audiovisual consumption. This was clearly demonstrated by a New Zealand team in a long-term longitudinal study[662]. More than 1000 individuals were followed from 5 to 32 years. Statistical analyses revealed, in the authors' own words, that "childhood television exposure was a better predictor of adult body mass index[a] and fitness[b] than adult exposure, and television exposure remained a significant predictor of these conditions after adjustment for adult viewing time. After adjustment for adult viewing time, the odds of adult obesity increased by a factor of 1.25 and the odds of poor physical fitness increased by a factor of 1.4 for each average weekday hour of television viewing during childhood [5-15 years]." In other words, take two brothers, one of whom (F2) watches 2 hours of television a day between the ages of 5 and 15, while the other (F1) is content with half. Make sure that this difference disappears as soon as they enter adolescence, so that our two brothers spend the same number of hours watching television at age 16. At age 32, F2 will have, compared to F1, 25% more chances of being obese and 40% more chances of being in poor physical condition. For those who are not bothered by these figures, the authors of the study propose a reformulation of their results, along a different axis. The American Pediatric Association recommends limiting children's exposure time to 2 hours per night. Children who exceeded this recommendation were 50% more likely to be obese at age 32. This link between childhood (and/or adolescent) audiovisual exposure and subsequent obesity has been confirmed by several other similar studies[196,235,663]. In one particularly interesting study, the authors showed that the long-term influence of television on weight was mainly related to the intake of commercial programs rich in advertising messages[664]. After controlling for a large number of potential covariates, each hour spent by children aged 6 years and younger watching such programs was associated with an increase of more than 10% in body mass index over 5 years. It is of course tempting to relate this result to another observation showing, after controlling for a large matrix of sociodemographic, psychological, and personal covariates, that each

---

a. This index is obtained by dividing weight by height squared. It is a standard marker of the level of overweight.

b. Calculated from the maximum oxygen consumption (adjusted for weight) during a stress test.

hour of television consumed before age 3 increased the amount of *junk food* (soda, snacks) ingested by the child at age 10 by 10%.[448]

In theory, the long-term influences just outlined could rest on a dual pillar involving the early emergence of both sedentary lifestyle habits[448] and maladaptive food preferences. Regarding the latter, it is now widely accepted that taste inclinations developed in early childhood tend to persist into adulthood[16,163,638,665,666]. In other words, what you eat in your early years determines what you like to eat for the rest of your life. A behavioural study by a German team illustrates this point perfectly.[667] 133 adults in their thirties were subjected to two successive tasks. First, they were asked to answer a questionnaire in which the following item was embedded: "Were you breast-fed or bottle-fed as a baby? Second, they were asked to taste two types of ketchup, one normal, the other vanilla flavored. The results showed that 71% of the breastfed subjects preferred the normal version, while 67% of the bottle-fed individuals preferred the vanilla version. This is a strange segmentation, but it is perfectly clear when you consider that most baby milks were vanilla flavored in Germany before the 1990s.

In the final analysis, beyond the dual subject of food preferences and lifestyle habits, the issue of obesity boils down to a simple energy problem. If an individual gets fat, it is simply because he or she ingests more calories than he or she burns[668]. In the light of this reality, it seems necessary, in order to understand the influence of television on body mass, to look at both the field of food intake and the field of physical expenditure. Let us start with this last point. A number of studies have tackled it head on over the last two decades. It turned out that the small window of opportunity had the disadvantage of only weakly soliciting the metabolic machinery while diverting the body from the most energy-consuming activities. In a frequently cited study, for example, it was shown in children aged 8 to 12 years that energy consumption was significantly lower in television viewing than in simple rest[669]. This is hardly surprising if we consider that cathode ray tube use profoundly reduces the volume of spontaneous motor activities. When a subject is simply sitting in an armchair, he/she agitates himself/herself, mobilizes his/her hands, scratches himself/herself and repositions himself/herself constantly. In contrast, when watching television, he hardly moves at all and is placed in a state of quasi-atony[637]. At the end of the day, an average of 210 kcal is lost each day to the metabolic boiler[669], the theoretical equivalent of 9 kilos of fat per year.[670] These kilos are all the more likely to be stored since the small television set also significantly reduces the resting metabolism, i.e. the number of calories burned by the body when it is not doing anything. This was shown in a recent study of 90 girls aged 7 to 12 years[671]. Among the latter, the small consumers (< 1 h/day) had a 17% increase in resting metabolism (1400 *versus* 1200 kcal/day) compared with their phone sisters (> 3 h/day). As impressive as this result is, it is hardly surprising. Indeed, we know that the resting metabolism depends on muscle mass, which is itself partly the result of physical activity. However, in both adults and children, television substantially reduces the time spent on sports and outdoor activities[12,63,243,246,672-676]. In this context, the screen not only deprives viewers of the acute energy expenditure associated with energy-intensive physical activity. It also deprives them of a more expensive basal metabolism, i.e. of an increased capacity of caloric dissipation throughout the day. Again, early experiences seem to be crucial in this area. Indeed, a recent study showed that each hour of television watched at 29 months reduced the amount of time spent on activities requiring physical effort by almost 10% at age 10.[448]

After the field of energy expenditure, let us look at the space of food intake. It appears that the more time an individual spends facing the post, the more he eats[642,651,652,677,678]. On this subject, a recent study showed, for example, in 12-year-old children, after taking into account a large matrix of sociodemographic, psychological and personal covariates (body mass index, overall food intake, age, sex, socioeconomic status, school performance, etc.), that each hour of television increased daily food intake by 167 kcal[679]. The first link in this massive increase occurs during the viewing phase. 90% of children aged 3-8 years consume solid foods or sweetened beverages while watching TV.[680] On average, among 8-18 year olds, nearly 15% of viewing time is spent with a fork in hand.[229] The food consumed then includes, through the use of a fork, a variety of other foods, such as fruit, vegetables, fruit juice, nuts and vegetables. The food consumed includes less raw vegetables, fruit or vegetables and more meat, deli meats, pizza, fried foods, salty snacks and sweet treats compared to meals or snacks away from the TV.[239,240,242,681] This difference is particularly alarming when compared to the time spent watching TV. This difference is all the more alarming because the feeling of satiety is delayed when an individual eats on automatic in front of a screen[682,683] or any other disturbing external stimulus (such as reading, radio, etc.)[684,685]. Therefore, when the small window is on, the individual not only eats less healthily, but also eats more[686,687]. For example, if instead of quietly enjoying your pizza in the kitchen, you choose to eat it in front of the news, you will increase your food intake by 260 kcal (36% more pizza)[688]. If you choose to replace the pizza with macaroni and cheese, the result will be roughly similar with an excess of 255 kcal (71% more pasta). If you drink water, your beverage intake will not change. However, if you choose soda, it will increase slightly (75 ml, or 30 kcal). Cumulated over a year, at a rate of one daily episode, these extra calories will represent 13 kilos of good fat, or, if we prefer (and if I believe the indications of the treadmill of my friend Caroline's gym), 1 hour and 15 minutes of fast walking per day for a woman of average build (58 kilos).

To make matters worse, the deleterious effect of television on satiety is not limited to the time of eating. It is clearly established that a subject who eats while watching television eats more quickly after the end of his or her meal[689] and in greater quantities[683,690]. This phenomenon finds its most credible explanation in a number of studies showing that the memory of the previous meal greatly influences subsequent food consumption[691,692]. Thus, for example, the less aware an individual is of what he or she ate at lunch, the more likely he or she is to eat a heavy snack at 4:00 pm[693,694]. The brain has been shown to have more difficulty remembering the qualitative and quantitative elements of the meal when the meal is eaten in the presence of a television.[690]

Regardless of the above factors, it also turns out that television encourages us to eat even when we are not hungry. As I will show in more detail in the last chapter, the brain is an organ that is both fabulously intelligent and hopelessly stupid. It does all sorts of things in a perfectly mechanical and automatic way, without informing the consciousness of the actions undertaken. For example, when it encounters an elderly person or words like *old man* and *grandfather*, it automatically decreases the speed of travel.[567,695,696] Similarly, when confronted with pleasant food stimuli, it sends signals of palatability[697]. This latter process accounts for the ability of audiovisual advertisements to trigger in the viewer first an artificial desire to eat and then an actual consumption behavior[698-701]. In a recent experiment, children aged 7 to 11 years were exposed, during a 14-minute cartoon, to two commercials for neutral products (games, records) or food products (cereals, potato chips, cakes)[702]. Participants were informed that they could nibble on snacks placed near them during viewing if they wished. Children who saw the food advertisements ate almost 50% more than their control peers. The same trend was observed in adult subjects. A subsequent study extended these results to soft drinks[703].

Of course, the power of advertising is not limited to the priming effects just described. It goes much deeper than that.[163,641,704-707] Around the world, food industry giants are the largest television advertisers. They spend billions of dollars each year.[163,708-710] Much of this money is targeted directly at children.[711] In a recent U.S. study, Gantz and colleagues analyzed 1,600 hours of programming "covering all genres of programming watched by children, not just children's programs, and then [they] combined a detailed analysis of advertising content with exposure data from a large national sample of children to determine how many ads children actually see based on the mix of programs they watch. The result of this absolutely titanic work speaks for itself. Children aged 2-7 see 4,400 food commercials each year. The 8-12 year olds are at 7,600 and the 13-17 year olds at 6,000. Within youth programs, half of the advertising coverage is devoted to food products. When considering all programs, food-related screens remain the most represented (~26%). 34% of food ads aimed at children and adolescents involve confectionery/biscuits/snacks (ice cream, candy, chips, cookies, etc.), 28% involve cereals, 10% involve fast food. For fruits and vegetables, the percentage of presentations is as high as 0%. These results are in line with a large number of other studies that have shown, with perfect unanimity, in countries as diverse as North America, Turkey, Germany, Australia, China, Italy, Greece, Sweden, Brazil, Spain, England and France, that advertising almost totally ignores fresh and healthy products in order to concentrate its enormous financial clout on the refined foods that obesity loves so much: cereals, fast food, sodas, cookies, confectionery, and the like.[247,680,712724] This focus is obviously not without consequences. It profoundly deteriorates the food preferences of young viewers, in the sense that they tend to appreciate, demand, buy and eat more *junk food*[a] the more they are exposed to massive advertising[247,646,657,679,717,725-733]. For example, after controlling for a large matrix of sociodemographic, psychological and personal covariates, a schoolchild who watches 2 or more hours of television daily is more likely than children who do not exceed this threshold to consume the main products of our advertising screens on a daily basis, including sweetened drinks (+131%), sweetened or salted snacks (+50%) and ready-made meals (such as pizza,

---

a. An expression that has now become part of the French language and literally means "rotten food, of poor quality".

meat pies, etc.; +40%). At the same time, they are substantially less likely to indulge in less promoted foods and to eat at least two servings of fruit (-42%) and vegetables (-13%) daily.[674] [674] These trends continue among adults[651,677,734] and across the so-called developed world[735]. This is hardly surprising. Indeed, the leaders of Nestlé, Ferrero, McDonald's, Coca-Cola, *PepsiCo* and Danone are neither stupid nor philanthropic. If they invest so much money in advertising space, it is because the martingale works. This effectiveness has not been a secret for a long time, as demonstrated by a superb study published more than 30 years ago by Joann Galst and Mary White[736]. These authors worked on a fairly simple protocol consisting of supervising a shopping session at the supermarket, while the mothers were accompanied by their children (aged 3-11). In half an hour, the children made an average of 15 requests, with a success rate of almost 50%. The number of requests was strongly correlated with the number of hours spent watching television. Not surprisingly, the products requested were those that were most heavily advertised (cereals, candy, sweetened drinks, ice cream, yogurt). Among young children who could not yet read, nearly 10% of the claims made did not directly mention a product category (cakes), but a brand name. The authors conclude, "A relationship exists between the reinforcing value of television commercials to children and their persistence in attempting to influence parental food purchases, and between the volume of exposure to commercial television and the number of attempts made to influence purchases." Since its formulation, this conclusion has been widely validated and generalized.[672,678,680,737-740] It is now clearly established that advertising has a direct effect on food group sales and viewer consumption behaviors.[16,218,646,678,739] The process operates at two levels. The process operates at a dual level, categorical and specific.[706,727] The *categorical* term indicates that the presentation of a given food product (cereal X) stimulates the purchase of all products in the same family (cereal X, Y, Z, etc.). The *specific* term states that the displayed brand (cereal X) is, however, chosen more frequently than its competing brands, when a choice is available. In relation to this last result, a study has, for example, shown that two 30-second spots for a given fruit juice were sufficient to multiply by 3 the probability that the child would specifically ask for this fruit juice rather than another similar drink, but which had not been advertised.[741] This selectivity effect is, of course, also due to the fact that it is not always possible to choose the same brand. Of course, this selectivity effect is extremely sensitive to the frequency of exposure. This has been very well demonstrated for large food brands such as McDonald's or Coca-Cola. In this case, the advertising hype is so intense that it distorts even the most primitive sensory perceptions of the spectators. For example, Thomas Robinson and his colleagues asked young children aged 3 to 8 years to compare the taste of various foods presented in pairs[742]. For each of these pairs, the same product was used but wrapped in either plain or McDonald's paper. The results showed clear differences between the two conditions. 59% of the children preferred McDonald's nuggets versus 18% who preferred the plain nuggets (the remaining 23% did not know). For fries, the scores were 77% and 13%. For drinks (milk or apple juice) it was 61% *versus* 21%. Even carrots were judged better by the children when they appeared in a paper of the brand in Ronald (54% versus 23%)! Interestingly, the greater the number of televisions in the child's home, the greater the effect observed. Similar biases are observed when subjects are confronted with products packaged in neutral boxes or decorated with well-known cartoon characters such as Dora, Scooby-Doo or Shrek[743]. For example, in a recent study, 55% of children preferred the taste of crackers in advertising packaging, compared to 7.5% who preferred anonymous cookies. More generally, 88% of children said that if given a choice, they would choose the character crackers over the others. This type of result obviously raises the question of causality. How can the presence of a simple logo on a package transform consumer taste to such an extent? The answer is as simple as it is hopeless. By dint of repetition, the logo no longer simply marks the package. It ends up by stamping the functioning of our neurons as well. This was recently demonstrated by a team from Baylor University in Texas[744]. The brain activity of a group of 67 adult subjects was recorded under two experimental conditions. In the first condition, known as "blind", the subjects drank two drinks in succession. One was Coke, the other Pepsi. The task was to determine which sample had the highest taste value. Behavioral observations showed that the subjects divided equally between these two brands. Neurophysiological recordings then indicated that the preferred beverage activated a small pleasure-related area in the front of the brain. In the second part of the experiment, called "semi-blind", the same tests were carried out, with one methodological detail: one of the drinks was clearly identified as Coke; the second was not labelled and could be either Coke or Pepsi. The behavioral results showed the existence, in this case, of a strong taste bias in favor of Coke. At the neurophysiological level, this majority preference was no longer translated by the activation of the previously identified "pleasure" area, but by the recruitment of a large network of areas known to be involved in the regulation of emotional and affective memory functions. Thus, the taste preference expressed by the subjects when the Coca-Cola brand was visible did not depend on pure sensory information, but on a combination of factors related to the memory of the brand and to the activation of positive feelings associated with this memory. The advertisement had literally written the brand into the subjects' neurons. However, as we shall see below, it is possible to manipulate this inscription, at least in children, by leading some Coke fans to choose a Pepsi from a dispenser[745]. To explain this change, one can argue that brand preference is still labile in children because of too little advertising. Alternatively, we can also think that the priming effect exerts a sufficiently strong pressure on our choices to lead us to punctually reverse a previously installed brand preference. This second possibility will probably not come as a great surprise to the 77% of adults who say, when questioned, that the small screen has a substantial influence on their children's food choices[237]. 237 Nor will it surprise the 66% of parents who acknowledge that their offspring regularly request food products in response to advertising exposure. 237 This type of demand turns into a whim in almost 10% of cases among the youngest children (3-8 years).

Although they are (it seems to me) both spectacular and convincing, the works presented above only tell part of the story. Indeed, they largely ignore all the hidden forms of advertising such as, for example, the placement of food products in films or audiovisual series. However, this practice is quite widespread, as a recent study in a leading medical journal has shown[746]. For their work, the authors extracted the 20 highest-rated productions at the US box office for each of the years from 1996 to 2005, i.e. a corpus of 200 films. Of these, 138 (69%) featured at least one food product. A total of 1,180 placements were identified, 427 of which were for food, 425 for beverages, and 328 for restaurant groups (such as Starbucks or McDonald's). For the food category, the foods featured were primarily candy/sweets (25%), salty snacks (21%), sweet treats/ desserts (12%) and breakfast cereals (11%). For the beverage category, 76% of the exposed beverages were in the high-calorie sweetened potion group. Finally, for the category of food groups, 62% of the firms displayed were from the fast-food division. The authors conclude: "More than two-thirds of popular films featured place-ments for food, beverages and restaurants. The overwhelming majority of these brand placements were for high-energy, nutritionally poor products. Movies provide a boulevard through which companies market foods with little nutritional value to consumers, including children and teens, who may not even be aware of the advertising." In short, if you are thinking, like my friend Veronique, "my daughter only sees DVDs, at least there are no ads", you will have to review your copy. And above all, don't think that these investments are innocent whims. They exert a phenomenal constraint on our behavior. A recent experiment, briefly mentioned above, shows this superbly[745]. A first "experimental" group of schoolchildren aged 6 to 12 was confronted with a piece of the film *Mommy, I missed the plane!* (*Home Alone*). In the chosen scene, a family was shown sitting around a table eating pizza while drinking milk and Pepsi-Cola. The latter brand was explicitly mentioned by an adult in the course of the action ("Fuller, go easy on the Pepsi"). A second identical control group saw a scene that was similar in every way, but without any reference to Pepsi-Cola. After viewing, the children were asked to leave the room and choose a drink, which could be either a Pepsi or a Coke. In England, the country where the experiment was conducted, the latter brand has 75% of the market compared to 25% for its competitor. The choices of the control group showed a distribution compatible with these figures: Coke 58%, Pepsi 42%. Conversely, the options of the experimental group revealed a clear reversal of this trend: Coke 38%, Pepsi 62%. In this case, no difference was observed between children who remembered seeing the brand and those who did not. This is the magic of product placements. They are able to manipulate our behavior in a totally unconscious way. An ingenious study by Shapiro and his colleagues clearly demonstrated this in the late 1990s[747]. Subjects were asked to focus their attention on a text presented on a screen under different conditions: (i) text and a small advertising banner representing a carrot or a can opener in the margin of the screen; (ii) text alone without an advertising banner. At the end of the experiment, subjects were presented with several banners and asked to indicate whether or not they had seen them during the exposure phase. Both experimental groups responded randomly. However, when the participants were asked to make a shopping list for food products or kitchen utensils, the members of the "advertising" group mentioned the target objects (carrot and can opener) twice as often as those of the "text only" group. The authors conclude: "Advertisers should be strongly encouraged by the results of this study. Our results indicate that an advertisement is capable of affecting future purchase decisions even if subjects, who are busy with another task, do not process the advertisement carefully and, thus, do not recall seeing the advertisement." Let's just say that what is encouraging for advertisers is not necessarily encouraging for our children, who continue to swell in an alarming way for their health, because the most intimate flaws of their brains are exploited without shame or reserve for commercial purposes. In its online version, the *Petit Larousse* defines rape as "the act of forcing, of coercing someone against their will".[748] It seems to me that the advertising practices just described are not far from this definition.

In response to the above problems, several countries have taken rather drastic measures. Sweden, for example, banned all advertising to individuals aged 12 and under as early as 1991 because it "sees advertising to children as morally and ethically unacceptable, as children have difficulty distinguishing between the motives of advertising and other modes of communication. In Flanders, Sweden, Denmark and Norway, all advertising is prohibited during and around children's programs.[197,707,749] In France, this common-sense measure has been adopted by the Ministry of Culture. In France, this common-sense measure was recently rejected by our deputies, under active pressure from the agri-food and advertising lobbies.[435] The added value of these economic fields justifies the ban on advertising. The added value of these economic fields justifies, let us hope, putting our children's health at risk and transferring the astronomical cost of a real health bomb to our social security (cf. *above*). One can of course argue that our dear politicians have established with the industrialists and advertisers, instead of a rigid ban, a concerted charter "to promote a diet and a physical activity favourable to health in the programs and the advertisements broadcasted on television"[750]. This choice would be justified, we are told, because the effect of the advertisement on obesity is by no means scientifically established. A press release co-signed by most of the major private media groups (TF1, M6, Canal +, Lagardère Active, etc.) proposes the following text: "Even though scientific studies and prohibition experiments [*sic*] carried out in several foreign countries have not yet demonstrated any correlation between obesity and television advertising, any prohibition measure would be misunderstood."[751] An idea widely taken up by the media historian Patrick Eveno, on the grounds that "overweight exists in all societies; but it becomes more frequent in populations that gain access to dietary comfort and abundance [...] If thinness became a canon of beauty for the elites in the second half of the 20th century, this "value" has not yet been transmitted throughout the social hierarchy, and advertising for chocolate bars and candy is not responsible for it. Frankly, for anyone who has taken the time to consult the almost absolute unanimity of the literature, this kind of assertion can only be deeply despairing[a]. Yet, in substance, these untruths should not surprise us too much. The tobacco industry had already acted, in its time, with the same intellectual dishonesty to assert that there was no established link between cigarettes and cancer[6]. That being said, let me nevertheless find strange the propensity of certain members of the Conseil supérieur de l'audiovisuel (CSA), such as Christine Kelly, president - excuse the pun - of the "Health and Sustainable Development" mission, to support and democratize this kind of pro-advertising nonsense[752]. According to this lady, "if the suppression of food advertising in children's programs is far from being an effective instrument in the fight against obesity, its economic consequences would on the other hand be certain on our structurally under-financed audiovisual sector: consequences on employment, on television channels, on the offer of programs for children and on the financing of the cinema. Let us recall, for the record, that before being appointed to the CSA by the President of the Senate, this journalist had been working for nine years on LCI (2000-2009), a subsidiary of the private group TF1[753]. It would obviously require pathological bad faith to suggest that such a professional affiliation could explain, even remotely, Ms. Kelly's position. In fact, if she takes up with such ardour the argument of her former employer, in defiance of the most elementary scientific evidence, it can only be pure coincidence.

On the substance, does the agreement in principle signed by our politicians have the slightest chance of being effective? Frankly, in the image of a scientific community that has almost unanimously denounced this "hand-sewn charter for advertising agencies"[754], I doubt it. There are several reasons for this. First, the tobacco, food and alcohol industries have clearly demonstrated that charters of good conduct often produce more than disappointing results.[247,713,755-758] This has been confirmed by the WHO, which has pointed out quite clearly that "to be effective, systems to regulate marketing must be based on sufficient incentives; in general, the effectiveness of the regulatory framework is proportional to the pressure exerted by the State.[759] Recently, a study by UFC-Que Choisir clearly validated this statement by showing that the food industry continued,

---

a. Again, for a review of the available evidence: [163,641,664,704-707].

despite its promises, to flood the programs most watched by children with advertisements for fatty, sugary and highly unbalanced products.[247] On another level, I am not sure that the addition of written slogans such as "For your health, avoid snacking between meals, www.mangerbouger. fr" would have any effect, especially on young children, many of whom will have the greatest difficulty reading the proposed text in the time allotted (especially if they have to give up looking at the images presented on the screen to do so). In the same vein, it does not seem to me that the invitation made to the channels to "make available to the public, in particular to the young public, programs on diet and physical activity" is very credible. For TF1, the basic volume imposed is indeed 10 hours per year, or 98 seconds per day. A nice joke! Finally, I do not see how a modification of the advertising in a more "ethical" direction, including, for example, a "promotion of good eating habits" and a "reference to nutritional equivalences and comparisons with fruits and vegetables", could modify the composition of the products presented. An excellent article in *Télérama* magazine illustrates this point perfectly.[760] In the words of this article, "manufacturers now claim to be working for a 'better balanced diet'. This is a mantra that advertisers repeat in every tone. We've gone from 'pleasure-pleasure' to 'pleasure-health'," says Gabriel Gaultier, director of the Leg agency. We're no longer selling a chocolate cream dessert, but a cream dessert with 4.5% milk, because it's good for growth." So Danone has made "plus-health" its strategic communication choice. When nutrition is used as a way to promote the company, without any legitimacy, I explode!" says nutritionist Béatrice de Reynal. Take the slogan of the Nutella ad, 'it's full of nuts and good milk for breakfast'. In a jar of Nutella there are 13% hazelnuts and 6% milk. The rest is saturated fat and sugar! As for Chocapic and company, the marketing people make it look like cereal. In fact, they are kibbles! The starch of the cereal has been industrially transformed into sugar. Some people go further and claim that their 'cereals' are rich in vitamins and minerals. But adding vitamin C to your cigarettes will not make them healthy!" Nutritionist Dominique Lanzmann-Petithory, 12 years with Lu before she slammed the door, never digested a promotional campaign for the apricot tray. "The advert said that by eating them, you are nourished by apricots. But we ingest 60% of sugar". To all this, one could add that many television programs and commercials feature characters with unsavory eating habits, but with impeccable dynamism and physical appearance, as if all this *junk food* could be consumed without weight or health risks[637,761]. As if being overweight were not really about food, but a lazy trait. "Eat" and "move" and you are safe. If your child is as fat as a monk, there's no need to deprive him of his favorite Chocapic or other BigMac. Just buy him sneakers (Nike of course, "like on TV"). Unfortunately, a recent study confirms that it doesn't really work like that. A child who eats junk food gets fatter, even if he or she plays sports[762].

To summarize, obesity has become a major public health problem in a few decades. Although it is not the only factor of this evolution, television cannot be exonerated from its heavy responsibility. Indeed, the more a viewer watches television, the more likely he/she is to be fat. This link, unanimously recognized by the scientific literature, is built on several complementary bases involving advertising pressure, extension of sedentary behaviors and disruption of the physiological signals of satiety. To effectively dissolve all these bases, there is no need for complicated measures. It is enough to turn off the television. In the long term, such a choice substantially reduces the risk of obesity and a wide range of health problems often associated with this pathology and, more generally, with sedentary behaviour: mortality[614,626-630], hypercholesterolemia[763], hypertension[764,765], cardiovascular accidents[614-617,627,630], cancers[627,630], arthritis[626] and diabetes[627,651,677,766]. Regarding the latter, for example, a recent study showed that adolescents who watched more than 2 hours of television per day were 3 times more likely to have abnormally high insulin levels than those who did not, after controlling for body mass index and a broad matrix of other covariates.[767] To make matters worse, we could also consider the possibility of a new study on the impact of television on the health of adolescents. To make matters worse, one could of course add to this long list of metabolic and weight disorders a wide range of psychological (self-esteem, depression, etc.)[768-770] and social (interpersonal relationships)[771] suffering. We could also add a few disorders not directly related to overweight, including asthma[772-774], photosensitive epilepsy[775] and autism[116].

*
**

Make the child a smoker... or close up store

James was a smoker, like 1.3 billion humans[776,777]. In 2009, he died of this habit, like 6 million other unfortunate people. For him, the grim reaper came in the form of cancer. It could just as easily have been a respiratory, vascular or cardiac accident[776-778]. At the age of 48, Jacques liked to emphasize that he did not believe in "that bullshit" and that his father had died of lung cancer without ever having smoked. This is a furiously popular argument, but it is terribly laughable when one considers that tobacco is the world's leading preventable disease factor[776-778]. Cigarettes kill more people than cerebrovascular disease or AIDS[778]. Every year, a country like Denmark is wiped off the world map because of tobacco[a].

Jacques had started smoking at 13, a pivotal age long considered a priority target by cigarette manufacturers[780,781]. This marketing choice has now been abandoned. Tobacco manufacturers have become "responsible" as shown by, among other examples, the declaration of intent posted on the Philip Morris International website: "Children who smoke risk becoming addicted and continuing to smoke as they grow up. They put themselves at risk for cardiovascular disease, lung cancer and other serious illnesses that may occur later in life. No one wants young people to smoke. [Governments can contribute to these efforts through legislation, by making it a criminal offence to sell cigarettes to children and by strictly enforcing it. [... We also believe that tobacco companies have an opportunity and a duty to contribute to the fight against youth smoking. [...] We are campaigning in many countries around the world for regulations that help prevent youth smoking. For example, where there is no legal age, we recommend that governments pass such legislation. We have done so in Indonesia and South Africa. We actively encourage all governments to enforce the legal age, arguing that for such a law to be effective, it must have a tangible impact on offending retailers. [We are not experts in education and you won't see us in the classroom.[782] "We do not promote our products to children and we do not use images or content that may appeal to minors.[783] This last commitment is strictly in line with the regulations now in place in most developed countries (although these are far from always respected).[778] In the European Union, the tobacco industry is not in a position to make any changes to its legislation. In the

---

a. Denmark has 5.5 million inhabitants[779].

European Union, for example, a directive purely and simply prohibits cigarette brands from all advertising and promotional activities in the audiovisual field.[784] In the United States, regulation is somewhat more restrictive than in Europe. In the United States, regulation is somewhat less restrictive, even though an agreement signed in 1998 stipulates (among other things) that manufacturers undertake not to launch any campaigns aimed at children and not to place any products in clips, films or audiovisual series.[785] The same manufacturers had already agreed to stop advertising in the United States. The same manufacturers had already committed themselves in 1989 to no longer pay for the explicit appearance of their brand in cinematographic productions[786]. Thus, for example, as Philip Morris explains, "we do not accept the promotion of our products in films or television programmes; we regularly decline such offers"[783]. I don't think anyone will be surprised to learn that such rhetoric is generally regarded with great caution by health authorities. A recent WHO report makes this clear. In the words of the report, "It takes a lot of cunning to sell a product that kills up to half of its consumers. Tobacco companies are among the world's best marketers and are increasingly working to circumvent advertising, promotion and sponsorship bans designed to reduce tobacco consumption. The tobacco industry claims that its advertising and promotion activities are not intended to increase sales or attract new consumers, but simply to reallocate the market among existing consumers. This is not true. Marketing and promotion increase tobacco sales and thus contribute to killing more people by encouraging smokers to smoke more and discouraging them from quitting. Marketing also encourages potential consumers, especially young people, to try cigarettes and become long-term customers. Advertising that targets youth and specific population subgroups is particularly effective.

In fact, many experts believe that the tobacco industry has little choice. They are condemned, if they want to survive, to recruit young smokers en masse. Once again, this conviction is clearly displayed in the writings of the WHO. According to this institution, "tobacco companies have long targeted young people to 'replace' smokers who die or quit. They know that the only hope for the future of their business is to get young people addicted. Anyone who uses tobacco can become addicted to nicotine, but those who don't start smoking before age 21 are unlikely to ever start. Experiencing a highly addictive product touted by the tobacco industry as a teenager can easily lead to a lifetime of addiction. The younger children are when they first smoke, the more likely they are to smoke regularly thereafter and the less likely they are to quit.

Thus, to summarize, the tobacco industry is faced with a cruel equation. On the one hand, they must comply with a certain number of ethical commitments and legislative texts in order not to risk being heavily condemned by the public authorities. On the other hand, they are obliged to circumvent the law and the given word if they do not want to disappear in the short term, for lack of customers. It is not easy to get out of this impasse. Fortunately, Lady Providence knows how to be good to her children. With a strange eagerness, the beautiful one chooses to appear to the cigar makers under the features of the noble seventh art. Thus, while the sinister clique of cancer-makers had been deprived, by law, of any promotional latitude, the American film studios zealously took up the propagandist torch. In the name (officially!) of the principle of reality and the sacrosanct freedom of expression[758,787], our friends made it their duty to flood their films with smoking scenes. Over the last decade, smoking scenes were featured in 70-75% of films, with an average number of presentations of 8-9 units[758,787-791]. It is worth noting that similar incidences have been reported for works broadcast in the European market[792,793], which is hardly surprising when one considers that America exports its films massively and serves as a general reference for world cinema production[758,794]. If smokers were to be portrayed in situations that were both well-founded and representative, this would undoubtedly be a lesser evil. Unfortunately, this is not the case. In fact, we are far from it. In the overwhelming majority of cases, the expression "smoking" does not seem to have any narrative basis. It appears in a totally "arbitrary" way, without illuminating the scenario or the psychology of the characters in the least[787]. When a smoker appears "for good reason," it is usually to spew out a good old-fashioned slimy stereotype.[787] You want to show a rebellious teenager, a stressed-out lawyer, a relentless cop, a troubled man? Try a little cigarette. Need to make a gorgeous blonde tease fatal? Try a revolutionary "do you have a light? Want to emphasize how much power your character has? Opt for a potent Havana. And so on. Is it really surprising that many of these stereotypes are uncritical of the messages used by the tobacco industry to recruit its customers?[795]

That said, the smoking scenes are not only overwhelmingly unnecessary to the story and/or pitifully stereotypical. They are also deeply biased. Indeed, among the smokers on the silver screen, there is a strong over-representation of "positive," sexually active, emotionally complex, intellectually strong, racially white, physically attractive, socially privileged, and professionally decisive characters.[787,791,796] This picture is clearly consistent with the way in which the "positive" characters are portrayed in the movies. This picture is obviously consistent with the observation that "stars" are very often at the forefront of the game when it comes to busting one[797,798]. The second knives are much further back. Unsurprisingly, a similar level of discretion (though much more pronounced) was identified with respect to the harmful influences of tobacco. Tobacco's harmful influences are hardly ever mentioned in feature films.[791,796] For example, Polansky and Glantz studied 479 films produced over the period 1999-2005. These films were unique in that they included at least one smoking reference and were allowed to be shown without restriction to viewers 13 years of age and older. The results of the study identified nearly 2,700 smoking scenes. They did not reveal any messages about the potential negative health effects of smoking[789]!

Of course, one would have to be profoundly naive to believe that the smoking hype that young viewers are subjected to is without consequence. In fact, the scientific literature shows with terrifying consistency that the more actors a teenager sees smoking on screen, the more likely he or she is to become a steady customer of our tobacco friends.[758,758,790,791,796] This phenomenon has been established for countries as culturally diverse as Canada and the United States. This phenomenon has been established for countries as culturally different as North America,[799-806] Germany,[792,793] Thailand,[807] Hong Kong,[808] New Zealand,[809] and Mexico.[810] And the least we can say is that the effects observed are not insignificant. To facilitate understanding of this point, it may be important to provide some technical details. Let us begin with the methodological aspect. Several approaches have been used. The most common was to divide the population into four quartiles, according to the volume of exposure to smoking scenes. Brackets 1 (T1) and 4 (T4) then contain the 25% of subjects with the least and most exposure, respectively (T2 and T3 fall in between). By comparing these bands, it is possible to define a smoking risk. Of course, for this measure to be meaningful, the potential effect of other socio-demographic, psychological and personal factors that may influence smoking risk (age, gender, economic level, education, smoking by parents, siblings and friends, school performance, self-esteem, propensity to rebel, alcohol consumption, etc.) must be taken into account at the statistical level. When all of this is taken into account, it appears that the "movie" factor almost triples the risk of a teenager succumbing to the charms of cigarettes. In other words, T4 subjects are almost 3 times more likely to start smoking than their T1[792,799,800,810] counterparts. T2 and T3 individuals are at intermediate levels (~ 2 and 2.5 respectively). For the avoidance of doubt, these measures are likely to be underestimates, given that the reference subjects (T1) themselves see a substantial dose of smoking on screen[93,94]. That said, and for those who are not struck by the magnitude of these numbers, there is another way to present the case. The question is: after controlling for potentially relevant covariates, what percentage of subjects started smoking because they saw actors smoking on screen? A study of young subjects (9-12 years) produced an estimate of 35%.[804] An earlier study, using older individuals (10-14 years) with higher volumes of exposure, produced a substantially higher measure: 52%.[802] The sheer astronomical nature of these effects will not, I think, escape anyone. To avoid any misunderstanding, it should be noted that the studies in question were published in leading medical journals (*Lancet, Pediatrics*), by internationally recognized scientific teams, after careful evaluation by several health and statistical specialists.

In response to the above data, it can of course be argued that the estimates presented are grossly misleading because an adolescent who starts smoking does not necessarily persist in his or her practice. To address this objection, the researchers focused on regular smokers. The results revealed a level of risk that was attenuated, but still substantial. Thus, after taking into account a large matrix of socio-demographic, psychological and personal covariates, it appears that the 25% of individuals who saw the most smoking scenes on screen (T4) were twice as likely to become established smokers as the 25% of individuals with the least exposure (T1)[792,801]. Similarly, it turns out that 35% of young adults (16-21 years old) become stable smokers because they were confronted, a few years earlier (10-14 years old), with films showing actors smoking.[803] It is interesting to note that this percentage was obtained by longitudinally following a cohort of individuals that had already shown that the film factor accounted for 52% of smoking initiation among adolescents (see previous paragraph). This continuity makes it possible to affirm that the overwhelming majority of those who try smoking because of a cinematographic factor, become regular smokers afterwards. For those who are still not convinced of the magnitude of the phenomenon, it should be noted that the film effect is more important for the development of chronic smoking than other factors that have long been known to be central, such as the consumption of friends or relatives.[803] However, it is rather a surprise that the film effect is not a factor in the development of chronic smoking. However, the good news is that the power of images to influence smoking seems to diminish significantly after adolescence.[811,812] This observation is consistent with the fact that the influence of images on smoking has been shown to be more important than that of other factors. This observation is consistent with the previously mentioned fact that young adults are statistically unlikely to start smoking if they have not already tried.[778]

In light of the foregoing, it seems legitimate to question the protective potential of possible prohibitive measures. The idea may seem questionable to some, on the grounds that there would be no point in prohibiting anything because children always end up seeing at the neighbor's what they were unable to see at home anyway[34,36]. This is an interesting fantasy, but it does not stand up to the test of facts. To understand this point, it is important to know that in the United States there is a category of films known as *R-Rated*, which individuals aged 17 and under can only see in the cinema in the company of an adult. These include films with violent or sexual content that many parents might consider rather harmless and which are frequently classified as "all audiences" in France. Examples include *A Fish Called Wanda, Shakespeare in Love, American Pie, Serial Noceurs, Sex and the City, Gran Torino, Gladiator, Rambo,* or *Mary at Any Price.*[813] [813] Restricted films have been found to contain a very high concentration of smoking references. At the same time, it has also been shown that adolescents subject to strict parental bans had, unlike their unconstrained peers, marginal exposure to *R-Rated* films[815]. Based on these observations, the researchers wondered whether smoking was lower than average among adolescents who were prevented by their parents from watching restricted movies. Several studies were conducted with the same positive result[809,816-819]. For example, in one large longitudinal study, 2,600 never-smoking adolescents aged 10-14 years were first subjected to a careful sociological survey and then re-contacted some time later (between 13 and 26 months). On the basis of the survey data, the participants were divided into 3 groups. The first group (19% of the sample) included subjects who, because of strict parental prohibitions, never watched *R-rated* movies. The second group (29% of the sample) included individuals who watched such films episodically. The third

(52% of the sample) included regular consumers with little or no parental control. After adjusting for a large set of potential covariates, it was found that adolescents in the "episodic" and "regular" groups were 2 and 3 times more likely, respectively, to have started smoking during the follow-up period than their "strictly constrained" counterparts. When the analysis was replicated using only those adolescents who were free of possible family influences to smoke, because their relatives did not smoke, the risk factors rose to 4 and 10! In other words, take two twins raised in a non-smoking environment under strictly identical conditions except that one of the two boys is prevented from watching *R-Rated* movies, while the other can watch whatever he wants. At the end of the day, the child left to his own devices is 10 times more likely to start smoking than his supervised brother. This being said, it may be important to point out that the competent commissions have gradually downgraded their evaluation criteria over the last 10 years, so that films that would previously have been rated *R-Rated* are now often defined as PG-13 (parents strongly warned, content potentially unsuitable for children under 13)[821,822]. Thus, there is a concern that there will be a significant expansion of smoking risks for teenagers who it seems reasonable to suggest are often allowed to view PG-13 works, even when they are banned from *R-Rated* films[791]. This fear undoubtedly echoes the observation that films rated PG-13 and below[a] have been the primary source of tobacco exposure for teens for some years now[788,789,796,814]. It is true that this problem does not arise in France, a country that blithely classifies many films identified as PG-13 in the United States as "all audiences" (which is hardly surprising given that the practice is already present for the *R-Rated* category; cf. *above*). *Avatar* is a recent example, with Sigourney Weaver as a scientist addicted to nicotine.[823] Of course, it is easy to talk about witch hunts and to ridicule the associations that denounce this kind of exhibition.[824] But it is also easy to attack these groups of supposed "witch hunters". It is easier to attack these groups of supposed bigots than to put pressure on film producers to obtain, for the use of those who want it, a clear indication of the smoking characteristics of a work[814,825]. However, in view of the data that has just been mentioned, it is high time that we collectively gave up our ideological posturing and (finally) began to think things through. This seems to me to be all the more

---

a. *PG-Rated*: parental supervision suggested, potentially unsuitable content for children.
G-Rated: general audience, acceptable for all ages.

necessary as tobacco impregnation operates in a largely unconscious way, at a level that it would be illusory to pretend to reach through some vague program of "education to images". Can't we ask ourselves, without risking any anathema, if *Avatar* and its followers are really worth multiplying by 10 the risk of seeing a teenager succumb to the sirens of tobacco and end up, at the end of 30 or 40 years, among the 6 million annual victims of Lady Cigarette? Can't we consider, without looking like a sad frog or a dangerous reactionary, that it would be legitimate to offer parents reliable information on the tobacco (and alcohol, and sexual) content of a film? Without this information, where is the educational freedom of parents? Once informed of the dangers to their offspring, parents may decide that the beauty of *Avatar* or any other movie makes the issue of smoking risk marginal. They may also decide, however, that no work is worth a child's health and that it is best to delay access to overly nicotine-laced films beyond the teenage years (critical for smoking initiation). In writing this, I do not feel that I am expressing a particularly retrograde or fundamentalist position!

Beyond what has just been said, the causal process that leads from film to smoking has yet to be questioned. According to several studies, the transition occurs mainly on the basis of a representational modification. In other words, the film leads adolescents to smoke by modifying their model of reality. In support of this thesis, it appears that the more smoking references a young viewer is exposed to, the more likely they are, first, to think that most adults smoke and, second, to develop positive expectations of smoking.[790,791,796] The development of positive expectations of smoking is, to a large extent, the result of the film's role in the development of the smoking behaviour of adolescents.[790,791,796] To a large extent, the development of these expectations seems to rely on the prescriptive role of "stars" who can define by their very aura what can be considered cool, sexy, hip, transgressive, or adult.[790,791,796] To illustrate, consider two non-smoking teenagers, one of whom likes Tom Cruise while the other is attracted to Leonardo DiCaprio. A seemingly benign difference, but nevertheless fundamental in terms of smoking. Indeed, DiCaprio is frequently presented smoking one in his films, which is not the case for Cruise. As a result, after controlling for relevant covariates, our DiCaprio fan is 16 times more likely than his Cruise fan counterpart to have a positive attitude toward smoking and to report being likely to smoke in the future[826]! This statement of susceptibility is a major predictor of actual smoking.

However, we should not believe that only children and teenagers are subject to the deleterious influence of tobacco images. It is true that the risk of seeing an adult of 25-30 years of age convert to the joys of smoking because he or she regularly sees his or her favorite actors smoking on the screen is practically nil. However, the probability of observing a resurgence of smoking in a confirmed, occasional or abstinent smoker after exposure to smoking stimuli is not negligible. Several studies have shown that the simple fact of seeing someone else smoke a cigarette on the screen creates a real impulse to smoke[828,829]. This is manifested on two levels. One is physiological, as has been established by measurements of body heat and electrodermal response markers830[a] . The other is behavioral. On this second point, a recent research study has provided results that are, to say the least, edifying[831]. Young adults (18-25 years old), smokers, were subjected to the viewing of a piece of a well-known film (e.g. *Bridget Jones' Diary*). The film was 8 minutes long and may or may not have included smoking scenes. After the session, each subject was instructed to wait 10 minutes outside the experimental room. No other cues were offered, and participants were of course unaware that they would be monitored during this break. Subjects who wished to smoke had to go out into the street. The day after the experiment, the participants were contacted by telephone. The results showed that, after controlling for a wide range of socio-demographic, psychological and personal covariates, the probability of seeing an individual go out for a cigarette during the break was more than tripled in the group that had seen the "smoking" clips. The probability of our guinea pig smoking a cigarette within 30 minutes of the end of the study was almost quadrupled. In other words, seeing people smoking on screen creates a kind of empathic need in viewers who smoke and are therefore much more likely to take a cigarette out of their pack during or after the exposure phase. Consistent with this conclusion, a recent study using a sample of nearly 200,000 individuals aged 15-49 years found that going to the movies at least once a month substantially increased the odds that an average person would be an active smoker, after controlling for

---

a. The electrodermal response determines the variations in the electrical resistance of the skin and informs the experimenter about the existence of possibly unconscious emotional disturbances. For example, subjects with brain damage may not explicitly recognize a relative in a photograph, whereas the electrodermal response shows a strong variation, thus indicating an implicit recognition of the face presented.

a large group of potential covariates. In quantitative terms, the increase in risk was 55% for women and 17% for men. The image incentive that emerges here could obviously play an important role in the process that leads light smokers to gradually increase their consumption and level of nicotine addiction[833].

Recently, a number of studies have shifted from the film field to the television space. This transition seemed natural enough insofar as tobacco is widely represented on television, in the form of films, series and *music videos*.[791] The results showed, after controlling for relevant covariates, that the more a teenager looked at tobacco, the more likely he or she was to be a smoker. The results showed, after controlling for relevant covariates, that the more television an adolescent watched, the more likely he or she was to smoke[834], to smoke heavily[835] and to smoke early[836]. The most comprehensive and impressive epidemiological study was conducted by Hancox and colleagues[196]. On the basis of long-term longitudinal work, they showed that 17% of smokers at age 26 had become smokers because of excessive television viewing between the ages of 5 and 15. The threshold of excess was then arbitrarily fixed at 120 minutes per day, which means that by limiting children's audiovisual consumption to 2 hours, parents would have reduced the number of smokers in the adult population by a substantial 17%. It is obviously probable, even if this calculation was not produced by the authors, that a more drastic reduction in access to the small screen would have resulted in even more spectacular effects.

Thus, smoking is a major public health problem. Many studies have shown that this problem originates during childhood and adolescence. Indeed, when an individual reaches adulthood without having smoked, he or she has every chance of never succumbing to the sirens of Lady Cigarette. Of all the factors that can lead a young person to smoke, exposure to smoking images in movies, TV shows and *music* videos is one of the most decisive. This is not a reactionary axiom or an opinion of a citizen, but an observation based on an impressive body of scientific work that has recently been recognized as indisputable by the World Health Organization[758,778] and the U.S. National Cancer Institute[791].

*
**

Drink more and earlier

Like obesity or tobacco, alcohol is a real economic and health scourge.[837-840] In Europe, each year, this substance is responsible for more than 1 in 10 deaths in the male population. This rate is roughly equivalent to that observed in North America. Women are less affected, with a prevalence of "only" 2% in both regions[837]. Clearly, if we reason, not simply in terms of mortality, but with reference to a "global burden of disease", the figures immediately take on a completely different aspect. Without going into too much technical detail, we can say that this burden of disease defines the number of years of healthy life lost due to a disease. The loss may be due to death or physical disability. International scientific publications and reports generally use the acronym DALY (Disability-Adjusted Life Year[841]) to describe these lost years. Large epidemiological studies have made it possible to evaluate the number of DALYs associated with each major disease family (stroke, AIDS, cancer, etc.) [841] It then appeared, on a European scale, for the male population, that diseases directly attributable to alcohol accounted for 17.3% of all DALYs (i.e., 17.3% of the total burden of disease!) North America was somewhat worse off with "only" 14.2%. Women, again, fared substantially better than their male counterparts with prevalences between 3% and 5%.[837]

In practice, the morbid effects of alcohol have a dual chronic and acute origin. At the chronic level, there are pathologies induced by long-term consumption, such as cirrhosis of the liver, cardiovascular diseases and a large number of cancers[837,838,842,843]. Acutely, there is damage from short-term ingestion that is known to significantly increase the risk of injury, motor vehicle accidents, suicidal behaviour, interpersonal violence, unsafe sexual behaviour and drowning[837,843-847]. These acute assaults are clearly the most easily spotted in the "News" sections of the mainstream news media, as a few recent headlines show: "Burned with gasoline by her drunken husband"[848], "Drunk, he kicks his pregnant wife"[849], "A baby in a coma after being hit by his drunken nurse"[850], "A drunken woman kills her infant by falling asleep on him"[851], "A 13-month-old baby in his stroller killed by a drunk driver"[852], "Two policemen killed by a drunk driver in Isère"[853], "Accident on the RN 9 that left five people dead: the driver was drunk"[854], "After celebrating his baccalaureate, a young man dies of an ethylic coma"[855], "Drinking: a teenager dies after a month in a coma"[856], "A teenager almost dies with 3.1 g of alcohol in the blood"[857], "The drunk teenager falls into the Loire [858], "Facebook party in Nantes: the dead man had 2.4 g of alcohol in the blood"[859]. "Alcohol among young people is becoming a national scourge"[860]. Etc.

Of course, many will object, despite the above, that one should be careful not to cast any aspersions because, when it comes to drinking, it is all a question of quantity. In support of this claim, several scientific studies have suggested that moderate alcohol consumption may have beneficial effects on morbid risk[843,861-863] through, in particular, the cardio-protective role of ethanol[861,864,865]. Although this result is still hotly debated[866,867], the *most* recent evidence seems to support the validity of the hypothesis[868]. However, this good news reaches its limit when the whole field of health is taken into account. Indeed, alcohol consumption which is supposed to be beneficial for the cardiovascular system turns out to be disastrous in terms of accidents[845,869,870] , cirrhosis of the liver[869] and cancers[842,869]. This variability in impact naturally makes it perilous to establish recommendations for use. A strictly safety-oriented approach might emphasize that the risks unquestionably outweigh the benefits, so that there is, as a WHO report recently stated, "no risk-free limit when it comes to drinking alcohol. On the other hand, an epidemiological position would be entitled to suggest that total abstinence is useless in the sense that it is not incongruous to consider acceptable a risk of very low magnitude. One could then admit, for example, that a 1% increase over a lifetime in the probability of dying from an alcohol-related accident or disease is quantitatively tolerable. In this case, the recommended consumption threshold would be set at around 20 grams of pure alcohol per day[845,869] or 2 x 10 cl bottles of red wine at 13.5º or 1.5 cans of 33 cl beer at 5º. This position is broadly consistent with most OECD countries, although they generally propose slightly lower limits for women (~20 g/day, or 2 so-called "standard" drinks) than for men (~30 g/day, or 3 "standard" drinks)[872,873]. However, this gender distinction seems highly debatable in the light of the most recent data[845,869]. However, it has the advantage, particularly in France, of not placing the average daily consumption per capita (~ 28 g)[874] too far from the maximum recommended consumption. In France, however, as the conclusions of a report by the Institut national de prévention et d'éducation pour la santé (INPES) point out, "53.5% of men and 21.2% of women have risky drinking habits, i.e., they drink more than the recommended amounts (21 standard glasses per week for men, 14 for women) and risk endangering their health in the medium or long term"[875].

It is probably worth noting at this point that the relatively consensual threshold of 20 grams of pure alcohol per day applies only to adults. It formally excludes the adolescent population. For the latter, in fact, specialists consider, almost unanimously, that the only safe consumption is zero[872,876,877]. The legislator has taken this into account by setting, in most countries of the world, a minimum age below which it is strictly forbidden to buy alcohol in retail stores or drinking establishments[878]. This age is, for example, 18 in France and 21 in the United States. From a strictly health perspective, this prohibition seems reasonable and sensible, to say the least. Indeed, adolescence seems to be more conducive to excess than to temperance. A joint report by the National Research Council and the American Institute of Medicine points out that "many adults assume that the potential risks and consequences of early drinking are more or less the same as in adults, but research suggests that the dangers of drinking in youth are magnified. For many, this magnification is paid for in cash at the Grim Reaper! For others, the journey takes them through the "wheelchair" box, the "prison" corridor, the "HIV" corridor or the "early pregnancy" section. These vicissitudes are hardly surprising for those who consider the main disorders induced in adolescents and young adults by episodes of binge drinking: road accidents, suicides, homicides, rapes, bodily injuries, violence, vandalism and risky sexual behaviour. Obviously, when the drinking process moves from occasional to chronic, other problems arise. These are psychological (anxiety, lowered self-esteem, aggression, behavioural problems), social (isolation), academic (school failure) and organic[872,877]. This last point is not the least alarming insofar as it refers to irreversible alterations in brain development which, contrary to what was believed for a long time, is very far from being completed by adolescence[880,881]. As if all this were not enough, it also turns out that early use strongly favours the emergence of late dependence[872,877,880]. Thus, for example, an adolescent who starts drinking before the age of 15 is, in the clinical sense of the term, 4 times more likely to become an alcoholic in adulthood than an individual whose consumption starts after the age of 20[882]. This trend is obviously all the more worrying as alcohol impregnation of the youngest age groups has reached an alarming level in many countries[872,879,883]. In France, for example, a recent European study of 15-16 year olds showed that in the 30 days prior to data collection, 64% of respondents had been drinking, 43% had drunk at a level considered dangerous (> 5 drinks) and 18% had drunk to the point of total drunkenness[879]. This state of drunkenness, 46% had in fact experienced it at least once in their lives. In 9% of cases, this experience had been consumed before the age of 14! In terms of consequences, the study clearly confirmed that alcohol had been the cause of many difficulties, including: accidents or injuries (14%), relationship conflicts with parents (12%) or friends (12%), school difficulties (10%), unprotected sex (7%) or sex they later regretted (7%), fights (12%) and trouble with the police (7%). This is a sobering set of figures, even if they do not (yet?) reach the heights recorded in other countries such as Germany, Austria or the UK. In the latter nation, for example, during the 30 days preceding their consultation, 70% of adolescents had been drinking, 54% had drunk to a level considered dangerous and 33% had drunk to the point of being totally drunk. Twenty-four percent of English youth had experienced this state of drunkenness before the age of 14. This is a far cry from marginal exposure.

Despite the magnitude of these figures, many countries apply much looser regulatory measures for alcohol than for tobacco. For example, in the European Union, while the promotion of tobacco is absolutely prohibited, alcohol advertising is simply subject to a series of restrictive criteria. These are 5[784] : "(a) not be specifically directed to minors and, in particular, depict minors consuming such beverages; (b) not associate the consumption of alcohol with improved physical performance or driving; (c) not create the impression that the consumption of alcohol promotes social or sexual success ; (d) not suggest that alcoholic beverages have therapeutic properties or have a stimulating, sedative, or anti-conflict effect; (e) not encourage binge drinking or portray abstinence or sobriety in a negative light; and (f) not emphasize as a positive quality of beverages their high alcohol content. " The same type of framework exists in the United States, but on a "voluntary" basis. In that country, the wine,[884] beer[885] and spirits[886] industries have collectively committed themselves to responsible advertising. Among the many measures set out, the most emblematic is undoubtedly the absence of any promotional campaign in media whose audience is composed of more than 30% of individuals aged 21 and under.[883] A measure of apparent moderation is that the advertising of alcoholic beverages is not permitted. A measure of apparent moderation which, however, is not without significant shortcomings. Indeed, 30% of a large audience can easily represent several million individuals. Consider, for example, the final of the American soccer championship (the famous Super Bowl). Typically, this competition brings together a hundred million viewers in front of the television[887], 25 to 30 million of whom are under the legal age to buy alcohol[888,889]. This is a real boon for the alcohol companies, which are jostling for attention and are among the biggest advertisers at the event[890,891]. Although our friends do not claim to be targeting a young audience, their screens are regularly at the top of the list of the most popular advertisements among teenagers[892-894]. This finding is reminiscent of earlier findings in the United States that 9-11 year olds identified the Budweiser frog almost as frequently as Bugs Bunny, while 8-12 year olds were more likely to name brands of beer than former presidents.[3] This is a rather sobering thought and seems to argue for the ineffectiveness of half measures in alcohol advertising. In line with this idea, some nations of the Old Continent have decided to go beyond the directives of the European Commission and adopt drastic prohibitions[895]. In France, for example, legislation prohibits all television advertising for beverages containing more than 1.2 degrees of alcohol[896]. This position is in line with the recommendations of most learned societies established in countries with partial regulation, such as England or the United States. These include the British Medical Association[897], the American Medical Association[898] and the American Academy of Pediatrics[87]. Recently, even the cautious WHO has decided to add its stone to the edifice by calling for strict regulation of alcohol marketing. According to this organization, "it is very difficult to target marketing to young adult consumers without exposing cohorts of adolescents under the legal minimum age to the same marketing strategies. Exposure of children and youth to appealing marketing is of particular concern, as is the targeting of new markets in developing and low- and middle-income countries where alcohol consumption is still low or abstinence rates are high. Both the content of commercial messages and the degree of exposure of young people to those messages are critical. The precautionary principle must be used to protect young people from these marketing techniques. 759 This recommendation obviously has a strong experimental basis. Indeed, the most recent scientific literature shows unambiguously that advertising, particularly in the audiovisual field, has a strong positive influence on the initiation and reinforcement of early drinking behaviour[641,755,897,899]. This conclusion is most clearly supported by some 15 longitudinal studies which have followed the fate of large groups of adolescents over several months or even years. Peter Anderson and his colleagues have recently summarized almost all of this research[900]. Their conclusion is clear: "Longitudinal studies consistently suggest that exposure to media and commercial communications about alcohol is associated with the likelihood that adolescents will initiate drinking and will increase their consumption if they are already drinkers." As an illustration of this general finding, consider, for example, work conducted by Rebecca Collins and colleagues[901]. These researchers followed 1,786 students during their 6th and 5th grade years. The results showed, after controlling for a large matrix of sociodemographic, psychological and personal covariates, that the quarter of individuals who had seen the most television ads for alcoholic products in the sixth grade were 27% more likely to have started drinking in the seventh grade, compared to the quarter of subjects with the least exposure. In another similar study, 2,250 seventh-graders were followed for one year.[902] The results of this study were similar to those of the other studies. Compared with the average for the study population, the 15% of subjects who had ingested the most commercial screens at age 12 had a 44% greater risk of having drunk beer and a 34% greater risk of having drunk wine at one year. Conversely, the 15% of students with the least exposure had these same risk factors at -30% and -25% respectively. These values were of course obtained after taking into account a large list of potential covariates.

Thus, taken together, the above evidence confirms that a strict ban on all audiovisual advertising of alcoholic beverages partially curbs the onset of drinking behavior among the youth population. Such a result is obviously encouraging. However, we must be careful not to exaggerate its significance. Alcohol does not need formal commercial screens to spread its message and influence the behavior of young viewers. All the content studies show that the collusion between Lady TV and Mr. Ethanol goes far beyond the framework of formal promotional communications. Alcohol is omnipresent on the small screen through prime time programs, *music* videos and film productions[755,877]. In the latter area, for example, it has been found that 80-90% of films at the U.S. and German box offices feature drinking scenes.[903-908] This range is even wider when one considers the number of films that feature drinking. This range is all the more alarming because Hollywood and its affiliates tend to portray alcohol use in a largely positive light[755,877,909]. Thus, when a character does imbibe, it is most often done in festive contexts and with impunity, i.e., without reference to the deleterious health influences of alcohol. This is hardly surprising if we consider that drinkers are often socially accomplished and humanly privileged individuals.

Obviously, the omnipresence, within the cinematographic field, of complacent alcoholic messages, is not without incidence on adolescent and infantile consumption. It is now clearly established that the more a young spectator sees actors playing with the bottle, the more likely he is to drink at an early age, in large quantities[904,905,907,908]. For example, a recent study measured the film exposure and drinking patterns of more than 5,500 students aged, on average, 13 years[904]. 904 After controlling for a wide range of potential covariates (age, gender, academic achievement, smoking status, propensity for rebellious behavior, parental and family alcohol use, etc.), the results showed that there was no significant difference between the two.), the results showed that the 25% of individuals who had seen the most alcoholic scenes on the screen were, compared to the 25% of individuals with the least exposure, 3 times more likely to have already drunk without their parents' knowledge and 2.6 times more likely to have been exposed to dangerous drinking (*binge-drinking*, = 5 drinks). Interestingly, the scientific team behind this research decided to continue their work by re-interviewing 2,700 students who had never drunk alcohol at the time of the initial assessment[905] after 1 to 2 years. After taking into account the covariates mentioned above, the results showed that the 25% of individuals who had seen the most alcohol at 13 years of age were twice as likely as the 25% of individuals with the least exposure to alcohol at 14 years of age to have drunk without their parents' knowledge, and 2.2 times as likely to have been exposed to hazardous drinking. For those who would not be struck by these values, a formulation of the results in terms of percentages of consumption should be more telling. To make this point, let us first consider those individuals who had seen the least amount of alcohol at age 13. It appears that 17% of them started drinking during the follow-up period. Next, let's ask what would have happened if the individuals in this low-exposure group had been subjected to the film diet of the most heavily hit youth. The answer is quite simple. 34% of the subjects would have tasted the pleasures of ethanol during the follow-up period, instead of 17%. If we reproduce the same reasoning for the area of dangerous consumption, we obtain percentages of 6% and 13%. These differences are clearly far from ridiculous.

In light of the preceding data, it seems legitimate to ask, as we have already done for tobacco, about the protective potential of possible prohibitive measures. To facilitate the understanding of this point, it should be recalled that in the United States there is a category of films known as

R-Rated, which individuals aged 17 and under can only see in the cinema in the company of an adult. It has been shown that teenagers with strict parental control have marginal exposure to these types of films. 815 It has also been found that these films contain more references to alcoholic beverages than general audience films. 906 Based on these observations, researchers investigated whether alcohol consumption was lower than average among youth who were prevented from viewing restricted films. The results were unanimously positive.[815-817,819] A recent longitudinal study by James Sargent's team is particularly impressive. These authors subjected nearly 3,600 never-drinking adolescents aged 10-14 years to a thorough sociological questionnaire. On the basis of this questionnaire, 4 cohorts were formed according to the level of parental control: (i) total prohibition of access to *R-Rated* films (20% of the sample); (ii) occasional confrontation tolerated (31% of the sample); (iii) viewing often allowed (28% of the sample); (iv) absolute permissiveness (21% of the sample). After a variable period of time ranging from 13 to 26 months, the members of these 4 cohorts were recontacted and submitted to a new questionnaire. The results showed that, after taking into account a wide range of sociodemographic, psychological and personal covariates (age, gender, socioeconomic status, propensity to rebellious behavior, school performance, self-esteem, parental and family alcohol use, etc.) that individuals who had "occasional", "frequent" or "free" access to *R-Rated* movies at age 13 were 3, 3.3 and 3.5 times more likely to have consumed alcohol during the follow-up period, respectively, than subjects who had been strictly prohibited. In compiling these data, however, Sargent and colleagues found that parental attitudes were not always stable over time. Indeed, between the initial questionnaire and the final evaluation, many adolescents had seen their usage instructions change substantially. When this parameter was added to the statistical model, the amplitude of the effects observed increased considerably. This point is easily understood when we focus on the experimental cohorts that were subjected to an unchanging parental instruction throughout the study. At the end of the second evaluation, individuals who had experienced "occasional", "frequent" or "free" access to *R-Rated* movies had 5.1, 5.6 and 7.3 times greater risks of alcohol consumption than strictly controlled subjects (these figures obviously take into account the influence of the socio-demographic, psychological and personal covariates mentioned above). Further analyses showed that the probability of an adolescent engaging in alcoholic behavior varied predictably when parents revised their position between the two survey periods. A relaxation of access conditions resulted in an increase in threat, whereas a tightening of access conditions resulted in a decrease in peril. This demonstration is essential because it irrefutably establishes the causal nature of the associations observed between cinematographic exposure and initiation of juvenile alcohol consumption. Recently, the protective character of prohibitive parental behaviours on adolescent alcohol use was generalized, by a German study, to the so-called "excessive use" behaviours[819]. In order to understand the logic of this study, it is important to know that our friends in Germany have introduced a system known as FSK-16 to designate productions that are forbidden in cinemas to children under the age of 16. After adjustment for a large set of socio-demographic, psychological and personal covariates, teenagers aged 10 to 15 years who had never consumed alcohol and who had complete freedom of access to FSK-16 works were almost 3 times more likely to engage in *binge-drinking* within 1 year than subjects of similar age who had been subjected to a strict prohibition. However, this effect may be underestimated because the instability of parental instructions could not be taken into account by the authors of this study.

At the end of the evidence so far stated, one could have hoped, carried by some optimism, that the alcoholic screens would limit their deleterious influence to the only future drinkers. Unfortunately, this is not the case. In fact, just like what happens with food or tobacco, it is now established that the simple fact of seeing a bottle of alcohol or an individual in the process of drinking triggers a strong desire to consume among confirmed users. This point was definitively demonstrated in 2009 by a Dutch research team.[910] Eighty young adults (18-29 years old) were invited to watch a 1-hour film. The film was interspersed with 2 commercials, each lasting 3.5 minutes. During the screening, the subjects were comfortably seated in a friendly room, facing a large flat screen. They underwent the experiment in pairs and had at their disposal drinks (wine, beer, soft drinks) as well as some snacks (chips, peanuts, etc.). 4 experimental conditions were explored. *Film/Advertising*: numerous alcoholic scenes in the film (*American Pie 2*) and advertisements for alcoholic beverages (2 spots randomly inserted during the 3.5-minute cut; it should be noted that in Holland, advertisements for alcohol are allowed in the cinema and on national television channels) *Film/NoPub*: many alcoholic scenes in the film and no advertisements for alcoholic drinks. *NoFilm/Pub*: few alcoholic scenes in the film (40 days 40 nights) and advertisements for alcoholic beverages. NoFilm/NoPub: Few alcoholic scenes in the film and no advertisements for alcoholic beverages. The results showed that the subjects subjected to the greatest number of alcoholic stimuli (Film/Pub) consumed twice as much alcohol during the hour of screening as the least exposed subjects (NoFilm/NoPub), i.e. the equivalent of 600 ml of beer (3 glasses) compared to only 300 ml (1.5 glasses). The intermediate exposure conditions (NoFilm/Pub and Film/NoPub) revealed median usage (around 2 glasses). It is therefore clear from these data that exposure to alcoholic scenes promotes drinking behavior among viewers. Whether the incitement comes from a film passage or a formal advertising screen does not change anything. This result is all the more worrying as this kind of phenomenon could play a self-reinforcing role that could lead, due to well-known habituation processes, to a progressive increase in consumption volumes.

To date, only a small number of studies have attempted to extend the results obtained in the film industry to the general field of television. These studies show unanimously that the more time a teenager spends watching television, the more likely he or she is, first, to start drinking at an early age and, second, to consume significant amounts of alcohol. For example, in a frequently cited study, 1,533 ninth graders (14 years of age) were followed for 18 months.[911] The results of this study showed that, after taking into account the results of the study, it was possible to determine whether or not they were drinking. It was found, after controlling for a wide range of socio-demographic, psychological and personal covariates, that each hour of television watched at age 14 increased the likelihood of a student drinking before age 16 by almost 10%. This percentage increased to more than 30% in subjects who concentrated their viewing time on *music* programs. The risk of acting out was particularly high when going out outside the family (bars, restaurants, discotheques, parties, etc.)[912]. They were also reinforced when the adolescent had a television in his room. To establish this last point, nearly 2,700 students aged on average 13 years and who had never drunk alcohol were followed for more than a year[905]. The results showed that, after controlling for a wide range of potential covariates, subjects with a television in their bedroom were 10% more likely to have started drinking, without their parents' knowledge, during the follow-up period. The risk of exposure to hazardous drinking was increased by 60%. In essence, these data are not surprising when one considers that subjects who have a television in

---

their room tend to spend substantially more time in front of the set and to have easier access to restricted content than their counterparts who do not have a television in their room.[435]

In summary, alcohol is a major public health problem. Every year, this substance causes millions of deaths and functional disabilities worldwide. While adults pay a heavy price for chronic diseases (cirrhosis, cancer, etc.), young people are hit more acutely (accidents, interpersonal violence, etc.). This overall difference does not mean, however, that juvenile alcohol use is without long-term effects. The earlier a person starts drinking, the more likely he or she is to become a heavy drinker as an adult. To make matters worse, during adolescence, ethanol intake significantly affects brain maturation and academic achievement. Of course, the consumption of alcohol, whether as a youth or as an adult, cannot be entirely attributed to television. However, this medium cannot be exempted from its responsibility. It contributes substantially to the initiation, development and maintenance of alcoholic behavior among viewers. Films, commercials, *music* videos, prime time programs, the inciting factors concern all genres and infect even the most innocent cartoons[913]. This omnipresence makes any targeted control totally utopian. Therefore, once again, the ultimate parental choice comes down to a simple dichotomy: take the risk of exposing children to a clearly identified health risk or turn off the set.

*
**

Sex, sex, sex and more sex

Obviously, there is no way to suggest here that sexuality is a pathology. That would be foolish. However, it should be emphasized that sex is not, far from it, a harmless practice in terms of health. Every year in France, to take just one example, tens of thousands of abortions and infectious sexual contaminations are observed[875,914,915]. Even if adolescents are not systematically the most affected by these scourges, they are still largely affected[916,917]. The latest available data on voluntary termination of pregnancy (abortion) illustrate this point perfectly, I believe. In 2007, nearly 13,500 minors under the age of 18 and 1% of girls between 15 and 17 had an abortion.[915] A similar percentage is found in the United States.

The same percentage is true for the United States, which in absolute terms represents nearly 80,000 procedures per year.[918] Of course, even though early pregnancies are almost systematically unwanted,[919] a substantial proportion of girls still forgo the abortion option and choose the path to motherhood. In France, in 2007, just over 4,200 adolescents aged 17 and under delivered a baby.[920] In the United States, the figure was 140,000. In the United States, the figure reached 140,000[918]. In relation to these data, it has been suggested that childbirth is psychologically easier than abortion for adolescent girls. 921 However, this position has been heavily criticized on what I believe to be eminently valid grounds.[922] In fact, it may well be that childbirth is more psychologically acceptable than abortion. In fact, the debate may well lack a satisfactory solution. On the one hand, it does appear that abortion significantly increases the risk of long-term psychological suffering in adolescents (depression, anxiety, suicidal behaviour, etc.)[921,923-925]. On the other hand, however, early motherhood has also been shown to be a significant risk factor for the outcomes of mothers and their children.[926] Perhaps the only viable solution to the problem would be to prevent the tens of thousands of unwanted teenage pregnancies that occur each year in France, the United States, and all developed nations. With respect to this objective, a reduction in the audiovisual exposure of the youngest children could prove to be highly effective. Indeed, television contributes directly to the propagation of harmful sexual beliefs and stereotypes within the youth population. The first symptom of this reality is the appalling ignorance displayed by adolescents about sexuality, contraception and venereal infections. For nearly 10 years, this has been repeatedly demonstrated in a large number of developed countries.[927-931] In France, for example, an exhaustive report on the state of sexual health in the United States was published. In France, in particular, a comprehensive report was published on the subject only a few months ago by the General Inspectorate of Social Affairs (IGAS)[932]. According to this organization, adults and adolescents are full of misconceptions, some of which are terribly dangerous. For example, 10 percent of 15- to 20-year-olds believe that oral contraceptives protect against sexually transmitted infections, including AIDS. Similarly, more than 60 percent of adults say that it is possible to have unprotected sex at certain times during the menstrual cycle without risk of pregnancy. This is how Sophiane was born in 2008. The mother of this charming young lady thought that a woman was only fertile around the fourteenth day after the beginning of her period. Missed! When she arrived, the proof of failure was 49 centimeters for 3.2 kilos.

At first glance, as the IGAS points out, this kind of wandering seems totally "paradoxical in a society where sexuality is omnipresent and where everyone claims to know everything about it from a very young age. However, the paradox quickly fades when one compares the large volume of pernicious information spaces with the low prevalence of sincere documentary sources. According to the IGAS, the imbalance is in fact so deep "that it is less a question [for the competent social bodies] of remedying an absence of information than of structuring and making reliable an overabundance of information, and of counterbalancing certain sources of misinformation: false ideas conveyed by peers and propagated in discussion forums, biased messages sent by the pornographic industry". To achieve mass education, two main recommendations are put forward. The first "emphasizes the need for comprehensive and continuous communication on sexual and reproductive health. The second one exhorts to respect the official texts related to sexual education in schools. Two paragons of truisms and, in the end, not a word about television and the media. This omission is all the more despairing because one would have to be totally naive to believe for a moment that a few prevention spots here and there and three statutory annual sex education sessions are likely to counterbalance the effect of the hundreds of hours of audiovisual programs that teenagers consume every year. In fact, two points seem to support this assertion. First, over the past 10 years, France, like most developed countries, has seen an impressive number of communication campaigns on contraception and sexuality.[932,934] Second, whether in France or in the United States, adolescents spontaneously identify schools and health personnel as important sources of information[929,935]. How can we not conclude, therefore, that the messages delivered by the school system and institutional campaigns are only very partially assimilated by young people and prove to be derisively effective in practice? This is an annoying observation, but one that does not seem to disturb our leaders, including the inimitable Roselyne Bachelot, Minister of Health and Sports, who recently declared: "Two-thirds of girls in the ninth grade still think that it is impossible to get pregnant the first time they have sex [...] With Luc Chatel, Minister of Education, we are going to put the emphasis on information in schools.[936] When a strategy fails, insist, the famous psychologist Paul Watzlawick told us in his time. Insist and "do more of the same". You will then have found the "ultrasolution" to "succeed at failing.

That said, it turns out that the main people concerned do not seem to be bothered by their own ignorance and the potential influence that the television screen could have on their practices. In fact, the overwhelming majority of our teenage friends consider themselves to be very well informed about sex and contraception. In fact, nearly 80% of these young people believe that television does not affect their own reproductive behaviour. However, this perception changes radically when the question is asked about the "I" and "You". In this case, 72% of 15-17 year-olds denounce the inciting action of television. This last position is, incidentally, quite similar to that of the parents. In fact, they repeatedly place inappropriate sexual content at the top of their list of media concerns[237,238]. More than 8 out of 10 adults think that television[237] and, more generally, the electronic media[238] push young people at an early age towards what the priest of my childhood used to call "the work of the flesh". As we shall see, most specialists and medical societies share this viewpoint[3,115,938-940]. However, there are a few dissonant positions outside the scientific field. Among these, some are of a consummate grotesqueness, as shown, for example, by this remark by Serge Tisseron, who wonders whether "the excessive way in which pornographic images are currently accused of disturbing young people might not be a way, for many adults, of trying to hide from themselves the terrible observation, made a few years ago, of the role played by families in sexual abuse"[34]. My arms fall off. Alexandre Lacroix's comment is, fortunately, more solid. According to this philosopher, "among all the intellectuals who criticize television today by deploring, in a serious tone of censor, its lust and its violence, I know more than one who formerly did not shine, in these domains precisely, by abstinence [...] One cannot make morals only when it suits us or when it serves our cause opportunely"[160]. The argument is not without merit and is certainly worth examining. However, the problem of sexuality on television goes far beyond the strict framework of morality. It also concerns, to a significant extent, as I propose to illustrate below, the health field.

To understand the influence of television on our sexual behavior, a first step is to question precisely the nature of the programs that animate our screens. In this field, the least we can say, in the light of a recent report published by Médiamétrie and IMCA (International Medias Consultants Associés), is that things come down to a relatively simple credo: "Sex,

sex and more sex"[941]! Yes, the small screen likes to titillate our libido and flatter our genesic papillae. Advertising, films, reality shows, entertainment, series, no field escapes the deluge[3,22,26,822,938,942-944]. The latest exhaustive study, carried out in the United States in 2005 under the aegis of the Kaiser Foundation, is edifying in this respect.[945] 70% of "all public" programs contain sexual references, with an average of 5 incidents per hour. For prime time broadcasts alone, these values reach 77% penetration (if you will forgive me for using this word in this instance) and 6 incidents per hour. Strikingly, health prevention messages related to the use of contraceptive methods and/or the possible negative consequences of unprotected sex only appear in an extreme minority of scenes with sexual content (4%). One might have hoped, of course, that these trends would be mitigated in programs with large youth audiences. This is not the case. The general figures reported above are perfectly representative of those assembled when only the favorite programs of adolescents are considered (70% penetration, 7 incidences per hour, 5% health messages). These include *American* Idol, *Desperate Housewives, Survivor, CSI, Lost, America's Next Top Model, The Simpsons, Without a Trace, 7th Heaven, Family Guy, The O.C., The Quintuplets,* and *Extreme Makeover: Home Edition.* A set of programs largely familiar to European and French broadcasters, which clearly suggests that the trends observed by the Kaiser Foundation in the United States must not be very far from those expressed on the Old Continent.

The carnal deluge that hits our screens is all the more annoying because it is almost universally accompanied by unrealistic representations of sexuality and other gender roles.[3,942,943,945947.] On television, the sexual act is a generalized norm, casually practiced, and shared almost half the time by individuals with no established relationship. Women are frequently represented as objects of desire or satisfaction. They are often portrayed as passive creatures, possibly intended to fill the airwaves in a purely decorative manner, like the famous Victoria Silvstedt in the program *Wheel of Fortune.* Almost systematically younger than their male partners, actresses often occupy in films or series strongly typified occupations (secretaries, nurses, domestic workers, housewives). Men, on the contrary, are represented in dominant, almost predatory postures. For them, the relationship to sex frequently defines the level of masculinity. From all of this, says Victor Strasburger in an excellent review of the literature, the viewer can draw several messages such as: "everyone has sex," "adults don't use contraceptives," "adults don't plan their sexual relationships," "married people frequently cheat on each other," "sex is a recreational sport," etc.[942]

Obviously, the omnipresence of sexual references on the small screen is not without consequences for the spectator. By dint of being hammered, audiovisual stereotypes end up irremediably altering the most intimate representations of the latter. The effect is moreover all the more profound that it generally operates without the knowledge of our poor brains. As Liliane Lurçat says, in agreement with the general theory of acculturation developed by Gerbner[72], "learning is done by impregnation: we do not know what we are learning"[25]. In other words, images literally end up, by dint of repetition, inscribing their truth at the heart of our unconscious. It is then very difficult to dislodge them. Try for example, if you doubt it, to convince a young anorexic girl that she is not fat and you will see to what extent reality has sometimes little hold on our intimate perceptions. A work already evoked shows all the relevance of this subject for the field of the sexual roles. Remember. Three sociologically comparable cities were studied[948]. Two received television (UniTel, MultiTel). The third had to be connected within 24 months (NoTel). The representations of two groups of 11- and 14-year-old schoolchildren were studied. It was shown that the NoTel subjects had, in the initial phase, a less stereotyped and more egalitarian perception of gender roles than their counterparts in the connected cities. Not surprisingly, the difference did not survive the introduction of NoTel.

Since the NoTel experiment, the effect of the small screen on sexual representations and gender stereotypes has been widely confirmed[3,641,942,944,949-954]. In the course of the experiments, it was shown, among other things, that the more television an adolescent watched, the more likely he or she was to: first, overestimate the prevalence of sexual relations among his or her peers; second, have unrealistic expectations regarding coitus; third, have a permissive view of sexuality; and fourth, feel significant pressure to act out. All of these elements can easily be found in the heart of the behavioral space. Indeed, it is now clearly established that the more time a young person spends in front of the television, the more likely he or she is to lose his or her virginity at an early age. A first indication of this association can be found in the comparative temporal evolution of audiovisual and sexual behaviors of the French. Among the latter, the age of first intercourse remained stable throughout the 1980s and 1990s. With the advent of the third millennium, things changed abruptly, and a significant drop was observed, first among men and then among women.[955] This decrease in the age of first intercourse is striking. Strikingly, this downward trend occurred at the same time as reality TV was being introduced[28] and the number of programs with sexual content was exploding.[945] Although there is no evidence of a sexual dimension to this decline, it is clear that it is not the case. Although this concomitance has no demonstrative dimension, it does not seem fortuitous. Indeed, it is significantly echoed in virtually every academic study to date that has examined the influence of television on the age of sexual debut.[3,641,942] As is often the case, the most convincing evidence of the influence of television on the age of sexual debut is that it has been shown to have a significant impact on the age of sexual debut. As is often the case, the most compelling evidence comes from longitudinal research[956-959]. One frequently cited study followed nearly 1800 adolescents aged 12 to 17 years for 1 year[959]. After taking into account a large matrix of sociodemographic, psychological and personal covariates, it was shown that the 10% of individuals who had seen the most sexual content on television were twice as likely to have experienced their first coitus during the follow-up period, compared with the 10% least exposed. When expressed differently, these data indicate that the small screen advanced the age of sexual initiation by 2 to 3 years. Indeed, the percentage of individuals who had bitten the apple was the same (~9%) among the most telephoned 12-year-olds and the least exposed 14-15-year-olds. Similar results were reported in a later study involving more than 4,800 16-year-olds[958]. Focusing on children whose parents discouraged them from having sex too early and after controlling for a large number of sociodemographic, psychological and personal covariates, this work showed that audiovisual consumption of more than 2 hours per day led to a 72% increase in the risk of coitus during the follow-up period. However, early sexual activity has serious health consequences. In particular, it is now clearly established that anticipation of first intercourse substantially increases the probability of pregnancy, contraceptive deficiencies, multiple relationships and infectious contamination[960-966]. For the latter, the risk factors are not only behavioral, but also biological in that puberty increases susceptibility to certain sexually transmitted diseases.[967,968]

Thus, to the slogan "Watching TV kills" which I had previously suggested (by sad irony) would have a place at the bottom of our screens, we could probably add other warnings such as: "Too many *music* videos expose you to AIDS" or "Watching TV can cause early pregnancy in your children". Before the whole of the "bobo" right-wing movement goes into action to denounce the horror of these abject sentences, it might be interesting to consider that each of them has recently been validated by rigorous scientific research[969,970]. Thus, for example, for the problem of pregnancy, Anita Chandra and her colleagues followed nearly 1,500 adolescent girls aged 12 to 17 for 3 years[969]. After taking into account a wide range of sociodemographic, psychological and personal covariates (age, sex, family structure, parents' education, school performance, long-term academic goals, desire to have children, desire to have children before 17, 18, 21 or 22 years of age, delinquent behaviour, etc.), the results showed that the problem of childbearing was more serious than that of pregnancy.), the results showed that the 10% of girls who had seen the most sexual content on television were 2-3 times more likely to have become pregnant during the follow-up period than the 10% with the least exposure. Formulated differently, these data indicate that the small screen advanced the age of pregnancy by almost 4 years. Indeed, the probability of becoming pregnant was the same (~12%) among the most telephoned 16-year-olds and the least exposed 20-year-olds. Again, this is a far cry from a marginal effect.

Obviously, in sexual matters, the deleterious role of television is not limited to the sanitary questions which have just been mentioned. Beyond the problems of coital precocity, abortion and infectious contaminations, the small screen also deeply disturbs certain psychological foundations of our sexuality, of which the self-esteem and the image of the body. In these fields, even if few studies have strictly targeted the audiovisual field, it has been shown that the media have had an increasing tendency, for the last three or four decades, to portray atypical characters, characterized by excessively threadlike phenotypes for women and abnormally muscular ones for men[3,942,971-976]. This evolution can be easily measured, for example, through the phenomenon of beauty contests, which is dear to televisions all over the world. During the 1950s and 1970s, the winners of the Miss America pageant had a healthily normal body mass index. Thirty years later, we had fallen well below the threshold of undernutrition[977], to a level that the American Psychiatric Association has called anorexia[978]. A similar pattern was observed in the fashion world, to the point that measures were recently taken to ban models from the catwalk who were judged to be dangerously thin (a phenomenon that would affect 30 to 40% of female pretenders)[979].

Obviously, this celebration of extreme thinness is not limited to the graphic domain. It is accompanied by a wide cognitive pounding. Thus, in the audiovisual field, pathologically thin or muscular physiques, totally inaccessible to the overwhelming majority of viewers, are readily associated with stereotypes of normality, success, dominance, intelligence and will. This is in contrast to the image of "fat people" that our screens devalue with gusto and represent in abnormally small numbers as lonely, weak, neglected, lazy, perverse, slanderous, spineless and of course abulic[971,973,974,980] individuals. Not surprisingly, these messages have been found to profoundly affect how viewers judge, on a comparative basis, their own body appearance[971,973,974,981-983]. The more an individual is confronted with media stereotypes, the more likely he or she is to see himself or herself, regardless of any objective reality, as ugly, fat, and unattractive, which, let's face it, is not conducive to the development of a fulfilled sexuality. The clearest demonstration of these representational distortions was provided recently by Grabe and his colleagues in a synthesis (meta-analysis) of data from nearly 80 studies[981] on the female population. According to the conclusions of this work: "Media exposure is linked to women's generalized dissatisfaction with their bodies, to an increase in investment in appearance and to an increase in the acceptance of unhealthy eating behaviors. These effects appear robust: they are present across multiple outcomes and are demonstrated in both experimental and correlational studies." Ultimately, these kinds of distortions promote the emergence of not only psychological distress (depression, low self-esteem, anxiety)[984-987] but also eating pathologies (anorexia, bulimia, purging behaviors, etc.)[97,986,988-994]. Although this last point is not directly related to the issues of sexuality that concern us here, it may be interesting to mention it briefly through a particularly striking study in which the eating behaviors of Fijian adolescents in the province of Nadroga were compared just before and 3 years after the arrival of television[995]. The idea of this work was all the more appealing to the researchers because the Nadroga community, in its original condition, favored "generous" body types, which were synonymous with affluence. The arrival of the post changed profoundly this inclination. By the grace of our brave little window, 74% of young Fijian women suddenly discovered they were too fat. Between the beginning and the end of the experiment, the percentage of teenage girls who went on a diet went from zero to 69%. The number of girls who adopted vomiting as a weight control strategy rose from 0% to 11%. Extensive qualitative interviews confirmed the causal role of television in these changes. These data are reminiscent of my daughter-in-law Charlotte's reaction to a low-calorie diet at the age of 7, at a height of 126 centimeters and a weight of 19 kilograms (!), after watching a youth program on television[996]. A worrying behaviour, to say the least, which unfortunately does not seem to be isolated if we are to believe an article recently published in a general public health magazine[997]. However, according to the child psychiatrist recruited by this magazine to reassure the masses, there is really nothing to worry about: "Children are capable of understanding that what they see on the screen does not reflect reality and that cartoons [such as the *Winx*, which present "real sexed-up characters with long legs, a slim waistline and enhanced breasts"] are part of an imaginary world. Same thing for the silhouette of the actresses of series. It is the result of full-time work: sport, restrictive diet and sometimes surgery."[998] In short, leave your kids in front of the TV, there is no risk. At 8 years old, the child is clear-sighted enough to guess that many actresses are fake and that Brad Pitt's superb calves in the film *Troy* belong in fact to an anonymous double. Patrick Eveno, "media historian", confirms valiantly the thesis of the harmlessness of television on the pretext that Empress Sissi was anorexic at a time when television did not yet exist (which probably allows us to affirm that smoking does not give cancer because there were cancer patients long before tobacco reached our countries). When confronted with the realities of the scientific literature, this pitiful nonsense leaves one dreaming. Once again, I find it disturbing that all these specialists are so light-hearted, convinced, no doubt, that a medical or academic title is enough to transform a counter opinion into an irrefutable truth.

In summary, sexuality is an essential dimension of human nature. However, when certain basic health rules are not respected, pleasure quickly turns into severe affliction. It is clear that television is not solely responsible for the tens of thousands of infectious contaminations, abortions and unwanted pregnancies that occur every year in Europe and the United States. However, it is clear that this medium cannot be exempted from its heavy and undeniable responsibility. On the screen, sex is omnipresent. Films, commercials, *music* videos, prime time programs, no field is spared. This ubiquity deeply alters, and often unconsciously, the sexual representations of teenagers, in the direction of a greater permissiveness. The more a young person focuses on the target, the more he or she is persuaded that sex is an acceptable recreational practice, devoid of risk and universally spread among his or her peers. This combination leads to a marked lowering of the age of first intercourse. Unfortunately, early sex is not a very good thing. It greatly increases the risks of infectious contaminations and unwanted pregnancies. But television seems to love this from the depths of its vile voyeurism, if the latest fashionable program showing poor, out-of-date teenagers sadly struggling in the midst of a maternal role that they are clearly not prepared to assume is anything to go by. To all these points, we must add a wide range of psychological problems, which are alarming to say the least, linked to the effects of television on body image and self-esteem.

*
**

Between Morpheus and Star Ac', you have to choose

As the decades progress, we sleep less. Children, adults and teenagers, we are all in chronic sleep debt after having seen our nights shortened by 90 to 120 minutes over the last 30 to 50 years[1001-1004]. These numbers are alarming. In fact, sleep deprivation is now so widespread that it can no longer be compensated for by simply extending the time spent asleep during weekends or rest periods[187,1002,1005-1008]. The latest studies show that we have in fact been tending to sleep less at weekends for some years now[1005,1007] and that deferred compensation at weekends maintains, in any case, irregular sleep/wake rhythms associated with poor quality sleep[1002]. The length and quality of our nights are essential elements of our good health. Although the causal link is not always easy to see on a day-to-day basis, it has been clearly established by dozens of rigorous studies that chronic sleep deprivation has devastating effects on our bodies[1002,1003]. Among the most commonly observed scourges are obesity[1009-1014], diabetes[1011,1013], hypertension[1015,1016], depression[1017], disturbances in brain development[1018], the emergence of suicidal behaviors[1017,1019], the collapse of immune defenses[1020,1021], increase in certain cancers (e.g. breast cancer)[1022-1025], exacerbation of physical pain[1026], increased risk of accidents at work[1027,1028] and on the road[187,1029-1032], use of psychotropic substances including alcohol, nicotine and caffeine[1033]. To this long list should also be added severe impairment of emotional

---

and cognitive functioning[1034-1036], as well as deterioration in learning and memory skills[1037,1038], which ultimately produces a marked deterioration in school performance[445,1039]. Perhaps it is important to note here that it is not necessary to vary sleep time massively to significantly disrupt cognitive mechanics. Lengthen or shorten your children's night by about 30 minutes from the usual level (which is probably already insufficient) and you will see a significant change in the intellectual performance of your children.[444]

Obviously, it is not enough to state that the length of our nights has collapsed over the last 30 years to conclude that the small screen has a deleterious effect. A great number of non-television factors could explain this phenomenon, such as, for example, the increase in transportation time or the development of women's work, which obliges the family to carry out in the evening some of the household and administrative tasks that the woman used to do alone during the day. In line with the importance of these non-television factors, 90% of parents say, when questioned, that the small screen only marginally affects their offspring's nights[442] ; 30% say that it has sleeping properties[185,202]; and 75% report that it is an integral part of the routine that leads the child into the arms of Morpheus[442]. This last argument is frequently found on specialized 24-hour channels, such as BabyFirst, which claim that "evening programs soothe your child to prepare him for sleep.[1040] Clearly, if all of these ideas were true, rooms with televisions should fall asleep earlier and more easily than rooms without them. This is not the case, on the contrary. In fact, compared to their control peers, children and adolescents with televisions in their bedrooms fall asleep later, have shorter nights, have impaired sleep quality and experience greater daytime fatigue[189,441,442,1041,1042]. If you put a television in a 5-year-old's room, at age 11 this will result, after taking into account a large list of potential covariates (age, sex, socioeconomic status, etc.), in an almost threefold increase in the risk of the child suffering from sleep disorders in the broad sense (irregular nights, nightmares, difficulty in falling asleep, etc.) and more than a twofold increase in the likelihood that he or she will struggle to put off the fateful moment of going to bed.[442] This result can be compared with adolescent practices. In fact, the subjects in this population who think that television has a narcotic effect and fall asleep staring at the screen concede nearly 45 minutes of sleep each night to their unconnected counterparts[1041]. This represents a deficit of almost 3 nights per month. A colossal figure!

In view of the preceding elements, one should not believe that only alcove televisions are dangerous. They certainly have a magnifying power, but this power is not intrinsic. It reflects a simple facilitation of use. When the TV is in a bedroom, we watch it more and later which mechanically accentuates the harmful influences of the set on sleep. However, these influences are present regardless of the place of consumption (living room, kitchen, etc.). In agreement with this assertion, several recent studies have shown, both in children and adults, that sleep duration is inversely proportional to the time spent in front of the screen[178,189,441-443,1043]. In other words, the more TV an individual watches, the less sleep they get. It could of course be suggested that this association is in fact a reverse causality. It would then not be the television that would affect sleepiness, but the sleep disorders that would lead the people with insomnia to spend more time in front of the screen. This explanation does not hold for at least four reasons. First, when television began to spread in the early 1950s, bedtime immediately shifted by nearly 30 minutes on weeknights for children who lived in an equipped home[463]. Second, when exposure to the set is voluntarily reduced, sleep duration rises rapidly. For example, an increase of more than 1 hour in daily sleep time was observed in Japanese students who were asked to keep their television consumption below 30 minutes per day[446]. Thirdly, it is clearly established that exposure to violent, exciting, anxiety-provoking or stressful audiovisual content (films, series, sports, games, etc.) provokes excitatory physiological responses that are detrimental to the sleep process[443,1001,1044]. In other words, setting the nervous system on fire before slipping under the comforter is the best way to delay the arrival of sleep and thus shorten the duration of sleep for all those who must get up at a fixed time because of school or professional obligations. Finally, fourthly, it has been shown that television, through its hegemonic domination of pre-sleep time, is the main decision-maker of our bedtime.[178] Clearly, when an individual is in front of the screen, lights out is not timed according to the physiological markers of need, but according to the end of the program watched. In this respect, a recent study showed that the bedtime peak was independent of the time of awakening and occurred just after 10 p.m. in the United States,[178] which typically corresponds to the time of completion of early evening programs.[1045] In fact, remarkably, the peak of bedtime was not related to the time of awakening but to the time of completion of the program. Remarkably, moreover, when primetime content ends earlier, viewers' nights get substantially longer. Researchers have used a particular American feature to show this. In this country, several time zones coexist and prime time programs do not start at the same time everywhere (for example, there is generally a one-hour difference between Boston - *Eastern Time* - and Chicago - *Central Time*[1046]). The difference is as high as 15 percent between the two regions, and the difference between the two regions is as high as 20 percent. The difference averages 15 to 20 minutes,[1047] which is quite substantial for an undifferentiated population that includes a substantial number of individuals who did not watch the primetime program because they were working, reading a book, or dining out with friends. This being said, it is perhaps interesting to point out here that the alignment of bedtimes with audiovisual schedules could also explain the link recently observed, in very young children aged 3 and under, between television consumption and variability in bedtime schedules[539]. It is tempting to speculate that the start time of the nap or night will be more irregular if it depends on an external audiovisual circumstance (end of DVD or TV program), rather than on a predefined temporal marker (at such and such a fixed time, in bed). Irregularity of bedtime has a strong negative effect on the sleep process[539,1002].

Beyond what has just been said, it must also be stressed that the deleterious influence of the small screen is not limited to the quantitative field. It also concerns the space of qualitative variables. The more a child watches television, the more likely he or she is to have restless nights, with parasomnia, anxiety attacks, difficulty in falling asleep, refusal to go to bed, nightmares and/or multiple awakenings[441-443,463,1048]. Thus, for example, after taking into account a large matrix of sociodemographic, psychological and personal covariates, it appears that 5- to 6-year-old schoolchildren are 3 times more likely to express sleep disorders if they are exposed to content intended for adults, but nevertheless labeled "all audiences" in many cases (television news, series, films, etc.). Somewhat unexpectedly, this effect is present, in similar magnitudes, whether the child is actively (paying attention to the TV) or passively (doing something else while the parents are watching TV) watching the screen[443]. It is tempting to associate these results with the potentially anxiety-provoking power, for the youngest viewers, of programs commonly watched by adults[435]. It is tempting to associate these results with the potential anxiety-provoking power of programs commonly watched by adults for the youngest viewers.[435] In this respect, several studies have shown that exposing children to programs that were not intended for them can generate significant anxiety in them, which is often expressed by refusing to sleep and/or producing recurrent nightmares.[442,1049-1053] These behaviours can persist for months or even years. These behaviors can persist for months[1049,1051,1054] and can be determined in preschool subjects by apparently harmless audiovisual content such as, for example, the cartoon *The Incredible Hulk* or the character of E.T.[1049,1054]. This brave extraterrestrial actually provoked an intense reaction of fear in my daughter Valentine when she was only 4 years old. After watching a part of the film at her cousin's house, the little girl had a restless sleep and unusual nightmares for several days. These have now been resolved. However, since this episode, almost a year ago, Valentine has adamantly refused to sleep unless all the closets in her room are carefully inspected and closed before lights out (the movie segment that caused her fear actually showed E.T. hiding in a closet). This type of reaction does not appear to be isolated. More than a quarter of adults say they have retained fears related to certain audiovisual content from their childhood[1051]. In practice, nearly 10% of parents say that television generates at least one nightmare for their children aged 5 to 11 each week[442]. At the same time, one-third of 13-year-olds admit to having regular bad dreams because of television.[150] These prevalences are far from being the same as the prevalence of bad dreams in children. These prevalences are far from trivial.

As if all this were not enough, longitudinal work has recently shown that the negative influences of television operate over the long term.[440] Thus, after taking into account a large list of potential covariates, it appears that 14-year-old adolescents who have never had sleep disorders and who watch television for 3 hours a day or more are twice as likely as their peers with consumption of less than 1 hour a day to develop sleep disorders at ages 16 and 22. Reducing the level of exposure between the ages of 14 and 16 reduces the risk by half. Beyond the age of 16, the effect becomes irreversible and the reduction in exposure time is ineffective. *Irreversible*, this word alone should sound a terrible alarm for us all.

Thus, sleep is an essential component of our somatic, emotional and cognitive functioning. However, it appears clearly that television has a strong negative influence on the length and quality of our nights. Children, teenagers, adults, no one is spared. However, it would be enough for us to give up wasting 2 or 3 hours each evening in front of TF1, M6 or France 2 to see our relationship with our friend Morpheus improve and our sleep debt disappear. Such an evolution would eventually allow us to substantially reduce the risk that we or our children will suffer from obesity, diabetes, hypertension, depression, immune deficiencies, suicidal desires, road accidents, alcoholism, attention disorders, school failure, etc. Benefits that are, it seems to me, largely worth the dismissal of Lady Television.

*
**

To conclude

Thus, we can see that television is not the harmless leisure activity that parents imagine it to be and that is described by the *ad hoc* specialists of the media bien-pensance. The small screen poses a major problem of public health. How many obese people, disabled people, HIV positive people, juvenile abortions, cirrhosis of the liver, lung cancer, heart attacks will it take for this reality to penetrate the inertia of our brains? Let's repeat it once again: our early experiences condition a large part of our adult life. A teenager who meets the bottle prematurely increases massively his chances of having a lifelong problem with alcoholism; a child who is overweight because of risky food choices increases substantially his chances of knowing, once grown up, the torments of obesity; a teenager who loses her virginity at an early age has a significantly increased chance of contracting sexually transmitted diseases and becoming pregnant; a kid who starts smoking before 18 has every chance of continuing to do so afterwards; a young person who does not get enough sleep greatly increases his or her chances of experiencing serious health and cognitive problems. In all these areas, television has a profoundly negative impact. This statement is not a hypothesis. It is, to date, a scientifically proven result. Therefore, things are quite simple: if you want to preserve as much as possible the health and the future of your children, then do not let them grow up next to a TV!

Chapter IV

TV cultivates fear and violence

"If there is one calamity to be wary of today, aside from the resurgence of Nazism, it is television."

(Françoise Sagan, novelist[1055])

"Despite the consensus among experts, the popular press does not seem to be delivering the message to the general public that media violence helps produce a more violent society...This inaccurate portrayal by the popular press may account for a controversy that persists when the debate should have been over long ago, in the same way that the cigarette/cancer controversy persisted long after the scientific community knew that smoking caused cancer."

(Craig Anderson and Brad Bushman,
professors of psychology, University of Iowa[1056])

"Exposure to media violence...represents a significant health risk to children and adolescents. Extensive scientific evidence indicates that media violence can contribute to aggressive behavior, desensitization to violence, nightmares, and fear of being victimized."

(American Academy of Pediatrics[1057])

The effect of violent audiovisual programs on the psyche and behavior of viewers has been widely studied by scientists around the world for more than 60 years. However, in this field, the research effort has not been expressed in a linear way. It took shape mainly between the beginning of the sixties and the end of the eighties. Since the latter date, the investment of specialists has slowly waned to almost zero. Today, only a small number of very long-term longitudinal studies still manage to find a place in leading international journals[1058,1059]. In essence, this progressive disaffection is not surprising. It merely confirms the gradual exhaustion of the problematic field and the unanimous conviction that everything has been said[1060]. In fact, since the beginning of the two thousand years, it is mainly to the diffusion of this reality that researchers in the field have been attached. The least one can say is that these specialists have not skimped on the clarity of their formulations. "The scientific debate intended to determine whether media violence increases aggressive and violent behavior is basically over." (Craig Anderson and colleagues[1061]) "There is clear evidence that exposure to media violence contributes significantly to real-world violence." (Ellen Wartella and colleagues[1062]) "Research conducted over the past 50 years leads to the conclusion that television violence affects viewers' attitudes, values, and behaviors. In general, there appear to be three main classes of effects: aggression, desensitization, and fear." (John Murray[1063]) "The conclusion of public health organizations, based on more than 30 years of research, is that watching violent entertainment can lead to increased aggressive attitudes, values, and behavior, particularly in children. The effects are measurable and long-lasting." (Joint statement of 6 major American medical associations[1064]) "The evidence is now clear and compelling: media violence is one of the causal factors in actual aggression and violence. As a result, pediatricians and parents must act." (American Academy of Pediatrics[1057]) "The accumulated body of evidence is consistent and clear - violence on television causes an increase in aggressive and violent behavior." (Rowell Huesmann and Laramie Taylor[1065]) "The controversy should be over." (Victor Strasburger[1066]) Perhaps the ultimate evidence for this reality lies, today, in the development of neuroimaging work.[1067-1070] Indeed, these bear direct witness to the fact that researchers have moved beyond the evidence problem (do violent images alter behavior?) to the causality question (how do violent images alter behavior?).

In view of the preceding observations, one might have expected that the message delivered to the general public by the media would be absolutely clear. This is not the case, on the contrary. Against all odds, "the entertainment industry and selected critics continue to deny the evidence"[1066]. In fact, the more scientists pile up confirmations, the more the media *vulgum pecus* displays its skepticism. This point was clearly demonstrated by Bushman and Anderson in a quantitative study conducted in response to a series of articles in several prominent media outlets, including *Newsweek* and the *New York Times*.[124] Prior to publishing this study, our two researchers were able to identify the most important scientific findings in the field. Prior to publishing this study, the two researchers obviously tried to strike a blow at various mainstream media outlets.

However, the latter remained unmoved. Like many of their colleagues, Bushman and Anderson were politely told to go play it safe. In desperation, the two men finally decided to publish their arguments in a scientific journal familiar only to specialists. The average citizen never heard of the controversy. The position expressed by the journalistic world and its army of complacent pipe-ologists remained the gospel. This observation is all the more annoying because it is not limited to the United States. Many other countries, including France, offer fertile ground for the delirious tribunes of hucksters from all horizons. Among the favourite arguments of these good people is the inescapable theory of the scapegoat.[44,288,1071] According to this theory, television is not the only thing that is harmful to the public. According to this theory, television is nothing more than an expiatory victim designated for popular vindication in order to exonerate the social body from its responsibilities. "For lack of identifying the "real culprits", says us for example the sociologist Judith Lazar, one falls back on the "ideal culprits". Television seems to be one of these illusory culprits."[1071] An idea recently taken up by Patrick Eveno. According to this media historian, there is "a recurrent theme that attributes to the media the cause of society's misfortunes. Thus, at the beginning of the twentieth century, the sociologist Gabriel de Tarde provoked a wide-ranging media debate by accusing the press, through its accounts of crime, of developing criminality.[288] To this kind of discourse we can, I think, make two remarks. Firstly, it is not because an eminent sociologist was perhaps mistaken more than a century ago in relation to the written press that scientists are mistaken today in reference to television. Second, as scholars have repeatedly stated, no serious individual has ever scapegoated the media or claimed that television is the sole or even primary source of the violent behaviors that permeate our society.[1057,1061,1072,1073] In the words of Rowell Huesy, "The media is a powerful tool for the prevention of violence. In the words of Rowell Huesmann and Laramie Taylor, for example, "no respectable researcher suggests that media violence is 'the' cause of violent behavior."[1065] [1065] The only thing that scientists dare to say is that television is a significant factor in violence and that it would be a shame not to act on this causal lever, which is relatively accessible compared to other, deeper social determinants (poverty, education, living environment, etc.)[1057,1061,1065,1072,1073]. From the depths of my great naivety, this position seems to me neither scandalous, nor imbecilic, nor, above all, of a nature to blame the media for "the cause of society's misfortunes".

In support of the scapegoat fable, there is usually also the tale of scientific uncertainty. It is then suggested that the effects of media violence on the behavior of the spectator are in no way proven. This idea was notably supported not so long ago by Catherine Tasca, who declared, when she was Minister of Culture, that "scientists are far from establishing a mechanical link between the violence of images and the evolution of children's behaviour".[1074] This idea was later reaffirmed by the French Minister of Culture, Catherine Tasca. This idea was later reaffirmed in a more direct way through the assertion that "the majority of researchers say that there is no link"[1075]. And those who dare to say otherwise are necessarily dishonest[1076]. In fact, all these scoundrels hide a devious project. They want, like Blandine Kriegel (coordinator of a noted official report on violence on television [117]), to "worry in order to control" and they do not hesitate, in order to support their fallacious conclusions, to select "certain research at the expense of others"[38]. 38 I must admit that this last argument is fatally beautiful. The ultimate recourse of bad faith, it nimbly takes up the wing of conspiracy theories by implying that there exists, "somewhere", a dissident literature that the contemptuous of media violence would slyly pass over in silence. This kind of projection has already proven itself in many fields, including global warming, the consequences of homoparenting, the effects of alternating custody and (of course) the association between cancer and smoking. Often, researchers are not interested in the problem, judging that it would not be appropriate to waste public money on such vain controversies. Sometimes, however, the pressure becomes so great that the scientific community has no choice but to stand up for its integrity. This is precisely what happened with audiovisual violence. In this field, the counter-offensive has been based on a systematic identification of the allegedly "forgotten" research. As a result, according to figures published by the American Academy of Pediatrics, "more than 3,500 research studies have examined the association between media violence and violent behavior; all but 8 have shown a positive relationship. This percentage, which is quite staggering for human science research, is not surprising in view of previous analyses based on so-called meta-analytical approaches. These are commonly used by researchers to combine a large number of independent observations in a single "giant" study. The ultimate goal is to determine whether an effect is present, "in the aggregate", beyond possible local variations. When this was done for the problem of violence on television, it was observed that there was a highly significant influence of violent images on the emergence of aggressive behaviour[3,423,1056,1061,1065,1073]. This result was all the more important because it was based on the evaluation of general, non-pathological populations. Such representativeness underscores, in the words of Rowell Huesmann and colleagues, that the brain processes that lead from violent images to aggressive behavior are "immutable and universal."[1059] This conclusion clearly invalidates the sadly widespread thesis of predisposition, of which we find traces, for example, in an interview with Mrs. Tasca, who docently declares that "the passage to the act only occurs in a predisposed public"[1075]. An assertion that is obviously shared by Catherine Muller and François Chemel, who certify with faith (but without a source, it must be said) that violent images "only represent a real danger in subjects who already have a certain pathology"[32]. In other words, and to quote Michael Stora, founder of an obscure "observatory of digital worlds in the human sciences", "images are taken as targets, but they are only revelations of already existing pathologies"[40]. All this is hardly serious, really... unless one considers that the famous [Dr] Knock was right when he exaltedly affirmed that "healthy people are sick people who ignore themselves"[1078]. Perhaps, after all, "every well-balanced spectator hides within him a sleeping psychopath". We shall have the opportunity to return to this idea below by addressing the central question of social *priming*[a]. Before doing so, however, I would like to discuss one last reproach made to the critics of audiovisual violence, and relating to the weakness of the influences observed.

In statistical terms, an effect can be both highly significant and hopelessly small. To illustrate this point, take, for example, 1,000 16-year-olds. Ask them to sprint 50 meters under two experimental conditions that require them to be either naked or wearing a 500 gram belt. In almost all subjects, performance will tend to deteriorate slightly in the second case. Therefore, if a statistical test is carried out to determine the effect of the load on motor performance, a very strong significance will be obtained in the presence of small chronometric variations. This type of dissociation has often been mentioned in relation to violent images. The idea then developed suggests that the effect exists, but that it is quantitatively marginal[38,1079].

---

a. In cognitive psychology, *priming* defines a type of paradigm in which the presentation of a prior stimulus (called a "primer"; e.g., words such as *force* or *effort*) influences the expression of a subsequent behavior (called a "target"; e.g., the vigor of the handshake to the experimenter at the end of the experiment). The priming is often presented to the subject subliminally (i.e., not consciously perceived).

A simple glance at the problem of large numbers is enough to disqualify this statement irrevocably. Indeed, it is clearly established that a locally minimal influence can have major consequences if it is applied to a large population and/or in a recurrent manner[124,1061,1080,1081]. To illustrate this point, suppose that the violence in a movie affects 1 in 1,000 viewers. If 10 million subjects see this film when it is released on television, we end up with 10,000 aggressive or violent acts on our hands. In line with this theoretical framework, Brandon Centerwall estimated the number of crimes attributable to television in the early 1990s on the basis of large-scale epidemiological data. According to his findings in the respected *Journal of the American Medical Association* (JAMA), "every violent act is clearly the result of a combination of forces acting in concert; poverty, crime, substance abuse, stress - of which early television exposure is only one dimension. Nevertheless, epidemiological evidence indicates that if, hypothetically, television technology had never been developed, there would be 10,000 fewer homicides, 70,000 fewer rapes, and 700,000 fewer assaults with injuries in the United States today each year. For those who find these figures extravagant, a quick look back at previously mentioned research may be of interest. In that work, three sociologically comparable cities were studied. Two of them received television (UniTel, MultiTel). The third had to be connected within 24 months (NoTel). The authors studied the behaviour of young primary school pupils while they were playing in the school yard during recess[1083]. Aggressive and violent behavior was classified along two axes, one physical (e.g., hitting, shoving, biting, etc.) and the other verbal (e.g., name calling, threats, altercations, etc.). The results showed that for NoTel, following the introduction of television, the number of verbal incidents doubled and the number of physical clashes almost tripled. No significant evolution was observed, over the same period, for the two other agglomerations (MultiTel and UniTel). It is difficult to conclude from this data that the television effect is marginal! An ultimate illustration of this reality comes from correlation studies. The principle consists in determining, under equal socio-demographic, psychological and personal conditions, whether children who consume the most violent audiovisual content produce a greater number of aggressive behaviors. This potential link is usually expressed as a coefficient r, which can vary between -1 (when one of the two variables increases, the other decreases in strict proportion), 0 (the two variables are independent) and 1 (the two variables vary in strict proportion). Typically, researchers have found coefficients between 0.2 and 0.4[1056,1061,1065,1084] depending on the studies, the indicators of aggression considered and the experimental approaches used. In mathematical terms, this means that 5-15% of the observed behavioral differences in violence between individuals are attributable to television[a] . In qualitative terms, this implies that the average association between violent images and aggressive behavior is almost as strong as the association between smoking and lung cancer. These two links are themselves stronger than those observed between lack of condom use and risk of infection with the AIDS virus, between early exposure to lead and the occurrence of intellectual disabilities, between calcium consumption and bone mass value, between use of nicotine patches and cessation of smoking behaviors, or between lack of administration of beta-blockers after a heart attack and risk of short-term mortality.[124,1086] Those who argue that the relationship between violence and aggressive behavior is not the same as the relationship between smoking and lung cancer are right. Would those who claim that the relationship between images and violent behavior is negligible argue that condom use has a minimal influence on the risk of HIV infection, or that the use of beta-blockers has a negligible effect on the survival of patients exposed to myocardial infarction, or that smoking only marginally increases the risk of developing lung cancer? I don't think so. But you can't defend one of these silly assertions without supporting them all.

Thus, in spite of the denials of the entertainment industry and its puppet masters, it is now clearly established that violent images affect the behavior of our children. This action takes three main forms: stimulation of violent and aggressive behavior; lowering of the threshold of tolerance to violence (i.e. desensitization); exacerbation of the feeling of insecurity. These diffe-rent points will be addressed successively in the following pages, after a brief overview of the omnipresence of violent images on television. The reader will perhaps find it surprising not to see developed also, within this chapter, the concept of catharsis according to which the spectators would purge themselves of their violent impulses by seeing these last ones put in scene on television. This idea of a "liberation by derivation" to use Henri Piéron's expression[604] is indeed very popular among the defenders of the right to creativity and audiovisual violence. If it does not appear here, it is simply because it does not enjoy any convincing experimental

---

a. The percentage of variance captured by the correlation is given by the square of the correlation coefficient[1085].

support[3,124,1054,1057] and that, according to the conclusion of a large synthesis work, "there is not the slightest beginning of convincing scientific data to support this theory [...] [which] can be forgotten"[423]. Victor Strasburger even goes so far as to speak of a "completely discredited theory" which owes its astonishing durability to the fact that it suits the film and audio-visual lobbies[3]. To date, among the thousands of studies carried out, none has been able to show, in accordance with the predictions of the cathartic purge model, that aggressive behaviour tends to decrease after exposure to violent audiovisual content.

*
**

Violence is good for business

Like sex, alcohol or tobacco, violence is omnipresent on television[3,423,1057,1061]. This observation is not new and I don't think it will surprise anyone. As early as 1988, *Le Point* denounced a real "telemassacre", after having asked a group of viewers to watch all the programs of the six channels of the time (TF1, Antenne 2, FR3, Canal +, La Cinq, M6) for one week (from Monday midnight to Sunday midnight).[1087] In the end, our volunteers counted the number of people who had been killed in the course of the week. In the end, our volunteers counted: 670 murders, 848 fights, 419 shootings, 15 rapes, 27 scenes of torture, 9 defenestrations, 14 kidnappings, 32 hostage-takings, etc. This serious trend was confirmed a few years later by a study of the Conseil supérieur de l'audiovisuel (CSA)[1088]. To make its point, this institution scrutinized a little over 109 hours of programs representing 194 broadcasts. The results showed that viewers ingested an average of 2 crimes and about 10 violent acts per hour, i.e., over the course of a year, for a typical television viewer who spends 3 hours and 30 minutes a day in front of the television set,[146] nearly 2,600 crimes and 13,000 violent acts. More than half of the dramas contained at least one crime sequence. In a large number of cases, the violent acts were committed by positive characters. Interestingly, and perhaps unexpectedly for some, these figures turned out to be quite similar to those published a few years later in the United States, in what remains to this day the most impressive content study of audiovisual violence[1089]. Over a period of three years, the authors dissected 10,000 hours of randomly selected programmes from 23 of the main American channels. The results showed that 60% of the programs contained acts of violence. These were repeated on average 6 times per hour (slightly less than in the CSA study). In about 1 case out of 2, the violence was presented in a realistic way and perpetrated by positive characters. It appeared to be acceptable and justified. Its immediate traumatic effects were frequently underestimated and its long-term negative consequences were almost never mentioned. In more than 7 out of 10 cases, the violence did not cause remorse, criticism or punishment. Strikingly, youth programs were by no means spared. 70% of them contained violent content, with 14 incidents per hour.[1090] That is more than 10,000 exposures per year for a child watching television for 2 hours a day.

Of course, not all audiovisual genres are equal when it comes to violence. Among the programs most affected are films, series and cartoons[1088,1089]. To this list we must also add the one that has been forgotten in previous content studies: news. The news contains a large number of violent sequences, usually presented in a sensational and emphatic manner[287,1091-1096]. By including news in its study protocol, a recent study identified, for Spanish television, no less than 18 violent incidents per hour of programming[1096]. This is a significant figure, which could also reflect, in part, an increase in violent content in recent years. In line with this idea, the CSA recently expressed concern about the dramatic increase in the number of programs on French channels that are not recommended for children under 10, 12, 16 or 18 years of age[1097]. According to Agnès Vincent-Deray, advisor in charge of the protection of minors within this institution, "the increase of programs on television likely to shock children is substantial and alarming [...] It is important that parents stop believing that their children are safe in front of the television". That's a clear statement.

Based on the observation that movies were among the most violent audiovisual programs, several authors have focused on the film industry. It was then shown that 90% of the most successful works at the American box-office contained violent content[822,1098-1100]. Unsurprisingly, the latter revealed the same biases as those previously observed for television programs: perpetration by positive characters, underestimation of the consequences, lack of remorse and punishment, etc. Some works, with their "positive" character, were not considered to be violent. Some works, labelled PG-13 in the United States ("content potentially unsuitable for children under 13") but classified as "all audiences" in France,[813] managed to include more than 100 explicitly violent acts (e.g., *The Mummy, James Bond: The World Is Not Enough, Charlie's Angels*, or *Mission Impossible 2*).[1100] In 30 years, films labelled PG-13 in the United States have become more and more popular. In 30 years, films labelled PG-13 and *R-Rated* ("forbidden in theatres for unaccompanied minors"), which represent a very large proportion of films at the American box office and are frequently free of any signage in France, have seen their violence load increase considerably[822].

In a recent work, a team from Dartmouth University looked at the issue of the most acute violence. The 100 highest-grossing U.S. box office films for each of the years from 1998 to 2002 were selected.[1101] From this selection, a group of 40 "extremely violent" films were identified. From this selection, a group of 40 "extremely violent" films were identified and submitted to more than 6,500 subjects aged 10-14 years. 21 films had been seen by more than 12% of the sample. At the top of the list was *Scary Movie* with nearly 50% of viewers! When the authors focused on 10-year-olds alone, they found that 25% of our young moviegoers had seen such profoundly and explicitly violent works as *Blade* (*1* and *2*), *Scream 3, Hollow Man, The Bride of Chucky, Scary Movie* or *Remember... Last Summer 2*. These observations are broadly consistent with those of a previous study that showed, on the basis of just over 50 films, that the most violent works at the box office were seen, on average, by 28% of subjects aged 10-14 years[1102]. A film like *Scream* was viewed by almost 40% of American 10-year-olds and 70% of 14-year-olds!

Thus, violence is omnipresent on our screens through films, series, cartoons and television news. Because of their propensity to consume all of these programs,[435] children are affected very early on. Before questioning the psychic and behavioral effects of such exposure, it might be interesting to briefly consider the question of origins. How is it that the film and audiovisual industries are so addicted to violence? Why is it that violence is so widely represented on our screens? The most commonly accepted answer to these questions refers to the dear God of ratings and to the general theme of "we give them what they want [...] it's not our fault if they are so stupid. In this framework, violence would not be imposed by the channels, but demanded by the viewer. The argument undoubtedly has some validity. However, it is by no means exhaustive and seems to leave out a large part of the equation. Indeed, several recent researches have shown that aggressive and brutal contents are, through the stress they impose on the brain, a real blessing for advertisers. Mr. Le Lay was perhaps thinking of this research when he mentioned, in a remark that has become a cult, these programs that are likely to "prepare" the brain in order to make it fully "available" for advertising breaks[23]. We know today that an individual subjected to emotional tensions registers better the messages that are imposed on him and proves to be more easily conditioned[1104-1106]. The effect is doubly interesting for food brands insofar as these tensions also encourage, through a certain number of biochemical mechanisms, the consumption of fatty and sweet products[1107-1110]. It is hard to believe that advertisers are unaware of these realities and are holding back from taking advantage of them. After all, it is necessary to be "realistic, basically, TF1's job is to help Coca-Cola, for example, to sell its product. If it proves necessary, to support this purpose, to stuff the air with a heap of violence, then it does not matter. It will always be time, if some accusing voices are raised, to delegate one or two complacent pipe-heads to denounce a cabal without foundation, intended to make of this poor television a convenient scapegoat. An argument that it is now more than time to refute precisely.

*
**

Violence calls for violence

To say that violent images influence our behavior does not imply, of course, that television is an infernal machine for producing psychopathic killers. It "just" means, if I may say so, that when a viewer is exposed to violent images, he becomes more aggressive. This aggressiveness can be measured in the short term by counting, for example, the number of slaps, altercations, blows and insults exchanged by children during a school recess[1083] or a field hockey game[1111]. It can also be assessed in the long term by counting the convictions for homicide, armed robbery or assault of adults who were, as children, heavy or light television consumers.[1058,1059] In what follows, these two dimensions of the problem can be assessed in the context of a more detailed analysis of the problem. In what follows, these two proximate and remote dimensions will be discussed in turn. This does not mean, however, that they are functionally independent. Indeed, it is quite possible that each punctual exposure increases the spectator's receptivity to violence, so that what was at the beginning only an ephemeral physiological reaction, is gradually transformed into a chronic psychological disposition. It is a bit like with tobacco. A single cigarette has only a minor and fleeting effect on the body. However, a single cigarette added to another one, day after day, for years, ends up abusing the vascular and pulmonary systems very severely.

Philosophically, we cherish the idea of free will. We like to think that our actions are the result of conscious, thoughtful decisions. Unfortunately, this is rarely the case even at the most basic level of behavior. Over the past 50 years, neuroscientists have accumulated evidence that our behaviors are constantly modulated by environmental factors of which we are not aware. It is now clearly established that our brain spends its time processing information without "telling" us; and to be honest, this is rather good news. Indeed, if everything that passes through the heart of our neurons were to reach consciousness, the mind would very quickly become saturated and unable to function. To execute a simple gripping movement, for example, we would have to determine the spatial trajectory to be taken, the speed to be used, the muscles to be activated, the points of contact to be used, the number of fingers to be mobilized, the gripping force to be developed, etc.[567,1112] This would be impossible and it would be enough to drive us crazy. To get out of it, the brain has no choice. It must restrict the volume of information delivered to the consciousness. This implies, to put it very schematically, that most of our decisions are taken without our ego being informed. We can cite numerous examples of this phenomenon, at all levels of the behavioral pyramid. At the most basic physiological level, for example, when we observe a fellow human being running, our breathing rate increases[1113], when we see our neighbor's hand pierced with a needle, the muscles of our own hand lower their excitability threshold[1114], when we attend an arm wrestling match our biceps contract[1115,1116], when we see an apple on a table or watch someone else grasp an object, our brain automatically activates the neuronal populations involved in the act of grasping[567,1117], when the environment contains food[701,702], tobacco[828,829] or alcohol[910] stimuli, this arouses in us the desire to consume these products, and when we are confronted in a subliminal way with words such as *strength, power* or *effort*, this pushes us to produce more vigorous movements[1118]. This last result is particularly interesting insofar as it opens the way to the quite fascinating field of conceptual *priming*. The basic idea is quite simple: specific environmental stimuli activate particular brain representations which in turn activate particular behaviors. To illustrate the validity of this process, the researchers developed a double-triggered protocol in which subjects must: first, construct correct sentences from different word lists (or perform some task that serves as a pretext for the delivery of subliminal visual stimuli) and second, take part in a social interaction that is apparently unrelated to the initial task. This framework has served as a model for several dozen experiments. Almost all of these experiments have revealed the very strong capacity of environmental *priming* to manipulate our behaviour[695,1119]. By way of illustration, let us just mention two studies directly related to the problem of aggression. In the first, subjects were initially confronted with lists of words evoking either hostile or neutral behaviours.[1120] They were then asked to inflict electric shocks on a stranger (in fact an actor) when the latter answered incorrectly to a question put to him. The level of shock was left to the subjects' discretion on a scale of 1 to 10. Individuals in the "hostile" group used shock levels that were on average 50% higher than their counterparts in the "neutral" group (3.3 *versus* 2.2). In a second, roughly similar study, the word lists presented evoked the concepts of politeness or rudeness[696]. At the end of their linguistic work, participants had to signal their departure to the experimenter while the latter was (unluckily!) in the middle of a discussion. 63% of the individuals in the "rudeness" group interrupted the exchange, compared to only 17% of the subjects in the "politeness" group. In another part of the same study, white students were asked to perform a tedious task on a computer. Before each trial, the face of either a black or Caucasian individual was subliminally presented on the screen. At the end of the experiment, the computer suddenly displayed an error message. The experimenter would then intervene and explain to the student that he or she had to start over. Subjects who had seen black faces showed substantially greater hostility and rejection than their counterparts exposed to Caucasian stimuli. To explain these results, the authors pointed to the existence of negative racial stereotypes, on the basis of which white subjects developed hostile reactions to their black counterparts.

In view of these data, the capacity of violent images to generate aggressive behaviour in the viewer should no longer appear as an unlikely curiosity, but as the inescapable expression of a universal neurophysiological process. In this respect, one might think that it is rather prudent to mobilize a certain aggressive potential in response to violent contexts. In fact, it is not at all excluded that reactive aggressiveness could have constituted, in our ancestors, an evolutionary trait favourable to survival. With a bit of luck, in a few thousand years, television will have overcome this aptitude and our brains will have been definitively transformed into flaccid apathetic phlyctenes, insensitive to the stimuli of the world. While waiting for the advent of this blessed period, we will unfortunately have to make do for a while with energetic neurons, quick to transform perceived violence into produced aggression. The scientific literature leaves no doubt on this point[3,423,1056,1057,1061,1063,1065,1073]. In a frequently cited study, Kaj Björkqvist, for example, observed 5-6 year olds in a playroom after they had watched neutral or violent videos. The results showed that individuals in the "violent" group were significantly more likely to push, hit and provoke their peers than individuals in the "neutral" group. A similar observation was reported by Wendy Josephson in 7-8 year olds who were invited to play a game of field field hockey after viewing neutral or violent images[1111]. In another study, Ivar Lovaas reached the same conclusion using an indirect measure of aggression[1122]. Subjects aged 4 to 6 years were allowed to play with two small automatons. The first one dropped a ball in a maze. The second showed a doll hitting its neighbor with a stick. The children who had been subjected to violent images before being allowed access to the experimental room used the doll on average twice as often as the individuals who had been confronted with the neutral video. Liebert and Baron used a comparable protocol to measure the effect of violent audiovisual content on the desire to harm others[1123]. Children aged 5-9 years were given the choice of helping or penalizing the playful activity of a conspecific visible in an adjacent room. Exposure to violent images significantly increased the willingness to harm, compared to a control situation involving the viewing of a neutral video. In another interesting study, Jacques-Philippe Leyens and his colleagues showed violent or neutral films to institutionalized delinquent adolescents. The results revealed a very significant increase in the number of physical assaults in situations of violent images[1124]. The same phenomenon was observed with a non-offending student population. They were randomly divided into two groups and exposed to four films, either violent or neutral, on four consecutive days. The day after the last screening, all of them were engaged in a behavioral study apparently unrelated to the original film experience. When placed in a position to harm the experimenter, the students who had watched the violent films were substantially more hostile and aggressive than their counterparts in the neutral group. This result was observed independently of the experimenter's initially friendly or aggressive behavior. The authors conclude, "These results show that prolonged exposure to gratuitously violent movies is capable of (a) escalating violence in men and women who have been provoked, and (b) perhaps more importantly, eliciting such behavior in men and women who have not been provoked."[1125] Examples like these can be found in the literature by the hundreds. Their aggregation in large meta-analyses leaves no doubt as to the deleterious role of violent content on the emergence of aggressive behaviour[1126-1128]. It should be noted that this conclusion has recently been generalized to the field of so-called "indirect" violence, which occurs, for example, when an individual takes credit for a colleague's work, when a student exposes compromising photos of her roommate in public, or when an unseemly servant takes advantage of the weakness of elderly employers to rob them.[1129]

Unsurprisingly, the experimental effects just described are clearly expressed in correlation studies intended to determine whether there is an increase in aggressiveness in subjects who consume the most violent images and/or television (which amounts to roughly the same thing, given that the small screen is full of violent content). In just over 50 years, dozens of studies have provided a positive answer to this question after taking into account a more or less important matrix of sociodemographic, psychological and personal covariates[3,423,1056,1057,1061,1063,1065,1073]. By aggregating a large number of these studies, regardless of the aggression variables considered, Haejung Paik and George Comstock identified a correlation of around 0.4[1126], equivalent to that observed between smoking and lung cancer.[124] When the analysis was restricted to physical violence against others, the strength of the link fell slightly to just over 0.3. When the experimental approach was constrained to the maximum to consider only criminal violence, the relationship fell to around 0.15. This last figure may seem low. This last figure may seem low. However, it is more important than the link generally found between early lead exposure and the emergence of long-term cognitive disorders. It is just less than the one identified between lack of condom use and infection with the AIDS virus.[124] Of course, with enough bad faith, it can be argued that the correlation studies reported here do not allow for any causal inference. The argument then suggests that the observed relationship between violent images and violent behavior simply reflects the natural appetite of violent individuals for violent programs. If this idea is correct, then one might predict that the magnitude of aggressive behavior should not change, for a given population, when the volume of audiovisual consumption is experimentally modulated. This prediction does not hold. Indeed, the experimental data reported in the previous paragraph clearly show that exposure to violent content significantly increases the prevalence of violent behavior in the viewer. Moreover, it appears that the frequency of aggressive behavior decreases when the time spent in front of the screen decreases. This has been demonstrated by Thomas Robinson and his colleagues in 9-year-old schoolchildren. By decreasing the amount of time spent watching television, these authors recorded a significant decrease in aggressive behaviour by the children during recess over a period of six months. This modification was of course not observed for a reference group that did not modify its cathodic exposure.

The fact that a child becomes less aggressive when his or her audiovisual consumption decreases does not mean, unfortunately, that television is a totally reversible wound. The same is true for television as for tobacco. When the exposure stops, the risk of disease decreases rapidly. However, it may not return to a controlled state for years or even decades. For example, for a man who quits smoking at 60, 50, 40 and 30 years of age, the cumulative risk of developing lung cancer at 75 years of age is 10%, 6%, 3% and 2%, respectively, compared to a control population of non-smokers.[1131] For television, it is the same as for smoking. The same is true for television. Several longitudinal studies have shown, in children and adolescents, that violent images spread their influence well beyond the time of viewing. For example, in a recent study, Dimitri Christakis and Frederick Zimmerman followed nearly 400 children to determine whether exposure to violent programs between 24 and 60 months of age favored the occurrence of antisocial behaviors 5 years later (propensity to lie, cheat, disobey, damage, talk back to teachers, etc.)[1132]. After controlling for the initial level of antisociality and a large number of sociodemographic, psychological and personal covariates (age, sex, ethnic origin, parents' education, physical punishment, father's presence at home, cognitive stimulation, etc.), the results showed that, for boys, each hour of violent programmes consumed daily before 60 months increased the probability of observing antisocial behaviour by more than 4 times at 5 years. The effect was not significant for girls. However, this gender difference was not validated in another study, conducted on a larger sample (1266 subjects), by the same authors, in order to determine whether children who had watched the most television at 4 years of age had an increased tendency to bully and abuse their classmates between the ages of 6 and 11 years.[1133] The answer to this question turned out to be no. The answer to this question was largely positive. After controlling for initial bullying behaviors and a large matrix of sociodemographic, psychological, and personal covariates, the results showed that each hour of television viewing in kindergarten increased the likelihood of oppressive peer behavior in elementary school by nearly 10%.

Similar data to those just mentioned were published in two longitudinal studies involving, in their initial phase, children of school age rather than preschool age. It was then established, after taking into account the initial level of aggressiveness of the participants and a broad spectrum of potential covariates, that exposure to violent images between the ages of 6 and 10 predicted the occurrence of aggressive behaviour at the age of 10[1134,1135] or 15[1059]. In the latter case, for example, it was shown that the 20% of young adult males who had consumed the most violent images between the ages of 6 and 10 were twice as likely as the rest of the population of the same sex to have physically abused their spouses, 3.5 times as likely to have been convicted of a crime, and 1.5 times as likely to have been fined for a traffic offence (not including parking). Women were 2.5 times more likely to have assaulted their spouse by throwing an object in his or her face, 5 times more likely to have physically assaulted another adult, and 2 times more likely to have committed a criminal offence.

For a long time, scientists believed that the long-term influence of violent images occurred primarily through early exposure. Underlying this belief was the idea that the social representations and behavioral patterns that form the basis of our relationship to the world are acquired primarily during childhood.[1056] Recently, a review by Brad Bushman and Rowell Huesmann found that the influence of violent images on children's development is not only the result of early exposure to them, but also the result of their exposure. Recently, a review by Brad Bushman and Rowell Huesmann invalidated this hypothesis by showing that the long-term influence of violent images was attenuated, but nonetheless very significant in adult subjects[1084]. This result, based on the aggregation of several hundred studies prior to 2001, has since been confirmed by a large-scale study published in the journal Science[1058]. After controlling for participants' initial level of aggression and a wide range of sociode-mographic, psychological and personal covariates, this work showed two things. First, the more time an adolescent spends facing the post at age 14, the greater the likelihood of expressing aggressive behaviors at age 16 or 22. Second, the more time a young adult spends in front of the post at age 22, the greater the likelihood of expressing aggressive behavior at age 30. In relation to this last point, for example, it was reported that subjects who had watched television between 1 and 3 hours per day at age 22 were 1.5 times more likely to physically or verbally assault another person and 2.5 times more likely to be involved in a fight than individuals who had watched less than 1 hour. These data clearly show that violent images act in a cumulative way. Children, teenagers, adults, no one is safe from a deluge by which each subsequent exposure reinforces the damage already done by previous consumption.

Thus, exposure to violent images increases the frequency of aggressive behavior in the viewer, both in the short and long term. These effects are attested to by experimental, correlative and longitudinal studies. Functionally, short-term influences seem to be based mainly on *priming* effects, whereas long-term actions seem to be based more on vicarious learning processes[1061,1065,1084]. The hypothesis is that, in the latter case, the viewer ends up internalizing and reproducing the aggressive patterns that his screen vomits out with inexorable regularity. Of course, this transition would be largely threatened if it were not accompanied by a double feeling of acceptability and normality. This is where a second major process of long-term audiovisual influence comes in: habituation[1059]. This process, well known to physiologists[1136], is considered in detail in the next section.

*
**

Violence pushes the boundaries of the unacceptable

Traditionally, habituation is defined as "a decrease in a behavioral response resulting from repeated stimulation and not based on sensory adaptation, sensory fatigue, or motor fatigue. This phenomenon accounts, among other examples, for the behavior of the child who gradually loses interest in the brand new toy you have just given him, for the indifference of the husband whose wife gradually becomes transparent, or for the astonishing metamorphosis of Nadja, a young nurse trainee who was deeply gagged during her first visit to neurosurgery and who ended up devouring a rare tartar in the local restaurant after a month. Over the last 50 years, many authors have asked whether it would be legitimate to add to this list the progressive desensitization to violence of telephone users. The answer is now known. It is clearly positive[3,423,1061,1138]. Indeed, it is now established that the more violent images a subject sees, the less emotional reaction he or she has to these images[1070,1139,1140], the less inclined he or she is (even if he or she risks absolutely nothing) to come to the aid of a stranger who is a victim of violence[1141-1144] and the less empathetic he or she is towards the victims of brutal aggression[1145-1147]. Among the most frequently cited studies on the subject is one conducted more than three decades ago by Victor Cline and his colleagues[1139]. In this work, children aged 5 to 14 were selected according to their audio-visual consumption: some watched less than 4 hours of TV per week, others more than 25 hours. During the experiment, the authors collected physiological signals of emotional activity (blood pressure, electrodermal response[a]), while the participants watched a 14-minute film consisting of alternating non-violent and violent scenes. The results showed that children with the least exposure to television reacted significantly more strongly to violent images than did their counterparts who watched television. These data could not reflect sampling or familiarity bias, since no difference in reactivity was observed between children for nonviolent content. They could only be explained by the existence of habituation to violent images in the most television-addicted individuals. Since its formulation, this conclusion has been generalized to short-term expo-sure by the teams of Jordan Grafman[1070] and Margaret Thomas.[140] In the latter case, for example, the authors conducted their experiment in two stages. First, 8-10 year old children and college students were exposed to either a violent or non-violent action film. Second, all subjects were asked to watch a video of an actual assault. The results were identical in both study populations. They showed that the physiological markers of emotional response were strongly attenuated in the subjects who had seen the violent film during the initial phase of the experiment. Further

---

a. See note p. 156.

analysis indicated, in agreement with the findings of Victor Cline's team (see *above*), that individuals who watched less television reacted more intensely than their fellow television viewers during the first phase of the experiment, when the violent film was shown.

In another series of studies, the concrete effect of the desensitization process was clearly demonstrated by Ronald Drabman's team with 8-9 year old school children[1142-1144]. At the beginning of the experiment, the children were led past an empty room equipped with a video camera and told that a little girl and a little boy would soon come and play. Then, the subjects were taken to a projection room and exposed to one of three experimental conditions: no film, violent film, non-violent film. At the end of the session, the experimenter would argue that he had to make an urgent phone call to ask the children to watch the little girl and boy on the TV screen who were supposedly playing in the next room. In reality, the children (who, it goes without saying, were doing the experiment individually), were watching a pre-filmed video in which two subjects, aged 4 and 5, were about to shout at each other, threaten each other, smash each other's toys, chase each other and finally fight. When the experimenter left, he said he was going to his office and insisted on being notified immediately if there was any problem. The results showed that the students who had initially watched a violent film waited until a much later stage of conflict than their counterparts in the control groups (no film or non-violent film) to notify the experimenter. In general, exposure to violent audiovisual content led children to ignore the precursor signals of physical aggression and to act only after the latter had occurred.

In a recent study, Kostas Fanti and his colleagues used a sophisticated mathematical approach to generalize the previous data and identify precisely the temporal dynamics of the habituation process to violent images[1148]. After confirming the validity of the phenomenon, these authors showed that the accumulation of violent stimuli generated a double cognitive movement. First, the subjects took more and more pleasure in seeing the images presented. Second, they felt less and less empathy towards the victims. This latter observation directly parallels the findings of other more specific work showing that men exposed to violent images tend to be more accepting of physical and emotional abuse of women.[1145,1147] A work by Charles Mullin and Daniel Linz is particularly edifying in this respect[1146]. Faculty students were exposed to a horror film every other day for six days, for a total of three films[a]. The films contained a particularly heavy load of sadistic violence against women. Three days after the final screening, the subjects were exposed to videos in which female victims of actual violent assaults recounted their ordeal in detail. The results showed that, compared to a control group that had not participated in the initial screenings, the students who had been exposed to the horror films felt less empathy for the victims, who were willingly presented as responsible for their misfortune. These victims also had the severity of the trauma they experienced greatly minimized. In other words, take educated individuals, subject them to violent images involving sadistic behavior directed at a woman, and our merry men will end up explaining to you without blushing that rape victims are sluts who had it coming to them, and that it's really not that bad anyway. I must admit that I have often been appalled by the prevalence of this kind of discourse. Perhaps this is the beginning of an explanation! TV not only makes us stupid, sick and violent, it also leads us to think like sad bastards.

Beyond the behavioral results mentioned so far, it seems interesting to ask how a process of habituation to violent images can be organized at the neuronal level. This question has been addressed by Christopher Kelly and his colleagues at Columbia University. These researchers, who specialize in functional magnetic resonance imaging (fMRI[b]), recorded the brain activity of adult subjects while they were watching either non-violent or violent video clips[1068]. In the latter case, the data revealed a gradual decrease in activity in certain frontal regions involved in the control of aggressive behavior. In other words, it was as if the repetition of violent images ended up partially inhibiting the structures that allow the brain to regulate its belligerent impulses. A recent study by Jordan Grafman's team clarified this observation by suggesting that these neuro-physiological changes probably reflected a progressive exhaustion of the emotional response to violent images.[1070] In another study, carried out in parallel, this same team also showed that the adolescents most frequently exposed to violent audiovisual content displayed subtle developmental abnormalities in certain frontal structures known to be both late maturing in humans and involved in the regulation of aggressive behaviour.[1069] This result is hardly surprising given that the brain's ability to regulate aggres-

---

a. *Maniac, Friday the 13th, The Bloody Drill.*
b. fMRI. This technique makes it possible to establish a map of the areas activated or inhibited in the brain during the performance of a given task.

---

sive behaviour is also a key factor in the development of the brain. This finding is not surprising, given that brain anatomy varies greatly according to the experiences of the individual.[64]

Thus, being exposed to violent images creates a progressive state of desensitization in the viewer. The violent act then becomes both easier to contemplate and easier to perpetrate. This double process can only contribute to make our societies substantially more violent and brutal.

*
**

Violence feeds fear

Mrs. T. lives in a small village deep in the Auvergne. This affable 67 year old retired lady never goes to the city, "because with all these young people and all that we hear... I used to go there," she says shyly when pushed a little, "but now, you understand, with these gangs hanging around, we are no longer at peace. Yet Mrs. T. has never been assaulted, she doesn't know anyone who has, she has never seen a "gang" in her life and the city of Le Puy-en-Velay that she is now afraid to walk through is far from being a cut-throat. Every day our sixty-year-old spends most of her time watching television. The newspaper is, by far, her favorite program.

Nathalie is an active and busy woman. Nevertheless, she refuses to let her 14 year old daughter go out alone in the streets of Lyon. Every evening, for example, a nanny comes to wait for the teenager at the school exit. Nathalie admits to being worried "because of everything that is going on". When asked what she means by this expression, this attentive mother evokes "the madmen on the loose, like those who push people in the subway". She also mentions "all those rapes and pedophiles. And then there are the gangs in the suburbs, the drivers, it's really dangerous for a kid, especially if she's cute. Is it useful to specify that Nathalie has never been assaulted, raped or been the victim of a serious traffic accident and that she can't name anyone in her close circle of acquaintances who has undergone this kind of ordeal? In fact, everything this woman knows about insecurity, road psychopaths and bloodthirsty gangs that haunt our cities, she owes to television. "What planet do you live on, don't you ever watch the news?"

was her answer to most of my questions. It must be said that Nathalie is an avid television viewer. She "loves" TV shows (*CSI, FBI: Missing, Bones*) and watches the news every night "to know what's going on, because with my job I don't have much time to read the paper". As if it was unthinkable to use the 30 minutes devoted to the 20 hours of TF1 or France 2 to read *Le Monde, Le Figaro, Libération, La Croix* or *Aujourd'hui en France*. The fact is well known: reading the newspaper takes time; watching TV, not at all!

In November 2005, violent riots broke out in the suburbs of Paris.[1149] I learned about this on television while in a bar in the United States. I learned about it on television, while I was in a bar in the United States. I was waiting quietly for friends when my eye was drawn to the screen on the wall in front of me. There were images of desolation, burned buildings and hooded hordes. The commentators were talking about civil war, curfews, sending in troops, angry Muslim youth, and the failure of the integration policy. The subtitle of the report stated unequivocally "France is burning"! I was taken aback and immediately decided to call my relatives, who were surprised, to say the least, at my extreme concern. Paris was still there, the Hexagon was not burning and no civil war seemed to be on the agenda.

These few examples illustrate quite well, I believe, what scholars mean when they refer to the so-called "acculturation" theory[a]. In its most common sense, this theory suggests two things. First, television shows us a world that is sometimes far removed from objective reality. Second, this unreal world strongly influences our perception of the real world[1049,1151-1153]. In operational terms, this means that "those who spend more time watching television are more likely to perceive the real world in a way that reflects the most common and recurrent messages of the television world, compared to those who watch less television but are otherwise comparable in terms of their key demographic characteristics. Since its formulation nearly 40 years ago, this hypothesis has received extensive experimental support, particularly in the area of violence.[1049,1151-1153] The first salvo was fired by George F. Schwartz, who was the author of the first study on the subject. The first salvo was fired by George Gerbner and his team. These authors showed, as early as the mid-1970s, that telephagia led to an exaggerated sense of victimization, distrust and social mispercep-

---

a. The Anglo-Saxons speak of *cultivation*. This concept seems to me to be quite close to the notion of acculturation understood as "modifications that occur in a cultural group [concerning the way of acting, perceiving, judging, working, thinking, speaking] as a result of permanent contact with a group belonging to another culture".[542]

tions about criminal prevalence[1154-1157]. For example, in an early study, it was found that the more television an individual watched, the more he or she overestimated the chances of being assaulted, while subscribing to statements such as "most people cannot be trusted. 1158 These patterns were observed regardless of gender, education level, or propensity to consult print media. The phenomenon is now known as the "big bad world syndrome.

Since Gerbner's initial work, dozens of studies have confirmed the acculturation thesis[1049,1151-1153]. Among these, some have looked at audio-visual consumption as a whole, without distinction of content. It was then shown that the more an individual watched television, the more he or she perceived the world as a hostile place, full of violence and danger[1159,1160]. Based on this observation, more precise work was undertaken to determine, if I may say so, the deleterious potential of different programs. Not surprisingly, the results indicated that newscasts[1093,1161,1162], law enforcement programs[1161-1164] and crime shows[1161,1162] were particularly conducive to the development of a sense of insecurity. In support of this point, one study showed, for example, that fear of being mugged increased in proportion to the time spent watching local news programs. This feeling was perfectly irrational, i.e. independent of the actual level of local delinquency[1093]. In the same vein, another study found that mothers who ingested the most violent or criminal content tended to overestimate the general level of crime and, as a result, greatly increased the amount of warning they gave their offspring.[1165] This result clearly echoes the findings of the study on the impact of crime on children. This finding certainly echoes another study showing that children subjected to stories of kidnapping display a more intense fear of abduction[1166]. In line with this observation, a fairly old work, which academic ethics committees would surely forbid from now on, had moreover been able to show that it was possible to experimentally increase the fear of being victimized in a group of subjects repeatedly exposed to action films, naturally rich in violent content[1167]. As if all this were not enough, it was also established that the emergence of a feeling of insecurity led to the development of largely conservative political positions. Indeed, programmatic types with a violent or criminal content lead subjects not only to overestimate their chances of being victimized, but also (and especially) to defend the death penalty, repressive policies, and the individual right to own weapons with regard to delinquency[1159,1161].

Among all the studies carried out with reference to the acculturation thesis, there is one that seems to me particularly eloquent. The authors were interested in "the great fear of 1994"[1095]. Behind this expression lies a mysterious statistical break in the evolution of what our American friends consider to be the most important problem facing their country[a]. Between 1978 and 1992, a small average of 2-5% of people mentioned crime as a major concern. At the end of that period, the proportion inexplicably exploded. It reached 9% in 1993 and 52% in 1994. It then began to fall back slightly: 27% in 1995, 25% in 1996, 23% in 1997 and 20% in 1998. This development seemed all the more curious to observers since FBI statistics had shown a decrease in crime, especially violent crime, during the decade 1990-2000.[1168] The response to this paradox was to be to ask the question: "What is the nature of the problem? The answer to this paradox was found in the audiovisual field. The fear of Americans had evolved in parallel with the prevalence of crime-related content (length, place, number) in the television news. These had exploded in 1994 before falling back, without however returning to the original reference level of the years 1990-1992. The authors conclude: "The great fear of 1994 was more a fear of the television news than a fear based on real-world crime".[1095] Precise content analyses showed that the increase in the number of items devoted to violence in 1994 reflected to a large extent the extensive coverage of particularly sordid news items, including, for example, the murder of the ex-wife of soccer player O.J. Simpson. The relative plateau reached after 1995, compared to the period 1990-1992, reflected a more general phenomenon, reflecting the increasingly chronic penetration of violence in the news.[1169] In the United States, over the decade 1990-2000, the number of news stories in the media increased by more than half. Over the decade 1990-2000, in the United States, murder stories increased by more than 500% in the newscasts of the major broadcast networks. Over the same period, the number of homicides recorded by the FBI fell by 40%.[1169] It is tempting to relate these figures to other more general data showing that in the United States, nearly 90% of the crimes presented in crime shows are violent, whereas in reality this proportion is just over 10%.[114] The fact that the number of crimes presented in crime shows is not the same as the number of homicides recorded by the FBI. As Michael Medved somewhat provocatively puts it, if the frequency of violent crime were the same

---

a. The exact question respondents were asked was, "What do you think is the most important issue facing our country today?"

in the physical world as in the audiovisual world, "then in just 50 days, everyone in the United States would be killed and the last survivor could turn off the TV. However, these obvious facts do not prevent our hexagonal pipeaulogues from asserting without blushing that television helps "to raise awareness, by showing the world as it is, in its reality, which is not always easy to accept [...] Of course, we would all prefer the world to be a vast Disneyland, in which 'everyone is beautiful, everyone is nice'. We would be happy all the time, there would be only joy and pleasure to live in. It turns out that this is not the case [...] It is like if you want to renovate your apartment. You are obliged to establish an inventory of fixtures and a provisional budget. If your report is not precise or lacks realism [...], in the end, you will not have the expected result or it will cost you much more than expected. To grow up is to understand this and accept it. Between laughter and dismay, I confess, my heart sways.

Independently of the acculturation thesis itself, a number of studies have examined the capacity of violent images to produce short- and long-term fear reactions in the viewer. The vast majority of these studies were conducted on children. They revealed, with a remarkable unanimity, that violent contents were carriers of a deep anxiogenic power[1049,1054,1170]. A study carried out on more than 2,200 schoolchildren aged 8 to 11 years showed, for example, after taking into account a large number of potential covariates, that the most telephoned children obtained significantly higher scores on tests of anxiety and depression[1171]. Other studies, already mentioned, also revealed a link between audiovisual exposure and the occurrence of nightmares in children and adolescents[442,1050,1051]. In some cases, the fears generated by the content viewed proved so intense that they required psychiatric treatment[1052,1172,1173]. The best documented example concerns two 10-year-old schoolchildren who developed post-traumatic stress disorder after being exposed to a particularly credible horror film[1053]. One of these children, for example, "expressed a fear of ghosts, witches and the dark. He talked about them constantly and sought reassurance. He suffered from panic attacks, refused to go up the stairs alone and slept with the light on. He had nightmares and daytime flashbacks and would bang his head to remove thoughts of ghosts. These kinds of reactions have since been observed, to varying degrees, in large child and adolescent populations after exposure to news reports of particularly catastrophic events such as the Challenger space shuttle explosion,[174] the Oklahoma City bombing,[175,1176] or the terrorist attack of September 11, 2001.[1177] In the latter case, nearly 35% of the children and teenagers who had been exposed to the bombing had experienced the bombing. In the latter case, nearly 35% of children developed palpable stress. The severity of the symptoms observed was found to be correlated with the volume of audiovisual exposure. These disorders can persist for years[1176].

Of course, the content that is likely to frighten children varies with their age. The youngest children (2-6 years old) express alarm reactions more easily in response to events that are perceptually disturbing because of their sound and/or graphic aspects. Ghosts, monsters, witches and strange noises easily provoke fear in these subjects. This fear can then originate, for example, from characters as harmless and grotesque as *The Incredible Hulk* or *E.T. the extraterrestrial*[1178]. Older subjects (7-12 years) are less sensitive to these perceptual attributes. They respond more readily to scenes of explicit violence, especially if the scenes are realistic as they appear to be in the news. As children grow older, they also become more sensitive to abstract fears and events that "might happen. For example, it has been shown that schoolchildren aged 3 to 12 showed fewer anxiety reactions than teenagers aged 13 to 18 after watching a TV movie about a small group of men who survived a nuclear attack (*The Day After*).[1179]

Thus, the fact of being exposed to violent or catastrophic images can produce in the spectator, especially if he is young, long term anxieties. These can be born from a brutal exposure to a particularly frightening content. In extreme cases, this acute mode of intoxication can result in real post-traumatic stress requiring psychiatric treatment. In general however, the anxiogenic effect of television operates according to a more diffuse logic. It is built by accumulation to lead to what George Gerbner named opportunely a "syndrome of the big bad world". By dint of bathing in a cesspool of violent images, made of kidnappings, murders, fights, robberies, torture, rapes and thefts, the viewer ends up persuading himself that the world is infinitely more dangerous, more perfidious and more brutal than it really is. This leads our happy cathodic quidam to take protective measures, to proclaim his belief in capital punishment, to buy weapons and to display rather conservative political opinions. By the way, let's not fool ourselves, many elected officials have perfectly understood the rules of the game. When an election or a problem arises, it is not uncommon to see the issue of insecurity reappear in the media spotlight. Recently, in a radio show, a listener said, in anger, that our government could not be so cynical. I was reminded of Cherie Blair, who wrote a book about how her husband, Tony, had had a miscarriage, which was leaked to the press as a political strategy. I couldn't believe it," Mrs. Blair wrote. I was standing there bleeding and they [Tony Blair and Alastair Campbell, his communications advisor] were talking about what was going to be in the papers. I put the phone down and just lay there staring at the ceiling as the pain started to grip me.[1180] As Corey Robin has shown in a superb book,[1181] individuals who can sit on their wife's pain and the death of her fetus have little qualms about waving the security rag when it serves their purposes. The 2004 election campaign that ensured George Bush's re-election as President of the United States is ample evidence of this.[1181] In the months leading up to the vote, the United States and Canada had a number of issues to consider. In the months leading up to the vote, every quiver to the contrary was countered by a timely terrorist alert. When the head of the Weapons of Mass Destruction Search Mission said he had found nothing in Iraq, the Bush administration responded within three days with a possible chemical attack on the bus and train systems. When incriminating photos surfaced of the vile treatment of Abu Ghraib prisoners, the Bush administration responded within five days by declaring that virtually all of al-Qaeda's planned provisions for attacking the United States were now operational. When John Kerry appeared to be rising in the polls after announcing his running mate, the Bush administration responded within two days by saying that an al Qaeda attack was imminent. When the Democratic convention was launched in Boston, the Bush administration immediately responded by declaring a state of alert, claiming that terrorists were preparing to blow up several targets in New York, New Jersey and Washington, DC. Of course, all the television stations in the country broadcast all these alarming announcements, which suddenly ceased - needless to say - the day after George W. Bush Jr. was re-elected. Strangely enough, the same type of phenomenon occurred in France just before the 2002 presidential election, when Jacques Chirac succeeded in imposing the theme of insecurity as a central issue in the campaign.[43,287] In this case, however, television did not broadcast the issue of insecurity. In this case, however, television not only relayed the movement, it accompanied and amplified it with ardour[287,1182-1184]; such an ardour that some observers did not hesitate to evoke a veritable "security madness"[287], which could only "create alarmism and a quasi-paranoid impression of being surrounded by danger, even in the most peaceful and remote countryside, as soon as it is served by television"[1182]. The fact is that during the six weeks preceding the first round of voting, the TF1 and France 2 news channels engaged in a veritable race for gloom and doom[287,1182-1184]. During this period, no less than 314 subjects related to insecurity were presented with great dramatization, that is, an average of 52 reports per week (maximum 89, minimum 38). During the first week of the inter-election period, this prevalence suddenly dropped to 3 units. The following week did not do much better, with 15 small stories[1183]. This was a dramatic drop that could not, of course, be linked to any change in actual crime. If the orientation of the television news had changed so much, it was because the channels had proceeded, in the words of Julien Terral, who produced an exhaustive academic study on the subject, to a "severe editorial reframing"[1183]. Information that would have made the headlines on the evening news just before the election disappeared completely from the screens. For example, in 2002, on the eve of the first round of the presidential election, TF1 and France 2 made a big deal out of the story of a 70-year-old man who was beaten up, in the words of the presenter Jean-Pierre Pernaut, by "two thugs who were trying to rob him of money. The victim appeared before the cameras with a swollen face and trembling voice[287,1184]. The effect was striking. A few months later, this drama was repeated when a vulnerable pensioner was beaten to death by drifting youth. The story did not even make the news; neither France 2 nor TF1 mentioned it[287]! Different times, different customs. This does not mean, however, that TF1 or France 2 actively sought in 2002 to manipulate the vote of voters or to alter the course of democratic debate. It is likely, as Hélène Risser[287] and Laurent Joffrin[43] suggest, that these two channels simply seized, out of commercial interest, on a security theme that was necessarily buoyant because it was at the center of the political debate. Once Lionel Jospin was eliminated from the game, this theme ceased to be a campaign issue and therefore a relevant subject for television. This being said, it seems obvious to me, in view of the experimental data cited earlier in this chapter, that Jacques Chirac succeeded, by leading television to avidly seize the security issue, in creating a feeling of insecurity favorable to the development of his campaign. Indeed, fear is a powerful factor of influence[1181,1185]. The more it penetrates the mind, the more likely it is that the individual will be receptive to the security rhetoric (used by Jacques Chirac in 2002) and resistant to the suspicions of laxity (attributed to Lionel Jospin at the same time). The latest developments in our political life suggest that the electoralist thread of insecurity still has a bright future ahead of it[1186,1187].

*
**

To conclude

Thus, it appears that the deleterious effect of television on aggressiveness is today solidly established from a scientific point of view. All the studies published over the last 15 years state it loud and clear. Overall, three major effects of violent audiovisual content have been demonstrated: (1) desensitization: the viewer gradually learns to tolerate increasingly high levels of violence without batting an eyelid; (2) big bad world syndrome: the viewer gradually becomes convinced that the surrounding world is hostile and dangerous; (3) aggressiveness: the viewer behaves more violently and aggressively, both in the short and long term. No argument could be made in favor of the cathartic thesis that viewers purge their violent impulses by seeing them staged on television.

Despite all this data, the mainstream media, politicians and *ad hoc* pseudo-specialists keep saying that the effect of violent images is unproven, that there is no consensus among researchers, that the problem concerns only a few predisposed psychopaths, etc. These statements are incomprehensible. They show at best a profound incompetence and at worst a nauseating bad faith. Of course, television is not responsible for all the violence that pours out of our societies every day. Of course other factors play a decisive role (poverty, parental abuse, etc.). However, the fact is there, inescapable: by reducing our exposure to violent content, we would contribute to creating a significantly less violent world. To say otherwise is either a denial of reality or an intellectual swindle.

CONCLUSION

A LITTLE LESS TV MEANS A LOT MORE LIFE

"Ha! ha! the Compromises,
Prejudices, cowardice!... That I pact? Never, never! - Ah! there you are,
you, the Sottish!
- I know well that in the end you will put me down; No matter: I fight! I
fight! I fight!"

(Edmond Rostand, Cyrano de Bergerac[1188])

"Opposing all the enslavements that modernity can produce will become the prerogative of a few minds miraculously kept awake."
(Natacha Polony, journalist, associate professor of modern literature[81])

"Conscience is much more than the thorn, it is the dagger in the flesh."
(Cioran, writer and philosopher[1189])

This summer, my wife, myself and the children spent our vacations in a beautiful little village in the Auvergne region of France in a family house we bought a few years ago. Since we moved in, all the surrounding buildings have gradually been clad with ugly satellite dishes. Our walls are now the exception in their ostensible virginity. "I have a satellite dish that I don't use anymore and that I can give you if you want," even suggested a neighbor to whom we didn't ask anything. "When you don't come often, it's true that it's expensive," she added, convinced that our reluctance could only be financial. People really have a hard time conceiving that one can choose, in all conscience, to live without TV. And the least we can say is that, from this point of view, children are remarkably ordinary people. Take Lea, for example. This charming little 9-year-old girl was deeply shocked when she realized that her friend Charlotte (our daughter) didn't have a TV. "But how do you watch in the kitchen?" said Lea, assuming, I suppose, that no TV just meant no TV in the bedroom. "No no," Charlotte resumed, "we don't have one at home, my parents don't want to." A long silence followed, finally punctuated by a disarming reply of which children have the secret: "You know, you can come and see at my place if you want my dad he is nice *and* he will let you watch.

Indeed, it is difficult to doubt this parental authorization when one examines little Léa's summer schedule. This one illustrates, I fear, to the point of caricature, the subject of this book and the terrible price that our children pay on the screen. In the morning, Léa "couldn't" come and play with Charlotte, because there was *Foudre* from 10 to 11 o'clock on France 2, and then just after that *Plus belle la vie* on France 3. In the afternoon, our young phone caller left the beach at 6pm to avoid missing *Secret Story* on TF1. In the evening, at the time of the dinner, all his family met in front of the television news. The day would then end with two or three episodes of some series, preferably American. At the very least, this stacking represented 5 hours of daily exposure, that is to say for 2 months of summer, 300 hours in total equivalent to nearly 19 days of watch time[a]. 19 days! 19 days of life and dozens of formative experiences vanished forever in the meanders of the cathodic nothingness. 19 polluted days, filled with smoking, drinking, sexual and consumerist incitements. A real disaster whose magnitude can only be really apprehended by comparing the schedules of Léa and Charlotte[b]. During her vacations, the latter was forced to occupy herself, without the help of television. She had to build activities, find play partners, adapt her projects to the weather conditions, etc. In the end, the hours Léa wasted watching *Foudre*, *Plus belle la vie*, *Les Experts*, *Desperate Housewives* or *Secret Story* were used by Charlotte to sleep, swim, dream, ride her bike, chase butterflies, bake cakes, feed the neighbor's donkeys or simply read a book. Concerning this last point, for example, I had slipped into the lady's luggage a book on French history that I thought was very well done[1190]. She opened it without enthusiasm on a morning heavy with an abysmal boredom. A boredom that obviously would never have seen the light of day if a TV had been present. Quickly, Charlotte entered the story that was proposed to her. She devoured it in a few days with obvious pleasure and immediately asked for a book on Joan of Arc and the Middle Ages. Several times she turned into an excellent storyteller for her 4 year old sister who asked her about the pictures in the book. The book then became a pretext for all sorts of games, exchanges and shared time. Prehistory saw the birth of a hut in the garden and strange

---

a. Calculated on an average basis of 8 hours of sleep per night.
b. Of course, this is not to make Charlotte a model. She is a perfectly ordinary little girl who acts like any other girl of her age in her situation.

frescoes on the wall of the garage (better, when you don't have a TV, to opt for watercolors!). Celtic times transformed the girls into mistletoe-gathering druids and potion-makers. The revolutionary period led to the building of a guillotine with Ken and Barbie in the respective roles of Louis XVI and Marie-Antoinette. None of these moments were experienced as chores or work. Yet each of them contributed directly to reinforcing the social, cultural, lexical, artistic, cognitive and physical skills of the girls. If a TV had been present, much of this learning would have been lost and replaced by comatose time. Of course, one can say that 300 hours, after all, is not much. Yet, on the scale of a child's life, those few summer units represent a total of nearly 13,000 hours[a]. 13,000 hours of formative activities gained by Charlotte and lost by Lea, which makes 812 days of waking life[b], or if you prefer, more than two full years of learning, one of which is in the space of the active and the other in the field of the passive. Confronted with these divergences, one cannot be surprised, I believe, at the profound differences that already exist between our two schoolgirls. Charlotte is rather healthy, well-adjusted, patient with her sister, solid at school and at ease in the community. Léa, on the other hand, has repeated her CM1. She reads with difficulty, is noticeably overweight, seems unable to talk to her little brother without vilifying him, and seems very proud of having already tried to smoke "like the grown-ups. To say that television alone accounts for all these differences would be foolish. However, it would be even more foolish to say that television does not play a role, or that it operates in a marginal way! Indeed, the hundreds of studies presented throughout this book leave no doubt that TV negatively affects the viewer's health, attention, intelligence, academic achievement, willingness to work, aggressiveness and capacity for empathy. Those who say the opposite can be divided into two categories: the ignorant who, hiding behind an academic title, feel exempt from any research work and deliver their beliefs as revealed truths; the swindlers who, familiar with the media world from which they benefit, are ready to make any intellectual compromise in order not to saw off the branch on which they are sitting.

In practice, ignoramuses and swindlers would hardly be a nuisance if they did not constantly have an open microphone and if they were not given as much - or even more - credit by many journalists than the

---

a. Calculated on a rather low average viewing time of 1 h/day between 0 and 4 years old and 2 h 15/day between 4 and 18 years old[435].
b. Calculated on an average basis of 8 hours of sleep per night.

---

most rigorous scientists who are actively working on the question of television influences and know every nook and cranny of the specialized literature[124]. Of course, fairness requires that all the opposing views be presented. But these must also be well-founded and supported. If this principle of fairness is violated, then any notion of impartiality disappears and the public is irreparably cheated. Of course, one can argue that researchers have, in the past, demonstrated their incredible capacity to make mistakes and to say anything. This is true, no one disputes it[1191]. However, it must be pointed out that the great errors of our scientific history have flourished, either on the erroneous interpretation of heavily fragmented facts, or on the existence of uncertain experimental observations (i.e. sometimes white, sometimes black, sometimes grey)[1192,1193]. However, the subject of television does not fit into either of these two boxes. The current body of data is both massive in its scope and consistent in its propensity to point to the deleterious effects of the small screen on thought, health, fear and sociability. In this context, the risks of error are not in the reality of the facts, but in the detail of the possible interpretations. For example, more than 99% of the available experimental work shows that viewers are more aggressive after seeing violent images. This is a fact. In practice, this fact can be explained in different ways (e.g. *priming* process; general arousal mechanism; imitation; etc.). Each of these explanations may of course be valid or erroneous. For a scientist, this is important. For a parent who must choose whether or not to expose his or her children to television, it is profoundly secondary. Indeed, substantive interpretative disagreements do not change the fact that television makes the viewer violent and aggressive. In a general way, this example accounts for what happens for the whole of the thematic fields approached within the preceding chapters. The subject could have been intelligence, language, school success, alcoholism, obesity, risky sexual behavior or sleep. Therefore, for all these dimensions, we should not expect any refutation of the principle of deleterious action of television in the years to come. At the most, we will learn that certain mechanisms of action were not those initially described. It does not matter, really. Basically, it will not change the fact that the small screen is a major ontogenetic disaster and that it is preferable to keep our children as far away as possible from its presence.

*
**

This work is now nearing completion. All the elements that, it seems to me, should be put on the table for discussion have been put on the table, without any cautelization or ambiguity. I hope that this approach will contribute to balance a debate that has been largely confiscated by the guardians of the television temple. Clearly, when I began writing this text, I had not planned to produce a list of "final recommendations". Indeed, I thought that it was up to each person to define his or her own position, according to singular arbitrations. For example, some parents may think that if they don't give themselves some quiet time on weekends by sticking their kid in front of the screen, they will develop a significant irritability whose effects will be much more harmful than those of television. Similarly, a single mother may say to herself that she prefers to entrust her son to a loving neighbor, but with a contagious telephagia, rather than to an unknown nanny or to an impersonal nursery. These choices are legitimate and belong to the sphere of individual responsibility. However, every time I finish a lecture on the problem of television influences, people come to me and ask me to summarize my position and give them some sort of "takeaway"[a] on which to anchor their thoughts. In these moments, I am often asked if I am "really" in favor of a strict ban, if there cannot be a good use of television, or if one should abruptly take away the TV from a child who has been used to watching it for years. As a final conclusion to this work, I will try to address these issues by proposing five major recommendations that I think can be made on the basis of the elements presented in this book.

First, TV has a strong negative impact on cognitive development (and aging), sleep, academic achievement, health, aggressiveness, and intra- and extra-familial sociability. Although there are (rare) good programs, there is no "good use" of the small screen. Indeed, when it is available, people turn it on syncretically and do not manage (except in very exceptional cases) to target their consumption precisely. This is particularly true for children and teenagers who are exposed to totally inappropriate programs at a very early age. The best solution seems to me to be, without any doubt, zero TV.

Second, if a TV is to be present in the home, it should never be in the bedroom, especially for a child or teenager.

____

a. What the English call a "*take-home message*".

Third, during the first five or six years of life, all audiovisual exposure should be strictly forbidden by parents, since television disturbs sleep, promotes long-term obesity and interferes with the intellectual, emotional, physical and social development of the child. The deficits acquired in these last domains at the first ages of the existence are very often irreversible. The problem includes both foreground exposure (the child watches TV directly) and background exposure (the child is simply present in the room when the parents are watching TV).

Fourth, among elementary and middle school students, television viewing should in all cases be kept below 3-4 hours per week (this figure includes video use, of course). The programs watched should be free of risky health content (alcohol, tobacco, violence, sexuality, food). Parents should be particularly adamant about advertising exposure, whether explicit (cuts) or implicit (product placement). Children and adolescents should never eat in front of the television, watch it at night before going to sleep or in the morning before leaving for school. It is clear that young people sometimes have access to a TV at their friends' homes. However, this opportunity for consumption is limited and in no way justifies the elimination of rules for use within the home.

Fifth, adults who have reached the age of majority and have been vaccinated can do what they want, it is nobody's business. However, these adults should not forget that television is a factor of social isolation and that it exposes the viewer to major morbid risks because of its propensity to encourage a sedentary lifestyle, the cognitive decline inherent in the aging process, the appearance of degenerative cerebral pathologies (Alzheimer's) and risky behaviors (tobacco, alcohol, violence, sexuality).

I hope that everyone will find in these recommendations some food for thought. On a personal level, I can only hope that a collective awareness will be reached that would revoke forever the exorbitant power enjoyed today by the clique of brain sellers. In light of the scientific data available, it seems unthinkable to me that we continue to entrust our children for more than 2 hours a day to the influences of a media as profoundly harmful as television. It directly affects human development in all its intellectual, emotional, social and somatic dimensions. I hope that this reality can be heard. If it is not, at least we will no longer be able to say that we did not know.

Notes

1. CÉLINE L.-F., *Cahiers Céline 2 : Céline et l'actualité littéraire. 1957-1961*, Gallimard, 1976, quoted *in* DOURNON J.-Y., *Grand dictionnaire des citations françaises*, Acropole, 1982, p. 798.

2. LACROIX A., "Finally a good reason to throw away your TV", *Philosophy magazine*, n° 37, March 2010, p. 3.

3. STRASBURGER V.C., "Children, adolescents, and the media," *Curr. Probl. Pediatr. Adolesc. Health Care*, 34, 54, 56, 92-93.

4. CHRISTAKIS D.A. *et al*, "Media as a public health issue," *Arch. Pediatr. Adolesc. Med*, n° 160, 2006, p. 445 *and passim*.

5. ROWLAND W., "A modest proposal: the class-action case against television", *Int. J. Media Cult Politics*, n° 1, 2005, p. 149 *and passim*.

6. GLANTZ S.A. *et al*, *The Cigarette Papers*, University of California Press, 1998.

7. SMITH R., "Television addiction", *in* BRYANT J. *et al* (eds.), *Perspectives on Media Effects*, Lawrence Erlbaum, 1986, p. 109 *and passim*.

8. KUBEY R., "Television dependence, diagnosis and prevention", *in* MACBETH T.M. (ed.), *Tuning in to Young Viewers: Social Science Perspectives on Television*, Sage Publications, 1996, p. 221 *and passim*.

9. KUBEY R. *et al*, "Television addiction is no mere metaphor", *Sci. Am.* n° 286, 2002, p. 74 *and passim*.

10. MCILLWRAITH R.D., " I'm addicted to television: the personality, imagination, and TV watching patterns of self-identified TV addicts ", *J. Broadcast Electronic Media*, n° 42, 1998, p. 371 *and passim*.

11. CONLIN M., "America's reality-TV addiction," businessweek. com, January 30, 2003, accessed December 2, 2010, http://www. businessweek.com/bwdaily/dnflash/jan2003/nf20030130_ 8408.htm.

12. PUTNAM R., *Bowling Alone*, Simon & Schuster, 2000.

13. KLEIN N., *No Logo*, Picador, 2000.

14. LINN S., *Consuming Kids*, Anchor Books, 2004.

15. QUART A., *Branded*, Basic Books, 2003.

16. SCHOR J.B., *Born to Buy*, Scribner, 2004.

17. MAHLER V., *Souriez, vous êtes ciblés*, Albin Michel, 2007.

18. BÉNILDE M., *On achète bien les cerveaux*, Raisons d'agir, 2007.

19. BOHLER S., *150 petites expériences de psychologie des médias*, Dunod, 2008, p. 4.

20. VINCENT C., "Peut-on tromper le cerveau pour la bonne cause?", lemonde.fr, August 8, 2009, accessed August 28, 2009, http://www. lemonde.fr/archives/article/2009/08/08/peuton-tromper-le-cerveau-pour-la-bonne-cause_1226801_0.html.

21. "vuàlatélé n° 1," Syndicat national de la publicité télévisée newsletter, n° 1, October 2003, accessed January 5, 2009, http://www.snptv.org/plus-tv/2003/vualateleN1.pdf.

22. GEORGE P. *et al*, *Le Neuromarketing en action. Talking and selling to the brain*, Eyrolles, 2010, p. 46.

23. Patrick Le Lay, chairman and CEO of TF1, quoted *in* "L'affaire Le Lay", *Télérama*, 11-17 September 2004, p. 9.

24. DUFOUR D.R., " Télévision, socialisation, subjectivation : le rôle du troisième parent ", *Le Débat*, n° 132, 2004, p. 195 *and passim*.

25. LURÇAT L., *Des enfances volées par la télévision. Le temps prisonnier*, François-Xavier de Guibert, 2004, 3rd ed., pp. 16, 48, 173, 175.

26. AMALOU F., *Le Livre noir de la pub. Quand la communication va trop loin*, Stock, 2001.

27. INGLEBY R *et al*, "UNCROC and the prevention of childhood obesity: the right not to have food advertisements on television", *J. Law Med*, n° 16, 2008, p. 49 *and passim*.

28. MEYER M., *Le Livre noir de la télévision*, Grasset, 2006, 4th cover, pp. 15 and 484.

29. WINN M., *The Plug-in-Drug*, Penguin Group, 2002, corrected edition, pp. 29 (BBC), 97 (survey), 151, 129-130, 204-205.

30. "Tom Cruise and Steven Spielberg Watch Their Kids," actustar.com, October 1, 2002, accessed September 25, 2010, http://www.actustar.com/Actualites/11092/tomcruise-et-steven-spielberg-surveillent-leurs-enfants.

31. "Madonna forbids her children to watch TV and eat candy so they don't go crazy," 20minutes.fr, April 26, 2008, accessed September 25,

2010, http://www.20minutes.fr/ article/227821/People-Madonna-interdict-a-ses-enfants-tele-and-candy-so-they-don't-go-crazy.php

32. MULLER C. *et al*, *Grandir avec la télé*, Marabout, 2007, 4th cover, pp. 10, 21, 57, 74, 109-110, 112-113, 114, 119, 185-186, 188, 193

33. FERRY L., " Actes de la journée thématique " La télévision pour quoi faire ? ", Commission des affaires culturelles du Sénat. Session of 11 June 2003, pp. 39-42; access 26 September 2010, http://www.senat.fr/rap/r02-352/r02-3521.pdf, pp. 40-41.

34. TISSERON S., *Les Bienfaits des images*, Odile Jacob, 2002, pp. 8, 11, 12, 46, 128, 130, 163-168, 187, 190, 228-229, 231.

35. ELKABBACH J.P., "Journalist and former President and CEO of France Télévisions", proceedings of the thematic day "La télévision pour quoi faire?" organized by the Senate's Cultural Affairs Commission, session of June 11, 2003, p. 14, accessed September 26, 2010, http://www.senat.fr/rap/r02-352/r02-3521.pdf.

36. Emmanuelle Guilbart, president of the Gulli youth channel, quoted *in* DESBORDES J.P., *Mon enfant n'est pas un cœur de cible*, Actes Sud, 2007, pp. 192-194.

37. MIÈGE B., " Une question à dépasser : celle de l'influence de la télévision et des médias de masse ", *in* COURBET D. *et al.* (sous la direction de), *La Télévision et ses influences*, De Boeck, 2003, pp. 113, 114, 120.

38. TISSERON S., " Inquiéter pour contrôler ", *Le Monde diplomatique*, January 2003, accessed September 26, 2010, http://www.monde-diplomatique.fr/2003/01/TISSERON/9894.

39. TISSERON S., *Enfants sous influence : les écrans rendent-ils les jeunes violents*, Armand Colin, 2000, p. 111.

40. STORA M., *Les Écrans ça rend accro... ça reste à prouver*, Hachette Littératures, 2007, 4ᵉ de couverture, pp. 8, 12, 14, 21-22, 23, 39, 103, 115.

41. BOUZOU V., *Le Vrai Visage de la téléréalité*, Jouvence, 2007, pp. 26-27, 89.

42. HALBERSTADT-HARARI S., *La Télé déchaînée*, Flammarion, 2009, pp. 21-24.

43. JOFFRIN L., *Média Paranoïa*, Éditions du Seuil, 2009, pp. 114, 123.

44. Dominique Poussier, director of the youth unit of TF1, quoted *in* DESBORDES J.P., *Mon enfant n'est pas un cœur de cible*, Actes Sud, 2007, pp. 49-53.

45. CHOMSKY N., *Media Control: The Spectacular Achievements of Propaganda*, Seven Stories Press, 2003, 2nd ed.

46. HERMAN E. *et al*, *Manufacturing Consent*, Pantheon, 2002.

47. POPPER K.R., " Une loi pour la télévision ", *in* POPPER K.R. *et al.* (under the direction of), *La Télévision, un danger pour la démocratie*, 10-18, coll. "Bibliothèques", 1996, p. 19 *and passim*.

48. BOURDIEU P., *Sur la télévision*, Raisons d'agir, 1996.

49. LURÇAT L., *Violence à la télé. L'enfant fasciné*, Syros, 1989.

50. LURÇAT L., *Le Jeune Enfant devant les apparences télévisuelles*, Desclée de Brouwer, 1994, 2nd edition.

51. LURÇAT L., *À cinq ans, seul avec Goldorak. Le jeune enfant et la télévision*, Syros, 1981, 2nd ed.

52. POSTMAN N., *Amusing Ourselves to Death: Public Discourse in the Age of Show Business*, Penguin, 1985.

53. DUFOUR D.R., "Vivre en troupeau en se pensant libres", *Le Monde diplomatique*, January 2008, accessed 25 September 2010, http://www.monde-diplomatique.fr/2008/ 01/DUFOUR/15491.

54. BENTOLILA A., *Tout sur l'école*, Odile Jacob, 2004, pp. 17, 19, 20-23, 71, 73, 81, 84, 93, 110.

55. KASSER T., *The High Price of Materialism*, MIT Press, 2002.

56. "L'affaire Le Lay", *Télérama*, 11-17 September 2004.

57. DESBORDES J.P., *Mon enfant n'est pas un cœur de cible*, Actes Sud, 2007.

58. KUBEY R. *et al*, "Media and the family", *in* SINGER D.G. *et al* (eds.), *Handbook of Children and the Media*, Sage Publications, 2001, p. 323 *and passim*.

59. "L'environnement médiatique des jeunes de 0 à 18 ans: que transmettons-nous à nos enfants?", CIEM, report in response to the mission entrusted by Ségolène Royal, Minister Delegate for the Family, Children and the Handicapped, May 2002, access 25 September 2010, http://www.cemea.asso.fr/IMG/rapportCIEM.pdf, pp. 7 and 46.

60. JOST F., *Comprendre la télévision et ses programmes*, Armand Colin, 2009, 2nd ed., p. 36.

61. See Chapters III and IV for a detailed discussion.

62. BOORSTIN D., *Histoire des Américains*, Robert Laffont, 1991.

63. MACBETH WILLIAMS T. *et al*, "Television and other leisure activities", *in* MACBETH WILLIAMS T. (ed.), *The Impact of Television: A Natural*

Experiment in Three Communities, Academic Press, 1986, p. 143 *and passim.*

64. See Chapter II for a detailed discussion.

65. HEALY J.M., *Endangered Minds*, Simon & Schuster Paperbacks, 1990, p. 316.

66. CHALL J.S., *Stages of Reading Development*, McGraw-Hill, 1983.

67. DOLAN R.J., "Emotion, cognition, and behavior", *Science*, n° 298, 2002, p. 1191 *and passim.*

68. LABAR K.S. *et al*, "Cognitive neuroscience of emotional memory", *Nat. Rev. Neurosci.* 2006;7:54 *and passim.*

69. LEDOUX J.E., " Emotion: clues from the brain ", *Annu. Rev. Psychol*, n° 46, 1995, p. 209 *and passim.*

70. VON GOETHE J.W., *Faust*, translated from the German by Gérard de Nerval, digitized work, online departmental media library, Conseil général du Haut-Rhin, access November 2, 2008, http://www.mediatheque.cg68.fr/livre_num/faust.pdf, p. 28.

71. SOKAL A. *et al*, *Impostures intellectuelles*, Odile Jacob, 1997.

72. See Chapter IV for a detailed discussion.

73. ZORN F., *Mars*, Gallimard, 1979, pp. 39-42.

74. "Bilan de campagne Maaf," stratégies.fr, October 2, 2008, accessed October 17, 2009, http://www.strategies.fr/actualites/marques/103010W/bilan-de-campagne-maaf.html; "Maaf, France's favorite TV ad," stratégies.fr, January 26, 2005, accessed October 17, 2009, http://www.strategies.fr/actualites/marques/r83243W/maaf-publicitetv-preferee-des-francais.html.

75. *Coeur océan*, France 2, youth programs (KD2A), August 13, 2008.

76. "Nicolas Sarkozy and Michel Onfray. Confidences entre ennemis", *Philosophie magazine*, April 8, 2007.

77. For an excellent critical review: JORDAN B., *Les Imposteurs de la génétique*, Éditions du Seuil, 2000.

78. BRIGHELLI J.P., *La Fabrique du crétin*, Gallimard, 2005, p. 124.

79. KOSKINIDOU Z., "Les Grecs veulent comprendre", *Métro*, 10 December 2008, p. 4.

80. HALIMI S. *et al*, *L'opinion ça se travaille*, Agone, 2006, 5th ed.

81. POLONY N., *Nos enfants gâchés*, Lattès, 2005, pp. 21-22, 44, 66, 92, 164-166, 193.

82. *The Game of Death*, France 2, March 17, 2010, 8:35 pm.

83. Patrick, 52 years old, quoted *in* "Ce *Jeu de la mort* qui fait peur", *Le Journal du dimanche*, 14 March 2010, p. 13.

84. DURANT-PARENTI C., "Deux préadolescents mis en examen pour le viol d'une fillette", LePoint.fr, May 16, 2008, access on October 8, 2008: http://www.lepoint.fr/actualitessociete/deux-preadolescents-mis-en-examen-pour-le-viol-d-une-fillette/920/0/246037.

85. FLOOD M., "The harms of pornography exposure among children and young people," *Child Abuse Rev* 18 (2009): 384ff.

86. AMERICAN ACADEMY OF PEDIATRICS, "Committee on public education, media education," *Pediatrics*, n° 104, 1999, p. 341 *et passim*.

87. AMERICAN ACADEMY OF PEDIATRICS, "Children, adolescents, and television," *Pediatrics*, n° 107, 2001, p. 423 *and passim*.

88. DELION P. *et al*, "Un moratoire pour les bébés téléphages", *Le Monde*, 26 October 2007.

89. GAMBOTTI C., *Brèves de pouvoir : petits meurtres sémantiques entre amis, alliés et adversaires*, Bourin, 2008, p. 93.

90. Stéphane Chomant, general delegate of the association of the Friends of the François-Mitterrand Institute, quoted *in* "La Star Ac fait couiner le Marais", libération.fr, 19 September 2008, accessed 26 September 2010, http://www.liberation.fr/societe/010113189-la-staracfait-couiner-le-marais.

91. "Nonce Paolini sets the limits," TVMag.com, August 26, 2009, accessed August 27, 2009, http://www.tvmag.com/programme-tv/article/mercato/46668/nonce-paolini-assumela-tele-realite.html?meId=3.

92. SAINT-EXUPÉRY A., *Le Petit Prince*, Gallimard, coll. "Folio", 1999, p. 76.

93. ROSE G., "Sick individuals and sick populations", *Int. J. Epidemiol*, n° 14, 1985, p. 32 *and passim*.

94. HANCOX R.J. *et al*, "Watching television is associated with childhood obesity: but is it clinically important?", *Int. J. Obes.(Lond.)*, n° 30, 2006, p. 171 *et passim*.

95. RIEDL R., "Les conséquences de la pensée causale", *in* WATZLAWICK P. (under the direction of), *L'Invention de la réalité*, 1988, Éditions du Seuil, p. 79 *and passim*.

96. HANCOX R.J. *et al*, "Association of television viewing during childhood with poor educational achievement," *Arch. Pediatr. Adolesc. Med*, 159, 614 *et al.*

97. "Eating disorders, body image and the media," British Medical Association, 2000.

98. ANSCHUTZ D.J. *et al*, "Exposure to slim images in mass media: television commercials as reminders of restriction in restrained eaters", *Health Psychol*, n° 27, 2008, p. 401 *and passim*.

99. ANSCHUTZ D.J. *et al*, "The bold and the beautiful. Influence of body size of televised media models on body dissatisfaction and actual food intake," *Appetite*, n° 51, 2008, p. 530 *et passim*.

100. FIELD A.E. *et al*, "Peer, parent, and media influences on the development of weight concerns and frequent dieting among preadolescent and adolescent girls and boys," *Pediatrics*, n° 107, 2001, p. 54 *and passim*.

101. JORDAN A., "The role of media in children's development: an ecological perspective," *J. Dev. Behav. Pediatr*, 25, 196 *et al.*

102. KILBOURNE J., *Deadly Persuasion: Why Women and Girls Must Fight the Addictive Power of Advertising*, Free Press, 1999.

103. MALONEY M.J. *et al*, "Dieting behavior and eating attitudes in children," *Pediatrics*, n° 84, 1989, p. 482 *et passim*.

104. PETRIE K.J. *et al*, "Influence of television on demand for cosmetic surgery," *Med. J. Aust.* 2008;189:244 *et al.*

105. MARKEY C.N. *et al*, "A correlational and experimental examination of reality television viewing and interest in cosmetic surgery," *Body Image*, n° 7, 2010, p. 165 *et passim*.

106. See Chapter III for a detailed discussion.

107. FOGEL J. *et al*, "Soap operas and talk shows on television are associated with poorer cognition in older women," *South. Med. J.*, n° 99, 2006, p. 226 *and passim*.

108. LINDSTROM H.A. *et al*, "The relationships between television viewing in midlife and the development of Alzheimer's disease in a case-control study," *Brain Cogn.* n° 58, 2005, p. 157 *et passim*.

109. AKBARALY T.N. *et al*, "Leisure activities and the risk of dementia in the elderly: results from the Three-City Study," *Neurology*, n° 73, 2009, p. 854 *et passim*.

110. KRAMER A.F. *et al*, "Environmental influences on cognitive and brain plasticity during aging," *J. Gerontol. A. Biol. Sci. Med. Sci.* n° 59, 2004, pp. M940-M957.

111. MILGRAM N.W. *et al*, "Neuroprotective effects of cognitive enrichment," *Ageing Res. Rev.* 5 (2006): 354ff.

112. CALVERT S.L., "Children as consumers: advertising and marketing", *Fut.Child*, n° 18, 2008, p. 205 *and passim*.

113. JENNINGS N.A. *et al*, "Advertising and consumer development", *in* PECORA N. *et al* (eds), *Children and Television*, LEA, 2007, p. 149 *and passim*.

114. SCHOR J.B., *The Overspent American*, Harper Perennial, 1998.

115. KAPPOS A.D., "The impact of electronic media on mental and somatic children's health," *Int. J. Hyg. Environ. Health*, n° 210, 2007, p. 555 *et passim*.

116. WALDMAN M. *et al*, "Does television cause autism?", Johnson School Research Paper Series n°s 1-7, Cornell University, December 2006, accessed September 26, 2010, http://forum.johnson.cornell.edu/faculty/waldman/AUTISM-WALDMANNICHOLSON-ADILOV.pdf.

117. KRIEGEL B., " La violence à la télévision, rapport de la mission présidée par Blandine Kriegel à M. Jean-Jacques Aillagon, ministre de la Culture et de la Communication ", Ministère de la Culture et de la Communication, novembre 2002, accès 16 novembre 2008, http://lesrapports.ladocumentationfrancaise.fr/BRP/024000584/0000.pdf.

118. DESCHAMPS S., " Actes de la journée thématique " La télévision pour quoi faire ? ", Commission des affaires culturelles du Sénat, séance du 11 juin 2003, p. 36 ; accès 26 septembre 2010, http://www.senat.fr/rap/r02-352/r02-3521.pdf.

119. SARDOU E., "Proceedings of the thematic day "Television for what purpose?", Commission of Cultural Affairs of the Senate, session of June 11, 2003, pp. 31-32; access September 26, 2010, http://www.senat.fr/rap/r02-352/r02-3521.pdf.

120. HUESMANN L.R. *et al*, *Television and the Aggressive Child: A Cross National Comparison*, Lawrence Erlbaum, 1986.

121. GROEBEL J., "Media violence in a cross-cultural perspective", *in* SINGER D.G. *et al* (eds.), *Handbook of Children and the Media*, 2001, Sage Publications, pp. 255, 262 *et passim*.

122. CARLSSON U. *et al*, *Children and Media Violence: Yearbook from the Unesco International Clearinghouse on Children and Violence on the Screen*, Nordicom, 1998.

123. GROEBEL J., "The Unesco global study on violence: report presented to the director-general of the Unesco", *in* CARLSSON U. *et al.* (eds.), *Children and Media Violence: Yearbook from the Unesco International*

Clearinghouse on Children and Violence on the Screen, 1998, Nordicom, pp. 181-183

124. BUSHMAN B.J. *et al*, "Media violence and the American public. Scientific facts versus media misinformation," *Am. Psychol.* n° 56, 2001, pp. 477, 479 (Michael Medved) *et passim*.

125. GARRISSON M.M. *et al*, "A teacher in the living room," The Henry Kaiser Family Foundation, Access 18 December 2008, http://www.kff.org/entmedia/upload/7427.pdf, pp. 14, 37, 41.

126. BabyTV, accessed September 26, 2010, http://www.babytvchannel.fr/view_program. aspx?l=4&i=5&si=5&p=24.

127. BabyTV, accessed September 26, 2010, http://www.babytvchannel.fr/view_article. aspx?l=8&i=29&si=19.

128. ZIMMERMAN F.J. *et al*, "Associations between media viewing and language development in children under age 2 years", *J. Pediatr.*, n° 151, 2007, p. 364 *and passim*.

129. CHONCHAIYA W. *et al*, "Television viewing associates with delayed language development", *Acta Paediatr.* n° 97, 2008, pp. 977 *and passim*.

130. ANDERSON D.R. *et al*, "Television and very young children," *Am. Behav. Sci.* 48 (2005): 505 *et al*.

131. TANIMURA M. *et al*, "Television viewing, reduced parental utterance, and delayed speech development in infants and young children," *Arch. Pediatr. Adolesc. Med.* 161 (2007): 618 *et al*.

132. VANDEWATER E.A. *et al*, "Time well spent? Relating television use to children's free-time activities," *Pediatrics*, n° 117, 2006, pp. e181-e191.

133. CHRISTAKIS D.A. *et al*, "Audible television and decreased adult words, infant vocalizations, and conversational turns: a population-based study," *Arch. Pediatr. Adolesc. Med*, n° 163, 2009, p. 554 *et passim*.

134. KIRKORIAN H.L. *et al*, "The impact of background television on parent-child interaction," *Child Dev.* n° 80, 2009, p. 1350 *et passim*.

135. BLOOM P., *How Children Learn the Meaning of Words*, MIT Press, 2000.

136. VENEZIANO E., "Interaction, conversation and language acquisition in the first three years of life", *in* KAIL M. *et al.* (ed.), *Language Acquisition. Le langage en émergence. De la naissance à trois ans*, PUF, 2000, p. 231 *and passim*.

137. BORNSTEIN M.H. *et al*, "Maternal responsiveness and cognitive development in children," *New Dir. Child Dev.* 1989, p. 49 *and passim*.

138. OLSON S.L. *et al*, "Mother-child interaction and children's speech progress: a longitudinal study of the first two years", *Merrill-Palmer Q*, n° 32, 1986, p. 1 *and passim.*

139. TAMIS-LEMONDA C.S. *et al*, "Maternal responsiveness and children's achievement of language milestones," *Child Dev*, n° 72, 2001, p. 748 *and passim.*

140. ROWE M.L. *et al*, "Differences in early gesture explain SES disparities in child vocabulary size at school entry," *Science*, n° 323, 2009, p. 951 *and passim.*

141. ROWE M.L. *et al*, "Early gesture selectively predicts later language learning", *Dev. Sci.* 12, 2009, p. 182 *and passim.*

142. ZIMMERMAN F.J. *et al*, "Teaching by listening: the importance of adult-child conversations to language development", *Pediatrics*, n° 124, 2009, p. 342 *and passim.*

143. HART B. *et al*, *Meaningful Differences in the Everyday Experience of Young American Children*, Brooks, 1995.

144. KUHL P.K. *et al*, "Foreign-language experience in infancy: effects of short-term exposure and social interaction on phonetic learning," *Proc. Natl. Acad. Sci.USA*, n° 100, 2003, p. 9096 *et passim.*

145. THIRION M. *et al*, *Le Sommeil, le rêve et l'enfant*, Albin Michel, 2002.

146. "Médiamat annuel 2009," Médiamétrie, accessed September 26, 2010, http://www. mediametrie.fr/television/communiques/media-mat-annuel-2009.php?id=178.

147. "The French and their sleep," press kit, INPES, March 2008, accessed September 26, 2010, http://www.inpes.sante.fr/70000/dp/08/dp080310.pdf.

148. "Main social times during an average day by age. Enquête emploi du temps 1999," insee.fr, accessed September 26, 2010, http://www.insee.en/themes/tableau.asp?reg_id=0&ref_id=NATSOS05523.

149. "Life expectancy at birth and infant mortality rate," insee.fr, accessed September 26, 2010, http://www.insee.fr/fr/themes/tableau.asp?reg_id=0&ref_id= NATTEF02221.

150. "Total population by sex and age as of January 1, 2010, all of France," INSEE, access September 26, 2010, http://www.insee.fr/fr/themes/detail.asp?reg_id=0&ref_id=bilandemo&page=donnees-detaillees/bilan-demo/pop_age2b.htm.

151. DARCOS X., "Présentation des nouveaux programmes du primaire," Ministère de l'Éducation nationale, February 20, 2008, accessed

September 26, 2010, http://www.education. gouv.fr/cid21007/ presentation-des-nouveaux-programmes-du-primaire.html.

152. RIDEOUT V. *et al*, "Generation M: media in the lives of 8-18 year-olds," The Kaiser Family Foundation, January 2010, accessed 26 September 2010, http://www.kff.org/ entmedia/upload/8010.pdf.

153. Quoted *in* "Ten days without a screen!", leparisien.fr, May 19, 2008, accessed September 26, 2010, http://www.leparisien.fr/societe/ dix-jours-sans-ecran-19-05-2008-3298510123.php.

154. LEMOINE P., *S'ennuyer, quel bonheur*, Armand Colin, 2007.

155. TEBOUL R., " Plaidoyer pour l'ennui ", *La Lettre de l'enfance et de l'adolescence*,n° 60, 2005, p. 25 *and passim*.

156. For a superb little book on the subject for children: LABBÉ B. *et al*, *Prendre son temps et perdre son temps*, Milan Jeunesse, 2006.

157. CHRISTOFF K. *et al*, "Experience sampling during fMRI reveals default network and executive system contributions to mind wandering," *Proc. Natl. Acad. Sci.USA*, 2009.

158. DE UNAMUNO M., *Mist: A Tragicomic Novel*, University of Illinois Press, 2000, p. 49.

159. CIORAN, *Syllogismes de l'amertume*, Gallimard, coll. "Folio Essais", 1952, p. 60.

160. LACROIX A., *Le Téléviathan*, Flammarion, 2010, pp. 72-73, 94.

161. BRUCKNER P., *La Tentation de l'innocence*, Le Livre de poche, 1995, pp. 28, 89-90.

162. MEYROWITZ J., *No Sense of Place*, Oxford University Press, 1985, p. 245.

163. MCGINNIS J.M. *et al*, *Food Marketing to Children and Youth: Threat or Opportunity*, Committee on Food Marketing and the Diets of Children and Youth, The National Academies Press, 2006.

164. MICHELET S., "Trop de télé nuit gravement aux enfants", *Psychologies magazine*, January 2007.

165. GROEBEL J., "Media access and media use among 12-year-olds in the world", *in* VON FEILITZEN C. *et al* (eds.), *Children and Media, Image Education Participation: Yearbook from the Unesco International Clearinghouse on Children and Violence on the Screen*, Nordicom, 1999, p. 61 *and passim*.

166. VON FEILITZEN C., "Children's amount of TV viewing: statistics from ten countries", *in* VON FEILITZEN C. *et al* (eds.), *Children and Media, Image Education Participation: Yearbook from the Unesco*

International Clearinghouse on Children and Violence on the Screen, Nordicom, 1999, p. 69 *and passim.*

167. "Inequalities in young people's health. HBSC international report from the 2005/2006 survey," WHO, 2008, accessed September 26, 2010, http://www.euro. who.int/ data/assets/pdf_file/0005/53852/E91416.pdf.

168. "Young people's health in context. HBSC international report from the 2001/2002 survey," WHO, 2004, accessed September 26, 2010, http://www.euro.who. int/ data/assets/pdf_file/0008/110231/e82923.pdf.

169. COMSTOCK G. *et al*, "The use of television and other film-related media", *in* SINGER D.G. *et al* (eds.), *Handbook of Children and the Media*, 2001, Sage Publications, pp. 47, 67 *et passim.*

170. LARSON R.W. *et al. 1999*; How children and adolescents spend time across the world: work, play, and developmental opportunities. *Bull*, 125 (1999), 701 *et al.*

171. PAIK H., "The history of children's use of electronic media", *in* SINGER D.G. *et al.* (eds.), *Handbook of Children and the Media*, 2001, Sage Publications, p. 7 *and passim.*

172. "Household multimedia equipment by socio-professional category," insee.fr, SRCV-SILC 2007 survey, accessed September 26, 2010, http://www.insee.fr/ en/themes/tableau.asp?reg_id=0&ref_id=NATnon05140.

173. "Les enfants de l'écran," Médiamétrie, *Audiences: le mag*, April 24, 2008, accessed September 26, 2010, http://www.audiencelemag.com/?article=22&rub=1.

174. HESS F., "Still at risk: What students don't know, even now," A report from Common Core (Washington, DC), 2008, accessed September 26, 2010, http://www. commoncore.org/_docs/CCreport_stillatrisk.pdf.

175. SIMPSON A., "Winston Churchill didn't really exist, say teens," telegraph.co.uk, February 4, 2008, accessed September 26, 2010, http://www.telegraph.co.uk/news/uknews/ 1577511/Winston-Churchill-didnt-really-exist-say-teens.html.

176. LINDLOF T. *et al*, "Accomodation of video and television in the American family", *in* LULL J. (ed.), *World Families Watch Television*, Sage, 1988, p. 158 *and passim.*

177. LULL J., "The social uses of television", *Human Comm. Res.*, n° 6, 1980, p. 197 *and passim.*

178. BASNER M. *et al*, "Dubious bargain: trading sleep for Leno and Letterman," *Sleep*, n° 32, 2009, p. 747 *et passim.*

179. VOLATIER J.L., "Le repas traditionnel se porte encore bien", *Consommation et modes de vie*, Credoc, n° 132, 30 January 1999, accessed 26 September 2010, http://www. credoc.fr/pdf/4p/132.pdf.

180. HÉBEL P., "Le petit déjeuner anglo-saxon s'installe à peu à peu", *Consommation et modes de vie*, Credoc, n° 204, July 2007, access 26 September 2010, http://www. credoc.fr/pdf/4p/204.pdf.

181. "Great dates in the history of French television," jeanmarcmorandini. com, accessed September 26, 2010, http://www.jeanmarcmorandini. com/article-22289,1-lesgrandes-dates-de-l-histoire-de-la-television-francaise.html.

182. Canal+ Group, access 26 September 2010, http://www.canalplus-group.com/cid5202.htm.

183. DAGNAUD M., "L'enfant, la culture et la télévision," *Journal du CNRS*, n° 189, October 2005, accessed September 26, 2010, http://www2. cnrs.fr/journal/2472.htm.

184. See for some cautionary tales about using the remote: "Jamais d'accord devant la télé: ce qu'elles nous disent; ce qu'ils nous disent," *Femme actuelle*, June 15-21, 2009.

185. RIDEOUT V. *et al*, "The media family: electronic media in the lives of infants, toddlers, preschoolers and their parents," The Kaiser Family Foundation, May 2006, accessed September 26, 2010, http://www.kff. org/entmedia/upload/7500.pdf, pp. 4, 11, 14, 23.

186. INSERM, "Rapport collectif. Troubles des conduites chez l'enfant et l'adolescent (chapitre VII)," INSERM, 2005, accessed September 26, 2010, http://www.inserm.fr/ index.php/content/download/7154/55249/file/troubles+des+conduites.pdf.

187. "9th National Sleep Day, Results of the "Sleep and Rhythm of Life" Survey - INSV/BVA Healthcare," National Sleep and Vigilance Institute, March 18, 2009, accessed September 27, 2010, http://www. institut-sommeil-vigilance.org/documents/ Enquete-2009-Sommeil-rythme.ppt.

188. "*Kids' Attitudes 2005*. Where are the tweens going?", Ipsos, 2005, accessed September 26, 2010, http://www.ipsos.fr/CanalIpsos/articles/images/1627/diaporama.htm.

189. VAN DEN BULCK J., "Television viewing, computer game playing, and Internet use and self-reported time to bed and time out of bed in secondary-school children," *Sleep*, n° 27, 2004, p. 101 *et passim*.

190. "Baromètre annuel du rapport à l'école des enfants de quartiers populaires", Trajectoires-Reflex for AFEV, September 24, 2008, accessed September 27, 2010, http://www.afev.fr/file.php?id=7; the figure of 53% does not appear in the text of the study where only the values by gender are given (boys 61%, girls 46%). The overall percentage of 53% was given to me by Mr. Pascal Bavoux, the person in charge of the study.

191. WOODARD E.H. *et al*, "Media in the home: the fifth annual survey of parents and children," The Annenberg Policy Center, Survey Series n° 7, 2000, accessed 27 September 2010, http://www.annenbergpublicpolicycenter.org/Downloads/Media_ and_Developing_Child/mediasurvey/survey7.pdf.

192. ROBERTS D.F. *et al*, "Generation M: media in the lives of 8-18 year-olds," The Kaiser Family Foundation, March 2005, accessed September 27, 2010, http://www.kff.org/ entmedia/upload/Generation-M-Media-in-the-Lives-of-8-18-Year-olds-Report.pdf.

193. ROBERTS D.F. *et al*, "Kids and media: the new millennium," The Kaiser Family Foundation, November 1999, accessed 27 September 2010, http://www.kff.org/entmedia/ upload/Kids-Media-The-New-Millennium-Report.pdf.

194. CERTAIN L.K. *et al*, "Prevalence, correlates, and trajectory of television viewing among infants and toddlers," *Pediatrics*, n° 109, 2002, p. 634 *et passim*.

195. GORELY T. *et al*, "Couch kids: correlates of television viewing among youth", *Int. J. Behav. Med.* 2004;11:152, *et al*.

196. HANCOX R.J. *et al*, "Association between child and adolescent television viewing and adult health: a longitudinal birth cohort study", *Lancet*, n° 364, 2004, pp. 257, 261 *et passim*.

197. DAGNAUD M., *Enfants, consommation et publicité télévisée*, La Documentation française, 2003.

198. "Baby'Bus Report", Tns-Sofres, study on toddlers and TV - 63EN12T - June 2004.

199. BARR-ANDERSON D.J. *et al*, "Characteristics associated with older adolescents who have a television in their bedrooms," *Pediatrics*, n° 121, 2008, p. 718 *et passim*.

200. BORZEKOWSKI D.L. *et al*, "The remote, the mouse, and the n° 2 pencil," *Arch. Pediatr. Adolesc. Med.* n° 159 (2005): 607 *et al*.

201. DENNISON B.A. *et al*, "Television viewing and television in bedroom associated with overweight risk among low-income preschool children," *Pediatrics*, n° 109, 2002, p. 1028 *and passim*.

202. VANDEWATER E.A. *et al*, "Digital childhood: electronic media and technology use among infants, toddlers, and preschoolers," *Pediatrics*, n° 119, 2007, pp. e1006-e1015.

203. THOMPSON D.A. *et al*, "The association of maternal mental distress with television viewing in children under 3 years old," *Ambul. Ambul. pediatr.* 7 (2007): 32 *et al*.

204. BURDETTE H.L. *et al*, "Association of maternal obesity and depressive symptoms with television-viewing time in low-income preschool children," *Arch. Pediatr. Adolesc. Med*, n° 157, 2003, p. 894 *and passim*.

205. DESPLANQUES E., " Les jeunes zappent la télé ", *Télérama*, n° 3040, 16 April 2008.

206. See also: TAPSCOTT D., "Net geners come of age," businessweek. com, November 3, 2008, accessed September 27, 2010, http://www. businessweek.com/technology/content/ nov2008/tc2008111_448166. htm.

207. Dominique Pasquier, sociologist, quoted *in* DESPLANQUES E., "Les jeunes zappent la télé", *Télérama*, n° 3040, 16 April 2008.

208. STIEGLER B., *La Télécratie contre la démocratie*, Flammarion, 2006.

209. "Les Français à l'ère du numérique", *Contact* (Crédit Mutuel magazine), n° 55, March 2010.

210. Édouard Le Maréchal quoted *in* DESPLANQUES E., "Les jeunes zappent la télé", *Télérama*, n° 3040, 16 April 2008.

211. "Worldwide TV unaffected by the crisis," Médiamétrie, press release, EurodataTV Worldwide, March 16, 2010, accessed September 27, 2010, http://www. mediametrie.com/eurodatatv/communiques/ eurodata-tv-worldwide-one-television-year-in-the-world-2010-edition.php?id=223.

212. "Les chaînes dites 'historiques' font de la résistance", Médiamétrie, *Audience : le mag*, July 21, 2008, accessed September 27, 2010, http:// www.audiencelemag.com/? article=24&rub=1.

213. "Les petites chaînes de la TNT dament le pion aux grandes", *Aujourd'hui en France*, December 2, 2008.

214. "La TNT bouscule les mesures d'audience", *Aujourd'hui en France*, 3 September 2008.

215. "TNT: la petite faucheuse", *Libération*, May 31, 2008.

216. Roberts D.F. *et al. 2008*, "Trends in media use", *Fut. Child*, n° 18, 2008, pp. 11, 19 *and passim.*

217. "How teens use media. A Nielsen report on the myths and realities of teen media trends," The Nielsen Company, June 2009, accessed September 27, 2010, http://blog. nielsen.com/nielsenwire/reports/ nielsen_howteensusemedia_june09.pdf.

218. "vuàlatélé: the 2008-2009 guide," National Television Advertising Union Newsletter, No. 5, January 2008, accessed September 27, 2010, http://www. snptv.org/_files/actualites/files/actualites-898-375.pdf, p. 60.

219. DESPLANQUES E., "L'avenir de la télé publique passe-t-il par le net ?", *Télérama*, n° 3040, 16 April 2008.

220. PELLERIN M., "Ces émissions qui cartonnent sur Internet", *Aujourd'hui en France*, 11 August 2009.

221. "When the Internet plays on TV", *Aujourd'hui en France*, January 3, 2010.

222. JONES S. *et al*, "Generations online in 2009," Pew Research Center, January 28, 2009, accessed April 24, 2010, http://pewresearch.org/ pubs/1093/generations-online.

223. "La "catch-up TV" progresse," 20minutes.fr, October 7, 2008, accessed October 20, 2010, http://www.20minutes.fr/article/260352/Media-La-catch-up-TV-progresse.php.

224. "L'année TV 2009: les façons de regarder la télévision changent, la mesure d'audience avance," Médiamétrie, February 23, 2010, mediametrie.fr, accessed October 20, 2010, http://www.mediametrie. fr/television/communiques/l-annee-tv-2009-les-facons-deregarder-la-television-changent-la-mesure-d-audience-avance.php?id=211.

225. "To see this series, go to the web", *Aujourd'hui en France*, November 22, 2009.

226. "Neuf Cegetel releases first mobile phone-television with DTT receiver," AFP, March 20, 2008, accessed September 27, 2010, http:// afp.google.com/article/ALeq M5j_FTMHgfu7r_fStTnE84FPflYp5w.

227. "La télévision mobile personnelle: lancement repoussé à 2010," LePoint.fr, March 3, 2009, accessed September 27, 2010, http://www. lepoint.fr/actualites-technologie-internet/ television-mobile-personnelle-lancement-repousse-a-2010/1387/0/322188.

228. "TDF: "La télévision mobile personnelle dès la fin 2011", lefigaro.fr, June 8, 2010, accessed September 19, 2010, http://www.lefigaro.fr/

medias/2010/06/07/04002-20100607   ARTFIG00485-olivier-huart-invite-du-buzz-media-orange-le-figaro.php.

229. FOEHR U.G., "Media multitasking among youth: prevalence, predictors and pairings," The Kaiser Family Foundation, December 2006, accessed September 27, 2010, http://www.kff.org/entmedia/upload/7592.pdf.

230. LENHART A. *et al*, "Teenage life online," Pew Internet & American Life Project, June 2001, accessed September 27, 2010, http://www.pewinternet.org/~/media//Files/Reports/2001/PIP_Teens_Report.pdf.pdf, p. 10.

231. TAPSCOTT D., "How digital technology has changed the brain," businessweek.com, November 10, 2008, accessed September 27, 2010, http://www.businessweek.com/ technology/content/nov2008/tc2008117_034517.htm.

232. CHRISTAKIS D.A. *et al*, "Early television viewing is associated with protesting turning off the television at age 6," *MedGenMed*, n° 8, 2006, p. 63.

233. ZIMMERMAN F.J. *et al*, "Children's television viewing and cognitive outcomes: a longitudinal analysis of national data," *Arch. Pediatr. Adolesc. Med.* 159 (2005): 619 *et al*.

234. LANDHUIS C.E. *et al*, "Does childhood television viewing lead to attention problems in adolescence? Results from a prospective longitudinal study," *Pediatrics*, n° 120, 2007, p. 532 *et passim*.

235. PARSONS T.J. *et al*, "Television viewing and obesity: a prospective study in the 1958 British birth cohort," *Eur. J. Clin. Nutr.* 62 (2008): 1355 *et al*.

236. LEE S.J. *et al*, "Predicting children's media use in the U.S.A.: differences in cross-sectional and longitudinal analysis," *Br. J. Dev. Psychol*, n° 27, 2009, p. 123 *and passim*.

237. RIDEOUT V., "Parents, Media and Public Policy," The Kaiser Family Foundation, Fall 2004, accessed September 27, 2010, http://www.kff.org/entmedia/upload/ Parents-Media-and-Public-Policy-A-Kaiser-Family-Foundation-Survey-Report.pdf.

238. RIDEOUT V., "Parents, Children and Media," The Kaiser Family Foundation, June 2007, accessed September 27, 2010, http://www.kff.org/entmedia/upload/7638.pdf.

239. FITZPATRICK E. *et al*, "Positive effects of family dinner are undone by television viewing," *J. Am. Diet. Assoc.* 107 (2007): 666 *et al*.

240. COON K.A. *et al*, "Relationships between use of television during meals and children's food consumption patterns," *Pediatrics*, n° 107, 2001, p. E7.

241. MATHESON D.M. *et al*, "Children's food consumption during television viewing," *Am. J. Clin. Nutr.* 79 (2004): 1088 *et al*.

242. Gillman M.W. *et al. 2000;* Family dinner and diet quality among older children and adolescents. *Fam Med* 9 (2000): *235ff.*

243. RIDEOUT V.J. *et al*, "Zero to six: electronic media in the lives of infants, toddlers and preschoolers," The Kaiser Family Foundation, Fall 2003, accessed 27 September 2010, http://www.kff.org/entmedia/upload/ Zero-to-Six-Electronic-Media-in-the-Livesof-Infants-Toddlers-and-Preschoolers-PDF.pdf.

244. FEIERABEND D. *et al*, "Was Kinder sehen. Eine Analyse der Fernsehnutzung Drei-bis 13-Jähriger 2008," *Media Perspektiven*, n° 3, 2009, p. 113 *et passim.*

245. MYRTEK M. *et al*, "Physiological, behavioral, and psychological effects associated with television viewing in schoolboys: an exploratory study," *J. Early Adolesc.* 1996;16:301 *et al*.

246. Huston, A.C. *et al. 1999;* "How young children spend their time: television and other activities"; *Dev. Psychol.* 35 (1999): 912 *et al*.

247. "Marketing télévisé pour les produits alimentaires à destination des enfants," UFC-Que Choisir, December 2010, accessed December 7, 2010, http://www.quechoisir.org/content/ download/98841/845978/ file/marketing-televise-produits-alimentaires-enfants.pdf.

248. MOREAU C., "*Secret Story* judged too vulgar by the CSA", *Aujourd'hui en France*, August 8, 2009.

249. DEREUX S., "TF1 doit-elle arrêter *Secret Story* ?", *14 jours TV,* 22 August-4 September 2009.

250. "*Secret Story* / Cindy to FX: "T'es qu'un fils de p**e"", jeanmarcmorandini.com, access 27 August 2009, http://www.jeanmarcmorandini. com/article-29757-secret-story-cindya-fx-t-es-qu-un-fils-de-p-e. html.

251. "French language: attention, la télé tue!", tvmag.com, July 23, 2010, accessed September 27, 2010, http://www.tvmag.com/programme-tv/ article/information/54362/ langue-francaise-attention-la-tele-tue.html.

252. *The Punisher*, for synopsis and trailer, see allocine.fr, access 27 September 2010, http://www.allocine.fr/film/fichefilm_gen_cfilm=52410.html.

253. KOOLSTRA C.M. *et al*, "Viewing behavior of children and TV guidance by parents: A comparison of parent and child reports," *Communications*, n° 29, 2004, p. 179 *and passim.*

254. "La télévision à la maison : regard croisé des parents et des enfants," CSA / *La Croix* / Unapel, March 26, 2003, accessed September 27, 2010, http://www.csa-fr.com/fra/ dataset/data2003/opi20030130a.htm.

255. SCHMIDT K.L., "Public policy, family rules and children's media use in the home," The Annenberg Public Policy Center, Report Series n° 35, 2000, accessed September 27, 2010, http://www.annenbergpublicpolicycenter.org/Downloads/Media_and_Developing_Child/20000626_public_policy_Vchip_report.pdf.

256. BELPOIS M., "La pub pour les enfants à la télé : un problème de poids", *Télérama*, n° 3092, 15 April 2009.

257. "Les spots télévisés vantant les produits gras ou sucrés ne seront pas interdits", *Le Figaro*, March 11, 2009.

258. "Childhood Obesity: 23 Learned Societies and 17 Associations Call on MPs to Regulate Television Advertising of Food Products to Children," quechoisir.org, March 3, 2009, accessed September 27, 2010, http://www. quechoisir.org/communiques/23-societes-savantes-et-17-associations-appellent-les-deputesa-regulate-la-publicite-televisee-pour-produits-alimentaires-a-destination-desenfants/C4F95011F9960D2BC125756E0057FADC.htm.

259. FREUD A., *The Ego and Defense Mechanisms*, PUF, 2001, 15th ed.

260. IONESCU S. *et al*, *Les Mécanismes de défense. Theory and clinic*, Armand Colin, 2005.

261. LAPLANCHE J. *et al*, *Vocabulaire de la psychanalyse*, PUF, 1988, 9th edition, pp. 115 and 387.

262. "MédiaCabSat, press release, September 14, 2009 / February 28, 2010," mediametrie.fr, March 23, 2010, accessed April 6, 2010, http://www. mediametrie.fr/ television/communiques/l-audience-des-chaines-du-cable-et-de-canalsat-du-14-septembre2009-au-28-fevrier-2010. php?id=227.

263. "La télé mode d'emploi," parents.fr, accessed September 27, 2010, http:// www.parents.fr/ parent/life-practice/leisure-children/dossiers/tele-mode-d-emploi/(gid)/29696/(offset)/0/ (breve)/179875.

264. BERMEJO BERROS J., *Generation television*, De Boeck, 2007, pp. 224-225, 312.

---

265. ROBERTS D.F. *et al*, *Kids & Media in America*, Cambridge University Press, 2004.

266. ARENDT H., " La crise de l'éducation ", *in* ARENDT H. (under the direction of), *La Crise de la culture*, Gallimard, 1972, pp. 223, 233 *and passim*.

267. POLONY N., " Rendez-nous les petites filles modèles ! ", *Marianne*, 4-10 October 2008.

268. JORDAN A.B. *et al*, "Reducing children's television-viewing time: a qualitative study of parents and their children," *Pediatrics*, n° 118, 2006, pp. e1303-e1310.

269. ZIMMERMAN F.J. *et al*, "Television and DVD/video viewing in children younger than 2 years," *Arch. Pediatr. Adolesc. Med* 161 (2007): 473-477.

270. DAVISON W.P., "The third-person effect in communication", *Public Opin. Q*, n° 47, 1983, p. 1 *and passim*.

271. PERLOFF R.M., "The third-person effect", *in* BRYANT J. *et al.* (eds.), *Media Effects: Advances in Theory and Research*, Lawrence Erlbaum, 2002, p. 489 *and passim*.

272. PAUL B. *et al*, "The third-person effect: a meta-analysis of the perceptual hypothesis", *in* PREISS R. *et al* (eds.), *Mass Media Effects Research: Advances Through Meta-Analysis*, Lawrence Erlbaum, 2007, p. 81 *and passim*.

273. "Teens, sex and TV," The Kaiser Family Foundation, May 2002, accessed September 28, 2010, http://www.kff.org/entmedia/loader. cfm?url=/commonspot/security/getfile.cfm& PageID=14061.

274. IFOP-TV *Magazine* poll, August 2005, quoted *in* MEYER M., *Le Livre noir de la télévision*, Grasset, 2006, p. 21.

275. "Le documentaire, programme télé favori des Français", Ipsos / *France-Soir* poll, February 22, 2010, accessed June 20, 2010, http:// www.ipsos.fr/CanalIpsos/articles/2999. asp?rubId=23.

276. "L'image des chaînes de télévision au crible," ipsos.com, Canal Ipsos, March 21, 2002, accessed June 19, 2009, http://www.ipsos.fr/ CanalIpsos/articles/929.asp.

277. "60% of French people are dissatisfied with TV programs," Ipsos Channel, March 25, 2004, accessed September 28, 2010, http://www. ipsos.fr/CanalIpsos/articles/1315.asp?rubId=1315.

278. "Ifop Barometer," tele-2-semaines.fr, February 21, 2008, accessed June 19, 2009, http:// www.tele-2-semaines.fr/contenu_editorial/pages/

echos-tv/1609-exclusif-france-3-etfrance-5-chaines-preferees-des-francais.

279. "Discover the Top 100 Audiences of 2009," ozap.com, December 31, 2009, accessed September 28, 2010, http://www.ozap.com/actu/top-100-meilleures-audiences2009-television/318170.

280. "*Home*, le plus gros éco-événement de l'Histoire en libre accès sur YouTube," LePoint.fr, June 4, 2009, accessed January 20, 2010, http://www.lepoint.fr/actualitescinema/2009-06-04/yann-arthus-bertrand-home-le-plus-gros-eco-evenement-de-l-histoireen-libre-acces-sur/903/0/349245.

281. "TF1 achieved the 100 best ratings in 2007," 20minutes.fr, January 1, 2008, accessed June 19, 2009, http://www.20minutes.fr/article/203784/Media-TF1-a-realise-en2007-les-100-meilleures-audiences.php.

282. "TF1 falls, the group sees a 9% drop in sales in 2009," lefigaro.fr, February 12, 2009, accessed September 28, 2010, http://www.lefigaro.fr/societes/2009/ 02/19/04015-20090219ARTFIG00365-tf1-chute-le-groupe-voit-une-baisse-de-9-de ses-ventes-en-2009-.php.

283. "TF1 rafle 96 des 100 meilleures audiences 2009," lefigaro.fr, 31 December 2009, accessed January 1 2010, http://www.lefigaro.fr/medias/2009/12/31/04002-20091231 ARTFIG00277-tf1-rafle-96-des-100-meilleures-audiences-2009-.php.

284. "98 of the Top 100 Audiences 2006 for TF1," TF1.lci.fr, January 2, 2007, accessed September 28, 2010, http://lci.tf1.fr/economie/medias/2007-01/100-meilleuresaudiences-2006-pour-tf1-4881447.html.

285. "Faible audience pour Nicolas Sarkozy," liberation.fr, 25 April 2008, accessed 19 June 2009, http://www.liberation.fr/actualite/010127129-faible-audience-pour-nicolas-sarkozy.

286. "12.1 million viewers for Nicolas Sarkozy's interview," 7.4 million on TF1 and 4.7 million on France 2, AFP, September 24, 2009, accessed September 28, 2010, http://www.google.com/hostednews/afp/article/ALeqM5iHpLZAo6z9JPGGVB3P8wGXY vfZnw.

287. RISSER H., *L'Audimat à mort*, Éditions du Seuil, 2004, pp. 63, 170, 174, 182, 186, 231, 240 (Jean-Pierre Pernaut), 242.

288. EVENO P., *Les Médias sont-ils sous influence ?*, Larousse, 2008, pp. 12, 41, 88-89.

289. MANDER J., *Four Arguments for the Elimination of Television*, Perennial, 1978, pp. 241-242.

290. MCKIBBEN B., *The Age of Missing Information*, Random House, 1992, pp. 40-41, 48, 75 (Wolfang Bayer), 77, 213-216, 219 (UNESCO).

291. CANEL-DEPITRE B., "L'expérience de la consommation d'images et la construction identitaire", 6e congrès "Les tendances du marketing en Europe", Paris, 26-27 January 2007, available online, access 19 June 2009, http://www.escp-eap.net/conferences/ marketing/2007_cp/ Materiali/Paper/Fr/CanelDepitre.pdf.

292. *L'Odyssée de l'espèce*, description available on france3.fr, access 28 September 2010, http://odysseedelespece.france3.fr/.

293. "Nos lointains ancêtres, stars de la télé," RFI, January 10, 2005, accessed September 12, 2010, http://www.rfi.fr/actufr/articles/061/ article_33143.asp.

294. CALVET L.J. *et al*, *Les Mots de Nicolas Sarkozy*, Éditions du Seuil, 2008.

295. SCHUCK N., "Sarkozy malmène le français", *Aujourd'hui en France*, March 22, 2009.

296. LE BEL P., *"Madame, Monsieur, Bonsoir..." Les dessous du premier JT de France*, Éditions du Panama, 2007, p. 107.

297. Quoted in *Closer*, n° 209, June 13-19, 2009, pp. 72-73.

298. "*Pékin Express* : M6 cernée par les soupcons de tricherie," LePoint.fr, March 10, 2008, accessed December 1, 2009, http://www.lepoint.fr/ actualites-medias/2008-03-11/ polemique-pekin-express-m6-cernee-par-les-soupcons-de-tricherie/1253/0/228146.

299. "*Pékin Express* controversy: M6 did not file a complaint!", jeanmarc-morandini.com, June 18, 2009, accessed December 1, 2009, http:// www.jeanmarcmorandini.com/ article-16304-polemique-pekin-ex-press-m6-n-a-porte-plainte.html.

300. "La cérémonie était truquée", *Libération*, August 13, 2008.

301. "La retransmission de la cérémonie d'ouverture était truquée", *Aujourd'hui en France*, August 13, 2008.

302. "*Le Grand Frère* : et si TF1 avait tout écrit à l'avance...", leParisien.fr, November 30, 2009, accessed December 1, 2009, http://www.lepari-sien.fr/loisirs-et-spectacles/le-grandfrere-et-si-tf-1-avait-tout-ecrit-a-l-avance-30-11-2009-728554.php.

303. " Bidon ? Regardez comment TF1 monte *Le Grand Frère*," lepost.fr, November 30, 2009, accessed December 1, 2009, http://www.lepost.fr/ article/2009/11/30/ 1817454_comment-tf1-bidonne-le-grand-frere.html.

304. "*Le Grand Frère*, Dylan sequencer, filming from October 29 to November 7, 2009," leParisien.fr, November 30, 2009, accessed December 1, 2009,

http://preview.leparisien.fr/complements/2009/11/30/729097_sequencier-le-grand-frere.pdf.

305.SIGMAN A., "Visual voodoo: the biological impact of watching TV," *Biologist*, n° 54, 2007, p. 12 *and passim*.

306.HUSTON A.C. *et al*, "Communicating more than content: formal features of children's television programs," *J. Commun.* 31, 1981, p. 32 *and passim*.

307.BERLYNE D.E., *Conflict, Arousal and Curiosity*, McGraw-Hill, 1960.

308.RICHARDS J.E. *et al*, "Attentional inertia in children's extended looking at television," *Adv. Child. Dev. Behav*, 32, 163 *et al*.

309.ANDERSON D.R. *et al*, "Attentional inertia reduces distractibility during young children's TV viewing," *Child. Dev.* 58 (1987): 798 *et al*.

310.ANDERSON D.R. *et al*, "Watching children watch television", *in* HALE G. *et al* (eds.), *Attention and Cognitive Development*, Plenum, 1979, pp. 331, 339 *and passim*.

311.BICKAM D.S. *et al*, "Attention, comprehension and the educational influences of television", *in* SINGER D.G. *et al* (eds.), *Handbook of Children and the Media*, Sage Publications, 2001, p. 101 *and passim*.

312.LANG A. *et al*, "The effects of edits on arousal, attention and memory for television messages," *J. Broadcast Electronic Media*, n° 44, 2000, p. 94 *and passim*.

313.LANG A. *et al*, "The effects of production pacing and arousing content on the information processing of television messages," *J. Broadcast Electronic Media*, n° 43, 1999, p. 451 *et passim*.

314.ANDERSON D.R. *et al*, "The effects of TV program comprehensibility on preschool children's visual attention to television," *Child. Dev.* 52 (1981): *151ff*.

315.LORCH E.P. *et al*, "The relationship of visual attention to children's comprehension of television", *Child Dev.* n° 50, 1979, p. 722 *and passim*.

316.Thierry Ardisson, talk-show host and producer, quoted *in* RISSER H., *L'Audimat à mort*, Éditions du Seuil, 2004, p. 67.

317. ADATTO K., "The incredible shrinking sound bite," *The New Republic*, May 28, 1990, accessed June 20, 2009, http://www.arts.mcgill.ca/programs/history/faculty/TROYWEB/ Courseweb/TheIncredibleShrinkingSoundBite.pdf.

318.See also: ROSEN R., "For overloaded eyes and ears, bite makes right bite makes right," *New York Times*, June 10, 1990, accessed June 20, 2009, http://www.nytimes.com/ 1990/06/10/arts/tv-view-for-overloaded-eyes-and-ears-bite-makes-right-bite-makes-right.html.

319. LA MENNAIS F. DE, *Œuvres complètes. Volume VI*, Cailleux et Cie, 1836, p. 407.

320. Didier Daeninckx, quoted *in* "L'affaire Le Lay", *Télérama*, 11-17 September 2004, p. 16.

321. ROQUEFORT B. DE, *Dictionnaire étymologique de la langue française*, Decourchant, 1829, definition p. 62.

322. MASCHINO M.T., *L'École de la lâcheté*, Flammarion, coll. "J'ai lu", 2007, pp. 7 and 16.

323. BOUTONNET R., *Journal d'une institutrice clandestine*, Ramsay/ Poche, 2005.

324. COMBES F. *et al*, *La Destruction de la culture*, Delga, 2005 (in particular chapter I), pp. 25 and 39.

325. LE BRIS M., *Et vos enfants ne sauront pas lire... ni compter*, Stock, 2004.

326. MOREL G. *et al*, *L'Horreur pédagogique*, Ramsay, 1999.

327. ABENSOUR C. *et al*, *De la destruction du savoir en temps de paix*, Mille et une nuits, 2007.

328. KHALDI E. *et al*, *Main basse sur l'école publique*, Demopolis, 2008.

329. COURBET J., "Ça peut vous arriver", RTL, April 7, 2010.

330. "Scientology: dissolution required," jdd.fr, June 15, 2009, accessed September 28, 2010, http://www.lejdd.fr/Societe/Actualite/ Scientologie-Dissolution-requise-17338/.

331. Personal communication Martine Taharo, health executive, member of the jury (2008).

332. For the video and story of the incident, see: "Justin Bieber humiliated on live TV! Watch," jeanmarcmorandini.com, May 5, 2010, accessed May 21, 2010, http://www. jeanmarcmorandini.com/article-38972-justin-bieber-humiliated-on-live-television-look. html.

333. M. Mathieu-Colas quoted *in* "Fautes en vrac... à la fac," nouvelObs.com, September 6, 2007, accessed September 28, 2010, http://hebdo.nouvelobs.com/sommaire/dossier/ 073519/fautes-en-vrac-a-la-fac.html.

334. MATHIEU-COLAS M., "Maîtrise du français", lefigaro.fr, March 11, 2008, accessed February 9, 2009, http://www.lefigaro.fr/ debats/2008/03/11/01005-20080311ARTFIG00399maitrise-du-francais-par-michel-mathieu-colas-.php.

335. CARLE G., "Mention très bien au bac et 30 fautes en dictée", leParisien.fr, 22 September 2006, accessed 9 February 2009, http://www. leparisien.fr/societe/mentiontres-bien-au-bac-et-30-fautes-en-dictee-22-09-2006-2007352449.php.

336. REVEILLON J.-M., "L'orthographe dans les copies d'invention", collective Sauver les lettres, October 2003, accessed February 9, 2009, http://www.sauv.net/orthoinvent.php.

337. LINARES J. DE, "Fautes en vrac... à la fac," nouvelObs.com, September 6, 2007, accessed September 28, 2010, http://hebdo.nouvelobs.com/sommaire/dossier/073519/fautesen-vrac-a-la-fac.html.

338. LECLAIR A., "Quand le langage SMS envahit les copies du bac", lefigaro.fr, May 19, 2008, accessed February 9, 2009, http://www.lefigaro.fr/actualites/2008/05/17/01001-20080517   ARTFIG00653-quand-le-langage-sms-envahit-les-copies-du-bac.php.

339. "Provisional results of the baccalaureate in metropolitan France and the overseas departments, June 2010 session," *Les Notes d'information - DEPP*, n° 10.10, July 2010, accessed September 28, 2010, http://www.education.gouv.fr/cid52534/resultats-provisoires-du-baccalaureat-session-de-juin-2010-france-metropolitaine-et-dom.html.

340. CAMUS R., *La Grande Déculturation*, Fayard, 2008.

341. ZEMMOUR E., "Z comme Zemmour", RTL, April 15, 2010, "It is the bac itself that no longer means anything. An exam that has a success rate of nearly 90% is no longer an exam, it's a gift, a myth, a smoke and mirrors."

342. REVEILLON J.-M., "Autopsy of a packet of ordinary baccalaureate copies", collective Sauver les lettres, 2003, accessed February 9, 2009, http://www.sauv.net/autopsiebac.php.

343. Patrick Porcheron quoted *in* "Les facs s'attaquent aux fautes d'orthographe", *Aujourd'hui en France*, October 4, 2010.

344. "Les facs s'attaquent aux fautes d'orthographe"; "Paris XIII université pionnière"; "Trop de fautes... pas de diplômes", *Aujourd'hui en France*, October 4, 2010.

345. "Rentrée 2008: évaluation du niveau d'orthographe et de grammaire des élèves entrant en classe de seconde," Sauver les lettres collective, January 2009, accessed July 1, 2009, http://www.sauv.net/eval2008analyse.php.

346. CONDILLAC E. DE, *Cours d'étude pour l'instruction du prince de Parme. Volume one*, Du Villard Fils et Nouffer, 1780.

347. "Literacy in the Information Age: Final Report of the International Adult Literacy Survey," OECD, 2000, accessed February 9, 2009, http://www.oecd.org/ dataoecd/24/62/39438013.pdf, citation p 11.

348. MURAT F., "L'évaluation des compétences des adultes : des méthodes en plein développement", *Éducation & Formation*, n° 78, 2008, p. 85 *et passim*.

349. "Reading as a Driver of Change (PISA 2000)," OECD, 2002, accessed February 9, 2009, http://www.pisa.oecd.org/dataoecd/43/33/33690971. pdf, p. 13, Table 8.5.

350. "L'école primaire, bilan des résultats de l'école," Haut Conseil de l'Éducation, 2007, accessed February 9, 2009, http://www.hce.education. fr/gallery_files/site/21/40.pdf, p. 7.

351. DAVIDENKOFF E., "Du CM2 au lycée, le niveau baisse", france-info. com, 31 January 2009, accessed 1 July 2009, http://www.france-info. com/spip.php?article245892 &theme=81&sous_theme=133.

352. "Lire, écrire, compter : les performances des élèves de CM2 à vingt ans d'intervalle 1987-2007," Direction de l'évaluation, de la prospective et de la performance, note d'information 08-38, December 2008, accessed June 30, 2009, http://media.education.gouv.fr/ file/2008/23/9/NI0838_41239.pdf, p. 1.

353. DEJONGHE V. *et al*, "Connaissance en français et en calcul des élèves des années 20 et d'aujourd'hui", *Dossiers d'éducation et formations*, n° 62, 1996.

354. MANESSE D. *et al, Orthographe : à qui la faute ?*, ESF, 2007.

355. "PISA 2006: science competencies for tomorrow's world (volume I: Analysis)," OECD, 2007, accessed 1 July 2009, http://www.oecd.org/ dataoecd/30/17/ 39703267.pdf.

356. "PISA 2006: science competencies for tomorrow's world (volume II: Data)," OECD, 2007, accessed July 1, 2009, http://www.oecd.org/ dataoecd/30/18/39703566.pdf.

357. "Overcoming Failure in Primary School," Institut Montaigne, April 2010, accessed May 5, 2010, http://www.institutmontaigne.org/ medias/documents/rapport_echec_scolaire.pdf.

358. "Maîtrise de la langue en seconde : la dégringolade prévisible se poursuit !", Sauver les lettres collective, January 27, 2009, accessed July 1, 2009, http://www.sauv.net/ fx090127.php.

359. BRANNON E.M., "The independence of language and mathematical reasoning," *Proc. Natl. Acad. Sci. USA*, n° 102, 2005, p. 3177 *et passim*.

360. VARLEY R.A. *et al*, "Agrammatic but numerate," *Proc. Natl. Acad. Sci. USA*, n° 102, 2005, p. 3519 *et passim*.

361.KAHN D.S., "How low can we go?", online.wsj.com, May 26, 2006, accessed September 29, 2010, http://online.wsj.com/article/ SB114861116410663937-search.html.

362.HAYES D.P. *et al*, "Schoolbook simplification and its relation to the decline in SAT-verbal scores," *Am. Educ. Res. J.*, n° 33, 1996, p. 489 *et passim*.

363.Nathalie Brion commenting on a study by the collective Sauver les lettres on the decline of spelling, in *On refait le monde*, RTL, 30 January 2009.

364.Clara Dupont-Monod commenting on a study by the collective Sauver les lettres on the decline of spelling, in *On refait le monde*, RTL, 30 January 2009.

365.See for example: CLOSETS F. DE, *Zéro faute. L'orthographe, une passion française*, Mille et une nuits, 2009.

366."Orthographe : zéro pointé aux diplômés", *Aujourd'hui en France*, September 28, 2009.

367.AMALOU F., "Les fautes d'orthographe deviennent un handicap pour faire carrière", *Le Monde*, 4 May 2006.

368.LEVY A., "L'enfer des handicapés de l'orthographe", LePoint.fr, June 28, 2007, accessed July 1, 2009, http://www.lepoint.fr/actualites-socie-te/2007-06-28/l-enfer-deshandicapes-de-l-orthographe/920/0/190124.

369.SÉRÈS A., "Les fautes d'orthographe inondent les entreprises", lefigaro. fr, 15 October 2007, accessed 1 July 2009, http://www.lefigaro.fr/actua-lite/2007/03/15/0100120070315ARTFIG90266-les_fautes_d_ortho-graphe_inondent_les_entreprises.php.

370.LINARES J. DE, "Stages d'orthographe dans les entreprises," nouve-lObs.com, September 6, 2007, accessed September 29, 2010, http:// hebdo.nouvelobs.com/hebdo/   parution/p2235/dossier/a353659-stages_dorthographe_dans_les_entreprises.html.

371."Donkey Science Finds Its Way Back," yahoo finance, March 29, 2010, accessed April 2, 2010, http://fr.biz.yahoo.com/29032010/395/ la-science-des-anesretrouve-ses-lettres-de-noblesse.html.

372.DOWNEY K., "Illiteracy slows American output," *Detroit News*, September 12, 1995.

373.GAUTIER-LOISEL M., "L'orthographe est un réel critère de sélection", *Aujourd'hui en France*, 28 September 2009.

374. "Zéro pointé en orthographe pour la rentrée de Luc Chatel," france-info.com, September 2, 2009, accessed September 5, 2009, http://www.france-info.com/spip.php? article337233&theme=9&sous_theme=43.

375. "Zéro pointé pour Luc Chatel," LePoint.fr, September 3, 2009, accessed September 3, 2009, http://www.lepoint.fr/actualites-societe/2009-09-03/education-nationale-zero-en-orthographe-pour-luc-chatel/920/0/373739.

376. BRIZARD C., "Le scandale de l'illettrisme," nouvelObs.com, September 6, 2007, accessed July 2, 2009, http://hebdo.nouvelobs.com/hebdo/parution/p2235/dossier/a353656le_scandale_de_lilletrisme.html.

377. Personal observation on a group of second year students.

378. LECLEC'H-LUCAS J. *et al, 1 000 problèmes : CM*, Hachette, 2001, p. 61.

379. POLONY N., "La fracture linguistique. Mais quel français parlent les adolescents?", *Marianne*, September 4, 2004.

380. LECHERBONNIER F., *Why do they want to kill French*, Albin Michel, 2005.

381. POTET F., "Vivre avec 400 mots", *Le Monde*, 19 March 2005.

382. CARRUTHERS P., *Language, Thought and Consciousness*, Cambridge University Press, 1996.

383. VYGOTSKY L.S., *Thought and Language*, MIT Press, 1962.

384. ORWELL G., *1984*, Gallimard, coll. "Folio", 1950, p. 396.

385. KLEMPERER V., *LTI. The Language of the Third Reich*, Albin Michel, 1996, pp. 38-39.

386. ECO U., *Cinq questions de morale*, Livre de poche, 2000, pp. 68-69.

387. HUXLEY A., *Return to the Brave New World*, Pocket, 1958, pp. 137-138 and 154.

388. HAZAN E., *LQR. La propagande au quotidien*, Raisons d'agir, 2006.

389. DELPORTE C., *Une histoire de la langue de bois*, Flammarion, 2009, p. 227.

390. See for a very entertaining discussion on this point: CHÉTOCHINE G., *Le Marketing des émotions*, Eyrolles, 2008.

391. "Information behaviour of the researcher of the future", University College London, study commissioned by the British Library and JISC, January 11, 2008, accessed March 24, 2009, http://www.bl.uk/news/pdf/googlegen.pdf, pp. 18 and 20.

392. "Young people, newspapers and new electronic media," ipsos.fr, March 18, 2006, accessed May 2, 2009, http://www.ipsos.fr/CanalIpsos/articles/images/1810/ slideshow.htm.

393. "The appropriation of new media by youth," Mediappro (with support from the European Commission), 2006, accessed May 3, 2009, http://www.mediappro.org/ publications/finalreport.pdf.

394. FOURGOUS J.M., "Réussir l'école numérique", report of the parliamentary mission of Jean-Michel Fourgous, deputy of Yvelines, on the modernization of the school by the digital technology, August 2009, access 23 August 2010, http://www.reussirlecolenumerique.fr/pdf/Rapport_mission_fourgous.pdf, p. 8.

395. BIENVAULT P., "Ces enfants nés avec une souris dans la main," la-croix.com, August 19, 2010, accessed August 23, 2010, http://www.la-croix.com/Ces-enfants-nes-avec-unesouris-dans-la-main/article/2436203/4076.

396. MINOUI D., "Iran : mystérieux assassinat d'un universitaire", *Le Figaro*, 13 January 2010.

397. "Ségolène Royal falls into the trap of Wikipedia," lefigaro.fr, June 8, 2010, accessed June 8, 2010, http://www.lefigaro.fr/politique/2010/06/08/01002-20100608ARTFIG 00346-segolene-royal-tombe-dans-le-piege-de-wikipedia.php.

398. pubmed, http://www.ncbi.nlm.nih.gov/sites/entrez.

399. THIRION P. *et al*, "Enquête sur les compétences documentaires et informnelles des étudiants qui accèdent à l'enseignement supérieur en communauté française de Belgique", EduDOC / Conseil interuniversitaire de la Communauté française de Belgique (CIUF), June 2008, access 24 March 2009, http://www.edudoc.be/synthese.pdf, pp. 4 and 18.

400. ARATANI L., "Teens can multitask, but what are costs?", washingtonpost.com, February 26, 2007, accessed March 24, 2009, http://www.washingtonpost.com/wp-dyn/ content/article/2007/02/25/AR2007022501600.html.

401. LOHR S., "Slow down, brave multitasker, and don't read this in traffic," nytimes.com, March 25, 2007, accessed March 24, 2009, http://www.nytimes.com/2007/ 03/25/business/25multi.html.

402. EDWARDS E., "Study shows ever more kids embrace a plugged-in lifestyle," washingtonpost.com, March 10, 2005, accessed March 24, 2009, http://www.washingtonpost. com/wp-dyn/articles/A22138-2005Mar9.html.

403. HEALY M., "We're all multitasking, but what's the cost?" latimes. com, July 19, 2004, accessed March 24, 2009, http://articles.latimes.com/2004/jul/19/health/hemultitasking19.

404. WALLIS C., "The multitasking generation," time.com, March 27, 2006, accessed March 24, 2009, http://www.time.com/time/magazine/article/0,9171,1174696,00.html.

405. MISEREY Y., "Multizappeurs mais bons à rien", lefigaro.fr, 26 August 2009, accessed 8 October 2010, http://www.lefigaro.fr/sciences/2009/08/27/01008-20090827ARTFIG 00007-multizappeurs-mais-bons-a-rien-.php.

406. GREENFIELD P.M., "Technology and informal education: what is taught, what is learned," *Science*, n° 323, 2009, p. 69 *and passim.*

407. HEMBROOKE H. *et al*, "The lecture and the laptop: multitasking in wireless learning environments," *J. Comput. High Educ.* n° 15, 2003, p. 46 *and passim.*

408. BERGEN L. *et al*, "How attention partitions itself during simultaneous message presentations," *Human Comm. Res* 31, 2005, p. 311 *and passim.*

409. BELLIENI C.V. *et al*, "Distracting effect of TV watching on children's reactivity", *Eur. J. Pediatr.* 2010.

410. MAROIS R. *et al*, "Capacity limits of information processing in the brain", *Trends Cogn. Sci.* 2005, n° 9, p. 296 *and passim.*

411. DUX P.E. *et al*, "Isolation of a central bottleneck of information processing with time-resolved FMRI," *Neuron*, n° 52, 2006, pp. 1109 *et passim.*

412. JIANG Y. *et al.* "Functional magnetic resonance imaging provides new constraints on theories of the psychological refractory period," *Psychol. Sci.* 15 (2004): 390 *et al.*

413. RUBINSTEIN J.S. *et al*, "Executive control of cognitive processes in task switching," *J. Exp. Psychol. Hum. Percept. Perform*, n° 27, 2001, p. 763 *et passim.*

414. PASHLER H., "Dual-task interference in simple tasks: data and theory," *Psychol. Bull*, n° 116, 1994, p. 220 *and passim.*

415. BRAVER T.S. *et al*, "The role of frontopolar cortex in subgoal processing during working memory", *Neuroimage*, n° 15, 2002, p. 523 *and passim.*

416. KOECHLIN E. *et al*, "The role of the anterior prefrontal cortex in human cognition", *Nature*, n° 399, 1999, p. 148 *and passim.*

417. FOERDE K. *et al*, "Modulation of competing memory systems by distraction," *Proc. Natl. Acad. Sci.USA*, n° 103, 2006, pp. 11778 *et passim.*

418. OPHIR E. *et al*, "Cognitive control in media multitaskers," *Proc. Natl. Acad. Sci. USA*, n° 106, 2009, pp. 15583 *et passim.*

419. POOL M.M. *et al*, "Background television as an inhibitor of performance on easy and difficult homework assignments", *Communication Research*, n° 27, 2000, p. 293 *and passim*.

420. POOL M.M. *et al*, "The impact of background radio or television on high school students' homework performance," *J. Commun.* n° 53, 2003, p. 74 *and passim*.

421. POOL M.M. *et al*, "Distraction effects of background soap operas on homework performance: an experimental study enriched with observational data", *Educ. Psychol.* 23 (2003): *361ff.*

422. ARMSTRONG G.B. *et al*, "Background television as an inhibitor of cognitive processing", *Human Comm. Res* 16, 1990, p. 355 *and passim*.

423. BUSHMAN B.J. *et al*, "Effect of televised violence on aggression," *in* SINGER D.G. *et al* (eds.), *Handbook of Children and the Media*, Sage Publications, 2001, pp. 223, 236 *and passim*.

424. "Digest of education statistics 2008," US Department of Education, NCES 2009-020, March 2009, accessed July 21, 2009, http://nces.ed.gov/pubs2009/ 2009020.pdf.

425. MACBETH WILLIAMS T., *The Impact of Television: A Natural Experiment in Three Communities*, Academic Press, 1986.

426. CORTEEN R.S. *et al*, "Television and reading skills", *in* MACBETH WILLIAMS T. (ed.), *The Impact of Television: A Natural Experiment in Three Communities*, Academic Press, 1986, p. 39 *and passim*.

427. JOHNSON P. *et al*, "Remediation", *in* BARR R. *et al* (eds.), *Handbook of Reading Research*, Longman, 1991, vol. II, p. 984 *and passim*.

428. JUEL C., "Learning to read and write: a longitudinal study of 54 children from first through fourth grades," *J. Educ. Psychol*, 80 (1988), 437ff.

429. COMSTOCK G., "Television and the American child", *in* HEDLEY C.N. *et al.* (eds.), *Thinking and Literacy: The Mind at Work*, LEA, 1995, pp. 101, 102, 119 *and passim*.

430. SCHMIDT M.E. *et al*, "Media and attention, cognition and school achievement," *Fut. Child*, n° 18, 2008, p. 63 *and passim*.

431. SCHMIDT M.E. *et al*, "The impact of television on cognitive development and educational achievement", *in* PECORA N. *et al* (eds), *Children and Television*, LEA, 2007, p. 65 *and passim*.

432. VAN EVRA J., *Television and Child Development*, Lawrence Erlbaum Associates, 2004.

---

433. WRIGHT J.C. *et al*, "The relations of early television viewing to school readiness and vocabulary of children from low-income families," *Child Dev.* n° 72, 2001, p. 1347 *and passim*.

434. ANDERSON D.R. *et al*, "Early childhood television viewing and adolescent behavior: the recontact study," *Monogr. Soc. Res. Child Dev.* 66 (2001): 1 *and passim*.

435. See Chapter I for a detailed discussion.

436. ZILL N., "Does Sesame Street enhance school readiness: evidence from a national survey of children?" *in* FISH S.M. *et al.* (eds.), *"G" Is for "Growing": Thirty Years of Research on Children and Sesame Street,* LEA, 2001, p. 115 *et passim*.

437. GADBERRY S., "Effects of restricting first graders' TV viewing on leisure time use, IQ change, and cognitive style," *J. Appl. Dev. Psychol,* n° 1, 1980, p. 45 *et passim*.

438. JOHNSON J.G. *et al*, "Extensive television viewing and the development of attention and learning difficulties during adolescence," *Arch. Pediatr. Adolesc. Med.* 161 (2007): 480 *et al.*

439. SHARIF I, *et al*, "Effect of visual media use on school performance: a prospective study," *J. Adolesc. Health*, n° 46, 2010, p. 52 *et passim*.

440. JOHNSON J.G. *et al*, "Association between television viewing and sleep problems during adolescence and early adulthood," *Arch. Pediatr. Adolesc. Med.* 158 (2004): 562 *et al.*

441. LI S. *et al*, "The impact of media use on sleep patterns and sleep disorders among school-aged children in China," *Sleep*, n° 30, 2007, p. 361 *et passim*.

442. OWENS J *et al*, "Television-viewing habits and sleep disturbance in school children," *Pediatrics*, n° 104, 1999, p. e27.

443. PAAVONEN E.J. *et al*, "TV exposure associated with sleep disturbances in 5 to 6-year-old children," *J. Sleep Res*, n° 15, 2006, p. 154 *et passim*.

444. SADEH A. *et al*, "The effects of sleep restriction and extension on school-age children: what a difference an hour makes," *Child Dev.* 74 (2003): 444 *et al.*

445. WOLFSON A.R. *et al*, "Understanding adolescents' sleep patterns and school performance: a critical appraisal," *Sleep Med. Rev.* 7 (2003): 491 *et al.*

446. ASAOKA S. *et al*, "Does television viewing cause delayed and/or irregular sleep-wake patterns?", *Sleep Biol. Rhythms*, n° 5, 2007, p. 23 *and passim*.

447. ENNEMOSER M. *et al*, "Relations of television viewing and reading: findings from a 4-year longitudinal study," *Journal of Educational Psychology*, n° 99, 2007, p. 349 *et passim*.

448. PAGANI L.S. *et al*, "Prospective associations between early childhood television exposure and academic, psychosocial, and physical well-being by middle childhood," *Arch. Pediatr. Adolesc. Med*, n° 164, 2010, p. 425 *et passim*.

449. WINTERSTEIN P. *et al*, "Medienkonsum und passivrauchen bei vorschulkindern", *Kinder und Jugendarzt*, n° 37, 2006, p. 205 *and passim*.

450. SHIN N., "Exploring pathways from television viewing to academic achievement in school age children," *J. Genet. Psychol.* 165 (2004): 367 *and passim*.

451. WILLIAMS P.A. *et al*, "The impact of leisure-time television on school learning: a research synthesis," *Am. Educ. Res. J.*, n° 19, 1982, p. 19 *and passim*.

452. "Le soutien scolaire : un business très juteux," TF1, 8 p.m. news, August 25, 2009, accessed September 29, 2010, http://videos.tf1.fr/jt-20h/le-soutien-scolaire-unbusiness-tres-juteux-4525052.html.

453. "Les fausses promesses du soutien scolaire", *Envoyé spécial*, France 2, January 22, 2009.

454. RUEFF J., "Des petits cours qui rapportent gros", liberation.fr, March 10, 2004, accessed August 30, 2009, http://www.liberation.fr/vous/0101481258-des-petits-cours-quirapportent-gros.

455. RAMADIER S., "Soutien scolaire : le gros business des petits cours", lesechos.fr, September 1, 2004, accessed August 30, 2009, http://archives.lesechos.fr/archives/2004/ LesEchos/19234-47-ECH.htm

456. "Soutien scolaire : un bon business", *Alternatives économiques*, n° 266, February 2008.

457. DUCKWORTH A.L. *et al*, "Self-discipline outdoes IQ in predicting academic performance of adolescents," *Psychol. Sci.* 16 (2005): 939 *et al*.

458. COOPER H., "Synthesis of research on homework", *Educ. Leadersh.*, n° 47, 1991, p. 85 *and passim*.

459. PASCHAL R.A. *et al*, "The effects of homework on learning: a quantitative synthesis", *J. Educ. Res* 78, 1984, p. 97 *and passim*.

460. CHOUINARD R. *et al*, "Les devoirs, corvée inutile ou élément essentiel de la réussite scolaire ?", *Rev. Sci. Edu*, n° 32, 2006, p. 307 *et passim*.

461. SCHRAMM W. *et al*, *Television in the Lives of Our Children*, Stanford University Press, 1961.

462. FURU T., *Television and Children's Life: A Before-After Study*, Japan Broadcasting Corp, 1962.

463. MACCOBY E.E., "Television: its impact on school children", *Public Opin. Q*, n° 15, 1951, p. 421 *and passim*.

464. WIECHA J.L. *et al*, "Household television access: associations with screen time, reading, and homework among youth," *Ambul. Pediatr.* 2001;1:244 *and passim*.

465. DONNAT O. *et al*, "Approche générationnelle des pratiques culturelles et médiatiques", DEPS, Ministère de la Culture et de la Communication, June 2007, access 21 September 2009, http://www2.culture.gouv.fr/culture/deps/2008/pdf/Cprospective07_3.pdf, p. 1.

466. ROBINSON J.P., "Television's impact on everyday life: some cross-national evidence", *in* RUBINSTEIN E.A. *et al* (eds.), *Television and Social Behavior. Reports and Papers, Vol. IV, Television in Day-to-Day Life: Patterns of Use*, US Government Printing Office, 1972, p. 410 *and passim*.

467. PARKER E.B., "The Effects of Television on Public Library Circulation," *Public Opin. Q*, n° 27, 1963, p. 578 *and passim*.

468. WOLFE D.A. *et al*, "A parent-administered program to reduce children's television viewing," *J. Appl. Behav. Anal.* 17 (1984): 267 *et al*.

469. KOOLSTRA C.M. *et al*, "Television's impact on children's reading comprehension and decoding skills: a 3-year panel study", *Read. Res. Q*, n° 32, 1997, p. 128 *and passim*.

470. VANDEWATER E.A. *et al*, "When the television is always on: heavy television exposure and young children's development," *Am. Behav. Sci.* 48 (2005): 562 *et al*.

471. DONNAT O., *Les Pratiques culturelles des Français à l'ère numérique. Enquête 2008*, La Découverte, 2009.

472. TOMOPOULOS S *et al*, "Is exposure to media intended for preschool children associated with less parent-child shared reading aloud and teaching activities?", *Ambul. Ambul. pediatr.* 7 (2007): 18 *and passim*.

473. SNOW C. *et al*, *Preventing Reading Difficulties in Young Children*, National Academy Press, 1998.

474. KRUGMAN H., "Brain wave measures of media involvement", *J. Adver. Res* 11, 1971, p. 3 *and passim*.

475. FEATHERMAN G. *et al*, "Electroencephalographic and electroocu-lographic correlates of television watching. Final Technical Report," National Science Foundation Student-Oriented Studies, Hampshire College, Amherst, MA, 1979.

476. WEINSTEIN S. *et al*, "Brain activity responses to magazine and televi-sion advertising," *J. Adver. Res.* 20 (1980), p. 57 *and passim.*

477. SALOMON G., "Television is 'easy' and print is 'tough': the differential investment of mental effort in learning as a function of perceptions and attribution," *J. Educ. Psychol*, n° 76, 1984, p. 647 *and passim.*

478. CHAULET G., *Fantômette contre le géant*, Hachette, 2006.

479. BENTOLILA A., "La maternelle : au front des inégalités linguistiques et sociales", report commissioned by Xavier Darcos, Minister of National Education, Ministry of National Education, December 2007, accessed 5 October 2009, http://ia73.acgrenoble.fr/IMG/rapport_Bentolila_maternelle.pdf.

480. LANCHON A., "Ne les obligez pas à lire !", *Psychologies magazine*, n° 247, December 2005.

481. *Voici*, n° 1143, October 2-8, 2009, p. 63 *and passim.*

482. KISHIMOTO M., *Naruto*, n° 29, Kana, 2007.

483. MICHAUDON H., "La lecture, une affaire de famille", *INSEE Première*, n° 777, 2001.

484. "Une cagnotte pour les lycéens qui ne sèchent plus les cours," lePa-risien.fr, October 2, 2009, accessed October 11, 2009, http://www.leparisien.fr/societe/une-cagnotte-pour-leslyceens-qui-ne-sechent-plus-les-cours-02-10-2009-659222.php.

485. "Marseille. Places de soccer contre présence en cours", lci.tf1.fr, 5October 2009, access 11 October 2009, http://lci.tf1.fr/france/societe/2009-10/places-de-foot-contre-presenceen-cours-4887943.html.

486. FISHER M., "Desperation time in D.C.: school is money?", washing-tonpost.com, August 22, 2008, accessed October 11, 2009, http://voices.washingtonpost.com/rawfisher/ 2008/08/desperation_time_in_dc_school.html.

487. Europe 1, *La Matinale*, June 9, 2009.

488. GIOVANNINI S. *et al*, "Parent-and teacher-reported behavior problems of first graders," *Prax. Kinderpsychol. Kinderpsychiatr.* 2005;54:104, *et al.*

489. LEGRAND C. *et al*, "Nos enfants ont-ils perdu le goût d'apprendre?", la-croix. com, November 12, 2003, accessed October 15, 2009, http://www.la-croix. com/parentsenfants/article/index.jsp?docId=2209252&rubId=24303.

490. CLERC S., *Au secours ! Sauvons notre école*, Oh Éditions, 2008, pp. 142-145.

491. TESTEFORT J.P., "Des miettes de philosophie", *in* ABENSOUR C. *et al* (under the direction of), *De la destruction du savoir en temps de paix*, Mille et une nuits, 2007, pp. 279, 283 *and passim.*

492. ANDERSON D.R. *et al*, "The impact on children's education: television's influence on cognitive development," US Department of Education, Office of Educational Research and Improvement, Working paper n° 2, accessed December 11, 2010, http://www.eric. ed.gov/PDFS/ED295271.pdf.

493. SINGER J.L. *et al*, "Family patterns and television viewing as predictors of children's beliefs and aggression," *J. Commun.* n° 34, 1984, p. 73 *and passim.*

494. KOOLSTRA C.M. *et al*, "Longitudinal effects of television on children's leisure-time reading: a test of three explanatory models," *Hum. Commun. Res.* 23 (1996), p. 4 *and passim.*

495. Anderson C.C. *et al. 1978*; "The effect of TV viewing on the educational performance of elementary school children", *Alberta J. Educ. Alberta J. Educ. Res.* 24 (1978): *156ff.*

496. LEVINE L.E. *et al*, "Television viewing and attentional abilities in fourth and fifth grade children", *J. Appl. Dev. Psychol,* 21, 667 *et al.*

497. CHRISTAKIS D.A. *et al*, "Early television exposure and subsequent attentional problems in children," *Pediatrics,* n° 113, 2004, p. 708 *et passim.*

498. CHRISTAKIS D.A., "The effects of infant media usage: what do we know and what should we learn?", *Acta Paediatr.*, n° 98, 2009, p. 8 *and passim.*

499. ZIMMERMAN F.J. *et al*, "Associations between content types of early media exposure and subsequent attentional problems," *Pediatrics,* n° 120, 2007, p. 986 *et passim.*

500. LAWSON K.R. *et al*, "Early focused attention predicts outcome for children born prematurely," *J. Dev. Behav. Pediatr.* 25 (2004): 399, 404 *et al.*

501. COLOMBO J. *et al*, "A cognitive neuroscience approach to individual differences in infant cognition", *in* RICHARDS J.E. (ed.), *Cognitive*

Neuroscience of Attention: A Developmental Perspective, Lawrence Erlbaum, 1998, p. 363 *and passim.*

502. NELSON C.A. *et al*, "A cognitive neuroscience perspective on the relation between attention and memory development", *in* RICHARDS J.E. (ed.), *Cognitive Neuroscience of Attention: A Developmental Perspective*, Lawrence Erlbaum, 1998, p. 327 *and passim.*

503. RUFF H.A. *et al*, *Attention in Early Development*, Oxford University Press, 1996.

504. HARTMANN T., *Beyond ADD: Hunting for Reasons in the Past and Present*, Underwood, 1996.

505. SINGER J.L., "The power and limits of television: a cognitive-affective analysis", *in* TANNENBAUM P. (under the direction of), *The Entertainment Function of Television*, Lawrence Erlbaum, 1980, p. 312 *and passim.*

506. LEONTIEV A.N., "The development of voluntary attention in the child", *in* LLOYD P. *et al* (eds.), *Lev Vygotsky: Critical Assessments*, Routledge, 1999, p. 89 *and passim.*

507. BROWN R.G. *et al*, "Internal versus external cues and the control of attention in Parkinson's disease," *Brain*, n° 111, 1988, p. 323 *et passim.*

508. LANDAU A.N. *et al*, "Different effects of voluntary and involuntary attention on EEG activity in the gamma band," *J. Neurosci.* n° 27, 2007, p. 11986 *et passim.*

509. VALKENBURG P.M., "Television and the child developing imagination", *in* SINGER D.G. *et al* (eds.), *Handbook of Children and the Media*, Sage Publications, 2001, p. 121 *and passim.*

510. CHRISTAKIS D.A. *et al*, "Effect of block play on language acquisition and attention in toddlers: a pilot randomized controlled trial," *Arch. Pediatr. Adolesc. Med* 161 (2007): 967 *et al.*

511. SINGER J.L., "Cognitive and affective implications of imaginative play in childhood", *in* LEWIS M. (ed.), *Child and Adolescent Psychiatry: A Comprehensive Textbook*, Lippincott Williams & Wilkins, 2002, 3rd ed.

512. TERENZINI P. *et al*, "Influences affecting the development of students' critical thinking skills," *Research in Higher Education*, n° 36, 1995, p. 23 *and passim.*

513. SHMUKLER D., "Preschool Imaginative Play Predisposition and Its Relationship to Subsequent Third Grade Assessment," *Imagin. Cogn. Pers.* 2 (1982): *231ff.*

514. SCHMIDT M.E. *et al*, "The effects of background television on the toy play behavior of very young children," *Child Dev.* n° 79, 2008, p. 1137 *et passim*.

515. RUFF H.A. *et al*, "Long-term stability of individual differences in sustained attention in the early years," *Child Dev.* 61 (1990): 60ff.

516. LAWSON K.R. *et al*, "Early attention and negative emotionality predict later cognitive and behavioral function," *Int. J. Behav. Dev.* 28, 2004, p. 157 *and passim*.

517. HANDEN B.L. *et al*, "A playroom observation procedure to assess children with mental retardation and ADHD", *J. Abnorm.Child Psychol.*, n° 26, 1998, p. 269 *and passim*.

518. FADEN V.B. *et al*, "Maternal substance use during pregnancy and developmental outcome at age three," *J. Subst. Abuse*, n° 12, 2000, p. 329 *and passim*.

519. VIG S., "Young children's object play: a window on development," *J. Dev. Phys. Disabil*, n° 19, 2007, p. 201 *and passim*.

520. WESTBY C., "A scale for assessing development of children's play," *in* GITLIN-WEINER K. *et al. (eds.)*, *Play Diagnosis and Assessment*, Wiley, 2000, 2nd ed. p. 15 *et passim*.

521. PIAGET J., *La Naissance de l'intelligence chez l'enfant*, Delachaux et Niestlé, 1977, 9th ed.

522. TOMOPOULOS S. *et al*, "Books, toys, parent-child interaction, and development in young Latino children," *Ambul. Pediatr.* 2006;6:72, *et al.*

523. WALLON H., *De l'acte à la pensée*, Flammarion, 1970, p. 9.

524. LYYTINEN P. *et al*, "Language and symbolic play in toddlers," *Int. J. Behav. Dev.* 21 (1997): 289ff.

525. MCCUNE L., "A normative study of representational play at the transition to language", *Dev. Psychol.* 31 (1995): *198ff.*

526. TAMIS-LE MONDA C.S. *et al*, "Specificity in mother-toddler language-play relations across the second year", *Dev. Psychol.* 30 (1994): 283ff.

527. OGURA T., "A longitudinal study of the relationship between early language development and play development," *J. Child Lang.* n° 18, 1991, p. 273 *et passim*.

528. BRUNER J., *Child's Talk: Learning to Use Language*, WW Norton & Company, 1983.

529. WECHSLER D., *Wais-III* (French translation), ECPA, 2000, see in particular Appendix C.

530. AUBIN G. *et al*, *Neuropsychologie de la mémoire de travail*, Solal, 2007.

531. GAONAC'H D. *et al*, *Mémoire et fonctionnement cognitif. La mémoire de travail*, Armand Colin, 2000.

532. COURAGE M.L. *et al*, "When the television is on: the impact of infant-directed video on 6- and 18-month-olds' attention during toy play and on parent-infant interaction," *Infant Behav. Dev.* n° 33, 2010, p. 176 *and passim*.

533. SCHRECKENBERG G. *et al*, "Neural plasticity of MUS musculus in response to disharmonic sound," *Bull. N. J. Acad. Sci.* n° 32, 1987, p. 77 *and passim*.

534. WACHS T.D., "Noise in the nursery: ambient background noise and early development," *Child Environ. Q*, n° 3, 1986, p. 23 *and passim*.

535. WACHS T.D. *et al*, *Early Experience and Human Development*, Plenum Press, 1982.

536. ANDERSON D.R. *et al*, "Television viewing at home: age trends in visual attention and time with TV", *Child Dev.* n° 57, 1986, p. 1024 *and passim*.

537. ANDERSON D.R. *et al*, "Young children's attention to *Sesame Street*," *Child Dev.* 47 (1976): 806ff.

538. SCHMIDT K.L., "Infants, toddlers, and television: the ecology of the home," *Zero to Three*, n° 22, 2001, p. 17 *and passim*.

539. THOMPSON D.A. *et al*, "The association between television viewing and irregular sleep schedules among children less than 3 years of age," *Pediatrics*, n° 116, 2005, p. 851 *et passim*.

540. CHRISTAKIS D.A. *et al*, "Preschool-aged children's television viewing in child care settings," *Pediatrics*, n° 124, 2009, pp. 1627 *et passim*.

541. BabyFirst, accessed October 2, 2010, http://babyfirsttv.com/fr/parents.asp?xml_id= 1627&subXml_id=1775.

542. "Trésor de la langue française informatisé," atilf, CNRS, Universities of Nancy 1 and 2, accessed October 2, 2010, http://atilf.atilf.fr/tlf.htm.

543. DESMURGET M., *Mad in U.S.A.*, Max Milo, 2008.

544. GILLIE O., "Crucial data was faked by eminent psychologist", *The Sunday Times*, October 24, 1976.

545. BROAD W. *et al*, *Betrayers of the Truth*, Simon & Schuster, 1982.

546. GOULD S.J., *La Mal-Mesure de l'homme*, Odile Jacob, 1997.

547. JUDSON H.F., *The Great Betrayal*, Harcourt, 2004.

548. KOHN A., *The False Prophets*, Barnes & Noble, 1986.

549. HEBB D.O., "The effects of early experience on problem solving at maturity", *Am. Psychol*, n° 2, 1947, p. 306 *and passim*.

550. HUBEL D.H. *et al*, "The period of susceptibility to the physiological effects of unilateral eye closure in kittens," *J. Physiol*, n° 206, 1970, p. 419 *et passim*.

551. WIESEL T.N. *et al*, "Extent of recovery from the effects of visual deprivation in kittens," *J. Neurophysiol*, n° 28, 1965, p. 1060 *et passim*.

552. GREENOUGH W.T. *et al*, "Experience and brain development", *Child Dev.* n° 58, 1987, p. 539 *and passim*.

553. VAN PRAAG H. *et al*, "Neural consequences of environmental enrichment", *Nat. Rev. Neurosci.* n° 1, 2000, p. 191 *and passim*.

554. PERRY B.D., "Childhood experience and the expression of genetic potential: what childhood neglect tells us about nature and nurture", *Brain and Mind*, n° 3, 2002, p. 79 *and passim*.

555. MOHAMMED A.H. *et al*, "Environmental enrichment and the brain," *Prog. Brain Res* 138, 2002, p. 109 *and passim*.

556. SALE A. *et al*, "Enrich the environment to empower the brain," *Trends Neurosci.* n° 32, 2009, p. 233 *and passim*.

557. TURNER A.M. *et al*, "Differential rearing effects on rat visual cortex synapses. I. Synaptic and neuronal density and synapses per neuron," *Brain Res.* n° 329, 1985, p. 195 *and passim*.

558. BENNETT E.L. *et al*, "Chemical and anatomical plasticity brain," *Science*, n° 146, 1964, p. 610 *and passim*.

559. VAN IJZENDOORN M.H. *et al*, "Adoption and cognitive development: a meta-analytic comparison of adopted and nonadopted children's IQ and school performance," *Psychol. Bull*, 131 (2005): 301.

560. See for the most recent example: RYMER R., *Genie. A Scientific Tragedy*, HarperPerennial, 1994.

561. GRIMSHAW G.M. *et al*, "First-language acquisition in adolescence: evidence for a critical period for verbal language development", *Brain Lang*, n° 63, 1998, p. 237 *and passim*.

562. DUYME M. *et al*, "How can we boost IQs of 'dull children'? : a late adoption study," *Proc. Natl. Acad. Sci. USA*, n° 96, 1999, p. 8790 *et passim*.

563. SCHWEINHART L.J. *et al*, *Lifetime Effects: The High/Scope Perry Preschool Study Through Age 40, Monographs of the High/Scope Educational Research Foundation*, High/Scope Press, 2005, Volume XIV.

564. CAMPBELL F.A. *et al*, "The development of cognitive and academic abilities: growth curves from an early childhood educational experiment", *Dev. Psychol.* 37 (2001): *231ff*.

565. REYNOLDS A.J., *Success in Early Intervention. The Chicago Child-Parent Centers*, University of Nebraska Press, 2000.

566. See for a detailed summary: SCHWEINHART L.J., "The High/Scope Perry Preschool Study through age 40: summary, conclusions and frequently asked questions," High/Scope Educational Research Foundation, 2006, accessed December 17, 2009, http://www.highscope.org/file/Research/PerryProject/3_specialsummary%20col%2006%2007.pdf.

567. DESMURGET M., *Imitation and motor learning*, Solal, 2006.

568. DOLLE J.M. *et al*, *Ces enfants qui n'apprennent pas*, Éditions du Centurion, 1989.

569. DANSET A., *Éléments de psychologie du développement*, Armand Colin, 1983.

570. DOLLE J.M., *Pour comprendre Jean Piaget*, Dunod, 1999, p. 48.

571. SACHS J. *et al*, "Language learning with restricted input: case studies of two hearing children of deaf parents", *Appl. Psycholinguist*, n° 2, 1981, p. 33 *and passim*.

572. NAIGLES L.R. *et al*, "Television as incidental language teacher", *in* SINGER D.G. *et al*.

573. (ed.), *Handbook of Children and the Media*, 2001, Sage Publications, p. 135 *and passim*.

574. BOYSSON-BARDIES B. DE *et al*, "A crosslinguistic investigation of vowel formants in babbling," *J. Child Lang.* n° 16, 1989, p. 1 *and passim*.

575. BOYSSON-BARDIES B. DE *et al*, "Discernible differences in the babbling of infants according to target language," *J. Child Lang.* 1984, 11, 1 *and passim*.

576. FORGAYS D.G. *et al*, "The nature of the effect of free-environmental experience in the rat", *J. Comp. Physiol Psychol*, n° 45, 1952, p. 322 *and passim*.

577. FERCHMIN P.A. *et al*, "Direct contact with enriched environment is required to alter cerebral weights in rats," *J. Comp. Physiol Psychol*, n° 88, 1975, p. 360 *and passim*.

578. HELD R. *et al*, "Movement-produced stimulation in the development of visually guided behavior," *J. Comp. Physiol Psychol*, n° 56, 1963, p. 872 *and passim*.

579. BARR R. *et al*, "Developmental changes in imitation from television during infancy," *Child Dev.* n° 70 (1999): 1067ff.

580. HAYNE H. *et al*, "Imitation from television by 24and 30-month-olds," *Dev. Sci.* 6 (2003): 254 *et al*.

581. TROSETH G.L. *et al*, "The medium can obscure the message: young children's understanding of video", *Child. Child Dev.* 69 (1998): *950ff*.

582. SCHMIDT K.L. *et al*, "Television and reality: toddlers' use of visual information from video to guide behavior," *Media Psychol.* 4 (2002): 51ff.

583. SCHMIDT K.L. *et al*, "Two-year-olds' object retrieval based on television: testing a perceptual account," *Media Psychol.* 9 (2007): 389 *et al*.

584. BabyFirst, accessed October 2, 2010, http://www.babyfirst.fr/parents. asp. BabyTV, accessed January 6, 2010, http://www.babytvchannel.fr/ view_article.aspx?l= 8&i=72&si=60.

585. BOYSSON-BARDIES B. DE, *Comment la parole vient aux enfants*, Odile Jacob, 1996.

586. ROBB M.B. *et al*, "Just a talking book? Word learning from watching baby videos," *Br. J. Dev. Psychol*, n° 27, 2009, p. 27 *and passim*.

587. RICHERT R.A. *et al*, "Word learning from baby videos," *Arch. Pediatr. Adolesc. Med*, n° 164, 2010, p. 432 *et passim*.

588. LOACHE J.S. DE *et al*, "Do babies learn from baby media?", *Psychol. Sci.* n° 21, 2010, p. 1570 *et passim*.

589. KRCMAR M. *et al*, "Can toddlers learn vocabulary from television? An experimental approach", *Media Psychol*, n° 10, 2007, p. 41 *and passim*.

590. KOOLSTRA C.M. *et al.* "Children's vocabulary acquisition in a foreign language through watching subtitled television programs at home," *Education Tech. Res. Dev.* 47 (1999): 51ff.

591. VAN LOMMEL S. *et al*, "Foreign-grammar acquisition while watching subtitled television programs," *Br. J. Educ. Psychol*, n° 76, 2006, p. 243 *and passim*.

592. SCHOON I. *et al*, "Children's language ability and psychosocial development: a 29-year follow-up study," *Pediatrics*, n° 126, 2010, pp. e73-e80 *et passim*.

593. SCHOON I. *et al*, "Childhood language skills and adult literacy: a 29-year follow-up study," *Pediatrics*, n° 125, 2010, pp. e459-e466 *and passim*.

594. DEHAENE-LAMBERTZ G. *et al*, "Bases cérébrales de l'acquisition du langage", *in* KAIL M. *et al* (under the direction of), *L'Acquisition du langage. Le langage en émergence. De la naissance à trois ans*, 2000, PUF, pp. 61, 65 *and passim*.

595.BabyFirst, accessed January 14, 2010, http://www.babyfirst.fr/programs.asp?xml_id= 1601&subXml_id=1670.

596.BabyFirst, accessed January 14, 2010, http://www.babyfirst.fr/programs.asp?xml_id= 1605&subXml_id=1909.

597.BabyFirst, accessed January 14, 2010, http://www.babyfirst.fr/programs.asp?xml_id= 1599&subXml_id=1913.

598.BabyFirst, accessed January 14, 2010, http://www.babyfirst.fr/programs.asp?xml_id= 1603&subXml_id=1896.

599.BabyFirst, accessed January 19, 2010, http://www.babyfirst.fr/programs.asp?xml_id= 1603&subXml_id=1888.

600.ROWE M.L. *et al. 2008*, "Learning words by hand: gesture's role in predicting vocabulary development", *First. Lang* 28 (2008): *182ff.*

601.CHOUINARD M.M. *et al*, "Adult reformulations of child errors as negative evidence", *J. Child Lang.* 2003; 30: 637 *and passim.*

602.MENDELSOHN A.L. *et al*, "Infant television and video exposure associated with limited parent-child verbal interactions in low socioeconomic status households," *Arch. Pediatr. Adolesc. Med*, n° 162, 2008, p. 411 *et passim.*

603.RISLEY T. *et al*, "Promoting early language development," *in* WATT N.F. *et al* (eds), *The Crisis in Youth Mental Health: Critical Issues and Effective Programs, Volume IV, Early Intervention Programs and Policies*, Praeger, 2006, p. 83 *et al.*

604.PIÉRON H., *Vocabulaire de la psychologie*, PUF, 1987, 7th ed.

605.HARRISON L.F. *et al*, "Television and cognitive development", *in* MACBETH WILLIAMS T. (ed.), *The Impact of Television: A Natural Experiment in Three Communities*, Academic Press, 1986, p. 87 *and passim.*

606.MELINE C.W., "Does the medium matter?", *J. Commun.* n° 26, 1976, p. 81 *and passim.*

607.GREENFIELD P. *et al*, "Is the medium the message? An experimental comparison of the effects of radio and television on imagination," *J. Appl. Dev. Psychol*, n° 7, 1986, p. 201 *and passim.*

608.GREENFIELD P. *et al*, "Radio vs. television: their cognitive impact on children of different socioeconomic and ethnic groups," *J. Commun.* 1988, n° 38, p. 71 *and passim.*

609.VALKENBURG P.M. *et al*, "Children's creative imagination in response to radio and television stories," *J. Commun.* n° 47, 1997, p. 21 *and passim.*

610. BETTELHEIM B., "Parents vs. television", *Redbook*, November 1963.

611. HARRIS D.B., *Children's Drawings as a Measure of Intellectual Maturity*, Harcourt Brace & World, 1963.

612. OHAYON D., "Regarder la télé... tue !", Chronique info médias, France Info, January 12, 2010, accessed September 2, 2010, http://www.france-info.com/chroniquesinfo-tele-2010-01-12-regarder-la-tele-tue-391387-81-168.html.

613. MOKDAD A.H. *et al*, "Actual causes of death in the United States, 2000," *JAMA*, n° 291, 2004, p. 1238 *et passim*.

614. DUNSTAN D.W. *et al*, "Television viewing time and mortality: the Australian diabetes, obesity and lifestyle study (AusDiab)," *Circulation*, n° 121, 2010, p. 384 *et passim*.

615. THORP A.A. *et al*, "Deleterious associations of sitting time and television viewing time with cardiometabolic risk biomarkers: Australian diabetes, obesity and lifestyle (AusDiab) study 2004-2005," *Diabetes Care*, n° 33, 2010, p. 327 *and passim*.

616. WIJNDAELE K. *et al*, "Television viewing time independently predicts all-cause and cardiovascular mortality: the EPIC Norfolk Study", *Int. J. Epidemiol*, 2010.

617. WIJNDAELE K. *et al*, "Increased cardiometabolic risk is associated with increased TV viewing time," *Med. Sci. Sports Exerc.* n° 42, 2010, p. 1511 *et passim*.

618. BAUGHCUM A.E. *et al*, "Maternal perceptions of overweight preschool children," *Pediatrics*, n° 106, 2000, p. 1380 *and passim*.

619. CAMPBELL M.W. *et al*, "Maternal concern and perceptions of overweight in Australian preschool-aged children," *Med. Aust J*, n° 184, 2006, p. 274 *and passim*.

620. WAKE M *et al*, "Parent-reported health status of overweight and obese Australian primary school children: a cross-sectional population survey," *Int. J. Obes. Relat. Metab. Disorder* 26 (2002): 717 *et al.*

621. JAIN A. *et al*, "Why don't low-income mothers worry about their preschoolers being overweight?", *Pediatrics*, n° 107, 2001, p. 1138 *and passim*.

622. DEITEL M., "Overweight and obesity worldwide now estimated to involve 1.7 billion people," *Obes. Surg* 13 (2003): 329 *et al.*

623. FLEGAL K.M. *et al*, "Prevalence and trends in obesity among US adults, 1999-2008," *JAMA*, n° 303, 2010, p. 235 *and passim*.

624. OGDEN C.L. *et al*, "Prevalence of high body mass index in US children and adolescents, 2007-2008," *JAMA*, n° 303, 2010, p. 242 *et passim.*

625. "National Nutrition and Health Study ENNS, 2006," Institut de veille sanitaire, December 2007, accessed February 3, 2010, http://www.invs.sante.fr/publications/2007/nutrition_ enns/RAPP_INST_ENNS_Web.pdf.

626. BELLANGER T.M. *et al*, "Obesity related morbidity and mortality," *J. La State Med. Soc.* n° 157, Spec. n° 1, 2005, pp. S42-S49.

627. KOPELMAN P.G., "Obesity as a medical problem," *Nature*, n° 404, 2000, p. 635 *and passim.*

628. BRAY G.A., "Health hazards of obesity," *Endocrinol. Metab. Clin. North Am.* 1996;25:907 *et al.*

629. ALLISON D.B. *et al*, "Annual deaths attributable to obesity in the United States," *JAMA*, n° 282, 1999, p. 1530 *et passim.*

630. BANEGAS J.R. *et al*, "A simple estimate of mortality attributable to excess weight in the European Union", *Eur. J. Clin. Nutr.* n° 57, 2003, p. 201 *and passim.*

631. "Main causes of death," INSEE, 2006, accessed February 3, 2009, http://www.insee.fr/fr/themes/tableau.asp?reg_id=0&ref_id=NATFPS06205.

632. STURM R., "The effects of obesity, smoking, and drinking on medical problems and costs," *Health Aff.(Millwood)*, n° 21, 2002, p. 245 *et passim.*

633. "The surgeon general's call to action to prevent and decrease overweight and obesity," US Department of Health and Human Services, 2001, accessed February 25, 2010, http://www.surgeongeneral.gov/topics/obesity/calltoaction/CalltoAction.pdf.

634. Consumer Price Index Inflation Calculator, Bureau of Labor Statistics, accessed February 25, 2010, http://www.bls.gov/data/inflation_calculator.htm.

635. US Census Bureau, http://www.census.gov/main/www/popclock.html.

636. Banque de France, http://www.banque-france.fr/fr/statistiques/taux/paritesquotidiennes.htm.

637. COON K.A. *et al. 2002;* "Television and children's consumption patterns. A review of the literature," *Minerva Pediatr.* 54 (2002): 423 *et al.*

638. LUDWIG D.S. *et al*, "Programming obesity in childhood," *Lancet*, n° 364, 2004, p. 226 *and passim.*

639. "The role of media in childhood obesity," The Henry Kaiser Family Foundation, February 2004, accessed February 4, 2010, http://www.kff.org/entmedia/upload/The-Role-OfMedia-in-Childhood-Obesity.pdf.

640. JORDAN A., "Heavy television viewing and childhood obesity," *J. Child Media*, n° 1, 2007, p. 45 *and passim*.

641. ESCOBAR-CHAVES S. *et al*, "Media and risky behavior", *Fut. Child*, n° 18, 2008, p. 147 *and passim*.

642. CHAPUT J.P. *et al*, "Modern sedentary activities promote overconsumption of food in our current obesogenic environment," *Obes. Rev.* 2010.

643. MORGENSTERN M. *et al*, "Relation between socioeconomic status and body mass index: evidence of an indirect path via television use," *Arch. Pediatr. Adolesc. Med*, n° 163, 2009, p. 731 *et passim*.

644. JACKSON D.M. *et al*, "Increased television viewing is associated with elevated body fatness but not with lower total energy expenditure in children," *Am. J. Clin. Nutr.* n° 89, 2009, p. 1031 *and passim*.

645. FOSTER J.A. *et al*, "Altering TV viewing habits: an unexplored strategy for adult obesity intervention?" *Am. J. Health Behavior* 30 (2006): 3, *et al.*

646. UTTER J *et al*, "Associations between television viewing and consumption of commonly advertised foods among New Zealand children and young adolescents," *Public Health Nutr.* 2006;9:606ff.

647. BOWMAN S.A., "Television-viewing characteristics of adults: correlations to eating practices and overweight and health status," *Prev. Chronic. Dis.* 2006;3:A38.

648. KUEPPER-NYBELEN J. *et al*, "Major differences in prevalence of overweight according to nationality in preschool children living in Germany: determinants and public health implications," *Arch. Dis. Child*, n° 90, 2005, p. 359 *et passim*.

649. JANSSEN I *et al*, "Comparison of overweight and obesity prevalence in school-aged youth from 34 countries and their relationships with physical activity and dietary patterns," *Obes. Rev* 6, 2005, p. 123 *and passim*.

650. JANSSEN I *et al*, "Overweight and obesity in Canadian adolescents and their associations with dietary habits and physical activity patterns," *J. Adolesc. Health* 35 (2004): 360 *et al.*

651. HU F.B. *et al*, "Television watching and other sedentary behaviors in relation to risk of obesity and type 2 diabetes mellitus in women," *JAMA*, n° 289, 2003, pp. 1785 *et passim*.

652. CRESPO C.J. *et al*, "Television watching, energy intake, and obesity in US children: results from the third National Health and Nutrition

Examination Survey, 1988-1994," *Arch. Pediatr. Adolesc. Med,* n° 155, 2001, p. 360 *et passim.*

653. ANDERSEN R.E. *et al,* "Relationship of physical activity and television watching with body weight and level of fatness among children: results from the Third National Health and Nutrition Examination Survey," *JAMA,* n° 279, 1998, p. 938 *et passim.*

654. OBARZANEK E. *et al,* "Energy intake and physical activity in relation to indexes of body fat: the National Heart, Lung, and Blood Institute Growth and Health Study," *Am. J. Clin. Nutr.* n° 60, 1994, p. 15 *and passim.*

655. DIETZ W.H. Jr *et al,* "Do we fatten our children at the television set? Obesity and television viewing in children and adolescents," *Pediatrics,* n° 75, 1985, p. 807 *and passim.*

656. GORTMAKER S.L. *et al,* "Television viewing as a cause of increasing obesity among children in the United States, 1986-1990," *Arch. Pediatr. Adolesc. Med* 150 (1996): 356 *et al.*

657. LOWRY R. *et al.* "Television viewing and its associations with overweight, sedentary lifestyle, and insufficient consumption of fruits and vegetables among US high school students: differences by race, ethnicity, and gender," *J. Sch. Health,* n° 72, 2002, p. 413 *et passim.*

658. LUMENG J.C. *et al,* "Television exposure and overweight risk in preschoolers," *Arch. Pediatr. Adolesc. Med,* n° 160, 2006, p. 417 *et passim.*

659. EPSTEIN L.H. *et al,* "A randomized trial of the effects of reducing television viewing and computer use on body mass index in young children," *Arch. Pediatr. Adolesc. Med,* n° 162, 2008, p. 239 *and passim.*

660. DOAK C.M. *et al,* "The prevention of overweight and obesity in children and adolescents: a review of interventions and programmes," *Obes. Rev.* 7 (2006): 111 *et al.*

661. ROBINSON T.N., "Reducing children's television viewing to prevent obesity: a randomized controlled trial," *JAMA,* n° 282, 1999, p. 1561 *et passim.*

662. LANDHUIS C.E *et al,* "Programming obesity and poor fitness: the long-term impact of childhood television", *Obesity (Silver Spring),* n° 16, 2008, pp. 1457, 1459 *et passim.*

663. VINER R.M. *et al,* "Television viewing in early childhood predicts adult body mass index," *J. Pediatr.* 2005;147:429 *and passim.*

664. ZIMMERMAN F.J. *et al*, "Associations of television content type and obesity in children," *Am. J. Public Health,* n° 100, 2010, p. 334 *et passim.*

665. BIRCH L.L., "Development of food preferences", *Annu. Rev. Nutr.* 19 (1999): 41 *and passim.*

666. KELDER S.H. *et al*, "Longitudinal tracking of adolescent smoking, physical activity, and food choice behaviors," *Am. J. Public Health,* n° 84, 1994, p. 1121 *et passim.*

667. HALLER R. *et al*, "The influence of early experience with vanillin on food preference later in life," *Chem. Senses,* n° 24, 1999, p. 465 *et passim.*

668. "He eats *junk food* and loses 12 kilos," metrofrance.com, access December 7, 2010, http://www.metrofrance.com/info/il-mange-de-la-junk-food-et-perd-12-kilos/ mjki!xKlKXmiP3haM/.

669. KLESGES R.C. *et al*, "Effects of television on metabolic rate: potential implications for childhood obesity," *Pediatrics,* n° 91, 1993, p. 281 *et passim.*

670. Hill J.O. *et al*, "Obesity and the environment: where do we go from here?" *Science,* n° 299, 2003, p. 853 *and passim.*

671. COOPER T.V. *et al*, "An assessment of obese and nonobese girls' metabolic rate during television viewing, reading, and resting," *Eat. Behav,* n° 7, 2006, p. 105 *et passim.*

672. BUIJZEN M. *et al*, "A test of three alternative hypotheses explaining the link between children's television viewing and weight status," *J. Child Media,* n° 2, 2008, p. 67 *and passim.*

673. BENNETT G.G. *et al*, "Television viewing and pedometer-determined physical activity among multiethnic residents of low-income housing," *Am. J. Public Health,* n° 96, 2006, p. 1681 *et passim.*

674. SALMON J *et al*, Television viewing habits associated with obesity risk factors: a survey of Melbourne schoolchildren, *Med. Aust.* 2006; n° 184, p. 64 *et passim.*

675. SALMON J *et al*, "The association between television viewing and overweight among Australian adults participating in varying levels of leisure-time physical activity," *Int. J. Obes. Relat. Metab. Disorder* 24 (2000): 600 *et al.*

676. JAGO R. *et al*, "BMI from 3-6 years of age is predicted by TV viewing and physical activity, not diet", *Int. J. Obes.(Lond.),* n° 29, 2005, p. 557 *et passim.*

677. HU F.B. *et al*, "Physical activity and television watching in relation to risk for type 2 diabetes mellitus in men," *Arch. Intern. Med*, n° 161, 2001, p. 1542 *et passim*.

678. TARAS H.L. *et al*, "Television's influence on children's diet and physical activity," *J. Dev. Behav. Pediatr.* 1989;10:176 *et al*.

679. WIECHA J.L. *et al*, "When children eat what they watch: impact of television viewing on dietary intake in youth," *Arch. Pediatr. Adolesc. Med*, n° 160, 2006, p. 436 *et passim*.

680. AKTAS ARNAS Y., "The effects of television food advertisement on children's food purchasing requests," *Pediatr. Int.*, n° 48, 2006, p. 138 *and passim*.

681. THOMSON M *et al*, "The association of television viewing with snacking behavior and body weight of young adults," *Am. J. Health Promot*, n° 22, 2008, p. 329 *and passim*.

682. TEMPLE J.L. *et al*, "Television watching increases motivated responding for food and energy intake in children," *Am. J. Clin. Nutr.* n° 85, 2007, p. 355 *and passim*.

683. BELLISSIMO N. *et al*, "Effect of television viewing at mealtime on food intake after a glucose preload in boys," *Pediatr. Res*, n° 61, 2007, p. 745 *et passim*.

684. EPSTEIN L.H. *et al*, "Allocation of attentional resources during habituation to food cues", *Psychophysiology*, n° 34, 1997, p. 59 *and passim*.

685. STROEBELE N. *et al*, "Listening to music while eating is related to increases in people's food intake and meal duration," *Appetite*, n° 47, 2006, p. 285 *and passim*.

686. BELLISLE F. *et al*, "Non food-related environmental stimuli induce increased meal intake in healthy women: comparison of television viewing versus listening to a recorded story in laboratory settings", *Appetite*, n° 43, 2004, p. 175 *et passim*.

687. HETHERINGTON M.M. *et al*, "Situational effects on meal intake: a comparison of eating alone and eating with others," *Physiol. Behav* 88 (2006): 498 *et al*.

688. BLASS E.M. *et al*, "On the road to obesity: television viewing increases intake of high-density foods," *Physiol. Behav* 88 (2006): 597 *et al*.

689. STROEBELE N. *et al*, "Television viewing is associated with an increase in meal frequency in humans," *Appetite*, n° 42, 2004, p. 111 *and passim*.

690. HIGGS S. *et al*, "Television watching during lunch increases afternoon snack intake of young women," *Appetite*, n° 52, 2009, p. 39 *and passim*.

691. HIGGS S., "Cognitive influences on food intake: the effects of manipulating memory for recent eating," *Physiol. Behav*, n° 94, 2008, p. 734 *et passim*.

692. HIGGS S., "Memory and its role in appetite regulation", *Physiol. Behav*, n° 85, 2005, p. 67 *and passim*.

693. HIGGS S., "Memory for recent eating and its influence on subsequent food intake," *Appetite*, n° 39, 2002, p. 159 *et passim*.

694. HIGGS S. *et al*, "Recall of recent lunch and its effect on subsequent snack intake," *Physiol. Behav*, n° 94, 2008, p. 454 *et passim*.

695. DIJKSTERHUIS A. *et al*, "The perception-behavior expressway: automatic effects of social perception on social behavior", *Adv. Exp. Soc. Psychol*, n° 33, 2001, p. 1 *and passim*.

696. BARGH J.A. *et al*, "Automaticity of social behavior: direct effects of trait construct and stereotype-activation on action", *J. Pers. Soc. Psychol*, n° 71, 1996, p. 230 *and passim*.

697. CORNELL C.E. *et al*, "Stimulus-induced eating when satiated", *Physiol. Behav*, n° 45, 1989, p. 695 *et passim*.

698. HALFORD J.C. *et al*, "Children's food preferences: effects of weight status, food type, branding and television food advertisements (commercials)", *Int. J. Pediatr. Obes*, n° 3, 2008, p. 31 *and passim*.

699. HALFORD J.C. *et al*, "Beyond-brand effect of television food advertisements on food choice in children: the effects of weight status," *Public Health Nutr* 2008;11:897 *et al*.

700. HALFORD J.C. *et al*, "Beyond-brand effect of television (TV) food advertisements/commercials on caloric intake and food choice of 5-7-year-old children," *Appetite*, n° 49, 2007, p. 263 *et passim*.

701. HALFORD J.C. *et al*, "Effect of television advertisements for foods on food consumption in children", *Appetite*, n° 42, 2004, p. 221 *and passim*.

702. HARRIS J.L. *et al*, "Priming effects of television food advertising on eating behavior," *Health Psychol*, n° 28, 2009, p. 404 *et passim*.

703. KOORDEMAN R *et al*, "Exposure to soda commercials affects sugar-sweetened soda consumption in young women. An observational experimental study," *Appetite*, n° 54, 2010, p. 619 *et passim*.

704. "The marketing of unhealthy food to children in Europe. A report of Phase 1 of the "Children, obesity and associated avoidable chronic diseases" project," European Heart Network, 2005, accessed October 3, 2010, http://www.ehnheart.org/downloads/ 47.html.

705.HARRIS J.L. *et al*, "A crisis in the marketplace: how food marketing contributes to childhood obesity and what can be done," *Annu. Rev. Public Health*, n° 30, 2009, p. 211 *and passim*.

706.HASTINGS G. *et al*, "Review of research on the effects of food promotion to children, Final Report for the Food Standards Agency," University of Strathclyde, September 2003, accessed 24 February 2010, http://www.food.gov.uk/multimedia/pdfs/ foodpromotiontochildren1.pdf.

707.STORY M. *et al*, "Food advertising and marketing directed at children and adolescents in the US," *Int. J. Behav. Nutr. Phys. Act.* 2004, n° 1, pp. 3, 14.

708."vuàlatélé n° 22," National Television Advertising Union Newsletter, February 2009, accessed February 23, 2010, http://www.snptv.org/_files/actualites/fichiers/ actualites-949-401.pdf.

709."The Media Guide," Dufresne Corrigan Scarlett, 2008.

710.DIBB S. *et al*, *A Spoonful of Sugar. Television Food Advertising Aimed at Children: An International Comparative Study*, Consumers International, 1996.

711."Marketing food to children and adolescents: a review of industry expenditures, activities, and self-regulation," Federal Trade Commission, Report to Congress, July 2008, last accessed February 23, 2010, http://www.ftc.gov/os/2008/07/ P064504foodmktingreport.pdf.

712.GANTZ W. *et al*, "Food for thought: television food advertising to children in the United States," The Kaiser Family Foundation, March 2007, accessed 23 February 2010, http://www.kff.org/entmedia/upload/7618.pdf, p. 1.

713.KUNKEL D. *et al*, "The impact of industry self-regulation on the nutritional quality of foods advertised on television to children," report ordered by Children Now, December 2009, accessed June 27, 2010, http://www.childrennow.org/uploads/ documents/adstudy_2009.pdf.

714.RADNITZ C. *et al*, "Food cues in children's television programs," *Appetite*, n° 52, 2009, p. 230 *and passim*.

715.POWELL L.M. *et al*, "Nutritional content of television food advertisements seen by children and adolescents in the United States," *Pediatrics*, n° 120, 2007, p. 576 *et passim*.

716.POWELL L.M. *et al*, "Adolescent exposure to food advertising on television," *Am. J. Prev. Med.* 33 (2007): S251-S256.

717.MALEYSSON F. *et al*, "Publicité télé. Écrans plats et ventres ronds", *Que Choisir*, n° 441, 2006, p. 26 *et passim*.

718. HARRISON K. *et al*, "Nutritional content of foods advertised during the television programs children watch most," *Am. J. Public Health*, n° 95, 2005, p. 1568 *et passim*.

719. BYRD-BREDBENNER C., "Saturday morning children's television advertising: a longitudinal content analysis," *Fam. Consum. Sci. Re. J.*, n° 30, 2002, p. 382 *and passim*.

720. BATADA A. *et al*, "9 out of 10 food advertisements shown during Saturday morning children's television programming are for foods high in fat, sodium, or added sugars, or low in nutrients," *J. Am. Diet. Assoc.* n° 108, 2008, p. 673 *and passim*.

721. GURAN T *et al*, "Content analysis of food advertising in Turkish television," *J. Paediatr. Child Health*, n° 46, 2010, p. 427 *et passim*.

722. KELLY B *et al*, Television food advertising to children: a global perspective, *Am. J. Public Health*, n° 100, 2010, p. 1730 *et passim*.

723. MINK M. *et al*, "Nutritional imbalance endorsed by televised food advertisements," *J. Am. Diet. Assoc.* n° 110, 2010, p. 904 *et passim*.

724. RODD H.D. *et al*, "Content analysis of children's television advertising in relation to dental health," *Br. Dent. J.*, n° 199, 2005, p. 710 *and passim*.

725. DIXON H.G. *et al*, "The effects of television advertisements for junk food versus nutritious food on children's food attitudes and preferences," *Soc. Sci. Med.* n° 65, 2007, p. 1311 *et passim*.

726. BOYNTON-JARRETT R *et al*, "Impact of television viewing patterns on fruit and vegetable consumption among adolescents," *Pediatrics*, n° 112, 2003, pp. 1321 *et passim*.

727. BUIJZEN M. *et al*, "Associations between children's television advertising exposure and their food consumption patterns: a household diary-survey study," *Appetite*, n° 50, 2008, p. 231 *et passim*.

728. FRENCH S.A. *et al.* "Fast food restaurant use among adolescents: associations with nutrient intake, food choices and behavioral and psychosocial variables," *Int. J. Obes. Relat. Metab. Disord*, n° 25, 2001, p. 1823 *et passim*.

729. KREMERS S.P. *et al*, "Adolescent screen-viewing behaviour is associated with consumption of sugar-sweetened beverages: the role of habit strength and perceived parental norms," *Appetite*, n° 48, 2007, p. 345 *et passim*.

730. MILLER S.A. *et al*, "Association between television viewing and poor diet quality in young children," *Int. J. Pediatr. Obes*, n° 3, 2008, p. 168 *et passim*.

731. PARVANTA S.A. *et al*, "Television use and snacking behaviors among children and adolescents in China," *J. Adolesc. Health*, n° 46, 2010, p. 339 *et passim*.

732. SIGNORIELLI N. *et al*, "Television and children's conception of nutrition: unhealthy messages", *Health Comm*, n° 4, 1992, p. 245 *and passim*.

733. SIGNORIELLI N. *et al*, "Television and children's conception of nutrition", *Health Comm*, n° 9, 1997, p. 289 *and passim*.

734. SCULLY M. *et al*, "Association between commercial television exposure and fast food consumption among adults," *Public Health Nutr.* n° 12, 2009, p. 105 *et passim*.

735. VEREECKEN C.A. *et al*, "Television viewing behaviour and associations with food habits in different countries," *Public Health Nutr* 2006;9:244 *and passim*.

736. GALST J.P. *et al*, "The unhealthy persuader: the reinforcing value of television and children's purchase-influencing attempts at the supermarket," *Child Dev.* n° 47, 1976, pp. 1089, 1094-1095 *et passim*.

737. CHAMBERLAIN L.J. *et al*, "Does children's screen time predict requests for advertised products? Cross-sectional and prospective analyses," *Arch. Pediatr. Adolesc. Med*, n° 160, 2006, p. 363 *et passim*.

738. GOLDBERG M.E. *et al*, "TV messages for snack and breakfast foods: do they influence children's preferences?", *J. Consum. Res.* 5 (1978): *73ff*.

739. GOLDBERG M.E., "A quasi-experiment assessing the effectiveness of TV advertising directed to children", *J. Market Res.*, n° 27, 1990, p. 445 *and passim*.

740. GORN G.J. *et al*, "Behavioral evidence of the effects of televised food messages on children," *J. Consum. Res.* 9 (1982): 200 *et al*.

741. BORZEKOWSKI D.L. *et al*, "The 30-second effect: an experiment revealing the impact of television commercials on food preferences of preschoolers," *J. Am. Diet. Assoc.* n° 101, 2001, p. 42 *and passim*.

742. ROBINSON T.N. *et al*, "Effects of fast food branding on young children's taste preferences," *Arch. Pediatr. Adolesc. Med*, n° 161, 2007, p. 792 *et passim*.

743. ROBERTO C.A. *et al*, "Influence of licensed characters on children's taste and snack preferences," *Pediatrics*, n° 126, 2010, p. 88 *and passim*.

744. MCCLURE S.M. *et al*, "Neural correlates of behavioral preference for culturally familiar drinks," *Neuron*, n° 44, 2004, p. 379 *et passim*.

745. Exploring children's choice: the reminder effect of product placement," *Psychol. Market,* n° 21, 2004, p. 699 *et passim.*

746. SUTHERLAND L.A. *et al,* "Prevalence of food and beverage brands in movies: 1996-2005," *Pediatrics,* n° 125, 2010, pp. 468, 473 *et passim.*

747. SHAPIRO S. *et al,* "The effects of incidental ad exposure on the formation of consideration sets," *J. Consum. Res.* 24 (1997): 94, 102, *et al.*

748. Larousse.fr, accessed February 25, 2010; http://www.larousse.fr/dictionnaires/francais/viol.

749. MIGNOT F. *et al, Les Enfants et la publicité télévisée,* La Documentation française, 2002.

750. Signing of the Charter to Promote Healthy Eating and Physical Activity in Television Programming and Advertising, February 18, 2009, accessed February 25, 2010, http://www.culture.gouv.fr/culture/actualites/ communiq/albanel/dpsante09.pdf.

751. "Charter on food advertising: significant and unprecedented commitments by audiovisual professionals," collective communiqué, February 19, 2009, accessed February 26, 2010, http://www.snptv.org/_files/actualites/fichiers/actualites-950-399.pdf.

752. KELLY C., "Lutte contre l'obésité infantile : les paradoxes de la télévision, partenaire d'une régulation à la française", lemonde.fr, February 17, 2010, accessed February 25, 2010, http://www.lemonde.fr/opinions/article/2010/02/17/lutte-contre-l-obesite-infantileles-paradoxes-de-la-television-partenaire-d-une-regulation-a-la-francaise-par-christine-kelly_1307382_3232.html.

753. "Biography of Christine Kelly," csa.fr, accessed March 17, 2010, http://www.csa.fr/ conseil/composition/college_conseillers_biographie_ck.php.

754. "23 Learned Societies and 17 Associations Call on Members of Parliament to Regulate Television Advertising of Food Products to Children," press release, March 3, 2009, accessed February 26, 2010, http://www.sfsp.fr/activites/file/ CP3mars.pdf.

755. ANDERSON P., "The impact of alcohol advertising: ELSA project report on the evidence to strengthen regulation to protect young people," National Foundation for Alcohol Prevention, May 2007, accessed May 20, 2010, http://www.stap.nl/content/ bestanden/elsa_4_report_on_impact.pdf.

756. "Youth exposure to alcohol advertising on television, 2001 to 2007," The Center on Alcohol Marketing and Youth, June 2008, accessed

October 3, 2010, http://www. camy.org/bin/c/o/Youth_Exposure_to_ Alcohol_Advertising_on_Television.pdf.

757. VENDRAME A. *et al*, "Assessment of self-regulatory code violations in Brazilian television beer advertisements," *J. Stud. Alcohol Drugs*, n° 71, 2010, p. 445 *et passim*.

758. "Smoke-free movies: from evidence to action," WHO, 2009, accessed April 19, 2010, http://whqlibdoc.who.int/publications/2009/9789241597937_eng.pdf.

759. "Strategies to reduce the harmful use of alcohol: draft global strategy," World Health Organization, Report A63/13 submitted to the 63rd World Health Assembly, March 25, 2010, accessed May 21, 2010, http://apps.who.int/gb/ebwha/pdf_files/WHA63/A63_13-fr.pdf, pp. 4 and 16.

760. BELPOIS M., "On se retrouve après une page spéciale obésité...", télérama.fr, 19 April 2009, accessed 26 February 2010, http://television.telerama.fr/television/on-se-retrouve-apresune-page-speciale-obesite,41780.php.

761. BAR-ON M.E., "The effects of television on child health: implications and recommendations," *Arch. Dis. Child*, n° 83, 2000, p. 289 *and passim*.

762. METCALF B.S. *et al*, "Fatness leads to inactivity, but inactivity does not lead to fatness: a longitudinal study in children (EarlyBird 45)," *Arch. Dis. Child*, 2010.

763. WONG N.D. *et al*, "Television viewing and pediatric hypercholesterolemia," *Pediatrics*, n° 90, 1992, p. 75 *and passim*.

764. MARTINEZ-GOMEZ D. *et al*, "Associations between sedentary behavior and blood pressure in young children," *Arch. Pediatr. Adolesc. Med*, n° 163, 2009, p. 724 *et passim*.

765. PARDEE P.E. *et al*, "Television viewing and hypertension in obese children," *Am. J. Prev. Med.* 2007;33:439 *et al*.

766. KRISHNAN S *et al*, "Physical activity and television watching in relation to risk of type 2 diabetes: the Black Women's Health Study," *Am. J. Epidemiol*, n° 169, 2009, p. 428 *et passim*.

767. HARDY L.L. *et al*, "Screen time and metabolic risk factors among adolescents," *Arch. Pediatr. Adolesc. Med*, n° 164, 2010, p. 643 *et passim*.

768. WANG F. *et al*, "The influence of childhood obesity on the development of self-esteem," *Health Rep.* n° 20, 2009, p. 21 *and passim*.

769. WANG F *et al*, "Self-esteem and cognitive development in the era of the childhood obesity epidemic," *Obes. Rev.* 9 (2008): 615 *et al*.

770. ERICKSON S.J. *et al*, "Are overweight children unhappy?: body mass index, depressive symptoms, and overweight concerns in elementary school children," *Arch. Pediatr. Adolesc. Med.* 154 (2000): 931 *et al.*

771. PITROU I. *et al*, "Child overweight, associated psychopathology, and social functioning: a French school-based survey in 6to 11-year-old children," *Obesity (Silver Spring)*, n° 18, 2010, p. 809 *et passim.*

772. CORBO G.M. *et al*, "Wheeze and asthma in children: associations with body mass index, sports, television viewing, and diet," *Epidemiology*, n° 19, 2008, p. 747 *et passim.*

773. SHERRIFF A. *et al*, "Association of duration of television viewing in early childhood with the subsequent development of asthma," *Thorax*, n° 64, 2009, p. 321 *et passim.*

774. VLASKI E *et al*, "Influence of physical activity and television-watching time on asthma and allergic rhinitis among young adolescents: preventive or aggravating?", *Allergol. Immunopathol(Madr.)*, n° 36, 2008, p. 247 *and passim.*

775. ISHIDA S. *et al*, "Photosensitive seizures provoked while viewing *Pocket Monsters*, a made-for-television animation program in Japan," *Epilepsia*, n° 39, 1998, p. 1340 *et passim.*

776. WIPFLI H *et al*, "Global economic and health benefits of tobacco control: part 2", *Clin. Pharmacol. Ther*, n° 86, 2009, p. 272 *and passim.*

777. WIPFLI H *et al*, "Global economic and health benefits of tobacco control: part 1", *Clin. Pharmacol. Ther*, n° 86, 2009, p. 263 *and passim.*

778. "WHO Report on the Global Tobacco Epidemic," WHO, 2008, accessed April 19, 2010, http://whqlibdoc.who.int/publications/2008/9789242596281_fre.pdf, pp. 21 and 36.

779. European Union website, accessed April 13, 2010, http://europa.eu/abc/european_ countries/eu_members/denmark/index_en.htm.

780. WEINSTEIN H., "R.J. Reynolds targeted kids, records show," latimes.com, January 15, 1998, accessed April 19, 2010, http://articles.latimes.com/1998/jan/15/news/mn-8487.

781. "Tobacco company marketing to kids," tobaccofreekids.org, July 2010, accessed October 3, 2010, http://www.tobaccofreekids.org/research/factsheets/pdf/0008.pdf.

782. "Youth Tobacco Prevention," Philip Morris International, access October 4, 2010, http://www.pmi.com/fra/about_us/how_we_operate/pages/youth_ smoking_prevention.aspx.

783. "Advertising and Marketing," Philip Morris International, access October 4, 2010, http://www.pmi.com/fra/tobacco_regulation/regulating_tobacco/pages/advertising_ and_marketing.aspx.

784. "Directive of 2010/13/EU of the European Parliament and of the Council of 10 March 2010," *Official Journal of the European Union*, April 15, 2010, access April 30, 2010, http://eurlex.europa.eu/LexUriServ/LexUriServ.do?uri=OJ:L:2010:095:0001:0024:FR:PDF.

785. "Master Settlement Agreement," Office of the Attorney General, access March 26, 2010, http://ag.ca.gov/tobacco/msa.php.

786. SARGENT J.D. *et al*, "Brand appearances in contemporary cinema films and contribution to global marketing of cigarettes", *Lancet*, n° 357, 2001, p. 29 *and passim*.

787. "Character smoking in top box office movies," American Legacy Foundation, October 18, 2007, accessed April 19, 2010, http://www.legacyforhealth.org/PDFPublications/ Character_Smoking_in_Top_Box_Office_Movies.pdf.

788. TITUS K. *et al*, "Smoking presentation trends in US movies 1991-2008," Breathe California of Sacramento-Emigrant Trails and the Center for Tobacco Control Research and Education, University of California San Francisco, February 2009, accessed April 19, 2010, http://escholarship.org/uc/item/30q9j424.

789. POLANSKY J.R. *et al*, "First-run smoking presentations in US movies 1999-2006," Center for Tobacco Control Research and Education, University of California San Francisco, April 2007, accessed April 19, 2010, http://escholarship.org/uc/item/67c514kh.

790. HEATHERTON T.F. *et al*, "Does watching smoking in movies promote teenage smoking?", *Curr. Dir. Psychol. Sci.* 2009;18:63, *et al*.

791. "The role of the media in promoting and reducing tobacco use," National Cancer Institute, Tobacco Control Monograph n° 19, US Department of Health and Human Services, National Institutes of Health, National Cancer Institute. NIH pub. n° 07-6242, June 2008, accessed October 4, 2010, http://cancercontrol.cancer.gov/ tcrb/monographs/19/m19_complete.pdf.

792. HANEWINKEL R. *et al*, "Exposure to smoking in popular contemporary movies and youth smoking in Germany," *Am. J. Prev. Med.* n° 32, 2007, p. 466 *et al*.

793.HANEWINKEL R *et al*, "Exposure to smoking in internationally distributed American movies and youth smoking in Germany: a cross-cultural cohort study," *Pediatrics*, n° 121, 2008, pp. e108-e117.

794.MILLER T. *et al*, *Global Hollywood 2*, BFI Publishing, 2005.

795.LING P.M. *et al*, "Why and how the tobacco industry sells cigarettes to young adults: evidence from industry documents," *Am. J. Public Health* 92 (2002): 908 *et al*.

796.CHARLESWORTH A. *et al*, "Smoking in the movies increases adolescent smoking: a review," *Pediatrics*, n° 116, 2005, pp. 1516 *et passim*.

797."Semi-annual report on tobacco in current movies," The thumbs up! thumbs down!, June 2004, accessed April 19, 2010, http://www.scenesmoking.org/docs/2004report.pdf.

798."Tobacco use in the movies, annual report card," The thumbs up! thumbs down!, 2005, accessed April 19, 2010, http://www.scenesmoking.org/ReportCard2004-05.pdf.

799.SARGENT J.D. *et al*, "Effect of seeing tobacco use in films on trying smoking among adolescents: cross sectional study," *BMJ*, n° 323, 2001, p. 1394 *et passim*.

800.SARGENT J.D. *et al*, "Exposure to movie smoking: its relation to smoking initiation among US adolescents," *Pediatrics*, n° 116, 2005, pp. 1183 *et passim*.

801.SARGENT J.D. *et al*, "Exposure to smoking depictions in movies: its association with established adolescent smoking," *Arch. Pediatr. Adolesc. Med* 161 (2007): 849 *et al*.

802.DALTON M.A. *et al*, "Effect of viewing smoking in movies on adolescent smoking initiation: a cohort study," *Lancet*, n° 362, 2003, p. 281 *et passim*.

803.DALTON M.A. *et al*, "Early exposure to movie smoking predicts established smoking by older teens and young adults," *Pediatrics*, n° 123, 2009, pp. e551-e558.

804.TITUS-ERNSTOFF L *et al*, "Longitudinal study of viewing smoking in movies and initiation of smoking by children," *Pediatrics*, n° 121, 2008, p. 15 *and passim*.

805.SARGENT J.D. *et al*, "Comparison of trends for adolescent smoking and smoking in movies, 1990-2007," *JAMA*, n° 301, 2009, pp. 2211 *et passim*.

806. PECHMANN C. *et al*, "Smoking scenes in movies and antismoking advertisements before movies: effects on youth", *J. Mark,* n° 63, 1999, p. 1 *and passim.*

807. GOLDBERG M.E. *et al*, "Cross-country attraction as a motivation for product consumption," *J. Bus. Res.* n° 55, 2002, p. 901 *and passim.*

808. GOLDBERG M.E., "American media and the smoking-related behaviors of Asian adolescents," *J. Advert. Res.* 43 (2003): 2 *and passim.*

809. LAUGESEN M *et al*, "R-rated film viewing and adolescent smoking," *Prev. Med* 45 (2007): 454 *et al.*

810. THRASHER J.F. *et al*, "Exposure to smoking imagery in popular films and adolescent smoking in Mexico," *Am. J. Prev. Med.* 35 (2008): 95 *et al.*

811. HUNT K *et al*, "An examination of the association between seeing smoking in films and tobacco use in young adults in the West of Scotland: cross-sectional study," *Health Educ. Res.* 24 (2009): 22 *et al.*

812. SONG A.V. *et al*, "Smoking in movies and increased smoking among young adults," *Am. J. Prev. Med.* 33 (2007): 396 *et al.*

813. For the American classification, see The Classification and Rating Administration (CARA), accessed October 4, 2010, http://www.filmratings.com/filmRatings_Cara/; for the French classification, see the website of the Centre national du cinéma et de l'image animée (database of the Commission de classification des films), accessed October 4, 2010, http://www.cnc.fr/Site/Template/A2.aspx?SELECTID=18&ID=19&t=1.

814. POLANSKY J.R. *et al*, "Two years later: are MPAA's tobacco labels protecting movie audiences?", Center for Tobacco Control Research and Education, University of California San Francisco, May 2009, accessed 19 April 2010, http://www.escholarship. org/uc/item/5sr9w2s1.

815. TANSKI S.E. *et al*, "Parental R-rated movie restriction and early-onset alcohol use," *J. Stud. Alcohol Drugs,* n° 71, 2010, p. 452 *et passim.*

816. DALTON M.A. *et al*, "Relation between parental restrictions on movies and adolescent use of tobacco and alcohol," *Eff. Clin. Pract* 5 (2002): 1, *et al.*

817. DALTON M.A. *et al*, "Parental rules and monitoring of children's movie viewing associated with children's risk for smoking and drinking," *Pediatrics,* n° 118, 2006, p. 1932 *et passim.*

818.JACKSON C. *et al*, "R-rated movies, bedroom televisions, and initiation of smoking by white and black adolescents," *Arch. Pediatr. Adolesc. Med*, n° 161, 2007, p. 260 *et passim*.

819.HANEWINKEL R. *et al*, "Longitudinal study of parental movie restriction on teen smoking and drinking in Germany", *Addiction*, n° 103, 2008, p. 1722 *et passim* (this study was carried out in Germany on the basis of the so-called FSK-16 films, which are not allowed to be shown in cinemas under the age of 16).

820.SARGENT J.D. *et al*, "Effect of parental R-rated movie restriction on adolescent smoking initiation: a prospective study," *Pediatrics*, n° 114, 2004, p. 149 *et passim*.

821.THOMPSON K.M. *et al*, "Violence, sex and profanity in films: correlation of movie ratings with content", *MedGenMed*, n° 6, 2004, p. 3.

822.NALKUR P.G. *et al*, "The effectiveness of the Motion Picture Association of America's rating system in screening explicit violence and sex in top-ranked movies from 1950 to 2006," *J. Adolesc. Health*, n° 47, 2010, p. 440 *et passim*.

823.CIEPLY M., "*Avatar* joins holiday movies that fail an antismoking test," nytimes.com, January 3, 2010, accessed April 13, 2010, http://www.nytimes.com/2010/01/04/business/ 04smoke.html.

824.LÉVY A., "*Avatar* seriously harms health?", libération.fr, January 6, 2010, accessed April 13, 2010, http://www.liberation.fr/culture/0101612145-avatar-nuit-gravement-ala-sante.

825.TICKLE J.J. *et al*, "Tobacco, alcohol, and other risk behaviors in film: how well do MPAA ratings distinguish content?", *J. Health Commun.* n° 14, 2009, p. 756 *et passim*.

826.TICKLE J.J. *et al*, "Favourite movie stars, their tobacco use in contemporary movies, and its association with adolescent smoking," *Tob. Control*, n° 10, 2001, p. 16 *and passim*.

827.PIERCE J.P. *et al*, "Validation of susceptibility as a predictor of which adolescents take up smoking in the United States," *Health Psychol*, 15 (1996), 355ff.

828.SARGENT J.D. *et al*, "Movie smoking and urge to smoke among adult smokers," *Nicotine Tob. Res.* 11 (2009): 1042 *et al*.

829.BAUMANN S.B. *et al*, "Smoking cues in a virtual world provoke craving in cigarette smokers," *Psychol. Addict. Behav* 20 (2006): 484 *et al*.

830.TONG C. *et al*, "Smoking-related videos for use in cue-induced craving paradigms," *Addict. Behav* 32 (2007): 3034 *et al*.

831. SHMUELI D. *et al*, "Effect of smoking scenes in films on immediate smoking: a randomized controlled study," *Am. J. Prev. Med.* n° 38, 2010, p. 351 *et passim*.

832. VISWANATH K. *et al*, "Movies and TV influence tobacco use in India: findings from a national survey", *PLoS.One.*, n° 5, 2010, p. e11365.

833. WATKINS S.S. *et al*, "Neural mechanisms underlying nicotine addiction: acute positive reinforcement and withdrawal", *Nicotine Tob. Res.* 2, 2000, p. 19 *et al*.

834. GIDWANI P.P. *et al*, "Television viewing and initiation of smoking among youth," *Pediatrics*, n° 110, 2002, p. 505 *et passim*.

835. GUTSCHOVEN K *et al*, Television viewing and smoking volume in adolescent smokers: a cross-sectional study, *Prev. Med* 39 (2004): 1093 *et al*.

836. GUTSCHOVEN K. *et al*, "Television viewing and age at smoking initiation: does a relationship exist between higher levels of television viewing and earlier onset of smoking?" *Nicotine Tob. Nicotine Tobacco Res.* 7 (2005): 381 *et al*.

837. REHM J *et al*, "Global burden of disease and injury and economic cost attributable to alcohol use and alcohol-use disorders," *Lancet*, n° 373, 2009, pp. 2223 *et passim*.

838. REHM J *et al*, "Alcohol use", *in* EZZATI M *et al* (eds), *Comparative Quantification of Health Risks. Global and Regional Burden of Disease Attributable to Selected Major Risk Factors*, WHO, 2004, vol. I, pp. 959.

839. THAVORNCHAROENSAP M. *et al*, "The economic impact of alcohol consumption: a systematic review," *Subst. Abuse Treat. Prev. Policy*, n° 4, 2009, p. 20.

840. "Global status report on alcohol 2004," WHO, 2004, accessed May 16, 2010, http:// www.who.int/substance_abuse/publications/global_status_report_2004_overview.pdf.

841. "The global burden of disease: 2004 update," WHO, 2008, accessed May 16, 2010, http://www.who.int/healthinfo/global_burden_disease/GBD_report_2004update_ full.pdf.

842. "Food, nutrition, physical activity, and the prevention of cancer: a global perspective," World Cancer Research Fund / American Institute for Cancer Research, 2007, accessed December 11, 2010, http://www.dietandcancerreport.org/.

843. CORRAO G *et al*, "A meta-analysis of alcohol consumption and the risk of 15 diseases," *Prev. Med* 38 (2004): 613 *et al*.

844. "Alcohol and Injuries," WHO, 2009, accessed May 16, 2010, http://www.who. int/substance_abuse/msbalcinuries.pdf.

845. Taylor B *et al*, Determination of lifetime injury mortality risk in Canada in 2002 by drinking amount per occasion and number of occasions, *Am. J. Epidemiol*, n° 168, 2008, p. 1119 *and passim*.

846. TAYLOR B. *et al*, "The more you drink, the harder you fall: a systematic review and meta-analysis of how acute alcohol consumption and injury or collision risk increase together," *Drug Alcohol Depend.* n° 110, 2010, p. 108 *et passim*.

847. REHM J *et al*, "The relationship of average volume of alcohol consumption and patterns of drinking to burden of disease: an overview", *Addiction*, n° 98, 2003, p. 1209 *and passim*.

848. leParisien.fr, November 21, 2009, accessed April 25, 2010, http://www.leparisien.fr/ seine-et-marne-77/brulee-a-l-essence-by-its-maribook-21-11-2009-719075.php.

849. LaProvence.com, October 20, 2009, accessed April 25, 2010, http://www.laprovence.com/ news/does-he-strike-his-wife-is-pregnant.

850. nouvelObs.com, Apr. 3, 2010, accessed Apr. 25, 2010, http://temps-reel.nouvelobs.com/ actualite/societe/20100403.OBS1863/un-bebe-dans-le-coma-apres-ete-frappe-by-sa-nourrice-ivre.html.

851. ouest-france.fr, January 22, 2010, accessed April 25, 2010, http://www.ouest-france.fr/actu/ actuLocale_-Une-femme-ivre-son-tue-en-sen-dormant-sur-le_63461236070-fils--44036-abd_filDMA.Htm.

852. LePoint.fr, April 10, 2010, accessed April 25, 2010, http://www.lepoint.fr/actualites-societe/ 2010-04-10/un-bebe-de-13-mois-dans-sa-poussette-tue-par-une-conductrice-ivre/ 920/0/442948.

853. lefigaro.fr, April 18, 2008, accessed April 25, 2010, http://www.lefigaro.fr/actualites/ 2008/04/18/01001-20080418ARTFIG00375-deux-policiers-tues-par-un-chauffardivre-en-isere.php.

854. MidiLibre.com, August 24, 2009, accessed April 25, 2010, http://www.midilibre.com/ articles/2009/08/24/BEZIERS-Beziers-Accident-de-la-RN-9-qui-a-fait-5-morts-leconducteur-etait-ivre-894235.php5.

855. LePoint.fr, July 6, 2008, accessed April 25, 2010, http://www.lepoint.fr/actualites-societe/ 2008-07-06/apres-avoir-fete-son-bac-un-jeune-homme-meur-d-un-coma-ethylique/920/ 0/258466.

856. 20minutes.ch, March 29, 2007, accessed April 25, 2010, http://www.20min.ch/ro/news/ monde/story/16030077.

857. elle.fr, November 2, 2009, accessed April 25, 2010, http://www.elle.fr/elle/Societe/News/ Une-ado-frole-la-mort-with-3-10g-of-alcohol-in-the-blood/.

858. ouest-france.fr, January 3, 2010, accessed April 25, 2010, http://www.ouest-france.fr/ actu/actuLocale_-L%E2%80%99adolescent-drinking-falls-in-the-Loire_-1211502-----44055-abd_actu.Htm.

859. 20minutes.fr, May 14, 2010, accessed May 16, 2010, http://www.20minutes.fr/article/ 404410/France-Apero-Facebook-de-Nantes-le-mort-avait-2-40-g-d-d-alcool-dans.php.

860. *France-Soir*, June 2, 2010.

861. KLATSKY A.L. *et al*, "Alcohol drinking and total mortality risk," *Ann. Epidemiol*, 2007, pp. S63-S67.

862. KLONER R.A. *et al*, "To drink or not to drink? That is the question," *Circulation*, n° 116, 2007, p. 1306 *et passim*.

863. DI CASTELNUOVO A. *et al*, "Alcohol dosing and total mortality in men and women: an updated meta-analysis of 34 prospective studies," *Arch. Intern. Med*, n° 166, 2006, p. 2437 *et passim*.

864. HVIDTFELDT U.A. *et al*, "Alcohol intake and risk of coronary heart disease in younger, middle-aged, and older adults," *Circulation*, n° 121, 2010, pp. 1589 *et passim*.

865. MUKAMAL K.J. *et al*, "Alcohol consumption and cardiovascular mortality among US adults, 1987 to 2002," *J. Am. Coll. cardiol.* n° 55, 2010, p. 1328 *et passim*.

866. FUCHS F.D. *et al*, "Is the cardioprotective effect of alcohol real?", *Alcohol*, n° 41, 2007, p. 399 *and passim*.

867. FILLMORE K.M. *et al*, "Moderate alcohol use and reduced mortality risk: systematic error in prospective studies and new hypotheses," *Ann. Epidemiol*, n° 17, 2007, pp. S16-S23.

868. KLATSKY A.L., "Alcohol and cardiovascular mortality: common sense and scientific truth," *J. Am. Cardiol Coll*, n° 55, 2010, p. 1336 *et passim*.

869. REHM J. *et al*, "Method for moderation: measuring lifetime risk of alcoholattributable mortality as a basis for drinking guidelines", *Int. J. Methods Psychiatr. Res.* 17 (2008): 141 *et al*.

870. BORGES G *et al*, "Multicentre study of acute alcohol use and non-fatal injuries: data from the WHO collaborative study on alcohol and injuries", *Bull. World Health Organ,* n° 84, 2006, p. 453 *and passim*.

871. "Framework for alcohol policy in the WHO European Region," WHO, 2006, accessed May 17, 2010, http://www.euro.who.int/document/ e88335.pdf, p. 15.

872. "Australian guidelines to reduce health risks from drinking alcohol," National Health and Medical Council, 2009, accessed May 17, 2010, http://www.nhmrc.gov.au/_files_ nhmrc/file/publications/ synopses/ds10-alcohol.pdf.

873. "A Practical Guide to Taking Stock of Your Alcohol Consumption," National Institute for Health Prevention and Education, document 210-05-111-B, accessed May 17, 2010, http://www.inpes.sante.fr/ CFESBases/catalogue/pdf/861.pdf.

874. "Tables de l'économie française," INSEE, 2010, accessed May 17, 2010, http:// www.insee.fr/fr/ffc/tef/tef2010/tef2010.pdf.

875. "Baromètre santé 2005: attitudes et comportements de santé," Institut national de prévention et d'éducation pour la santé, accessed May 17, 2010, http://www.ofdt. fr/BDD/publications/docs/BS2005_Alcohol. pdf, p. 121.

876. "The surgeon general's call to action to prevent and reduce underage drinking," Department of Health and Human Services, Office of the Surgeon General, 2007, accessed May 17, 2010, http://www. surgeongeneral.gov/topics/underagedrinking/ calltoaction.pdf.

877. BONNIE R.J. *et al, Reducing Underage Drinking: A Collective Responsibility. Committee on Developing a Strategy to Reduce and Prevent Underage Drinking*, National Research Council and Institute of Medicine, The National Academies Press, 2004, pp. 58-59.

878. "Minimum Age Limits Worldwide," International Center for Alcohol Policies, January 2010, accessed May 17, 2010, http://www.icap.org/ Table/MinimumAgeLimits Worldwide.

879. "The 2007 ESPAD report: substance use among students in 35 European countries, European School Survey Project on Alcohol and Other Drugs," European School Survey Project on Alcohol and Other Drugs, February 2009, accessed May 17, 2010, http://www.espad.org/ documents/Espad/ESPAD_reports/2007/The_2007_ESPAD_ Report-FULL_091006.pdf.

880. FADEN V. *et al*, "The effects of alcohol on physiological processes and biological development," *Alcohol Res. Health*, n° 28, 2005, p. 125 *et passim*.

881. TAFFE M.A. *et al*, "Long-lasting reduction in hippocampal neurogenesis by alcohol consumption in adolescent nonhuman primates," *Proc. Natl. Acad. Sci.USA*, n° 107, 2010, pp. 11104 *et passim*.

882. GRANT B.F. *et al*, "Age at onset of alcohol use and its association with DSM-IV alcohol abuse and dependence: results from the National Longitudinal Alcohol Epidemiologic Survey," *J. Subst. Abuse*, n° 9, 1997, p. 103 *et passim*.

883. "Self-regulation in the alcohol industry," Report of the Federal Trade Commission, June 2008, accessed May 18, 2010, http://www.ftc.gov/os/2008/06/080626 alcoholreport.pdf.

884. "Wine Institute Code of Advertising Standards," September 2005, accessed May 18, 2010, http://www.wineinstitute.org/initiatives/issuesandpolicy/adcode/details.

885. "Beer institute advertising and marketing code," January 2006, accessed May 18, 2010, http://www.beerinstitute.org/BeerInstitute/files/ccLibraryFiles/Filename/000000000384/ 2006ADCODE.pdf.

886. "Code of responsible practices for beverage alcohol advertising and marketing," Distilled Spirits Council of the United States, January 2009, accessed May 18, 2010, http://www.discus.org/pdf/61332_DISCUS.pdf.

887. "Record 106.5 million Americans watch Super Bowl," reuters.com, February 8, 2010, accessed May 18, 2010, http://www.reuters.com/article/idUSTRE6174AY20100208.

888. "Budweiser's Super Bowl beer ads fuel underage drinking," The Marin Institute, access May 18, 2010, http://www.marininstitute.org/alcohol_industry/ad_alert.htm.

889. "Youth video winners announced in Free The Bowl(TM) Contest," reuters.com, February 4, 2010, accessed October 4, 2010, http://www.reuters.com/article/idUS25361+ 05-Feb-2010+PRN20100205.

890. "Most Super Bowl viewers tune in for the commercials, Nielsen says," The Nielsen Company, January 20, 2010, accessed October 4, 2010, http://en-us.nielsen.com/content/ nielsen/en_us/news/news_releases/2010/january/most_super_bowl_viewers.html.

891. ELIOTT S., "Anheuser-Busch pushes the big beers for the Super Bowl," nytimes.com, January 22, 2008, accessed October 5, 2010, http://www.nytimes.com/2008/01/22/ business/media/22adco.html?_r=1&ref=alcoholic_beverages.

892. NEWMAN A.A., "Youngsters enjoy beer ads, arousing industry's critics," nytimes.com, February 13, 2006, accessed

October 5, 2010, http://query.nytimes.com/gst/fullpage. html?res=9501E3DD123EF930A25751C0A9609C8B63.

893. "Children vote beer commercials among their favorite Super Bowl ads," Drug Free Action Alliance, February 4, 2009, accessed October 5, 2010, http://www.drugfreeactionalliance. org/documents/SB09.pdf.

894. "Children vote beer commercials among their favorite Super Bowl ads," Drug Free Action Alliance, February 7, 2008, accessed October 5, 2010, http://www.drugfreeactionalliance. org/documents/super-bowlonlinepr.pdf.

895. "Comparative legislation studies. Alcohol advertising in Europe", National Assembly, July 2004, accessed June 1, 2010, http://www. assemblee-nationale.fr/ europe/comparisons/alcohol.asp.

896. "Decree n° 92-280 of March 27, 1992, Article 8. Modified by Decree n° 2003-960 of October 7, 2003 - Article 1," *JORF*, October 8, 2003 effective January 1, 2004, accessed October 5, 2010, http://www.legifrance. gouv.fr/affichTexteArticle.do;jsessionid=   5D4154105889D8BAD63 8B3F717FD5904.tpdjo14v_3?idArticle=LEGIARTI000006424478&-cidTexte=LEGITEXT000006078905&dateTexte=20100915.

897. "Under the influence. The damaging effect of alcohol marketing on young people," British Medical Association, September 2009, accessed May 16, 2010, http://www. bma.org.uk/images/underthein-fluence_tcm41-190062.pdf.

898. "Testimony to committee on underage drinking, the board on children, youth and families of the National Research Council and the Institute of Medicine: developing a strategy to reduce and prevent underage drinking," American Medical Association, November 18, 2002, accessed May 18, 2010, http://www.ama-assn.org/ama1/pub/ upload/mm/388/statementuad.pdf.

899. "Does marketing communication impact on the volume and patterns of consumption of alcoholic beverages, especially by young people? A review of longitudinal studies," scientific opinion of the Science Group of the European Alcohol and Health Forum, 2009, accessed June 9, 2010, http://ec.europa.eu/health/ph_determinants/life_style/ alcohol/Forum/docs/science_o01_en.pdf.

900. ANDERSON P. *et al*, "Impact of alcohol advertising and media exposure on adolescent alcohol use: a systematic review of longitudinal studies," *Alcohol Alcohol*, n° 44, 2009, pp. 1, 229 *et passim*.

901. COLLINS R.L. *et al*, "Early adolescent exposure to alcohol advertising and its relationship to underage drinking," *J. Adolesc. Health*, n° 40, 2007, p. 527 *and passim*.

902. STACY A.W. *et al*, "Exposure to televised alcohol ads and subsequent adolescent alcohol use," *Am. J. Health Behavior* 28 (2004): 498 *et al*.

903. EVERETT S.A. *et al*, "Tobacco and alcohol use in top-grossing American films," *J. Community Health*, n° 23, 1998, p. 317 *et passim*.

904. HANEWINKEL R *et al*, "Exposure to alcohol use in motion pictures and teen drinking in Germany," *Int. J. Epidemiol*, n° 36, 2007, p. 1068 *and passim*.

905. HANEWINKEL R *et al*, "Longitudinal study of exposure to entertainment media and alcohol use among German adolescents," *Pediatrics*, n° 123, 2009, p. 989 *et passim*.

906. DAL CIN S. *et al*, "Youth exposure to alcohol use and brand appearances in popular contemporary movies," *Addiction*, n° 103, 2008, p. 1925 *et passim*.

907. SARGENT J.D. *et al*, "Alcohol use in motion pictures and its relation with early-onset teen drinking," *J. Stud. Alcohol*, n° 67, 2006, p. 54 *and passim*.

908. WILLS T.A. *et al*, "Movie exposure to alcohol cues and adolescent alcohol problems: a longitudinal analysis in a national sample," *Psychol. Addict. Behav*, n° 23, 2009, p. 23 *and passim*.

909. LORCH E.P., "Health, drugs, and values," *in* PECORA N. *et al.* (eds.), *Children and Television*, LEA, 2007, p. 205 *and passim*.

910. ENGELS R.C. *et al*, "Alcohol portrayal on television affects actual drinking behavior," *Alcohol Alcohol*, n° 44, 2009, p. 244 *et passim*.

911. ROBINSON T.N. *et al.* 1998; Television and music video exposure and risk of adolescent alcohol use.

912. VAN DEN BULCK J. *et al*, "Television and music video exposure and adolescent alcohol use while going out," *Alcohol Alcohol*, n° 40, 2005, p. 249 *and passim*.

913. THOMPSON K.M. *et al*, "Depiction of alcohol, tobacco, and other substances in G-rated animated feature films," *Pediatrics,* n° 107, 2001, p. 1369 *et passim*.

914. IVS, "Surveillance du VIH-sida en France. Data from September 30, 2009," Institut de veille sanitaire, accessed June 15, 2010, http://www. invs.sante.fr/publications/2010/vih_sida_donnees_septembre_2009/ vih_sida_donnees_septembre_2009.pdf

915. Direction de la recherche des études de l'évaluation et des statistiques (DREES), "Les interruptions volontaires de grossesse en 2007", *Études et résultats*, n° 713, 2009.

916. SINGH S. *et al*, "Adolescent pregnancy and childbearing: levels and trends in developed countries," *Fam. Plann. Perspect.* 32, 2000, p. 14 *and passim*.

917. PANCHAUD C. *et al*, "Sexually transmitted diseases among adolescents in developed countries," *Fam. Plann. Perspect*, n° 32, 2000, pp. 24, 45 *and passim*.

918. "US teenage pregnancies, births and abortions: national and state trends and trends by race and ethnicity," Guttmacher Institute, January 2010, accessed July 2, 2010, http://www.guttmacher.org/pubs/USTPtrends.pdf.

919. FINER L.B. *et al*, "Disparities in rates of unintended pregnancy in the United States, 1994 and 2001," *Perspect. Sex Reprod. Health*, n° 38, 2006, p. 90 *and passim*.

920. "Live births by marital status and age of mother in completed years," Eurostat data for 2007, accessed October 6, 2010, http://epp.eurostat.ec.europa.eu/portal/page/portal/product_details/dataset?p_product_code=DEMO_ FAGEC.

921. COLEMAN P.K., "Resolution of unwanted pregnancy during adolescence through abortion versus childbirth: individual and family predictors and psychological consequences," *J. Youth Adolesc.*, n° 35, 2006, p. 903 *et passim*.

922. MAJOR B., "Psychological implications of abortion - highly charged and rife with misleading research", *CMAJ*, n° 168, 2003, p. 1257 *and passim*.

923. FERGUSSON D.M. *et al*, "Abortion and mental health disorders: evidence from a 30-year longitudinal study", *Br. J. Psychiatry*, n° 193, 2008, p. 444 *and passim*.

924. FERGUSSON D.M. *et al*, "Abortion in young women and subsequent mental health," *J. Child Psychol. Psychiatry*, 47 (2006), 16, *et al.*

925. PEDERSEN W., "Abortion and depression: a population-based longitudinal study of young women," *Scand. J. Public Health* 36 (2008): 424 *et al.*

926. SAVIO BEERS L.A. *et al*, "Approaching the adolescent-headed family: a review of teen parenting," *Curr. Probl. Pediatr. Adolesc. Health Care*, 39, 216 *et al.*

927. HAMANI Y *et al*, "Misconceptions about oral contraceptive pills among adolescents and physicians," *Hum. Reprod* 22 (2007): 3078 *et al.*

928. MOLLEN C.J. *et al*, "Assessing attitudes about emergency contraception among urban, minority adolescent girls: an in-depth interview study," *Pediatrics*, n° 122, 2008, pp. e395-e401.

929. KFF, "Sexsmarts: birth control and protection," The Kaiser Family Foundation, July 2004, accessed July 2, 2010, http://www.kff.org/entpartnerships/upload/SexSmarts-Birth-Control-and-Protection-Bruchure.pdf.

930. INPES, "Contraception: What do the French know?", National Institute for Prevention and Health Education, press kit, June 2007, accessed July 2, 2010, http://www.inpes.sante.fr/70000/dp/07/dp070605.pdf.

931. GOMEZ C.A. *et al*, "The development of sex-related knowledge, attitudes, perceived norms and behavior in a longitudinal cohort of middle school children," *in* ALBERT B. *et al* (eds), *14 and Younger. The Sexual Behavior of Young Adolescents*, National Campaign to Prevent Teen Pregnancy, 2003, p. 67 *and passim.*

932. IGAS, "La prévention des grossesses non désirées : information, éducation et communication," Inspection générale des affaires sociales, report RM2009-118A, October 2009, available online, access 6 October 2010, http://lesrapports. ladocumentationfrancaise.fr/BRP/104000048/0000.pdf, pp. 3 and 5.

933. "L'éducation à la sexualité dans les écoles, les collèges et les lycées," Ministère de la Jeunesse, de l'Éducation nationale et de la Recherche, Circular n° 2003-027 of February 17, 2003, accessed July 2, 2010, http://www.education.gouv.fr/botexte/ bo030227/MENE0300322C.htm.

934. For the latest campaign: "La pub qui met les hommes enceintes", lejdd.fr, access 2 July 2010, http://www.lejdd.fr/Societe/Sante/Actualite/La-pub-qui-met-leshommes-enceintes-185047/.

935. BENNIA-BOURAÏ S. *et al*, "Contraception and adolescence: a survey of 232 high school students (Caen)", *Medicine*, 2006, p. 84 *and passim.*

936. "Contraception: Bachelot wants to "put the package in the school environment," leParisien.fr, February 2, 2010, accessed July 3, 2010, http://www.leparisien.fr/societe/ contraception-bachelot-veut-mettre-le-paquet-dans-le-milieu-scolaire-02-02-2010800577.php.

937. WATZLAWICK P., *Comment réussir à échouer : trouver l'ultrasolution*, Éditions du Seuil, 1991.

938. AMERICAN ACADEMY OF PEDIATRICS, "Policy statement - sexuality, contraception, and the media," *Pediatrics*, n° 126, 2010, p. 576 *and passim*.

939. VILLANI S., "Impact of media on children and adolescents: a 10-year review of the research," *J. Am. Acad. Child Adolesc. Psychiatry*, 40, 392 *et al*.

940. STRASBURGER V.C. *et al*, "Health effects of media on children and adolescents," *Pediatrics*, n° 125, 2010, p. 756 *et passim*.

941. "Le jeu et le sexe haantent nos télés", lexpress.fr, April 1, 2008, accessed July 2, 2010, http://www.lexpress.fr/actualite/societe/le-jeu-et-le-sexe-hantent-nos-teles_471630.html.

942. STRASBURGER V.C., "Adolescents, sex, and the media: ooooo, baby, baby-a Q & A," *Adolesc. Med. Clin*, n° 16, 2005, pp. 269, 273, *and passim*.

943. WARD L.M., "Understanding the role of entertainment media in the sexual socialization of American youth: a review of empirical research," *Dev. Rev.* 23 (2003): 347ff.

944. DONNERSTEIN E. *et al*, "Sex in the media," *in* SINGER D.G. *et al* (eds.), *Handbook of Children and the Media*, 2001, Sage Publications, p. 289 *et passim*.

945. KUNKEL D. *et al*, "Sex on TV4," The Kaiser Family Foundation, November 2005, accessed July 2, 2010, http://www.kff.org/entmedia/upload/Sex-on-TV-4-Full-Report.pdf.

946. RIVADENEYRA R. *et al*, "The association between television-viewing behaviors and adolescent dating role attitudes and behaviors," *J. Adolesc.*, n° 31, 2008, p. 291 *et passim*.

947. "Fall Colors: prime time diversity report 2003-2004," Children Now, April 2004, accessed July 2, 2010, http://www.childrennow.org/uploads/documents/fall_colors_2003.pdf.

948. KIMBALL M.M., "Television and sex-role attitudes", *in* MACBETH WILLIAMS T. (ed.), *The Impact of Television: A Natural Experiment in Three Communities*, Academic Press, 1986, p. 265 *and passim*.

949. AUBREY J.S. *et al*, "Variety versus timing: gender differences in college students' sexual expectations as predicted by exposure to sexually oriented television", *Comm. Res.*, n° 30, 2003, p. 432 *and passim*.

950. Does television exposure affect emerging adults' attitudes and assumptions about sexual relationships? Correlational and experimental confirmation," *J. Youth Adolescence*, 31 (2002), 1 *and passim*.

951. WARD L.M. *et al*, "Using TV as a guide: associations between television viewing and adolescents' sexual attitudes and behavior," *J. Res. Adolesc.* 2006;16:133 *and passim.*

952. MARTINO S.C. *et al*, "It's better on TV: does television set teenagers up for regret following sexual initiation?", *Perspect. Sex Reprod. Health*, n° 41, 2009, p. 92 *and passim.*

953. FERRIS A.L. *et al*, "The content of reality dating shows and viewer perceptions of dating," *J. Commun.* n° 57, 2007, p. 490 *and passim.*

954. EYAL K. *et al*, "The effects of sex in television drama shows on emerging adults' sexual attitudes and moral judgments," *J. Broadcast Electronic Media*, n° 52, 2008, p. 161 *and passim.*

955. "First results of the CSF survey "Contexte de la sexualité en France", ANRS/Inserm/INED, press kit, March 13, 2007, accessed July 3, 2010, http:// www.anrs.fr/index.php/anrs/content/download/483/3662/ file/DP%2013%20mars% 2007%20-%20Premiers%20r%C3%A9sul- tats%20de%20l/%27enqu%C3%AAte% 20CSF.pdf.

956. PRICE M.N. *et al*, "When two isn't better than one: predictors of early sexual activity in adolescence using a cumulative risk model," *J. Youth Adolesc.*, n° 38, 2009, p. 1059 *et passim.*

957. BROWN J.D. *et al*, "Sexy media matter: exposure to sexual content in music, movies, television, and magazines predicts black and white adolescents' sexual behavior," *Pediatrics*, n° 117, 2006, p. 1018 *et passim.*

958. ASHBY S.L. *et al*, "Television viewing and risk of sexual initiation by young adolescents," *Arch. Pediatr. Adolesc. Med*, n° 160, 2006, p. 375 *and passim.*

959. COLLINS R.L. *et al*, "Watching sex on television predicts adolescent initiation of sexual behavior," *Pediatrics*, n° 114, 2004, pp. e280-e289.

960. KIRBY D. *et al*, "Sexual risk and protective factors," Education Training Research Associates and The National Campaign to Prevent Teen and Unplanned Pregnancy Report, November 2007, accessed July 3, 2010, http://www.thenationalcampaign.org/ ea2007/protective_factors_FULL. pdf

961. SANDFORT T.G. *et al*, "Long-term health correlates of timing of sexual debut: results from a national US study," *Am. J. Public Health*, n° 98, 2008, p. 155 *and passim.*

962. KAESTLE C.E. *et al*, "Young age at first sexual intercourse and sexually transmitted infections in adolescents and young adults," *Am. J. Epidemiol*, n° 161, 2005, p. 774 *and passim.*

963. SANTELLI J.S. *et al*, "Multiple sexual partners among US adolescents and young adults," *Fam. Plann. Perspect* 30 (1998): 271 *et al.*

964. Parker, A.L. *et al*, "Correlates and consequences of early initiation of sexual intercourse," *J. Sch. Health*, 64 (1994): 372 *et al.*

965. MOSHER W.D. *et al*, "Use of contraception and use of family planning services in the United States: 1982-2002," *Adv. Data*, 2004, p. 1 *and passim.*

966. FLANIGAN C., "Sexual activity among girls under 15," *in* ALBERT B. *et al.* (eds.), *14 and Younger. The Sexual Behavior of Young Adolescents*, 2003, National Campaign to Prevent Teen Pregnancy, p. 57 *and passim.*

967. JACOBSON D.L. *et al*, "Histologic development of cervical ectopy: relationship to reproductive hormones," *Sex Transm. Dis.* 27 (2000): 252 *et al.*

968. KAHN J.A. *et al*, "Mediators of the association between age of first sexual intercourse and subsequent human papillomavirus infection," *Pediatrics*, n° 109, 2002, p. E5.

969. CHANDRA A *et al. 2008;* "Does watching sex on television predict teen pregnancy? Findings from a national longitudinal survey of youth," *Pediatrics*, n° 122, 2008, p. 1047 *et passim.*

970. WINGOOD G.M. *et al*, "A prospective study of exposure to rap music videos and African American female adolescents' health," *Am. J. Public Health* 93 (2003): 437 *et al.*

971. HARRISON K., "Adolescent body image and eating in the media," *in* JAMIESON P.E. *et al.* (eds.), *The Changing Portrayal of Adolescents in the Media since 1950*, Oxford University Press, 2008, p. 165 *and passim.*

972. DERENNE J.L. *et al*, "Body image, media, and eating disorders," *Acad. Psychiatry*, n° 30, 2006, p. 257 *et passim.*

973. GROGAN S., *Body Image: Understanding Body Dissatisfaction in Men, Women and Children*, Routledge, 2008, 2nd ed.

974. WYKES M. *et al*, *The Media and Body Image*, Sage Publications, 2005.

975. POPE H.G. *et al*, *The Adonis Complex: The Secret Crisis of Male Body Obsession*, Free Press, 2000.

976. LEVINE M.P. *et al*, "Media as a context for the development of disordered eating," *in* SMOLAK M. *et al* (eds.), *The Developmental Psychopathology of Eating Disorders: Implications for Research, Prevention, and Treatment*, Lawrence Erlbaum Associates, 1996, p. 235 *et passim.*

TV Lobotomie

977.RUBINSTEIN S. *et al*, "Is Miss America an undernourished role model?", *JAMA*, n° 283, 2000, p. 1569.

978.AMERICAN PSYCHIATRIC ASSOCIATION, *Diagnostic and Statistical Manual for Mental Disorders. 4th Edition Text Revision (DSM-IV-TR)*, American Psychiatric Association, 2000.

979."Skinny models banned from catwalk," CNN.com, September 13, 2006, accessed July 10, 2010, http://edition.cnn.com/2006/WORLD/europe/09/13/spain.models/ index.html; "Skinniest models are banned from catwalk," timesonline, September 9, 2006, accessed July 10, 2010, http://www.timesonline.co.uk/tol/news/world/europe/article633568.ece.

980.PUHL R.M. *et al*, "The stigma of obesity: a review and update," *Obesity (Silver Spring)*, n° 17, 2009, p. 941 *et passim*.

981.GRABE S. *et al*, " The role of the media in body image concerns among women: a meta-analysis of experimental and correlational studies ", *Psychol. Bull*, n° 134, 2008, pp. 460, 471 *et passim*.

982.GROESZ L.M. *et al*, "The effect of experimental presentation of thin media images on body satisfaction: a meta-analytic review", *Int. J. Eat. Disord*, n° 31, 2002, p. 1 *and passim*.

983.AGLIATA D. *et al*, "The impact of media exposure on males' body image", *J. Soc. Clin. Psychol*, n° 23, 2004, p. 7 *and passim*.

984.GRABE S. *et al*, "Body objectification and depression in adolescents: the role of gender, shame, and rumination," *Psychol. Women Q*, 31, 175.

985.JOHNSON F *et al*, "Dietary restraint, body dissatisfaction, and psychological distress: a prospective analysis," *J. Abnorm. Psychol.* 114 (2005): *119ff*.

986.HAWKINS N *et al*, "The impact of exposure to the thin-ideal media image on women," *Eat. Eat Disorder* 12 (2004): 35ff.

987.PAXTON S.J. *et al*, "Body dissatisfaction prospectively predicts depressive mood and low self-esteem in adolescent girls and boys," *J. Clin. Child Adolesc. Psychol.* 35 (2006): 539 *et al*.

988.HOGAN M.J. *et al*, "Body image, eating disorders, and the media," *Adolesc. Med. State Art. Rev.* 19 (2008): 521 *et al*.

989.SPETTIGUE W. *et al*, "Eating disorders and the role of the media," *Can. Child Adolesc. Psychiatr. Rev.* 13 (2004): 16 *et al*.

990.NEUMARK-SZTAINER D. *et al*, "Does body satisfaction matter? Five-year longitudinal associations between body satisfaction and health behaviors in adolescent females and males," *J. Adolesc. Health*, n° 39, 2006, p. 244 *and passim*.

991. STICE E. *et al*, "Role of body dissatisfaction in the onset and maintenance of eating pathology: a synthesis of research findings", *J. Psychosom. Res.* 53 (2002): 985 *et al*.

992. CALADO M. *et al*, "The mass media exposure and disordered eating behaviours in Spanish secondary students", *Eur. Eat. Disord. Rev.* n° 18, 2010, p. 417 *et passim*.

993. MORIARTY C.M. *et al*, "Television exposure and disordered eating among children: a longitudinal panel study," *J. Commun.* n° 58, 2008, p. 361 *et passim*.

994. HARRISON K. *et al*, "The relationship between media consumption and eating disorders," *J. Commun.* n° 47, 1997, p. 40 *and passim*.

995. BECKER A.E. *et al*, "Eating behaviours and attitudes following prolonged exposure to television among ethnic Fijian adolescent girls," *Br. J. Psychiatry*, n° 180, 2002, p. 509 *et passim*.

996. See Introduction.

997. GARNIER C., "À 8 ans, elle veut faire un régime!", *Top Santé*, n° 238, July 2010.

998. Isabelle Nicolas, child psychiatrist, quoted *in* GARNIER C., " À 8 ans, elle veut faire un régime ! ", *Top Santé*, n° 238, July 2010, p. 136.

999. "Exposed: Brad's "puny" legacies," mailonline, accessed July 10, 2010, http://www. dailymail.co.uk/tvshowbiz/article-188530/Exposed-Brads-puny-legs.html.

1000. "16 and pregnant," MTV, accessed October 6, 2010, http://www.mtv. com/shows/16_ and_pregnant/season_1/series.jhtml; "16 ans et enceinte" for the French version, accessed October 6, 2010, http:// www.mtv.fr/emissions/16-ans-et-enceinte.

1001. ZIMMERMAN F.J., "Children's media use and sleep problems: issues and unanswered questions," The Kaiser Family Foundation, June 2008, accessed March 3, 2010, http://www.kff.org/entmedia/ upload/7674.pdf.

1002. GIORDANELLA J.P., " Rapport sur le thème du sommeil à M. Xavier Bertrand, Ministère de la Santé et des Solidarités ", Ministère de la Santé et des Solidarités, décembre 2006, accès 2 mars 2010, http:// lesrapports.ladocumentationfrancaise.fr/ BRP/064000899/0000.pdf

1003.	Institute of Medicine of the National Academies, *Sleep Disorders and Sleep Deprivation: An Unmet Public Health Problem*, The National Academies Press, 2006.

1004.	"9th National Sleep Day," press kit, National Sleep and Vigilance Institute, March 18, 2009, accessed March 3, 2010, http://www.institut-sommeil-vigilance.org/documents/Presse-JNS-2009.pdf.

1005.	"Health and safety," National Sleep Foundation, 2009, accessed March 3, 2010, http://www.sleepfoundation.org/article/sleep-america-polls/2009-health-and-safety.

1006.	"Children and sleep," National Sleep Foundation, 2004, accessed March 3, 2010, http://www.sleepfoundation.org/article/sleep-america-polls/2004-children-and-sleep.

1007.	"Adult sleep habits and style," National Sleep Foundation, 2005, accessed March 3, 2010, http://www.sleepfoundation.org/article/sleep-america-polls/2005-adult-sleephabits-and-styles.

1008.	"Teens and sleep," National Sleep Foundation, 2006, accessed March 3, 2010, http://www.sleepfoundation.org/article/sleep-america-polls/2006-teens-and-sleep.

1009.	HITZE B. *et al*, "Determinants and impact of sleep duration in children and adolescents: data of the Kiel Obesity Prevention Study," *Eur. J. Clin. Nutr.* 63 (2009): 739 *et al.*

1010.	NIXON G.M. *et al*, "Short sleep duration in middle childhood: risk factors and consequences," *Sleep*, n° 31, 2008, p. 71 *and passim.*

1011.	SPIEGEL K., "Sleep loss as a risk factor for obesity and diabetes", *Int. J. Pediatr. Obes,* n° 3, Suppl. n° 2, 2008, p. 27 *and passim.*

1012.	TAVERAS E.M. *et al*, "Short sleep duration in infancy and risk of childhood overweight," *Arch. Pediatr. Adolesc. Med,* n° 162, 2008, p. 305 *and passim.*

1013.	SPIEGEL K. *et al*, "Sleep loss: a novel risk factor for insulin resistance and type 2 diabetes," *J. Appl. Physiol,* n° 99, 2005, p. 2008 *and passim.*

1014.	VON KRIES R. *et al*, "Reduced risk for overweight and obesity in 5and 6-year-old children by duration of sleep - a cross-sectional study", *Int. J. Obes. Relat. Metab. Disord,* n° 26, 2002, p. 710 *and passim.*

1015.	GANGWISCH J.E. *et al*, "Short sleep duration as a risk factor for hypertension: analyses of the first National Health and Nutrition Examination Survey," *Hypertension,* n° 47, 2006, p. 833 *et passim.*

1016. GOTTLIEB D.J. *et al*, "Association of usual sleep duration with hypertension: the Sleep Heart Health Study," *Sleep*, n° 29, 2006, p. 1009 *et passim*.

1017. GANGWISCH J.E. *et al*, "Earlier parental set bedtimes as a protective factor against depression and suicidal ideation," *Sleep*, n° 33, 2010, p. 97 *and passim*.

1018. PEIRANO P.D. *et al*, "Sleep in brain development", *Biol. Res.* n° 40, 2007, p. 471 *and passim*.

1019. 1019. LIU X., "Sleep and adolescent suicidal behavior," *Sleep*, n° 27, 2004, p. 1351 *et passim*.

1020. 1020. BRYANT P.A. *et al*, "Sick and tired: does sleep have a vital role in the immune system?", *Nat. Rev. Immunol.* 2004;4:457 *et al*.

1021. IRWIN M. *et al*, "Partial sleep deprivation reduces natural killer cell activity in humans," *Psychosom. Med.* n° 56, 1994, p. 493 *and passim*.

1022. KAKIZAKI M *et al*, "Sleep duration and the risk of breast cancer: the Ohsaki Cohort Study", *Br. J. Cancer*, n° 99, 2008, p. 1502 *et passim*.

1023. VERKASALO P.K. *et al*, "Sleep duration and breast cancer: a prospective cohort study," *Cancer Res* 2005;65:9595 *et al*.

1024. WU A.H. *et al*, "Sleep duration, melatonin and breast cancer among Chinese women in Singapore," *Carcinogenesis*, n° 29, 2008, pp. 1244 *et passim*.

1025. SEPHTON S *et al*, "Circadian disruption in cancer: a neuroendocrine-immune pathway from stress to disease?", *Brain Behav. Immun.* 17 (2003): 321 *et al*.

1026. ROEHRS T. *et al*, "Sleep loss and REM sleep loss are hyperalgesic," *Sleep*, n° 29, 2006, p. 145 *et passim*.

1027. AKERSTEDT T. *et al*, "A prospective study of fatal occupational accidents - relationship to sleeping difficulties and occupational factors", *J. Sleep Res.* 2002, n° 11, p. 69 *et passim*.

1028. NAKATA A. *et al*, "Sleep-related risk of occupational injuries in Japanese small and medium-scale enterprises," *Ind. Health*, n° 43, 2005, p. 89 *and passim*.

1029. CONNOR J *et al*, "Driver sleepiness and risk of serious injury to car occupants: population based case control study", *BMJ*, n° 324, 2002, p. 1125.

1030. HORNE J *et al*, "Vehicle accidents related to sleep: a review", *Occup. Environ. Med*, n° 56, 1999, p. 289 *and passim*.

1031.   PHILIP P. *et al*, "Determinants of sleepiness in automobile drivers", *J. Psychosom. Res.* 41 (1995): 279 *et al*.

1032.   BONNET M.H. *et al*, "We are chronically sleep deprived," *Sleep*, n° 18, 1995, p. 908 *et passim*.

1033.   GIANNOTTI F. *et al*, "Circadian preference, sleep and daytime behaviour in adolescence", *J. Sleep Res*, n° 11, 2002, p. 191 *and passim*.

1034.   O'BRIEN L.M., "The neurocognitive effects of sleep disruption in children and adolescents," *Child Adolesc. Psychiatr. Clin. N. Am.* n° 18 (2009): 813 *et al*.

1035.   FALLONE G. *et al*, "Sleepiness in children and adolescents: clinical implications", *Sleep Med. Rev* 6, 2002, p. 287 *et al*.

1036.   DAHL R.E., "The impact of inadequate sleep on children's daytime cognitive function," *Semin. Pediatr. Neurol*, n° 3, 1996, p. 44 *and passim*.

1037.   HOFFMAN K.L. *et al*, "Sleep on it: cortical reorganization after-the-fact", *Trends Neurosci.* n° 25, 2002, p. 1 *and passim*.

1038.   MAQUET P., "The role of sleep in learning and memory", *Science*, n° 294, 2001, p. 1048 *and passim*.

1039.   CURCIO G. *et al*, "Sleep loss, learning capacity and academic performance," *Sleep Med. Rev.* n° 10, 2006, p. 323 *et passim*.

1040.   BabyFirst, access October 6, 2010, http://babyfirsttv.com/fr/content.asp?xml_id=1785.

1041.   EGGERMONT S. *et al*, "Nodding off or switching off? The use of popular media as a sleep aid in secondary-school children," *J. Paediatr. Child Health*, 42, 428 *et al*.

1042.   SHOCHAT T. *et al*, "Sleep patterns, electronic media exposure, and daytime sleep related behaviors among Israeli adolescents," *Acta Paediatr.* 2010.

1043.   CAIN N. *et al*, "Electronic media use and sleep in school-aged children and adolescents: a review," *Sleep Med*, n° 11, 2010, p. 735 *et passim*.

1044.   HIGUCHI S. *et al*, "Effects of VDT tasks with a bright display at night on melatonin, core temperature, heart rate, and sleepiness," *J. Appl. Physiol.* n° 94, 2003, p. 1773 *et passim*.

1045.   For example, for tonight - March 23, 2010 - prime time ends at 10:05 p.m. on virtually all major US networks including ABC, CBS, NBC, FOX, BBC, PBS, CW, CNN, access March 23, 2010, http://tv.yahoo.com/ listings?starttime=1269392400&provider=199).

1046.   HAMERMESH D.S. *et al*, "Cues for timing and coordination: lati-tude, letterman, and longitude," *J. Labor Econ.* n° 26, 2008, p. 223 *and passim.*

1047.   SILVA G.E. *et al*, "Relationship between reported and measured sleep times: the Sleep Heart Health Study (SHHS)," *J. Clin. Sleep Med.* 2007;3:622 *et al.*

1048.   TYNJALA J *et al*, "How young Europeans sleep", *Health Educ. Res.* 8 (1993): 69 *et al.*

1049.   WILSON B.J., "Media and children's aggression, fear and altruism", *Fut. Child* 18 (2008): *87ff.*

1050.   VAN DEN BULCK J., "Media use and dreaming: the relationship among television viewing, computer game play, and nightmares or pleasant dreams", *Dreaming*, n° 14, 2004, p. 43 *and passim.*

1051.   HARRISON K., "Tales from the screen: enduring fright reactions to scary media", *Media Psychol.* 1999, n° 1, p. 97 *and passim.*

1052.   MATHAI J., "An acute anxiety state in an adolescent precipitated by viewing a horror movie", *J. Adolesc.*, n° 6, 1983, p. 197 *and passim.*

1053.   SIMONS D. *et al*, "Post-traumatic stress disorder in children after television programmes", *BMJ*, n° 308, 1994, p. 389 *and passim.*

1054.   CANTOR J., "The media and children's fears, anxieties, and perception of danger," *in* SINGER D.G. *et al.* (eds.), *Handbook of Children and the Media*, Sage Publications, 2001, p. 207 *and passim.*

1055.   Françoise Sagan, quoted *in* LAMBRON M., " Bonsoir tristesse ", *Le Point,* 30 September 2004.

1056.   ANDERSON C.A. *et al*, "Psychology. The effects of media violence on society," *Science*, n° 295, 2002, p. 2377 *and passim.*

1057.   AMERICAN ACADEMY OF PEDIATRICS, "Policy statement - Media violence," *Pediatrics*, n° 124, 2009, p. 1495 *et passim.*

1058.   JOHNSON J.G. *et al*, "Television viewing and aggressive behavior during adolescence and adulthood," *Science*, n° 295, 2002, pp. 2468 *et passim.*

1059.   HUESMANN L.R. *et al*, "Longitudinal relations between children's exposure to TV violence and their aggressive and violent behavior in young adulthood: 1977-1992," *Dev. Psychol.* 39 (2003): 201, 218 *et al.*

1060.   SCHMIDT M.E. *et al*, "The effects of electronic media on children ages zero to six: a history of research," The Kaiser Family Foundation, January 2005, accessed October 6, 2010, http://www.kff.

org/entmedia/upload/The-Effects-of-Electronic-Media-onChildren-Ages-Zero-to-Six-A-History-of-Research-Issue-Brief.pdf.

1061.   ANDERSON C.A. *et al.* "The influence of media violence on youth," *Psychol. Sci. Public Interest* 4 (2003): *81ff.*

1062.   WARTELLA E. *et al,* "Children and television in the United States", *in* CARLSSON U. *et al* (eds.), *Children and Media Violence: Yearbook from the Unesco International Clearinghouse on Children and Violence on the Screen,* Nordicom, 1998, pp. 55, 58 *et passim.*

1063.   MURRAY J.P., "TV violence: research and controversy", *in* PECORAN. *et al* (eds), *Children and Television,* LEA, 2007, pp. 183, 193-194 *and passim.*

1064.   "Joint statement on the impact of entertainment violence on children," Congressional Public Health Summit, July 26, 2000, accessed July 30, 2010, http://www.aap.org/advocacy/releases/jstmtevc.htm.

1065.   HUESMANN L.R. *et al,* "The role of media violence in violent behavior," *Annu. Rev. Public Health,* n° 27, 2006, pp. 393, 394, 396 *et passim.*

1066.   STRASBURGER V.C., "Risky business: what primary care practitioners need to know about the influence of the media on adolescents," *Prim. Care,* n° 33, 2006, pp. 317, 321-322 *and passim.*

1067.   MURRAY J.P. *et al,* "Children's brain activations while viewing televised violence revealed by fMRI," *Media Psychol.* 8 (2006): 25ff.

1068.   KELLY C.R. *et al,* "Repeated exposure to media violence is associated with diminished response in an inhibitory frontolimbic network," *PLoS.One.,* n° 2, 2007, p. e1268.

1069.   STRENZIOK M. *et al,* "Lower lateral orbitofrontal cortex density associated with more frequent exposure to television and movie violence in male adolescents," *J. Adolesc. Health,* n° 46, 2010, p. 607 *et passim.*

1070.   STRENZIOK M. *et al,* "Fronto-parietal regulation of media violence exposure in adolescents: a multi-method study," *Soc. Cogn. Affect. Neurosci.* 2010.

1071.   LAZAR J., " La violence contagieuse? ", *Le Débat,* n° 94, 1997, p. 152 *and passim.*

1072.   STRASBURGER V.C., "Go ahead punk, make my day: it's time for pediatricians to take action against media violence," *Pediatrics,* n° 119, 2007, pp. e1398-e1399.

1073.   HUESMANN L.R., "The impact of electronic media violence: scientific theory and research," *J. Adolesc. Health*, 41 (2007), p. S6, *et passim*.

1074.   Catherine Tasca, quoted *in* GARRIGOS R. *et al*, " Contre la violence, pas de censure mais un médiateur ", libération.fr, April 10, 2002, accessed July 30, 2010, http://www.liberation.fr/medias/0101409179-contre-la-violence-pas-de-censuremais-un-mediateur.

1075.   Catherine Tasca, quoted *in* " Je suis hostile à la censure ", leParisien.fr, June 21, 2002, accessed July 10, 2010, http://www.leparisien.fr/faits-divers/je-suis-hostile-a-la-censure-21-06-2002-2003185041.php.

1076.   FREEDMAN J., *Media Violence and Its Effect on Aggression*, University of Toronto Press, 2002.

1077.   AMERICAN ACADEMY OF PEDIATRICS, "Media violence. Committee on Public Education," *Pediatrics*, n° 108, 2001, pp. 1222-1223 *and passim*.

1078.   ROMAINS J., *Knock ou Le Triomphe de la médecine*, Gallimard, coll. "Folio", 1972, act I, p. 31.

1079.   ANDERSON K., "The great TV violence hype", *Time*, July 12, 1993.

1080.   ABELSON R.P., "A variance explanation paradox: when a little is a lot", *Psychol. Bull*, n° 97, 1985, p. 129 *and passim*.

1081.   ROSENTHAL R., "Media violence, antisocial behavior, and the social consequences of small effects," *J. Soc. Issues*, n° 42, 1986, p. 141 *et passim*.

1082.   CENTERWALL B.S., "Television and violence. The scale of the problem and where to go from here," *JAMA*, n° 267, 1992, pp. 3059, 3061 *et passim*.

1083.   JOY L.A. *et al*, "Television and Children's Aggressive Behavior", *in* MACBETH WILLIAMS T. (ed.), *The Impact of Television: A Natural Experiment in Three Communities*, Academic Press, 1986, p. 303 *and passim*.

1084.   BUSHMAN B.J. *et al*, "Short-term and long-term effects of violent media on aggression in children and adults," *Arch. Pediatr. Adolesc. Med*, n° 160, 2006, p. 348 *and passim*.

1085.   HAYS W.L., *Statistics*, CBS College Publishing, 1981, 3rd ed.

1086.   BRADLEY E.H. *et al*, "Hospital quality for acute myocardial infarction: correlation among process measures and relationship with short-term mortality," *JAMA*, n° 296, 2006, p. 72 *and passim*.

1087.   "Télé-massacre", *Le Point*, n° 840, October 24, 1988.

1088.	"Survey on the representation of television violence", CSA surveys, November 1995.

1089.	FEDERMAN J., *National Television Violence Study*, Sage Publications, 1998, vol. III.

1090.	WILSON B.J. *et al*, "Violence in children's television programming: assessing the risks," *J. Commun.* 2002; 52: 5 *and passim*.

1091.	JOHNSON R.N., "Bad news revisited: the portrayal of violence, conflict, and suffering on television news", *Peace and Conflict*, n° 2, 1996, p. 201 *and passim*.

1092.	DORFMAN L. *et al*, "Youth and violence on local television news in California," *Am. J. Public Health*, n° 87, 1997, p. 1311 *and passim*.

1093.	ROMER D. *et al*, "Television news and the cultivation of fear of crime", *J. Commun.* n° 53, 2003, p. 88 *and passim*.

1094.	WALMA VAN DER MOLEN J.H., "Violence and suffering in television news: toward a broader conception of harmful television content for children," *Pediatrics*, n° 113, 2004, p. 1771 *and passim*.

1095.	LOWRY D.T. *et al*, "Setting the public fear agenda: longitudinal analysis of network TV crime reporting, public perceptions of crime, and FBI crime statistics," *J. Commun.* n° 53, 2003, p. 61 *and passim*.

1096.	FERNANDEZ-VILLANUEVA C. *et al*, "Broadcasting of violence on Spanish television: a quantitative panorama", *Aggress. Behav*, n° 32, 2006, p. 137 *and passim*.

1097.	BOUVET B. *et al*, "La télévision toujours plus violente", la-Croix. com, November 20, 2008, accessed August 2, 2010, http://www. la-croix.com/article/index.jsp?docId=2356564 &rubId=5548.

1098.	JENKINS L. et al, "An evaluation of the Motion Picture Association of America's treatment of violence in PG-, PG-13-, and *R-Rated* films," Pediatrics, n° 115, 2005, pp. e512-e517.

1099.	YOKOTA F. *et al*, "Violence in G-rated animated films," *JAMA*, n° 283, 2000, pp. 2716 *et passim*.

1100.	WEBB T. *et al*, "Violent entertainment pitched to adolescents: an analysis of PG-13 films", *Pediatrics*, n° 119, 2007, pp. e1219-e1229.

1101.	WORTH K.A. *et al*, "Exposure of US adolescents to extremely violent movies," *Pediatrics*, n° 122, 2008, p. 306 *and passim*.

1102.	SARGENT J.D. *et al*, "Adolescent exposure to extremely violent movies," *J. Adolesc. Health*, n° 31, 2002, p. 449 *and passim*.

1103.   SCHARRER E., "Should we be concerned about media violence?", *in* MAZZARELLA S.R. (ed.), *20 Questions About Youth and the Media*, Peter Lang Publishing, 2007, p. 117 *and passim*.

1104.   DUNCKO R. *et al*, "Acute exposure to stress improves performance in trace eyeblink conditioning and spatial learning tasks in healthy men," *Learn. Mem.* 14 (2007): 329.

1105.   JOELS M. *et al*, "Learning under stress: how does it work?", *Trends Cogn. Sci.* 2006, n° 10, p. 152 *and passim*.

1106.   HU H. et al, "Emotion enhances learning *via* norepinephrine regulation of AMPA-receptor trafficking," Cell, n° 131, 2007, p. 160 et passim.

1107.   DALLMAN M.F. *et al*, "Chronic stress and obesity: a new view of "comfort food"", *Proc. Natl. Acad. Sci.USA*, n° 100, 2003, p. 11696 *et passim*.

1108.   MACHT M. *et al*, "Immediate effects of chocolate on experimentally induced mood states," *Appetite*, n° 49, 2007, p. 667 *et passim*.

1109.   ADAM T.C. *et al*, "Stress, eating and the reward system," *Physiol. Behav*, n° 91, 2007, p. 449 *et passim*.

1110.   PECORARO N. *et al.* "Chronic stress promotes palatable feeding, which reduces signs of stress: feedforward and feedback effects of chronic stress," *Endocrinology*, n° 145, 2004, pp. 3754 *et passim*.

1111.   JOSEPHSON W.L., "Television violence and children's aggression: testing the priming, social script, and disinhibition predictions," *J. Pers. Soc. Psychol.* 53 (1987): 882 *et al.*

1112.   DESMURGET M. *et al*, "From eye to hand: planning goal-directed movements", *Neurosci. Biobehav. Rev.* 22, 1998, p. 761 *and passim*.

1113.   PACCALIN C. *et al*, "Changes in breathing during observation of effortful actions", *Brain Res*, n° 862, 2000, p. 194 *and passim*.

1114.   AVENANTI A. *et al*, "Transcranial magnetic stimulation highlights the sensorimotor side of empathy for pain," *Nat. Neurosci.* n° 8, 2005, p. 955 *and passim*.

1115.   BERGER S.M. *et al*, "Electromyographic activity during observational learning", *Am. J. Psychol*, n° 83, 1970, p. 86 *and passim*.

1116.   BERGER S.M. *et al*, "Some effects of a model's performance on an observer's electromyographic activity," *Am. J. Psychol*, n° 88, 1975, p. 263 *and passim*.

1117.   RIZZOLATTI G. *et al*, "The mirror-neuron system", *Annu. Rev. Neurosci.* n° 27, 2004, p. 169 *and passim*.

                                            TV Lobotomie

1118. AARTS H. *et al*, "Preparing and motivating behavior outside of awareness," *Science*, n° 319, 2008, p. 1639.

1119. FERGUSON M.J. *et al*, "How social perception can automatically influence behavior", *Trends Cogn. Sci*, n° 8, 2004, p. 33 *and passim*.

1120. CARVER C.S. *et al*, "Modeling: an analysis in terms of category accessibility", *J. Exp. Soc. Psychol*, n° 19, 1983, p. 403 *and passim*.

1121. BJÖRKQVIST K., "Violent films, anxiety, and aggression," Finnish Society of Sciences and Letters.

1122. LOVAAS O.I., "Effect of exposure to symbolic aggression on aggressive behavior," *Child Dev.* n° 32, 1961, p. 37 *and passim*.

1123. LIEBERT R.M. *et al*, "Short term effects of television aggression on children's aggressive behavior," *in* MURRAY J.P. *et al* (eds), *Television and Social Behavior. Reports and Papers, vol. II. Television and Social Learning*, US Government Printing Office, 1972, p. 181 *and passim*.

1124. LEYENS J.P. *et al*, "Effects of movie violence on aggression in a field setting as a function of group dominance and cohesion," *J. Pers. Soc. Psychol.* 32 (1975): *346ff.*

1125. ZILLMANN D. *et al*, "Effects of prolonged exposure to gratuitous media violence on provoked and unprovoked hostile behavior," *J. Appl. Soc. Psychol*, n° 29, 1999, p. 145 *et passim*.

1126. PAIK H. *et al*, "The effects of television violence on antisocial behavior: a meta-analysis", *Comm. Res* 21, 1994, p. 516 *and passim*.

1127. WOOD W. *et al*, "Effects of media violence on viewers' aggression in unconstrained social interaction," *Psychol. Bull*, 109, 371 *et al*.

1128. HEAROLD S., "A synthesis of 1043 effects of television on social behavior", *in* COMSTOCK G. (ed.), *Public Communication and Behavior, vol. I*, Academic Press, 1986, p. 65 *and passim*.

1129. COYNE S.M. *et al*, "Cruel intentions on television and in real life: can viewing indirect aggression increase viewers' subsequent indirect aggression?", *J. Exp. Child Psychol*, n° 88, 2004, p. 234 *and passim*.

1130. ROBINSON T.N. *et al*, "Effects of reducing children's television and video game use on aggressive behavior: a randomized controlled trial," *Arch. Pediatr. Adolesc. Pediatr. Adolesc. med.* 155 (2001): 17 *and passim*.

1131. PETO R *et al*, "Smoking, smoking cessation, and lung cancer in the UK since 1950: combination of national statistics with two case-control studies", *BMJ*, n° 321, 2000, p. 323 *et passim*.

1132.   CHRISTAKIS D.A. *et al*, "Violent television viewing during preschool is associated with antisocial behavior during school age," *Pediatrics*, n° 120, 2007, p. 993 *et passim*.

1133.   ZIMMERMAN F.J. *et al*, "Early cognitive stimulation, emotional support, and television watching as predictors of subsequent bullying among grade-school children," *Arch. Pediatr. Adolesc. Med.* n° 159 (2005): 384 *et al*.

1134.   ERON L.D. *et al*, "Does television violence cause aggression? *Psychol.* 27 (1972): 253ff.

1135.   LEFKOWITZ M.M. *et al*, *Growing Up to Be Violent: A Longitudinal Study of the Development of Aggression*, Pergamon Press, 1977.

1136.   "Special issue of neurobiology of learning and memory on habituation," *Neurobiol. Learn. Mem.* n° 92(2), 2009.

1137.   RANKIN C.H. *et al*, "Habituation revisited: an updated and revised description of the behavioral characteristics of habituation," *Neurobiol. Learn. Mem.* 92 (2009): 135-136 *et al*.

1138.   NIAS D.K., "Desensitization and media violence," *J. Psychosom. Res.* 23 (1979): 363ff.

1139.   CLINE V.B. *et al*, "Desensitization of children to television violence," *J. Pers. Soc. Psychol.* 1973;27:*360ff*.

1140.   THOMAS M.H. *et al*, "Desensitization to portrayals of real-life aggression as a function of exposure to television violence," *J. Pers. Soc. Psychol.* 35 (1977): 450ff.

1141.   MOLITOR F. *et al*, "Children's toleration of real-life aggression after exposure to media violence: a replication of the Drabman and Thomas studies", *Child Stud. Child Stud. J.*, 24, 191 *et al*.

1142.   DRABMAN R.S. *et al*, "Does media violence increase children's tolerance for real-life aggression?", *Dev. Psychol.* 1974;10:418 *et al*.

1143.   DRABMAN R.S. *et al*, "Does TV violence breed indifference?", *J. Commun.* n° 25, 1975, p. 86 *and passim*.

1144.   THOMAS R.H. *et al*, "Tolerance of real life aggression as a function of exposure to televised violence and age of the subject," *Merrill-Palmer Q*, n° 21, 1975, p. 227 *et passim*.

1145.   LINZ D.G. *et al*, "Effects of long-term exposure to violent and sexually degrading depictions of women," *J. Pers. Soc. Psychol.* 1988;55:758 *et al*.

1146.   MULLIN C.R. *et al*, "Desensitization and resensitization to violence against women: effects of exposure to sexually violent films on judgments of domestic violence victims", *J. Pers. Soc. Psychol.* 69 (1995): 449 *et al.*

1147. MALAMUTH N.M. *et al*, "The effects of mass media exposure on acceptance of violence against women: a field experiment," *J. Res. Pers.* 1981, 15, 436 *et al.*

1148. FANTI K.A. *et al*, "Desensitization to media violence over a short period of time," *Aggress. Behav.* 35 (2009): 179 *and passim.*

1149. MUCCHIELLI L. *et al*, *Quand les banlieues brûlent... : retour sur les émeutes de novembre 2005*, La Découverte, 2007, 2nd ed.

1150. "Banlieues: les violences vues depuis les États-Unis," TF1News, November 5, 2005, accessed September 8, 2010, http://lci.tf1.fr/monde/2005-11/banlieues-violences-vuesdepuis-etats-unis-4902322.html.

1151. MORGAN M., "What do young people learn about the world from watching television?" *in* MAZZARELLA S.R. (ed.), *20 Questions About Youth and the Media*, Peter Lang Publishing, 2007, p. 153 *and passim.*

1152. MORGAN M. *et al*, "The state of cultivation," *J. Broadcast Electronic Media*, n° 54, 2010, p. 337 *and passim.*

1153. MORGAN M. *et al*, "Growing up with television", *in* BRYANT J. *et al* (eds), *Media Effects: Advances in Theory and Research*, Routledge, 2009, 3rd edn, p. 34 *and passim.*

1154. GERBNER G. *et al*, "Cultural indicators: violence profile n° 9", *J. Commun.* n° 28, 1978, p. 176 *and passim.*

1155. GERBNER G. *et al*, "The 'mainstreaming' of America: violence profile n° 11," *J. Commun.* n° 30, 1980, p. 10 *and passim.*

1156. GERBNER G. *et al*, "The demonstration of power: violence profile n° 10", *J. Commun.* n° 29, 1979, p. 177 *and passim.*

1157. SIGNORIELLI N., "Television's mean and dangerous world: a continuation of the cultural indicators perspective", *in* SIGNORIELLI N. *et al.* (eds.), *Cultivation Analysis: New Directions in Media Effects Research*, Sage Publications, 1990, p. 85 *and passim*

1158. GERBNER G. *et al*, "Living with television: the violence profile", *J. Commun.* n° 26, 1976, p. 172 *and passim.*

1159. NABI R.L. *et al*, "Does television viewing relate to engagement in protective action against crime?", *Comm. Res.* 28, 2001, p. 802 *and passim.*

1160. VAN DEN BULCK J., "Research note: the relationship between television fiction and fear of crime", *European Journal of Communication*, n° 19, 2004, p. 239 *and passim.*

1161.   HOLBERT R.L. *et al*, "Fear, authority, and justice: crime-related TV viewing and endorsements of capital punishment and gun ownership," *Journalism Mass Comm. Q*, n° 81, 2004, p. 343 *et passim*.

1162.   ESCHHOLZ S. *et al*, "Television and fear of crime: program types, audience traits, and the mediating effect of perceived neighborhood racial composition," *Soc. Probl.*, n° 50, 2003, p. 395 *et passim*.

1163.   GOIDEL R.K. *et al*, "The impact of television viewing on perceptions of juvenile crime," *J. Broadcast Electronic Media*, n° 50, 2006, p. 119 *and passim*.

1164.   SALMI V. *et al*, "Crime victimization, exposure to crime news and social trust among adolescents," *Young*, n° 15, 2007, p. 255 *and passim*.

1165.   BUSSELLER.W., "Television exposure, perceived realism, and exemplar accessibility in the social judgment process," *Media Psychol.* 3 (2001): 43ff.

1166.   WILSON B.J. *et al*, "Children's and parents' fright reactions to kidnapping stories in the news," *Commun. Monogr.* n° 72 (2005): 46 *and passim*.

1167.   BRYANT J. *et al*, "Television viewing and anxiety - An experimental examination", *J. Commun.* n° 31, 1981, p. 106 *and passim*.

1168.   "Uniform crime reports," Federal Bureau of Investigation, accessed September 6, 2010, http://www.fbi.gov/ucr/ucr.htm.

1169.   CENTER FOR MEDIA AND PUBLIC AFFAIR, "The media at the millennium," *Media Monitor*, n° 14, 2000.

1170.   CANTOR J., *"Mommy I'm scared": How TV and Movies Frighten Children and What Can We Do to Protect Them*, Hartcourt Brace, 1998.

1171.   SINGER M.I. *et al.* "Viewing preferences, symptoms of psychological trauma, and violent behaviors among children who watch television," *J. Am. Acad. Child Adolesc. Psychiatry*, n° 37, 1998, p. 1041 *et passim*.

1172.   BOZZUTO J.C., "Cinematic neurosis following *The Exorcist*. Report of four cases", *J. Nerv. Ment. Dis*, n° 161, 1975, p. 43 *and passim*.

1173.   HAMILTON J.W., "Cinematic neurosis: a brief case report", *J. Am. Acad. psychoanal*, n° 6, 1978, p. 569 *and passim*.

1174.   TERR L.C. *et al*, "Children's symptoms in the wake of Challenger: a field study of distant-traumatic effects and an outline of related conditions," *Am. J. Psychiatry*, 156, 1536 *et al*.

1175.   PFEFFERBAUM B. *et al.* "Clinical needs assessment of middle and high school students following the 1995 Oklahoma City bombing," *Am. J. Psychiatry*, n° 156, 1999, p. 1069 *et passim*.

                                                                TV Lobotomie

1176.   PFEFFERBAUM B. *et al.* "Post-traumatic stress two years after the Oklahoma City bombing in youths geographically distant from the explosion," *Psychiatry*, n° 63, 2000, p. 358 *et passim*.

1177.   SCHUSTER M.A. *et al*, "A national survey of stress reactions after the September 11, 2001, terrorist attacks," *N. Engl. J. Med.* 2001, n° 345, p. 1507 *et passim*.

1178.   See Chapter III.

1179.   CANTOR J. *et al*, "Emotional responses to a televised nuclear Holocaust film", *Communic. Res.* 13 (1986): 257ff.

1180.   "Tony Blair used Cherie's grief to protect Iraq strategy," timesonline.co.uk, March 12, 2008, accessed September 6, 2010, http://www.timesonline.co.uk/tol/news/politics/article3913305.ece.

1181.   ROBIN C., *La Peur. History of a political idea*, Armand Colin, 2006.

1182.   MUZET D., *La Mal info*, Éditions de l'Aube, 2006, p. 23.

1183.   Terral J., *L'Insécurité au journal télévisé. La campagne présidentielle de 2002*, L'Harmattan, 2004, p. 37.

1184.   SCHNEIDERMANN D., *Le Cauchemar médiatique*, Denoël, 2003.

1185.   MAGGIORI R., "La peur un moyen de faire obéir les hommes", liberation.fr, 31 October 2009, accessed 8 September 2010, http://www.liberation.fr/societe/ 0101600340-la-peur-un-moyen-de-faire-obeir-les-hommes.

1186.   "The press denounces Sarkozy's 'one-upmanship' and 'diversion,'" lemonde.fr, August 2, 2010, accessed September 8, 2010, http://www.lemonde.fr/imprimer/article/2010/08/02/1394668.html.

1187.   AUFRAY A. *et al*, "La droite dégaine son arme sécuritaire", liberation.fr, 19 March 2010, accessed 8 September 2010, http://www.liberation.fr/politiques/0101625451-la-droite-degaine-son-arme-securitaire.

1188.   ROSTAND E., *Cyrano de Bergerac*, Larousse, coll. "Petits classiques", 2007, act V, scene VI.

1189.   CIORAN, *De l'inconvénient d'être né*, Gallimard, coll. "Folio essais", 1973, p. 61.

1190.   *Imagia. The history of France*, Fleurus, 2010.

1191.   BOORSTIN D., *Les Découvreurs*, Robert Laffont, 1988.

1192.   KUHN T., *The Structure of Scientific Revolutions*, University of Chicago Press, 1996, 3rd ed.

1193.   HELLMAN H., *Great Feuds in Science*, John Wiley & Sons, 1998.

Table of Contents